CodeMosaic

Learn AI-Driven Development and Modern Best Practices for Enterprise

Arpit Dwivedi

CodeMosaic: Learn AI-Driven Development and Modern Best Practices for Enterprise

Arpit Dwivedi
Lucknow, Uttar Pradesh, India

ISBN-13 (pbk): 979-8-8688-0275-1   ISBN-13 (electronic): 979-8-8688-0276-8
https://doi.org/10.1007/979-8-8688-0276-8

Managing Director, Apress Media LLC: Welmoed Spahr
Acquisitions Editor: Aditee Mirashi
Development Editor: James Markham
Editorial Assistant: Kripa Joseph

Cover designed by eStudioCalamar
Cover image designed by Freepik (www.freepik.com)

Distributed to the book trade worldwide by Springer Science+Business Media New York, 1 New York Plaza, Suite 4600, New York, NY 10004-1562, USA. Phone 1-800-SPRINGER, fax (201) 348-4505, e-mail orders-ny@springer-sbm.com, or visit www.springeronline.com. Apress Media, LLC is a California LLC and the sole member (owner) is Springer Science + Business Media Finance Inc (SSBM Finance Inc). SSBM Finance Inc is a **Delaware** corporation.

For information on translations, please e-mail booktranslations@springernature.com; for reprint, paperback, or audio rights, please e-mail bookpermissions@springernature.com.

Apress titles may be purchased in bulk for academic, corporate, or promotional use. eBook versions and licenses are also available for most titles. For more information, reference our Print and eBook Bulk Sales web page at http://www.apress.com/bulk-sales.

Any source code or other supplementary material referenced by the author in this book is available to readers on GitHub. For more detailed information, please visit https://www.apress.com/gp/services/source-code.

If disposing of this product, please recycle the paper

Table of Contents

About the Author

 **Arpit Dwivedi's** tech odyssey began as a Digital Specialist Engineer at Infosys, rapidly ascending to a Specialist Programmer role. His fervor for innovation steered him to Kline & Company as a Product Engineer, diving deep into full-stack development. Beyond corporate confines, Arpit's zeal for knowledge dissemination is evident in his writings across tech platforms and his personal blog. His commitment extends to open source contributions, leaving indelible marks on the tech canvas. His brainchild, DevIncept, an open source online community, stands testament to his vision, amassing over 9,000 LinkedIn followers. *CodeMosaic: Learn AI-Driven Development and Modern Best Practices for Enterprise* is Arpit's literary debut, encapsulating his mission to shepherd budding developers through the intricate maze of modern software craftsmanship.

About the Technical Reviewer

 **Ashish Singh** is a proficient full-stack developer specializing in Microsoft technologies, such as .NET, Azure DevOps, and Microsoft Azure. After obtaining his bachelor's degree in 2020, Ashish quickly advanced his career by taking on pivotal roles at Infosys and Neudesic, an IBM company, before his current role at BP (British Petroleum). His professional path has been characterized by a deep commitment to leveraging cutting-edge technologies to solve complex problems and enhance business efficiency.

At Infosys, Ashish excelled as a Power Programmer, where he honed his skills in MVC frameworks and Angular with Azure Cloud and Azure DevOps, preparing him for more sophisticated challenges. His subsequent position at Neudesic involved significant work with Microsoft platforms, which enriched his expertise in cloud and AI technologies. Now at BP, Ashish is working as an Engineering Specialist and focuses on integrating these technologies into secure and efficient software solutions. Beyond his technical endeavors, Ashish is an active participant in open source communities, contributing to various projects that reflect his dedication to collaborative development. He is also passionate about mentoring and guiding students and professionals alike, helping to demystify complex technical concepts and motivate the next generation of technologists. Ashish's extensive knowledge and community involvement make him a valued contributor in critiquing and understanding technical content across various domains.

PART I

Foundations and Smart Techniques

CHAPTER 1

Embarking on the Digital Odyssey

In the vast ocean of technology, where waves of information crash upon the shores of understanding, every developer needs a compass—a guide to navigate the treacherous waters of the digital age. This chapter is the starting point of our journey, one where we lay the foundation stones for the landmarks we'll explore in the forthcoming chapters. Here, we will traverse the paths that led us to the modern digital era, understand the landscapes of today's software development, and get a sneak peek into the tools that have become synonymous with modern programming. More importantly, this chapter will highlight the incredible power you wield as a developer and the impact you can make on the world.

The Digital Revolution: From Binary Beginnings to the Metaverse Era

We live in an era defined by rapid technological advancements. But how did we get here? The story of the digital revolution is filled with breakthroughs, from the invention of the transistor to the rise of the Internet. It's a tale of visionary individuals who transformed abstract concepts into tangible technologies, bringing about monumental shifts in how we communicate, work, and live. By understanding this journey, you'll appreciate the significant leaps we've taken and the foundation upon which modern development is built.

As software developers, we often live on the cutting edge, looking forward to the next breakthrough or technology that will shape our future. Yet, understanding our digital history can offer us invaluable perspectives. It roots our understanding, fuels our creativity, and gives us a profound appreciation for the tools at our fingertips.

© Arpit Dwivedi 2024
A. Dwivedi, *CodeMosaic*, https://doi.org/10.1007/979-8-8688-0276-8_1

Binary Beginnings

The earliest phase of digital evolution was when the world began to realize the transformative potential of computing.

- The invention of the transistor: the building block of modern electronic devices

- Mainframe computers and their dominance in the early digital age

Developer's Glimpse: Think about coding in this era as building foundational algorithms without the luxury of high-level programming languages. Punched cards, room-sized machines, and the thrill of executing the first few lines of code.

The Personal Computer Paradigm

Computers transitioned from mammoth structures to desktop fixtures.

- Apple's pioneering efforts with the Macintosh

- Microsoft's Windows: A GUI revolution, providing a more intuitive user interface

Developer's Glimpse: Visualizing software that's user-centric, designing applications that are intuitive yet powerful, and the start of debates on which platform to develop for.

The Connectivity Cascade

The birth of a global digital network.

- The invention of the Internet: ARPANET to the World Wide Web

- The rise of web browsers, making the Internet accessible to the non-tech savvy

Developer's Glimpse: Developing websites with HTML tables, the excitement of seeing your first website go live, and the dawn of web-based applications.

The Age of Mobility

Computers went from desks to pockets.

- Introduction of smartphones, led by Apple's iPhone
- The explosion of mobile applications with App Store and Play Store

Developer's Glimpse: Designing for mobile-first experiences, optimizing for touch interfaces, and the challenges of ensuring software performs seamlessly across a myriad of devices.

The AI Epoch

The age where data became the new oil.

- The rise of machine learning algorithms and their transformative potential.
- Cloud computing democratizes access to high computational power.

Developer's Glimpse: Delving into big data, training AI models, ensuring data privacy, and the shift from monolithic applications to microservices in the cloud.

The Metaverse Frontier

A futuristic realm where digital and physical realities intermingle.

- The emergence of augmented reality (AR) and virtual reality (VR) tools, changing how we perceive digital content
- Social platforms evolving into expansive, interconnected digital universes

Developer's Glimpse: Crafting rich, immersive experiences, understanding spatial computing, and the potential of creating entire worlds from lines of code.

Reflections on Our Digital Journey

The tapestry of the digital revolution is vast and intricate, weaving together countless innovations, pioneers, and transformative moments. Knowing these phases is more than just a retrospective look into our past. For developers and tech enthusiasts, it serves as

- **Context:** Understanding the foundations upon which today's technologies are built allows for deeper insights and a better appreciation of our tools' capabilities and limitations.

- **Inspiration:** Witnessing the exponential growth and transformative power of technology serves as a beacon of inspiration, urging us to push boundaries and envision the unimaginable.

- **Guidance:** The challenges, pitfalls, and successes of the past offer valuable lessons. They guide current decision-making, ensuring we move forward with both caution and ambition.

- **Connection:** It fosters a sense of belonging. To know history is to be part of a legacy, a continuum of innovators and thinkers pushing humanity forward.

In essence, the digital revolution's narrative is a testament to human spirit, creativity, and resilience. As we stand on the shoulders of digital giants, we're better equipped to shape the future, ensuring that the next chapter in our digital story is as groundbreaking as the ones that came before.

As we unravel the fabric of our digital past, it becomes evident how these technological advancements set the stage for modern development practices, influencing not just what we create but how we create it. This leads us to understand the landscape of modern development.

The Modern Development Landscape

As the years roll by, the world of software development continually shifts, much like tectonic plates reshaping the Earth's landscape. If we were to trace our steps back just a few decades, we'd find a drastically different setting.

Evolution of Software Development

From the clunky punch cards of yesteryears that dictated the instructions for massive mainframes, we've leapfrogged into an era where cloud platforms can be commanded with a few lines of code. This incredible journey highlights not just the technological advancements, but the evolution of developers' roles. Table 1-1 meticulously maps out the transformative epochs in the realm of software development.

Table 1-1. *Chronology of technical advancements*

Technology	Year Introduced	Details
Punch Cards	1950	Although punch cards were used since the 1800s, they became prominent in computing in the early 20th century.
The Internet	1960s	The concept of the internet began with ARPANET in the 1960s, with the World Wide Web becoming available in 1991.
BASIC	1964	Beginner's All-purpose Symbolic Instruction Code was created by John Kemeny and Thomas Kurtz at Dartmouth College.
C Language	1973	The C programming language was developed between 1969 and 1973 by Dennis Ritchie at Bell Labs.
Personal Computers	1975	The MITS Altair 8800 was released in 1975 and is considered the first commercially successful personal computer.
World Wide Web	1991	Tim Berners-Lee proposed the World Wide Web in 1989, which became publicly available in 1991.
Java	1995	Java programming language was released by Sun Microsystems.
Agile Manifesto	2001	The Agile Manifesto for software development was published in 2001, outlining principles for agile software development.
Git	2005	Git, the distributed version control system, was created by Linus Torvalds for Linux kernel development.
Cloud Computing	2006	The term "cloud computing" became common in 2006 when Amazon introduced the Elastic Compute Cloud (EC2) service. In 2008, Google launched its App Engine.
iPhone	2007	Apple Inc. introduced the first iPhone, revolutionizing the smartphone industry.
Android OS	2008	Google released the first version of the Android operating system after acquiring Android Inc. in 2005.
DevOps	Post-2009	The term DevOps started to become popular as a series of "devopsdays" conferences began in 2009.
Microsoft Azure	2010	Microsoft Azure, a cloud computing service, was launched by Microsoft in 2010.
GitHub Copilot	2021	GitHub Copilot was released as a plugin on the JetBrains marketplace on October 29, 2021.
OpenAI's GPT-3 Official Release	2022	OpenAI's GPT-3 was indeed released on November 30, 2022.

Beginning with the humble origins of punch cards in the 1950s, used for programming the behemoth mainframes of the era, it traces our ascent to the dawn of programming languages like BASIC and the birth of personal computers in the 1970s. The 1990s witnessed the phenomenal rise of the Internet and the World Wide Web, forever changing the way we connect and communicate. The dawn of the new millennium saw a proliferation of mobile apps, a testament to the shift in personal computing paradigms. This was soon followed by the genesis of modern platforms and tools like Android OS, iPhone, and Git, which revolutionized both user experience and development workflows. The most recent years have been marked by leaps in cloud computing and the advent of powerful AI technologies like OpenAI's GPT-3 in 2022. This table not only emphasizes the rapid pace of technological breakthroughs but also showcases the resilience and adaptability of developers in steering these innovations.

The Rise of Full-Stack Development

The era where developers were siloed into specific roles is waning. Now, a developer is expected to don multiple hats—designing the user interface, architecting the backend, and often even dabbling in database management or machine learning. This "Jack of All Trades" expectation has given birth to the Full-Stack Developer, a master of both the frontend visuals and the backend logic.

The Importance of Collaboration

Development today is akin to a well-coordinated orchestra. Each developer plays their part, but the magic truly happens when they all come together in harmony. Tools like Git haven't just facilitated collaboration; they've transformed it. The capability to merge ideas, to build on another's code seamlessly, has shifted the dynamics of software creation.

The Shift to Cloud and Microservices

With the advent of cloud giants—Azure, AWS, Google Cloud—the game's rules changed. The monolithic architectures of the past have fragmented into microservices, making applications more resilient, scalable, and maintainable. Serverless computing, where you only worry about your code and not the underlying infrastructure, has further streamlined and democratized development.

Figure 1-1 is a comparative diagram illustrating the fundamental differences and structure between Monolithic and Microservices Architectures. On the right, the Monolithic Architecture is depicted as a single, cohesive unit, where each component— web, app, code, and database—is tightly integrated. This structure presents challenges like tight coupling, scalability issues, and prolonged deployment times.

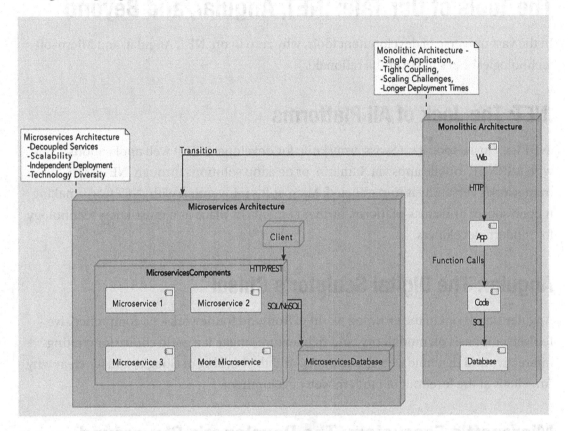

Figure 1-1. *Monolithic and microservices architectures*

Conversely, the Microservices Architecture on the left emphasizes decentralization. Each microservice operates as an independent entity, emphasizing decoupled services, scalability, and technology diversity. In this model, clients communicate with various microservices through HTTP/REST protocols, and these services might have their own databases, fostering independent deployment and more robust fault isolation.

The above diagram aptly portrays the transition many organizations are making from the monolithic model to the more modular and scalable microservices approach.

Navigating through this dynamic landscape requires not only versatile skills but also an arsenal of effective tools. Let's delve into the essential tools that complement our expertise in the next section, understanding their role in this modern ecosystem.

The Tools of Our Tale: .NET, Angular, and Beyond

In the vast universe of development tools, why zero in on .NET, Angular, and Microsoft technologies? Let's uncover the rationale.

.NET: The Jack of All Platforms

.NET isn't just a tool; it's a Swiss army knife for developers. Be it web applications with ASP.NET, mobile apps via Xamarin, or desktop solutions through .NET Core, the framework's versatility is unparalleled. Microsoft's reinvention with .NET Core, making it open source and cross-platform, further cements its place as a must-know technology for modern developers.

Angular: The Digital Sculptor's Chisel

Angular stands out in the crowded world of frontend frameworks. Its comprehensive toolset, emphasis on modularity, and rich features make it a go-to choice for crafting interactive and dynamic web applications. Add the backing of Google, and it's clear why Angular is at the forefront of modern web development.

Microsoft's Ecosystem: The Developer's Playground

But our tools don't end with .NET and Angular. Microsoft's expansive ecosystem offers a treasure trove of utilities that cater to every development need. Azure democratizes cloud computing, Visual Studio simplifies coding with its intelligent IDE, and GitHub fosters collaboration and version control. Each tool, each service, complements the other, forming a cohesive and powerful development environment.

Figure 1-2 is a vibrant mind map encapsulating Microsoft's multifaceted ecosystem, aptly termed "The Developer's Playground." At the heart of the diagram is Microsoft Tools, which branches out into distinct categories:

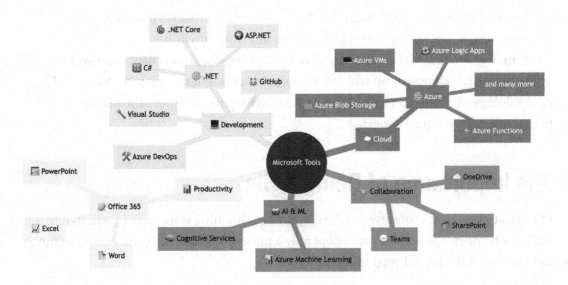

Figure 1-2. *The "Developer's Playground"*

1. **Development:** This arm highlights programming frameworks, languages, and tools, from the versatile .NET Core to the collaborative platform of GitHub. Key instruments like C#, Visual Studio, and Azure DevOps showcase Microsoft's commitment to developer-friendly environments.

2. **Cloud:** A testament to Microsoft's foray into cloud computing, with platforms like Azure Blob Storage, Azure Functions, and Azure Logic Apps leading the charge.

3. **Productivity:** This segment delves into the staple offerings of Microsoft, like Office 365, underscoring essential tools like Word, Excel, and PowerPoint that have become synonymous with workplace efficiency.

4. **AI and ML:** Microsoft's strides in artificial intelligence and machine learning are evident with offerings like Cognitive Services and Azure Machine Learning.

5. **Collaboration:** Focusing on teamwork and integrated workflows, this branch features tools like Teams, OneDrive, and SharePoint, pivotal for seamless remote collaborations and file sharing.

The above map succinctly captures the expanse of Microsoft's offerings, giving developers a plethora of tools and platforms to innovate and build.

Armed with these tools, developers are not just builders but artists, creating digital art. However, the canvas upon which they paint is not stagnant. The introduction of Agile methodologies has revolutionized this canvas, inviting us to explore the importance of being agile in development next.

The Importance of Being Agile

In the fast-paced world of software development, remaining stationary is akin to moving backward. The methodologies we adopt play a pivotal role in ensuring we move at the right speed, in the right direction. Enter Agile.

Agile: The Philosophy of Continuous Evolution

At its core, Agile isn't just a methodology; it's a mindset. It champions adaptability, customer feedback, and rapid iteration. The focus isn't just on building software but on delivering value continuously. Figure 1-3 illustrates the key steps in the Agile Development Cycle, emphasizing a continuous loop of planning, designing, developing, testing, reviewing, and iterating. We'll delve deeper into this later in Chapter 12, "Mosaic Tile 1: Setting up the Stage—Ideation and Boards."

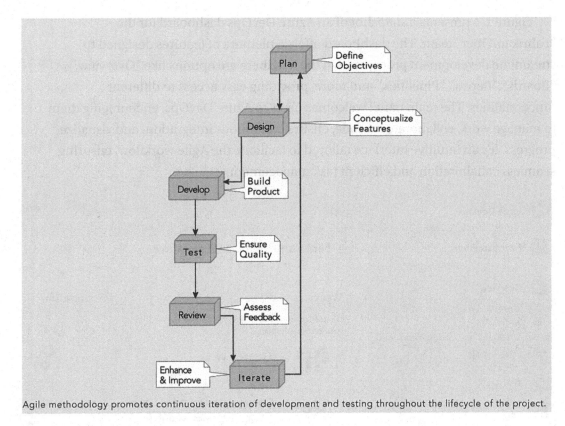

Agile methodology promotes continuous iteration of development and testing throughout the lifecycle of the project.

Figure 1-3. *Agile development cycle*

The Role of Azure Boards in Agile Development

Azure Boards aren't just tools; they're virtual command centers for Agile teams. They offer a visual platform to track work, backlog, and sprints, ensuring that the team remains on track and aligned. Whether it's breaking down features into user stories or tracking sprint progress with burndown charts, Azure Boards make the Agile process transparent and efficient.

A Glimpse into Azure Boards

Azure Boards weave the narrative of a project. Features, epics, user stories, and tasks can be visualized, tracked, and managed seamlessly. The integration capabilities, allowing it to work in tandem with tools like GitHub, mean that the entire development process can be overseen from a single pane of glass.

Figure 1-4 presents a snapshot of an Azure DevOps dashboard for the "FabrikamFiber" team. The dashboard offers a plethora of features designed to streamline development processes. On the left, there are options like "Overview," "Boards," "Repos," "Pipelines," and more, providing easy access to different functionalities. The main panel welcomes users to Azure DevOps, encouraging them to manage work, collaborate on code, ensure continuous integration, and visualize progress. It's an intuitive interface tailored to facilitate the Agile workflow, ensuring seamless collaboration and efficient task management.

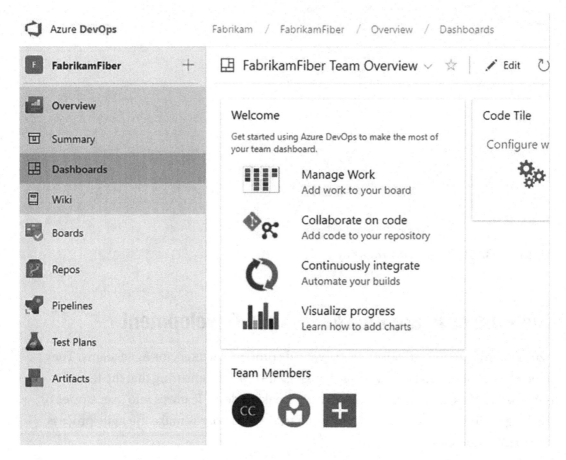

Figure 1-4. *Sample Azure DevOps dashboard*

Just as Agile methodologies have brought about a significant shift in development practices, there's another force redefining the boundaries of what's possible in development: Artificial Intelligence. Next, we explore AI's transformative influence in every aspect of development.

The Role of AI in Development

The tidal wave of AI isn't limited to chatbots or recommendation engines. Its ripples are being felt deeply in the realm of software development, aiding developers in every facet, from ideation to deployment.

Aide in Architecting and Designing

Before a single line of code is written, AI can aid in the design phase. Through predictive analytics and machine learning, it can forecast user behavior, helping in crafting user experiences that are both intuitive and engaging.

Databases: AI-Powered Efficiency

Gone are the days of manually tuning databases. AI can predict database loads, automate query optimizations, and even assist in structuring data more effectively.

AI and Development: Beyond Coding

Tools like GitHub Copilot are making waves, not just by suggesting code but understanding context. AI doesn't just understand what you're coding but why you're coding it. Whether it's recommending design patterns or highlighting potential pitfalls, AI is rapidly becoming the developer's right hand.

Automation Scripts: The Magic Wand of Development

Consider mundane tasks, like converting an Excel sheet into SQL tables. With an AI-driven Python script, what would take hours can be accomplished in minutes. These scripts understand data types, relationships, and even constraints, automating the tedious and letting developers focus on the innovation.

Figure 1-5 presents a comparative overview of two distinct methods for migrating Excel data to an SQL database.

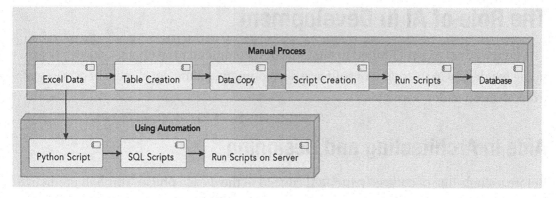

Figure 1-5. *Migrating Excel data to an SQL database*

The top half of the above flowchart outlines the manual process, which starts with raw Excel data. Following this, the data undergoes several stages including table creation, data copying, script creation, and script execution, before finally being stored in the database.

Conversely, the lower half of the flowchart emphasizes the benefits of automation. Here, Excel data is immediately processed using a Python script which then automatically generates the necessary SQL scripts. These scripts are subsequently executed on a server, ensuring a direct and efficient transfer of data to the database. This automated process significantly reduces the steps involved, showcasing its streamlined nature in comparison to the manual approach.

Crafting the Future: The Developer's Odyssey

As a developer, your role in the digital epoch is not confined to writing code. You are a modern-day pioneer, navigating uncharted technological realms. Each line of code is a stitch in the vast tapestry of the future, making your contribution far-reaching, beyond mere applications or software solutions.

Innovators at the Digital Frontier

You stand at the precipice of innovation. With each project, you don't just solve a problem; you unlock new potentials that could ripple through and disrupt technological norms. Your innovative spirit paves the way for new industries, propels economies, and even sparks global digital revolutions.

Architects of Digital Experiences

The digital realms you construct form the landscapes of tomorrow's online world. You're an architect of interconnected spaces, building not just platforms but experiences, fostering communities, and shaping digital interactions. These landscapes offer solace, convenience, and endless possibilities to billions, defining the very way humanity communicates, learns, and evolves.

Guardians of Ethical Technology

With great power comes great responsibility. Your role extends to being conscientious guardians of technology, ensuring ethical principles steer the digital age. You advocate for data privacy, fair regulations, and inclusivity, embedding these principles into the very code that will govern future societies and protect individuals' digital lives.

Educators and Mentors in the Digital Epoch

Your journey empowers you to become educators and mentors, passing on the torch of knowledge. By sharing your insights, experiences, and foresight, you're shaping the next generation of tech enthusiasts. You're not just fostering skilled professionals; you're nurturing visionary leaders who would carry on your legacy of innovation.

Harbingers of Societal Transformation

Your influence transcends digital spaces, instigating change in the tangible world. From healthcare, transportation, and education to how we interact with our environments, your creations catalyze societal transformation. You hold the keys to solving some of humanity's most pressing issues, harnessing technology as a force for positive change.

Embracing the Odyssey

Embrace your odyssey with pride and anticipation. The challenges will be monumental, but the rewards, profound. As you craft the future, remember: each challenge surmounted redraws the boundaries of what's possible; each innovation marks a step forward for humankind.

This journey you embark upon is not walked alone but shared with a global community of dreamers, innovators, and builders. Together, you are unstoppable, driving humanity forward into a future replete with possibilities yet to be imagined.

Conclusion

This chapter navigated through the evolution of technology, from its binary beginnings to the current era dominated by AI and the Metaverse. It underscored the transformative journey of digital technology, highlighting the developer's role as not just a participant but a creator within this expansive digital landscape. It lays the foundational understanding necessary for appreciating the depth and breadth of software development's past, present, and future.

Key Takeaways

- **Evolution of the Digital Era:** Our journey through technology began with simple computing machines and has arrived at an age of interconnected digital systems and artificial intelligence. Understanding this history is not just about appreciation but about learning from the past to innovate for the future.

- **The Toolbox of Modern Developers:** The landscape of software development is vast, with an array of languages, frameworks, and tools at our disposal. Mastery of these tools, from .NET to Angular, empowers us to build comprehensive, robust solutions for modern challenges.

- **Agility in Our Approach:** In a field that's constantly evolving, adaptability is key. Agile methodologies aren't just techniques; they're a mindset that, when embraced, keeps projects dynamic, team-centric, and ready to navigate change. Tools like Azure Boards reinforce this approach, embedding collaboration and flexibility at the heart of our projects.

- **AI: The Game-Changer:** Artificial intelligence is no longer just a concept; it's a reality reshaping our workflow. AI-driven tools like GitHub Copilot and ChatGPT are not replacing developers; they're enhancing our capabilities, handling repetitive tasks, and offering code suggestions, making room for more creative and complex problem-solving.

- **Beyond Coding—a Broader Impact:** As developers, we're not just behind-screen coding; we're at the forefront of building the future. Every line of code can contribute to societal shifts, whether it's through ethical tech, accessibility, or innovations that bridge digital divides. Our role extends into being guardians of digital landscapes, educators for future generations, and innovators of tech solutions that could one day change the world.

- **Crafting Tomorrow:** Our journey in tech is not solitary; it's a collective adventure. We are part of a community that thrives on sharing knowledge and ideas. Each challenge we overcome and every advancement we make is a step toward a future that we are responsible for shaping. It's a continuous cycle of learning, improving, and envisioning the unimaginable.

Transitioning into the Building Blocks of Software

As we conclude this chapter, our journey takes a more granular turn. From the broad strokes of digital history and the sweeping trends of technology, we pivot, focusing on the intricate building blocks that create the digital experiences around us. The next stage is about connecting the dots between the past lessons and the practical tasks we face as developers in the digital workspace.

Chapter 2, "Laying the Foundation: Pixels, Logic, and Data Streams" peels back the layers of software development, guiding us through the meticulous craft behind every application. We'll delve into the nuts and bolts of how vibrant pixels form the welcoming face of the digital frontier and unravel the complex logic that dictates the seamless functionality of the digital tools we rely on daily. Our exploration goes deeper as we dance with the streams of data that pulse through the veins of our systems, and we'll witness firsthand how artificial intelligence is becoming our indomitable ally in forging new digital wonders.

Prepare to transition from the macro to the micro, from revolution to evolution, and from concept to construction. We're about to navigate the fascinating labyrinth of creation in the digital realm, armed with historical insights, a peek into future possibilities, and a developer's toolbox brimming with potential. The forthcoming chapter is more than just a learning curve; it's the path to mastering the art and science of software development, the bedrock upon which we'll paint our digital tomorrow.

So, let's step forward. Beyond this horizon lies a world of logic and magic, data, and wonder. As architects, artisans, and visionaries, we're about to lay the foundational blocks of the digital landscapes of tomorrow.

CHAPTER 2

Laying the Foundation: Pixels, Logic, and Data Streams

As we peel back the layers of sophisticated software applications, a harmonious interplay between various components becomes apparent. In this chapter, you'll journey through the foundational elements—the vibrant pixels of the frontend, the intricate logic of the backend, and the ceaseless dance of data streams—that create the robust digital solutions we rely on. Furthermore, we'll unveil the transformative role of AI as a new collaborator in this domain, reshaping the traditional paradigms of development.

The Anatomy of an Application

Understanding the anatomy of an application is akin to unraveling the DNA of digital solutions. For developers, it's not just about writing code; it's about creating an orchestrated solution where every component plays a crucial role. Whether dealing with the aesthetics of design, the logic that drives functionality, or the server-client relationship that forms the backbone of data exchange, a clear comprehension of these elements defines the efficiency of the end product.

© Arpit Dwivedi 2024
A. Dwivedi, *CodeMosaic*, https://doi.org/10.1007/979-8-8688-0276-8_2

Decoding the Building Blocks

- **Design and User Experience (UX):** The journey begins with a thoughtfully designed user interface (UI), the gateway through which users interact with the application. A harmonious balance between visual elements and user experience is paramount.

  - **Wireframes to Reality:** The blueprint, usually a visual representation that outlines the skeletal framework of the application.

  - **Interactive Elements:** The tools that make an application intuitive, from navigation bars to transition animations, enhancing user engagement.

  - **Aesthetic Consistency:** Ensuring a visually cohesive narrative across the application, strengthening brand identity.

- **The Server-Client Model:** Central to web-based applications, this model is the interaction skeleton, facilitating communications between two parties.

  - **Understanding Servers and Clients:** Servers provide resources, including data or HTML files, while clients, like web browsers, request these resources.

  - **Communication Protocols:** HTTP/HTTPS, foundational for data exchange, outlining how messages are formatted and transmitted.

  - **Handling Requests and Responses:** The lifecycle of a client-server interaction, critical for developers to understand data flow.

- **Business Logic:** Residing in the server-side, this dictates the core operational rules, processed away from the client's reach, ensuring security and robust management.

- **Core Computations and Data Processing:** The hidden cogs and gears, managing everything from user authentication to operational workflows.

- **Backend Frameworks:** Tools like .NET Core that empower developers to construct complex, reliable, and scalable logic layers.

- **Data Management:** Here, systems like SQL Server come into play, handling the storage, retrieval, and manipulation of data structured across relational tables.

- **Efficient Querying:** Techniques ensuring quick and efficient data retrieval.

- **Data Integrity and Security:** Protocols and methodologies safeguarding information, responsibility, and necessity in the digital age.

Visualizing the Application Workflow

To solidify our understanding, envision an infographic detailing a user's interaction with an application, starting from their device (client), reaching out to the server, and how responses are generated and received. This visual journey underscores the interconnected nature of modern web applications.

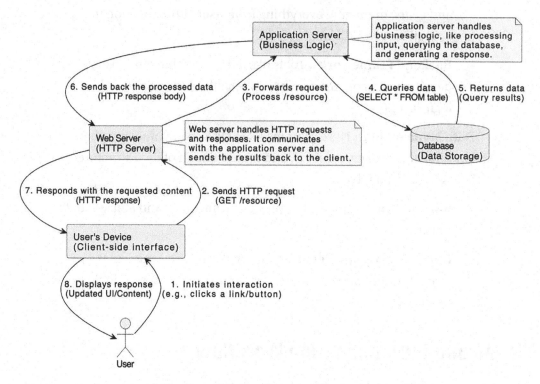

Figure 2-1. *Web application interaction workflow*

Certainly! Let's break down the Figure 2-1 from the perspective of the user:

1. **Initiating the Interaction:** At the very beginning, the user
   (depicted as a stick figure at the bottom left) takes action. This
   can be something as simple as clicking a button, selecting an item
   from a drop-down menu, or typing in a search query. This action
   sends a signal to the device they're using, indicating that they wish
   to interact with the web application.

2. **Requesting Information:** Once the user's device (labeled "User's
   Device (Client-side interface)") receives this signal, it packages
   up the user's request and sends it to the web server as an HTTP
   request. This request could be to retrieve a specific web page, post
   a comment, or request some data.

3. **Web Server's Role:** The "Web Server (HTTP Server)" receives the user's request. It is responsible for handling these HTTP requests and determining where they should go next. For some simple requests, the web server might return a result directly. But for more complex interactions, it passes the request on to the "Application Server (Business Logic)."

4. **Delving Deeper with the Application Server:** The Application Server is where much of the "thinking" occurs. It handles the business logic of the application. If the user's request requires data retrieval, the Application Server communicates with the "Database (Data Storage)." This could involve querying the database for specific data, like user profiles, product details, or content.

5. **Database's Contribution:** Once the Application Server makes a request, the Database searches its records and returns the requested data back to the Application Server. The Database serves as the repository for all persistent data in the application.

6. **Constructing the Response:** With the necessary data in hand, the Application Server processes it according to the application's business rules. It might format the data, perform calculations, or merge various data sources. Once ready, it sends the processed data back to the Web Server.

7. **Returning to the User:** The Web Server then takes this processed data, packages it into an HTTP response, and sends it back to the user's device.

8. **Final Display:** Finally, the user's device receives this HTTP response. The device then renders the response, updating the display with new content, visuals, or feedback based on the original request. The user sees this updated content and can either continue interacting with the application or move on to other tasks.

In essence, the diagram showcases a user's journey from initiating an action on their device, traveling through the intricate web of web servers, application servers, and databases, and culminating in the reception and display of the desired information or feedback.

💡 **Quick Byte!**   The rise of Single Page Applications (SPAs) has transformed the client-server interaction, leveraging techniques for faster, more responsive web experiences without constant page reloads.

In dissecting the intricate components that make up an application, we begin to see software development not just as a technical endeavor, but as a form of art. Each building block, from the visually engaging frontend to the robust backend, and the intelligent infusion of AI, plays a critical role in this digital masterpiece. As we pivot toward a more detailed exploration of the frontend, remember, this is where our digital solutions begin to take shape, directly influencing user engagement and satisfaction.

Pixels at Play: The Frontend

Frontend development is the art that gives life to logic, the visual symphony that users interact with. In the heart of this discipline, we find Angular, a platform that's both robust and versatile, transforming our code into interactive experiences. Here, we delve into Angular-centric practices, emphasizing the importance of visualization, security, and user-centric design in crafting interfaces that aren't just functional but also intuitive and secure.

Empathetic Design: Understanding User Needs

Creating an application isn't solely about fulfilling requirements; it's about connecting with the user on a human level.

- **The Role of Empathy in Design:** Tailoring experiences based on user needs and expectations.

- **Visualization Excellence:** Utilizing charts, diagrams, and interactive elements to present data in an understandable format, enhancing the user's cognitive experience.

- **Security in Design:** Implementing security measures from the ground up, making it an integral part of UI/UX without compromising on user friendliness.

Aesthetic and Functionality: Crafting with Angular

Angular isn't just a framework; it's a complete toolset that allows developers to build highly interactive and well-structured applications.

- **Component-Based Architecture:** Designing and coding with a component mindset, focusing on reusable, modular, and maintainable code practices.

- **Responsive Design with Angular:** Leveraging Angular's capabilities to create UI layouts that work seamlessly across devices, enhancing accessibility.

- **Visualization in Angular:** Exploring libraries compatible with Angular that help in creating dynamic, responsive, and interactive visualizations.

Best Practices in UI/UX: The Angular Way

Angular reshapes the approach to UI/UX, providing a structured and maintainable way of creating user experiences.

- **UI/UX Guidelines:** Adhering to proven best practices in the Angular ecosystem, ensuring applications are user-friendly, intuitive, and accessible.

- **Form Design and Validation:** Understanding the importance of form interaction, implementing real-time validation using Angular's reactive forms for better user engagement.

- **Routing and Navigation:** Crafting seamless navigation using Angular's Router Module, enhancing user experience and application performance.

Performance and Optimization: Keeping It Swift

In the online realm, speed and security are not just features but expectations. Angular steps in here, offering various optimization techniques.

- **Efficient Data Rendering:** Implementing techniques like lazy loading and trackBy for efficient rendering, significantly reducing load times.

- **State Management:** Ensuring consistency across components with state management libraries, offering predictable behavior within the application.

- **Security Measures:** Protecting user data with Angular's built-in security features, mitigating common security threats.

AI Integration: Smarter Interfaces

Integrating AI into Angular applications opens new frontiers, offering users smarter, more context-aware experiences.

- **Intelligent Experiences:** Using AI-driven components like chatbots integrated via Angular, for more dynamic user interactions.

- **Predictive UI:** Harnessing AI to predict user actions and preload anticipated data or layouts, making interactions seamless.

- **Enhancing Accessibility:** Utilizing AI to adapt interfaces in real-time for users with special needs, making applications truly inclusive.

As we encapsulate our dive into Angular-driven frontend development, we recognize the symbiotic relationship between technical efficiency and empathetic design. The frontend is more than what meets the eye; it's the gateway through which users touch the digital world we've crafted. With our insights into Angular, we're not just coding; we're architecting experiences. As we transition, we venture behind these experiences into the backbone of applications—the backend, where the logic embedded in our Angular components comes to life, securely and efficiently.

The Logic Labyrinth: The Backend

Behind the engaging visuals of an application lies the unsung hero: the backend, orchestrated significantly with .NET Core in our context. This robust framework from Microsoft powers the logic, the data handling, the authentication, and much more, ensuring our application is not just functional but also secure, scalable, and adaptable. Here, we explore the intricacies of backend development with .NET Core, understanding why its features form the bedrock of many modern applications.

Decoding .NET Core: Understanding the Framework

.NET Core emerges as a favorite for building high-performance, cross-platform applications, and here's why.

- **Cross-Platform Capabilities:** Write your code once and run it anywhere—the promise of .NET Core stands tall, offering increased flexibility and a broader audience reach.

- **Microservices Architecture:** Explore the support for microservices in .NET Core, allowing for scalability, isolation, and resilience in your application infrastructure.

- **High-Performance and C# Elegance:** Dive into the performance optimizations inherent to .NET Core and how C#, with its powerful features, complements the framework.

Seamless Data Handling

Data is the pulse of any application, and .NET Core provides sophisticated tools for handling it gracefully.

- **Entity Framework Core:** Delve into Microsoft's flagship ORM, understanding its role in querying and manipulating data with high-level abstraction.

- **Data Streaming and Real-Time Operations:** Learn about real-time data operations in .NET Core applications, vital for features like live notifications, messaging, and collaboration tools.

- **Secure Data Transactions:** Understand the security measures provided by .NET Core to ensure safe and reliable data transactions.

Authentication and Authorization: Security Essentials

Security isn't an afterthought; it's a foundational necessity. .NET Core places a strong emphasis on securing backend operations.

- **Identity and Access Management:** Implement robust security protocols with .NET Core Identity, managing user authentication and ensuring secure data access protocols.

- **OAuth and OpenID Connect:** Explore the standards supported by .NET Core for authenticating users via third parties, ensuring secure and convenient access controls.

- **Data Protection and Encryption:** Utilize .NET Core's cryptographic services to protect sensitive data both at rest and in transit.

Integration with Frontend: Bridging with Angular

The seamless integration between .NET Core and frontend technologies like Angular forms a full-stack developer's dream.

- **API Development and Integration:** Master the art of creating scalable, secure, and efficient APIs with .NET Core, consumed effortlessly by Angular frontend.

- **SignalR and Real-Time Communication:** Implement real-time functionality in your Angular app with .NET Core's SignalR, enhancing user experience with dynamic content.

- **Consistent Development Experience:** Enjoy the consistent, unified environment that the integration of .NET Core and Angular brings, streamlining workflow from frontend to backend.

Optimizing for Efficiency: Best Practices

Writing code is an art, and writing efficient, scalable code in .NET Core is a masterstroke.

- **Code Profiling and Performance Tuning:** Techniques for monitoring and improving the performance of your .NET Core applications.

- **Dependency Injection:** Utilize this pivotal practice in .NET Core for writing loosely coupled, maintainable, and testable code.

- **Error Handling and Logging:** Implement effective strategies for exception handling and logging, ensuring your backend processes are transparent and traceable.

The backend, especially one powered by .NET Core, is the linchpin holding our application together, processing, securing, and managing everything the user interacts with. As we conclude our exploration of the labyrinth that is the backend, we understand that it is more than just lines of code—it's the brain of our application. As we segue into our next topic, we'll see how this brain requires lifeblood—and that comes in the form of data. The journey ahead leads us into the dance of data, exploring how pivotal data management is in harmonizing the entire application's function.

Data's Dance

In the digital realm, data dictates the rhythm. Every feature, operation, and transaction hinges on how well the application manages data. It's here that SQL Server emerges as a maestro, conducting the flow of data with precision, ensuring integrity, performance, and security. Understanding the nuances of data management, particularly through SQL Server, is indispensable for developers, as it forms the heart that pumps life into the functionalities of any application.

Understanding SQL Server: Beyond Basic CRUD

SQL Server is not just a storage bin; it's a powerhouse for data processing, and understanding its capabilities can transform the way your applications handle data.

- **Optimized Data Storage:** Explore the structures, indexing, and data types in SQL Server that allow efficient storage and quick retrieval, critical for application performance.

- **Transactions and Concurrency Control:** Dive into how SQL Server manages multiple data accesses simultaneously, ensuring data integrity and consistency.

- **Advanced Queries and Data Retrieval:** Uncover the power behind complex queries, stored procedures, and views in fetching and manipulating data effectively.

- **Security Measures:** Understand SQL Server's robust security features, from encryption to user access controls, protecting sensitive data from threats.

Data in Motion: Streaming and Real-Time Insights

The modern application doesn't just store data; it interacts with it in real-time, necessitating developers to understand data streaming and real-time processing.

- **Stream Processing:** Learn about handling data on-the-fly, allowing for real-time insights and decision-making in your application.

- **Real-Time Data Integration:** Explore the tools and methodologies to integrate and synchronize data across different systems in real-time.

- **Analytics and Business Intelligence:** Harness SQL Server's capabilities for real-time analytics, transforming raw data into actionable insights.

Data Integrity and Disaster Recovery

Data is an asset, and like all assets, it needs to be protected and maintained. This section delves into ensuring data integrity and recovering from unforeseen disasters.

- **Backup Strategies:** Essential methodologies for backing up data, allowing for quick recovery and minimal downtime.

- **Ensuring Data Quality:** Techniques for maintaining data accuracy and consistency through constraints, triggers, and data validation practices.

- **Disaster Recovery Solutions:** Understand the mechanisms in SQL Server that safeguard against data loss in extreme scenarios.

Data and AI: Leveraging Data for Machine Learning

As AI and machine learning integrate deeper into applications, the role of data evolves, becoming the teacher to our machine learners.

- **Machine Learning with SQL Server:** Dive into SQL Server's machine learning services, allowing for predictive analytics and intelligent algorithms within your applications.

- **Data Mining and Predictive Analysis:** Utilizing your data for more than just information storage—uncover patterns, trends, and predictions.

- **Integrating with Azure AI:** Enhance capabilities by leveraging Azure's AI services, bringing advanced intelligence into your applications' fold.

Best Practices in Data Management

Managing data effectively is key to ensuring an application's speed, reliability, and consistency. Here we explore the best practices that all developers should embrace.

- **Database Design Principles:** Foundational rules for structuring a database efficiently, ensuring it's scalable, performant, and secure.

- **Performance Tuning:** Techniques for optimizing database performance, from query optimization to hardware and software configuration adjustments.

- **Data Compliance and Ethics:** Navigating the legal landscape of data usage, storage, and protection, ensuring your applications comply with global and regional regulations.

As we step back from the whirlwind dance of data, we realize its pivotal role in the entire ecosystem of our application. Effective data management, especially through a robust system like SQL Server, ensures our application is reliable, secure, and intelligent. But data doesn't stand alone. As we transition to the next segment, we prepare to meet the digital age's game-changer, AI, and explore how it's not just a tool but a collaborator, revolutionizing how we build, manage, and interact with our applications.

AI: The New Collaborator

In the tapestry of modern software development, AI stands out, not as a mere thread, but as a weaver itself, influencing how patterns come together. Understanding and harnessing AI's potential is no longer a futuristic concept but a necessary staple in a developer's toolkit. With innovations like ChatGPT and GitHub Copilot, AI has transitioned from being an abstract concept to a tangible partner in coding.

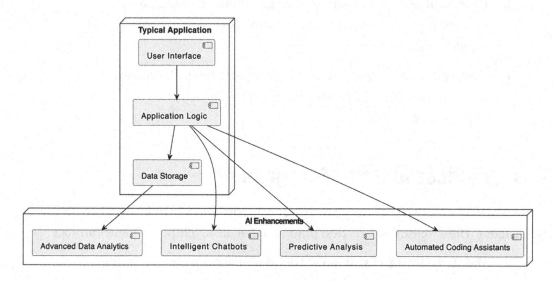

Figure 2-2. *Interaction points of AI in modern applications*

The preceding diagram showcases the integration of AI in modern applications. At its core is a typical application with user interface, Application Logic, and Data Storage layers. These components can be enhanced using AI capabilities, including Advanced Data Analytics, Intelligent Chatbots, Predictive Analysis, and Automated Coding Assistants, illustrating the transformative potential of AI in software development.

Demystifying AI in Development

Before we incorporate AI into our work, we must understand what it is, how it operates, and its implications in a development environment.

- **Understanding AI and Machine Learning:** Breaking down complex jargon to understand how these technologies learn, adapt, and predict.

- **AI's Role in Development:** How AI is shifting the developer's role from a creator to a supervisor and collaborator.

- **Ethical Implications:** Considerations and responsibilities that come with using AI, including fairness, accountability, and transparency.

ChatGPT: Revolutionizing Interactions

AI's role in enhancing user experience and interaction is exemplified by ChatGPT, a model that brings conversational intelligence to applications.

- **What Is ChatGPT?:** Understanding the mechanics behind this conversational marvel and how it learns from data.

- **Implementing ChatGPT in Applications:** From customer service to interactive interfaces, how ChatGPT can transform user interaction.

- **Limitations and Considerations:** Navigating the restrictions of AI in conversation, ensuring ethical and practical usage.

GitHub Copilot: Your AI Pair Programmer

Explore how GitHub Copilot is changing the game, assisting developers in writing code by providing suggestions and writing snippets of code.

- **Getting Started with GitHub Copilot:** Integrating this tool into your development environment and how to begin.

- **Real-World Applications:** Examples of how Copilot can speed up development, improve code quality, and assist in bug fixing.

- **Best Practices and Limitations:** Maximizing efficiency while understanding the tool's limitations in creativity and complex decision-making.

Enhancing Applications with AI

AI's influence permeates various facets of an application, significantly enhancing its capabilities and performance.

- **AI in User Experience:** Personalization, accessibility features, and intelligent interactions driven by AI.

- **Data Analysis and Predictions:** Using AI for deeper insights, trends prediction, and effective data utilization.

- **Security Enhancements:** AI's role in cybersecurity, fraud detection, and secure user authentication.

AI in Testing and Quality Assurance

AI not only aids in building applications but also plays a crucial role in testing, ensuring the final product is bug-free and high-quality.

- **Automated Testing:** Leverage AI to automate repetitive but necessary testing, increasing efficiency.

- **Bug Detection and Resolution:** Use AI's predictive nature to identify potential issues before they affect the application.

- **Continuous Improvement:** AI's role in consistent learning from application data to improve processes, features, and user satisfaction.

The integration of AI in development processes marks a revolutionary stride in how we approach creation and problem-solving in digital solutions. It is a dynamic, powerful collaborator, capable of propelling us into new realms of innovation. However, our journey doesn't end here. As we transition, we recognize that embracing AI's assistance fundamentally reshapes our approach, mindset, and the very nature of development challenges we can tackle. Thus, we move forward to understand the comprehensive process of crafting an application, bearing in mind that modern tools require a modern mindset.

Crafting an Application: The Process

Embarking on the journey of creating a software application is no less than an adventure, one filled with discovery, challenges, and innovative breakthroughs. For developers, particularly those stepping into the realm of web applications, understanding the roadmap to transforming an idea into a functional digital solution is paramount. This process is not linear but a cyclic, flexible approach known as Agile, promoting adaptive planning, evolutionary development, early delivery, and continual improvement.

The Agile Philosophy

Before diving into the stages, it's crucial to grasp the Agile mindset, a stark shift from traditional methods.

- **Principles of Agile:** Core beliefs that drive Agile projects, focusing on flexibility, customer satisfaction, and iterative progress.

- **Role of a Developer in Agile:** Shifting from solitary work to collaborative effort, understanding one's multifaceted role in a team.

- **Embracing Change:** Agile's strength lies in its adaptability to change, whether in requirements, technology, or end-user needs.

Starting with a Vision: Planning Your Application

The inception of any application is a vision, a problem to solve, or a service to provide. Here's how to approach it in Agile.

- **Conceptualizing the Problem:** Identifying the needs your web application will address.

- **Drafting User Stories and Use Cases:** Creating scenarios that your end users might encounter, ensuring your application caters to their needs.

- **Setting Up the Product Backlog:** Prioritizing features and tasks that will form the roadmap for your application's development cycles.

Design: Crafting User Experience and Architecture

Bridging the gap between imagination and reality requires design—both technical and aesthetic.

- **UI/UX Design:** The importance of intuitive design that ensures user engagement and satisfaction.

- **System Architecture Planning:** Laying out the technical blueprint, considering factors like scalability, data flow, and integration with other systems or technologies.

- **Design Reviews and Iterations:** Collaborative evaluation of designs, incorporating feedback, and iterating for improvement.

Development: Bringing Your Application to Life

This phase is where the magic happens—the actual building of the application.

- **Sprint Planning:** Breaking down the product backlog into manageable, executable components within time-framed "sprints."

- **Coding Best Practices:** Writing clean, efficient code, utilizing frameworks like .NET Core and languages suited to your application's requirements.

- **Regular Stand-Ups and Collaboration:** Daily meetings to discuss progress, hurdles, and collaborative solutions, keeping the team synchronized and focused.

Testing: Ensuring Functionality and Usability

No application is ready without rigorous testing to ensure it performs seamlessly and securely.

- **Types of Testing:** Implementing unit testing, integration testing, and user acceptance testing to ensure each piece and the whole system work flawlessly.

- **Iterative Testing:** Regular testing during development cycles to catch issues early and ensure quality in every sprint.

- **Feedback Incorporation:** Using feedback from testing phases to improve and adapt the application.

Deployment: Launching Your Solution

Putting your application out into the world for users to experience and benefit from.

- **Preparing for Launch:** Final reviews, pre-launch testing, and setting up environments for deployment.

- **Continuous Deployment Practices:** Automating the deployment process for quicker, efficient, and safer launches, ensuring that new features are smoothly integrated.

- **Monitoring and Quick Fixes:** Keeping an eye on the application's performance and being ready to make quick fixes as necessary.

Review and Iteration: The Cycle Continues

Post-launch doesn't mean the journey ends. Agile development is ongoing.

- **User Feedback and Analytics:** Gathering insights from users and application performance to understand how your application is received.

- **Retrospectives:** Reflecting on what went well and what didn't, and planning improvements for the next cycles.

- **Backlog Grooming for New Features:** Updating your product backlog with new features, enhancements, or fixes required.

Crafting a web application is an iterative journey of continuous learning and improvement. The Agile approach provides a structure that supports adaptability and a keen focus on delivering value to users. As we have seen, each phase of the process is interconnected, with feedback loops integrated at every step to ensure that the application evolves in tune with user needs and market trends.

Moving forward, we shift our attention from the process-oriented landscape of Agile to the personal realm of the developer. We will explore how the modern developer's mindset and approach must align with these methodical practices, ensuring not just the success of the project but also personal growth within this dynamic field.

The Developer's Mindset in the Modern Era

In the swiftly evolving realm of technology, where new frameworks, languages, and tools emerge rapidly, developers find themselves in an environment of perpetual learning. However, it's not just about acquiring technical skills. The modern developer's mindset—a blend of curiosity, adaptability, and a forward-thinking approach—is fundamental to thriving in this landscape. This section delves into the intrinsic qualities and attitudes that facilitate success in the contemporary development scene, especially when creating sophisticated web applications.

Cultivating a Growth Mindset

The path of a developer is one of lifelong learning. Here, we explore why maintaining a growth mindset is essential.

- **Embracing Challenges:** Viewing difficulties as opportunities to grow rather than insurmountable obstacles.

- **Perseverance over Quick Wins:** Understanding the value of resilience and sustained effort over seeking only fast, easy victories.

- **The Power of Yet:** Adopting the mentality that not knowing something doesn't mean failure; it simply means you haven't mastered it yet.

Adaptability in the Face of Change

Technology is anything but static. Developers must be quick to adapt, ready to discard old norms for more efficient, innovative solutions.

- **Staying Updated:** Keeping abreast of the latest technologies, trends, and best practices in the industry.

- **Flexibility with Tools and Technologies:** Willingness to switch tools or languages based on project requirements or market demands.

- **Responsive to Feedback:** Using constructive criticism from peers or users to refine solutions.

Thinking Beyond the Code

Successful developers recognize that their role extends beyond just coding. This section emphasizes holistic thinking that contributes to a project's overall success.

- **Understanding the Business:** Recognizing how your software fits into larger business goals and user needs.

- **Problem-Solving and Innovation:** Employing creative thinking to deliver unique solutions, not just writing code but innovating through it.

- **Collaboration and Communication:** Engaging with cross-functional teams, understanding the value of diverse perspectives in crafting holistic solutions.

Ethical Considerations and Responsible Development

In an age where software influences almost every aspect of our lives, ethical programming and responsibility take center stage.

- **Data Privacy and Security:** Prioritizing user data protection and understanding the legal and ethical implications of data handling.

- **Sustainable and Accessible Coding:** Crafting solutions considerate of environmental impact and accessible to diverse user groups.

- **Impact Awareness:** Recognizing the broader social and ethical impact of your software on communities and individuals.

Continuous Improvement and Professional Growth

Development doesn't cease with project completion; it's an ongoing cycle of improvement—for both the software and the developer.

- **Reflective Practice:** Regularly reviewing and reflecting on past projects to identify areas for personal and professional development.

- **Community Engagement:** Participating in developer communities for shared learning, mentorship, and staying connected with industry shifts.

- **Setting SMART Goals:** Establishing Specific, Measurable, Achievable, Relevant, and Time-bound objectives for continuous self-improvement.

As we encapsulate our exploration of the foundational elements of software development, it's clear that the journey doesn't end here. Being a proficient developer is not just about technical acumen; it's about cultivating a mindset equipped for continuous growth, adaptability, and a broader understanding of our societal impacts. As we transition into subsequent chapters, we carry forward this holistic perspective, delving deeper into specialized areas of development, new technologies, and the future of this ever-evolving field.

Examples

1. **Application Blueprint**

    Introduction

    Understanding the architecture of a web application is crucial for any developer. In this hands-on example, we create a simplified blueprint of an application. This visual aid helps you understand how the frontend, backend, and data layers interact, and how data flows through the system.

    The Blueprint

    Imagine an online bookstore. The user interacts with a sleek web page (frontend), which connects to a server (backend) that retrieves and processes data from a database.

Components

- **Frontend (User Interface):** Depicts book listings, shopping cart, etc.

- **Backend (Server-Side Operations):** Processes requests like "add to cart," "checkout," etc.

- **Database:** Stores information like "available books," "user data," and "purchase history."

- **AI-Enhanced Feature:** A book recommendation system based on user behavior.

- **Visualization:** Here is Application Blueprint (Figure 2-3), which sows how these components are connected.

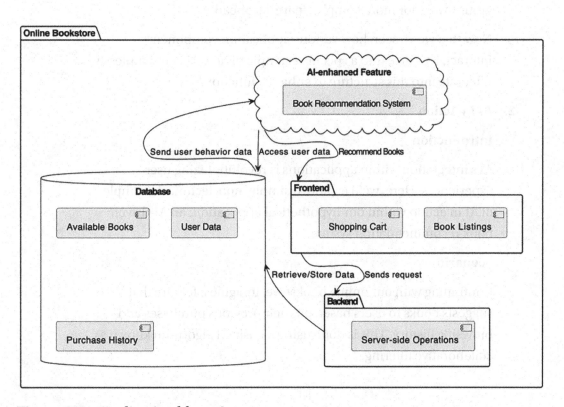

Figure 2-3. *Application blueprint*

Walkthrough

The diagram illustrates the blueprint of an "Online Bookstore" application. The database holds data on available books, user profiles, and purchase history. The frontend, which users interact with, features a shopping cart and book listings. User behavior data informs the AI-enhanced Book Recommendation System, which then provides tailored book suggestions. All data transactions between the frontend and the database are managed by the backend server-side operations.

Key Learning

This blueprint highlights the distinct roles of the application's layers and the importance of their interaction. It's a basic yet fundamental view of application architecture, laying the groundwork for more complex learning ahead.

Now that we've seen how various application components interact, let's dive into a specific example of how AI can seamlessly integrate into this structure to enhance functionality.

2. **AI in Action**

    Introduction

    AI's integration within applications is revolutionizing user experiences. Here, we'll explore a simple, non-technical example of AI in action within our hypothetical application: an AI-driven book recommendation system.

    Scenario

    Continuing with our online bookstore, imagine a feature that suggests books to users based on their previous purchases and browsing history. This is done using a basic AI algorithm known as collaborative filtering.

How It Works

- **Data Gathering:** The system collects data on user preferences through ratings, purchase history, and browsing patterns.

- **Analysis:** AI processes this data to identify patterns and relationships between users and products. For example, if User A likes Book X and User B likes Book X and Book Y, User A might also enjoy Book Y.

- **Recommendation:** Based on this analysis, the system predicts and displays books the user might be interested in, offering a personalized browsing experience.

Visualization

Figure 2-4 displays a user's interaction with a book browsing platform. As a user browses and views specific books on the frontend interface, book listings are fetched. When viewing a book, the system can request recommendations.

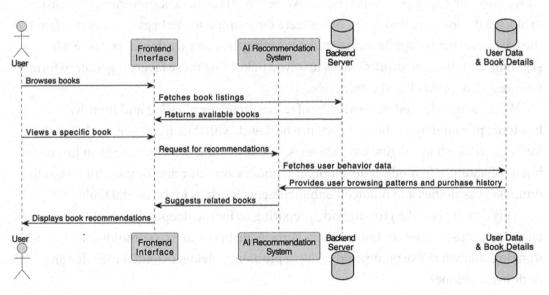

Figure 2-4. *AI in action*

The AI Recommendation System retrieves user behavior data and suggests related books based on browsing patterns and purchase history. The backend server facilitates these processes, accessing user data and book details as needed.

Why It Matters

This AI enhancement doesn't just boost sales by suggesting targeted options likely to appeal to the user. It also improves user satisfaction by personalizing the interface and interactions, catering to individual tastes and preferences.

Through these hands-on examples, we've seen the interconnectedness of application components and the transformative impact of AI on user experience. These practical insights lay the groundwork for deeper exploration and more complex project involvement.

Conclusion

As we draw the curtains on this chapter, we've embarked on a comprehensive journey, exploring the multifaceted realm of software development. We began by demystifying the basic structure of applications, understanding the pivotal roles played by each segment, and the delicate intricacies involved in knitting these layers together to form a seamless, functional digital experience.

We've acknowledged the criticality of an aesthetically pleasing and intuitive frontend, powered by a robust and secure backend, with data management being the fulcrum on which this digital balance rests. The revelation of AI as more than just a tool, but a collaborator in modern development, underscores our discussions, hinting at the limitless possibilities and nuanced enhancements it brings to the digital table.

This chapter lays the groundwork, preparing us for the deeper dive each subsequent chapter promises. It serves not only as a knowledge base but as a stimulus for critical thinking, analytical reasoning, and creative problem-solving, essential traits for any budding developer.

Key Takeaways

The Anatomy of an Application: Every application is a confluence of meticulously designed components, each crucial for the overall functionality and user experience. Understanding the interaction between these elements is foundational in software development.

Frontend—the User's Theater: The significance of a well-structured frontend extends beyond visuals; it's about crafting an intuitive, responsive, and accessible experience for every user, ensuring satisfaction and continued engagement.

Backend—the Logic Powerhouse: The backend is the operational hub of any application. Its efficiency, security, and ability to manage and process data effectively are paramount for the application's performance and reliability.

Data Management—the Keystone: Efficient data management strategies ensure speed, consistency, and accessibility of data, forming the backbone of user trust and application stability.

AI Integration—the Game-Changer: Embracing AI's potential transforms applications, making them more efficient, intelligent, and responsive, thereby enhancing user interaction and developer productivity.

Crafting an Application—an Art and Science: Building a digital solution is an iterative process of planning, designing, developing, testing, and deploying. Adherence to this process, guided by agile principles, ensures a balanced, effective, and quality product.

The Developer's Mindset: Continuous learning, adaptability, and a forward-thinking approach are non-negotiable traits for modern developers. Staying abreast of emerging technologies and methodologies is key to innovation and relevance in the ever-evolving tech landscape.

Each section of this chapter has been a stepping stone toward understanding the broader picture of software development. As we forge ahead, these learnings will become the building blocks for more advanced concepts, ensuring a holistic comprehension and mastery of creating effective, efficient, and innovative digital solutions.

Transitioning into Git Going

With the foundational understanding established in Chapter 2, we pivot toward Chapter 3, "Git Going: Time-Traveling with Code," where we explore the world of version control. This next chapter will transition from the theoretical underpinnings of application components and AI's role in development to the practical application of managing and collaborating on code effectively. Understanding Git becomes crucial as we delve deeper into software development practices, ensuring that readers are well-equipped to navigate the complexities of code management in a collaborative environment.

So, as we proceed, keep your mind agile, your curiosity piqued, and your passion for discovery undimmed. The world of application development is vast, complex, and wondrous, and we've only just scratched the surface.

Bonus Byte 1: Browser's Magic Mirror

In the vast landscape of web development, tools and technologies play a pivotal role in ensuring that developers can craft applications that are robust, optimized, and user-friendly. One such indispensable tool, often nestled discreetly within our browsers yet packed with immense power, is the **Browser Developer Tools**. Whether you're a seasoned developer or just starting out, these tools are the trusty companions you'll often turn to, the unsung heroes behind every successful web application.

The digital age has brought about a need for immediacy. We desire to understand, rectify, and enhance things in real time. The Browser Developer Tools are a testament to this very need. They allow developers to peek behind the curtains of a web page, offering insights into its structure, performance, and potential bottlenecks. From debugging unexpected behaviors to ensuring that a website performs optimally across different devices, these tools are the silent workhorses that ensure our web applications deliver the experience users expect. More than just tools, they are a window into the intricacies of web applications, helping developers unravel mysteries, optimize performance, and craft seamless user experiences.

As we delve deeper into the "Browser's Magic Mirror," our aim is twofold. Firstly, to provide you with a comprehensive overview of the functionalities and features that these developer tools offer. From understanding the Document Object Model (DOM) to analyzing network requests, we'll explore the breadth of capabilities these tools bring to the table. Secondly, we believe in the adage, "learning by doing." Therefore, interspersed within this exploration will be hands-on exercises, designed to provide you with practical experience and a deeper understanding of how to harness the power of browser developer tools effectively. By the end of this section, you'll not only appreciate the capabilities of these tools but also feel confident in leveraging them in your web development endeavors.

The Hidden Arsenal in Every Browser

Web browsers have long evolved from being mere gateways to the Internet to becoming sophisticated software platforms in their own right. While the average user interacts with a browser's surface, developers know there's a treasure trove of tools lying beneath, ready to be deployed. Let's embark on a journey to uncover this hidden arsenal.

1. **Google Chrome—Chrome DevTools**

   Chrome DevTools, integrated into Google Chrome, is one of the most popular developer tool sets. It offers a wide array of functionalities ranging from real-time DOM inspection, performance profiling, to even simulating network conditions. The user-friendly interface combined with continuous updates makes it a favorite among many developers.

2. **Mozilla Firefox—Firefox Developer Tools**

   Firefox, a stalwart in the browser industry, brings with it a set of robust developer tools. While it offers many of the same features as Chrome, it also introduces unique tools tailored for CSS Grid and Flexbox, making it a strong contender for frontend developers.

3. **Microsoft Edge—Edge DevTools**

    Built on the same engine as Chrome (Chromium), Microsoft
    Edge's developer tools are quite similar to Chrome DevTools but
    have their own set of unique features. Microsoft has been actively
    investing in enhancing these tools, ensuring they're on par, if not
    better, than its competitors.

4. **Apple Safari—Safari Web Inspector**

    Safari's Web Inspector, although less popular due to its macOS
    and iOS exclusivity, is incredibly powerful. It offers detailed
    insights into website performance, especially for sites that receive
    a significant amount of traffic from Apple devices. Its visual media
    query inspector and energy timeline are standout features.

    In essence, the choice of browser and its developer tools often
    boils down to personal preferences, specific project needs, and
    the unique features that a particular toolset offers. However,
    irrespective of the browser, one thing remains consistent—a
    powerful suite of developer tools lies beneath the surface, ready
    to assist, debug, and optimize. As we delve deeper, we'll uncover
    more about the magic these tools bring to the table and how they
    shape the modern web.

Elements Panel: Inspecting the DOM

Every website or web application we interact with is structured using the Document
Object Model (DOM). Think of the DOM as the blueprint of a website, detailing every
element, from text to images and buttons.

1. **Google Chrome and Microsoft Edge**

    Both offer a straightforward interface where you can hover over
    elements in the DOM to highlight them on the web page. You
    can also modify the HTML and CSS directly, seeing changes in
    real-time.

2. **Mozilla Firefox**

Firefox provides a unique color-coded representation of elements. Its standout feature is the box model visualizer, which graphically represents padding, borders, and margins.

3. **Apple Safari**

Safari's Elements tab is visually appealing and offers features similar to its counterparts. Its node filtering feature, which lets you quickly find elements, is a notable mention.

The ability to inspect and modify the DOM in real-time is invaluable. It aids in debugging, design tweaking, and understanding the structure of websites. It's the first step in the web development debugging process, allowing for rapid changes without altering the source code.

Console: Your Interactive Playground

The console is the Swiss Army knife for developers. It's more than just a space to view errors; it's an interactive shell for your web application.

Navigating the Console Across Browsers

1. **Google Chrome and Microsoft Edge**

Both offer a tabbed console, allowing you to filter by errors, warnings, and info. You can execute JavaScript on the fly, inspect variables, and even interact with the page's DOM directly.

2. **Mozilla Firefox**

Firefox's console boasts a unique inline variable viewer, letting you see variable values without having to hover or click. It's especially useful when dealing with arrays or objects.

3.   **Apple Safari**

Safari's console, while visually different, aligns in functionality with the rest. It offers a neat feature where you can save snippets of code to run them later.

Unlocking Potential

The console isn't just for debugging. It's a platform to test code snippets, log data, and even manipulate web page content in real-time. A deep understanding of the console accelerates debugging, enhances learning, and fosters experimentation.

Network Tab: Monitoring Web Traffic

Every website or application communicates with servers, fetching data, sending information, and loading resources. The Network tab provides a lens into this intricate dance of requests and responses.

1.   **Google Chrome and Microsoft Edge**

These browsers categorize network requests by type, such as XHR, JS, CSS, Img, etc. You can view details of each request, including headers, response payloads, and timing information. Their waterfall view is particularly useful for gauging loading sequences and delays.

2.   **Mozilla Firefox**

Firefox offers a similar categorized view with an additional feature: a throttling dropdown. This allows you to simulate different network speeds, helping test how your website behaves under various conditions.

3.   **Apple Safari**

Safari's Network tab, while consistent in core functionalities, offers a unique visual timeline, highlighting the duration and overlap of requests.

Understanding the network interactions of a website is crucial. It can help pinpoint inefficiencies, optimize loading times, and ensure that data is being sent and received correctly. Whether you're troubleshooting a slow-loading page or ensuring API calls are functioning, the Network tab is your diagnostic hub.

Sources: Diving Deep into Code

Behind every interactive web page lies a multitude of code files, scripts, stylesheets, and more. The Sources tab provides a structured view of these, allowing developers to navigate, edit, and debug with precision.

1. **Google Chrome and Microsoft Edge**

   Both offer an organized file explorer pane, enabling easy navigation through scripts, styles, and assets. Developers can set breakpoints, step through code, and watch variable values, facilitating a comprehensive debugging experience.

2. **Mozilla Firefox**

   Firefox's unique touch is its "Debugger" tab, which works in tandem with the Sources view. It offers a clear distinction between original source files and compiled ones, especially useful for modern frameworks and transpiled languages.

3. **Apple Safari**

   Safari's Resources pane provides a hierarchical view of files. Its debugging capabilities are on par with the rest, complete with breakpoints, call stacks, and scope chains.

   As web applications grow in complexity, having a robust debugging environment becomes paramount. The Sources tab, with its debugging capabilities, ensures that developers can trace issues, test solutions, and validate code behavior seamlessly.

Diverse Offerings of Browser Developer Tools

While we've explored some primary tools, browser developer tools have much more to offer:

- **Application Tab**

  Insights into storage mechanisms, such as cookies and local storage, ensuring smooth user sessions.

- **Security Tab**

  Details SSL certificates, highlights vulnerabilities, and offers secure interaction recommendations.

- **Performance Tab**

  Profiles resource loading times and highlights potential optimization areas for responsive web applications.

- **Memory Tab**

  Tools to analyze memory distributions and track potential leaks, ensuring efficient application performance.

- **Accessibility Tab**

  Ensures web applications are usable by everyone, offering audits and recommendations for inclusive web content.

  These tools, beyond just troubleshooting, are about understanding and optimizing. They stand as invaluable allies in crafting impeccable web experiences.

EXERCISE - BROWSER DEVELOPER TOOL

In the realm of web development, practical experience often speaks louder than theoretical knowledge. As we've delved into the intricacies of browser developer tools, it's now time to put that knowledge to the test. Through the following exercises, you'll gain hands-on experience with some of Chrome's most pivotal developer tools. By following along in Chrome, you'll ensure a consistent learning experience, although feel free to experiment in other browsers once you're comfortable. Each exercise is structured to provide a clear introduction, step-by-step guidance, and a means to verify your success. Let's dive in!

Delving into the DOM with the Elements Panel

The Elements panel is your gateway to the DOM, providing a real-time view and interaction platform for a web page's structure and styles. This exercise will familiarize you with its capabilities.

Steps to Proceed

1. Open your Chrome browser and navigate to a web page of your choice.

2. Right-click on a prominent element, such as a headline or button, and select "Inspect."

3. In the Elements panel, observe the highlighted code corresponding to the element you selected.

4. Try modifying the text content of the element directly within the panel.

Expected Outcome

You should see the changes reflected immediately on the web page. This showcases the power of real-time DOM manipulation using the Elements panel.

Interacting with the Console

The Console serves as an interactive playground for developers. It's a space where you can execute JavaScript, view logs, and debug in real-time.

Steps to Proceed

1. With Chrome open, use the shortcut **Ctrl + Shift + J** (or **Cmd + Option + J** on Mac) to open the developer tools directly to the Console tab.

2. In the console input line, type `console.log("Hello, World!");` and press Enter.

3. Next, try a basic arithmetic operation, such as **5 + 7**, and hit Enter.

Expected Outcome

You should first see the message "Hello, World!" printed in the console followed by the result **12** from the arithmetic operation. This demonstrates the console's capability to execute and display JavaScript.

Monitoring Web Traffic in the Network Tab

The Network tab provides insights into a web page's data interactions, showcasing every request and response in detail. This exercise will help you understand the flow of data in and out of a web page.

Steps to Proceed

1. In Chrome, navigate to a content-rich website or web application.

2. Open the developer tools and switch to the Network tab.

3. Reload the web page.

4. Observe the list of network requests, noting the various types and sizes.

Expected Outcome

You'll see a plethora of requests, each representing a file or resource loaded by the web page. By clicking on any request, you can view its details, such as headers, response content, and timing. This exercise underscores the complex web of interactions behind every modern web page.

As you work through these exercises, remember that the goal is exploration and understanding. The browser developer tools offer a vast landscape of features and capabilities. While these exercises provide a starting point, the true depth is realized through consistent use and experimentation. Happy exploring!

CHAPTER 3

Git Going: Time-Traveling with Code

In this chapter, you and I are about to embark on a remarkable adventure through the intricacies of code, stepping back into history and zooming into the future with the magic of version control. Picture this: a world where every mistake is just a stepping stone, where you can revisit your steps and perfect your journey, and where chaos morphs into harmony. That's the power we're harnessing together.

- **Unveiling the Magic:** Ever wondered why every expert developer emphasizes version control? It's the cornerstone of coding professionalism, and we're going to discover exactly why and how it's shaping the way we create digital marvels.

- **A Time Capsule of Code:** Think about a time machine, but for your code. We'll delve into how version control lets you track changes, revert to previous versions, and essentially, time-travel with your projects. It's your safety net and secret weapon, all rolled into one.

- **Collaboration, Not Chaos:** We'll see how version control transcends coding, bringing teams together, streamlining workflows, and setting the stage for the collaborative building. It's the unsung hero in a world where collective creation is the norm.

- **Future-Proofing Your Skills:** And it doesn't stop here. How is version control keeping pace with futuristic technologies like AI? There's a horizon to explore, and we're just getting started.

© Arpit Dwivedi 2024
A. Dwivedi, *CodeMosaic*, https://doi.org/10.1007/979-8-8688-0276-8_3

💡 **Quick Byte!**   The journey of version control started way back in 1972 with SCCS (Source Code Control System), marking the beginning of an era. That's nearly 50 years of innovation and enhancement!

So, are you ready to step into this realm, where every line of code contributes to a larger narrative, and every command writes a piece of history? Let's set the stage for a journey of learning, unlearning, and mastering the art of version control.

Version Control: The Why and How

Imagine yourself stepping into the shoes of Alex, a developer who's been working tirelessly on a project. Picture the chaos: hundreds of files, constant updates, and numerous team members editing, deleting, and adding code. Now, freeze that image. This chaotic world is about to get a lot more manageable as we journey through the realm of version control, the unsung hero in the life of developers like Alex and yourself.

The Evolution of Safeguarding Code

Join Alex, a budding developer, as they discover the fascinating evolution of safeguarding code. If you've ever tried to protect something important, you'll understand why developers over time have sought better ways to safeguard their code.

- **The Beginning: Manual Management**

  Alex started like any other developer, saving their code changes manually. They had a folder on their computer filled with files like "project-final.txt" and "project-final-UPDATED.txt." It was chaotic! Alex found it stressful to find the latest version or remember the changes made. They thought, "There must be a better way to organize this!"

- **Step Forward: Local Version Control Systems (LVCS)**

  After some research, Alex stumbled upon Local Version Control Systems. It was a game-changer! LVCS allowed them to maintain a history of their work on their computer. It was like a diary that recorded all the changes made. However, Alex realized its limitation when they wanted to collaborate with others—it was not designed for teamwork.

- **Joining Forces: Centralized Version Control Systems (CVCS)**

  As Alex joined more collaborative projects, they encountered Centralized Version Control Systems. Now, the code and its versions were stored on a central server where every team member could access and update it. It was revolutionary but came with its risks—if the central server crashed, everyone's work could be lost!

- **Strength in Numbers: Distributed Version Control Systems (DVCS)**

  The journey didn't stop there. Alex learned about Distributed Version Control Systems, where every collaborator had a complete history of the project on their computer. This approach meant that even if one computer crashed, the project could be recovered from others. "This is resilient teamwork!" Alex thought.

- **Today: Integration with Development Environments**

  Now, in the present day, Alex uses sophisticated systems that integrate version control with other development tools. They're part of a dynamic environment that supports coding, communication, and testing—all within a single setup. It's a far cry from the cluttered desktop folders they started with, and they couldn't be happier about the progress.

So as we can see in Figure 3-1, Alex's journey in safeguarding code mirrors the broader evolution in code management techniques.

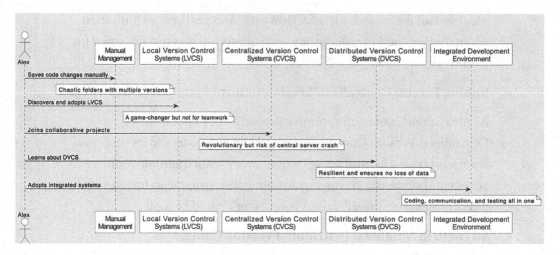

Figure 3-1. *Evolution of safeguarding code*

Beginning with the chaos of manual management, the advancements transitioned through Local, Centralized, and Distributed Version Control Systems, culminating in the holistic approach of Integrated Development Environments. This progression reflects a continuous quest for efficiency, collaboration, and resilience in the coding world. The accompanying diagram encapsulates this transformative journey, emphasizing the pivotal milestones in code safeguarding.

Why Version Control Is Unskippable

Alex's journey in the realm of coding took a more collaborative turn when they joined a development team that included Jamie, a seasoned lead developer, and Casey, another newcomer like Alex. This mix of experience and fresh perspectives brought to light the undeniable significance of version control systems (VCS) in software development.

- **Navigating Through Time**

   One afternoon, while trying to integrate a new feature, Alex inadvertently deleted several lines of critical code. Jamie, witnessing the panic in Alex's eyes, calmly introduced them to the concept of reverting changes using VCS. It was like having a time machine that could undo the mistake as if it never happened, saving the day.

- **Collaborative Harmony**

  The team often faced confusion in the initial days, with overlapping updates and conflicting codes. Observing the chaos, Jamie decided it was time to streamline the process using VCS. With each member's changes clearly documented and isolated, resolving conflicts became straightforward. Casey, who enjoyed playing the violin, likened it to an orchestra: every instrument (team member) contributes to the music (project), yet no sound (code) clashes.

- **Experiment Without Fear**

  Version control encouraged Alex and Casey to innovate. They learned to create "branches" for their experimental features, keeping the main project stable. This freedom led Alex to devise a successful optimization for the project, which Jamie praised and merged into the main code, acknowledging Alex's growing skills.

- **Accountability and Tracking Progress**

  The team grew appreciative of the VCS's role in documenting who made which changes and why. This clear record-keeping was invaluable in team reviews, helping everyone understand each contribution's context. It removed the guesswork and ensured credit was duly assigned, fostering a positive team environment.

- **Seamless Maintenance and Faster Recovery**

  A significant test came when users reported a serious bug. The team dove into the version history to identify when the bug was introduced. It was Casey's inadvertent error, but instead of blame, the team focused on learning from the mishap. With VCS, they quickly isolated the problem, rectified it, and pushed an update, turning a potential disaster into a smooth recovery and learning opportunity.

Through the eyes of Alex, Jamie, and Casey, it becomes evident that version control is an unskippable lifeline in the ever-evolving sphere of software development. It empowers teams to collaborate efficiently, innovate bravely, and maintain accountability, forming the backbone of any successful project.

Real-World Implications of Not Using Version Control

Imagine this: Alex, an enthusiastic new developer, is part of a budding project team at TechFusion Corp, working on their flagship product. The energy is palpable, and creativity abounds. However, the team operates without any version control system (VCS) in place, relying on manual code backups and email-based file sharing.

- **Tales of Catastrophe**

  One dreaded Monday, disaster strikes. A failed attempt at integrating new features has corrupted several core files, and the latest version of the project is irretrievable. Weeks of hard work—vanished! Alex and their teammates are in despair, sifting through a maze of disjointed files, trying to piece together the remnants of their efforts.

  In comes Charlie, a seasoned developer, witnessing the chaos unfolding. "I've seen this before," Charlie remarks, recounting tales from the industry's digital dungeons where the absence of version control led to project delays, financial losses, and dented reputations. "Without a dedicated VCS, you're walking a tightrope without a safety net," Charlie warns, emphasizing the precarious nature of their working method.

- **The Redemption Arc**

  The team, led by a visionary project lead, Jamie, decides enough is enough. It's time for a change—the introduction of a proper VCS. Jamie organizes training sessions, and the team learns about commits, branches, and merges. They set up repositories, start tracking their changes, and the quality of life improves drastically. The project gets back on track, and the team collaborates like a well-oiled machine.

  As Alex and the team reflect on these events, they realize the VCS did more than just save their code; it transformed their entire work culture. The tool brought in accountability, transparency, and confidence. No more fear of experimenting—the safety net of the VCS meant that they could innovate and explore without the risk of losing progress.

The journey from the brink of disaster to smooth sailing was tumultuous but enlightening. It demonstrated a universal truth in the world of software development: with the right practices in place, technology doesn't just facilitate work; it safeguards it. Through their ordeal, Alex's team learned that version control is not a luxury but an unskippable necessity in modern development.

The Psychology Behind Version Control

In the bustling environment of TechFusion Corp, Alex and the team are now more than familiar with the technical benefits of version control. However, there's another subtle yet profound impact that their new system introduces—a psychological one. The transition wasn't just about changing tools but also about evolving mindsets.

- **Cognitive Load and Efficiency**

    Before VCS, the team members were constantly stressed. They had to remember every change, who made it, and why. It was a cognitive burden, like juggling while riding a unicycle. However, with version control, this changed. The system tracked all modifications, freeing the mind from this immense mental load.

    Alex noticed that with fewer things to worry about, everyone was more focused and efficient. Ideas flowed more freely, and problem-solving became more about creativity than about remembering minutiae. This phenomenon wasn't just a happy accident. It's backed by psychology—when the brain has fewer mundane things to process, it can perform higher-order thinking tasks more effectively, fostering innovation.

- **Reducing Friction in Team Dynamics**

    Before, team collaborations were often tense. There were conflicts over overwritten changes and accountability issues, leading to a blame game. When they switched to VCS, these issues faded. Every change had a record, and every code snippet had an author.

    It was during a team meeting that Emma, the frontend specialist, remarked, "Have you noticed? Our discussions are more about 'how we can improve' rather than 'who did what.'" It was true. The

VCS, acting as an impartial record-keeper, had diffused the latent tension in the team, making collaborations more about constructive outcomes.

There was also newfound respect and understanding. For instance, when reviewing changes, colleagues weren't just seeing "what" was altered; they were understanding the "why" behind those alterations. This empathy, born from clearer communication and transparency, was a game-changer in team dynamics.

- **Comfort in Consistency**

  Implementing version control also introduced a consistent workflow structure, something that the human mind appreciates. Alex realized that the predictability of processes, the regularity of commits, and the systematic approach to merges created a rhythm that was comforting and reliable.

  As days turned into months, the team at TechFusion Corp discovered that version control was more than a system—it was a catalyst for a healthier, more harmonious work environment. It supported their mental well-being, fostered a collaborative spirit, and instilled a sense of security and confidence in their roles. Unbeknownst to them, adopting version control was nurturing their most crucial asset: their minds.

Looking Ahead: The Synergy of Version Control and Modern Technologies

In the heart of TechFusion Corp's innovation lab, Alex and the team were brainstorming their next big project. They had seamlessly adapted to the rhythms of version control, and it had markedly transformed their workflow and interactions. Amidst this progress, an intriguing question from their project manager, Jordan, shifted their collective gaze toward the horizon: "Where do we see the role of version control in the evolving landscape of tech innovations?"

- **Preparing for the Future**

Jordan's question lingered in the air, compelling each member to ponder. They had established that version control was indispensable in the current scenario, but technology was ever-evolving. What about the integration of Artificial Intelligence in software development? Or the burgeoning realm of Quantum Computing?

As they dived into spirited discussions, it became clear that version control wasn't static; it was dynamic, evolving with technological advancements. For instance, with AI-driven development, version control systems would need to adapt to track changes made by both human programmers and AI algorithms, maintaining a record of automated decisions and code modifications.

- **Embracing Enhanced Collaboration Tools**

Olivia, the team's cloud expert, chimed in, "Think about the explosion of remote work culture! We need version control systems robust enough to support real-time collaborations across continents, blending synchronous and asynchronous interactions seamlessly." The future hinted at version control transcending beyond code repositories, merging with project management tools to create holistic platforms that could handle complex project timelines, integrated team communications, and more.

- **A Glimpse into Distributed Version Control Systems (DVCS)**

This conversation naturally steered them toward the concept of Distributed Version Control Systems. Alex explained how traditional VCS relies on a central server, but DVCS, like Git, allows full copies of the source code on every developer's computer. The implications? Enhanced workflow flexibility and the freedom for developers to work offline, which was revolutionary.

The team was intrigued, realizing that their current knowledge was just scratching the surface of what version control could eventually become. The potential for integrating with virtual reality for code reviews, or employing blockchain for immutable change records, were just speculative ideas now, but they could be the next big leaps in version control evolution.

- **Transitioning to the Next Adventure: Git**

  As their session drew to a close, Jordan proposed, "Why don't we explore Git as our next step? It's the epitome of advanced version control, and it seems like the logical next step in our journey." Nods of agreement resonated around the room, a mix of excitement and curiosity filling the air.

The discussion had been an eye-opener. Version control wasn't an isolated element; it was part of a larger technological symphony, growing and adapting with each new era. As the team disbanded, Alex felt a surge of anticipation. They were not just developers but pioneers on the cusp of uncharted digital territories.

Version Control: The Why and How

After a productive day of coding and troubleshooting, Alex and the team relaxed in their designated lounge at the office, the hum of the vending machine providing a familiar backdrop. Their journey through the intricacies of version control had been enlightening, solidifying not just its necessity but its role as a cornerstone of efficient, collaborative development.

- **Recapitulation**

  "I think we all can agree now more than ever, version control isn't just a safety net; it's our silent guardian, a watchful protector," Jordan quipped, clearly pleased with his dramatic summary. Laughter echoed in the lounge, but they all nodded in agreement. Their recent discussions truly spotlighted the critical role version control plays in safeguarding their efforts and maintaining sanity in the workflow.

- **Embracing New Horizons**

  Casey, flipping through a tech magazine, chimed in, "And what's more exciting is thinking about the future. Imagine the mash-up of traditional version control systems with things like AI-driven development or real-time collaboration platforms!" The idea seemed ripped straight from science fiction, but with the pace of technological evolution, it felt within reach.

- **Seamless Transition to Git**

As the chatter subsided, Alex leaned in with a conspiratorial grin, lowering their voice as if about to reveal a secret. "Speaking of evolving technology, are you all ready to deep dive into something that's already taking these version control principles to the next level? Because, my friends, it's time we explore the world of Git."

The team perked up at the mention. While they had interacted with Git to varying degrees, none had truly unpacked its full potential. It was not merely a tool; for developers, it was akin to a time machine, an exciting blend of everything they had learned and so much more.

"We've laid the groundwork with version control," Alex continued, a hint of excitement bubbling beneath the calm exterior. "Now, let's see how Git amplifies these concepts and practically reads our minds to make development a breeze!"

As they wrapped up, the team felt a renewed sense of curiosity, ready to tackle the next segment of their journey. They had dissected the "why" and "how" of version control, and now they were stepping into the realm of "what's next" with Git.

Git: The Time Machine for Developers

Welcome aboard, fellow time travellers! In this chapter, you and I, along with our adventurous developer Alex and his enthusiastic team, embark on a journey through the intricacies of Git, a tool no less fascinating than a time machine. Imagine being able to leap through different stages of your code's history, revisit past versions, make parallel universes (branches, in Git terms), and even discard alternate realities that don't serve our purpose. Intriguing, isn't it?

Our journey begins with understanding why Git is not just another tool in a developer's arsenal but a time-space continuum manipulator for your projects. It allows you to navigate through your project's timeline, offering the freedom to explore without jeopardizing your project's current reality. With Git, making mistakes isn't a roadblock; it's a learning curve. You're allowed to experiment, make errors, and yet, with a few commands, restore harmony in your project's universe.

This expedition is not just about commands and concepts. It's about embracing a mindset that frees you from the linear constraints of time (version history) and space (your repository). Ready to strap in? Alex and the team are already tinkering with their newly installed Git, eager to explore. Together, we'll unravel how Git empowers you, the developer, to be the master of your code's past, present, and future.

Understanding Git's Core Philosophy

Welcome to the revolutionary world of Git, where we abandon the linear constraints of traditional version control and embrace a paradigm that transforms the way we think about our codebase. Imagine if you could work on your project like a time-travelling craftsman, able to revisit past decisions, explore new ideas in parallel timelines, and even rewrite a bit of history for the better. That's the power Git bestows upon Alex and his team, and now, they're all set for a journey of limitless creative freedom.

- **The Time Travel Analogy Continues**

  In the realm of Git, our adventurers don't move forward in a straight line. Instead, they explore a maze of possibilities, much like the intertwined timelines in science fiction epics. Every **commit** is a checkpoint, a bookmark in time they can return to, allowing them to venture down a different path or continue in the current direction, all without the fear of losing their way.

- **Immutable History and the Integrity of Snapshots**

  Here's the magic: every change Alex and his teammates make, every bit of code they alter, is captured as a unique snapshot in time—a **commit**. These commits are sacred, immutable records, much like how historians chronicle events, ensuring that none of their groundbreaking ideas get lost in the sands of time.

- **Distributed Version Control: Collaboration Without Constraints**

  The traditional ways of collaboration feel so... central, so limited. But with Git, it's like every member of Alex's team has their time machine, their copy of the entire world! They can make changes, big or small, without stepping on each other's toes. It's a dance of creativity that spans cities, countries, and continents, each contributing to a masterpiece asynchronously.

- **Branching: Parallel Universes in Development**

  What if, in another universe, Alex tried a different approach to a problem? Well, in the world of Git, these "what ifs" flourish in the form of branches. They're like parallel realities where different ideas can be tested and nurtured without altering the main timeline, ensuring the team's main project remains untouched and free from untested novelties.

- **Merging: Creating a Cohesive Narrative from Different Timelines**

  Once these alternate realities (branches) yield promising outcomes, how do they contribute to the primary vision? Through a process called "merging," the best of all timelines—these unique, creative solutions—are brought together, weaving a tapestry of collective genius into the main story.

- **The Importance of a Single Source of Truth**

  Despite the whirlwind of creativity, there's a core anchor in Git: the main branch. No matter how many branches proliferate, the main branch upholds the project's authentic narrative, serving as the single source of truth. It's the lighthouse guiding Alex and his team through the exhilarating storm of collective creation.

The leap into Git's philosophy is more than learning a new tool; it's about adopting a mindset. It's about seeing the coding landscape as a realm of endless possibilities, where collaboration, exploration, and innovation are not just welcomed but encouraged.

Ready to put theory into action? Stay tuned, as Alex and the team are about to dive into the practical ocean, sailing from the abstract horizon of "what" and "why" into the thrilling waters of "how." Up next, they gear up to set their very own coding universes into motion!

Hands-On: Setting Up for Time Travel

Alex and his team, each equipped with different operating systems, realized the importance of understanding the installation process across various platforms. It wasn't just about individual setup; knowing how to get Git up and running on any machine was crucial for helping colleagues, contributing to other projects, and ensuring a smooth, compatible workflow regardless of the hardware.

Preparing the Time Machine: Installing Git

Windows

- Alex, using a Windows machine, started by visiting the official Git website—`https://git-scm.com/`.

- He downloaded the latest version for Windows and ran the executable, following the on-screen instructions, a straightforward process even for beginners.

Mac

- Jamie, a dedicated Mac user, preferred using Homebrew. She opened the terminal and typed

  ```
  /bin/bash -c "$(curl -fsSL https://raw.githubusercontent.
  com/Homebrew/install/HEAD/install.sh)"
  ```

- After Homebrew was ready, she simply had to

  ```
  brew install git
  ```

Linux

- Sam, the Linux enthusiast of the group, used the standard package management tool. He opened the terminal and swiftly typed

  ```
  sudo apt update
  ```

  ```
  sudo apt install git
  ```

Everyone in the team followed these steps, relevant to their operating systems, ensuring they were on the same page, and ready for the challenges ahead.

Is Our Machine Ready? Verifying the Installation

Once installation was complete, the team needed to ensure their "time machines" were operational. They opened their command prompts or terminals and entered:

```
git --version
```

A moment of silence, and then the screen displayed the installed Git version, signaling they were ready to proceed.

Meeting Your Time-Travel Companion: Basic Git Commands

"Before we dive into different timelines, we need a map," Alex remarked, understanding the importance of orientation in this new landscape. Here's a cheat sheet (Figure 3-2), they put together for some basic Git commands, essentials for their upcoming voyage.

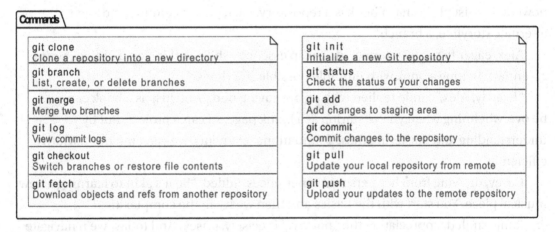

Figure 3-2. *Git basic cheat sheet*

Setting the Scene in Azure Repos

Kelly, who was proactive in collaboration, suggested they start preparing their Azure accounts for the projects and adventures ahead. They headed to **Azure DevOps** (https://dev.azure.com/) and set up their accounts, a move that they knew would pay off shortly.

Wrapping Up and Gearing Up

With the environment set up and a map in their hands, Alex and his team were brimming with excitement. They knew that their next step, cloning their first repository, would be a landmark event, setting them squarely on the path of professional-level development.

Repositories, Commits, and Branches

Amid the buzz of TechFusion Corp's dynamic office, Jamie stood poised next to a whiteboard, ready to delve deep into Git's core concepts: Repositories, Commits, and Branches. As the seasoned lead, Jamie had seen the transformative power of these tools firsthand and was eager to share this knowledge. Alex and Casey, the new entrants to the tech world, settled into their chairs with a mix of anticipation and curiosity.

"Imagine Git as a library," Jamie began, sketching a simple analogy to help the newcomers visualize. "Each book is a repository, each page a commit, and each alternate storyline, a branch."

Alex, eager to relate, interjected, "So, in essence, while working on a project, we're essentially writing a book with multiple possible storylines?"

"Exactly, Alex," Jamie replied with an approving nod. "And just as a book can be overwhelming when you're staring at a blank page, so can a project. But by understanding and mastering these foundational elements, we can craft our narrative efficiently."

Casey, drawing from her personal experiences, added, "So it's akin to learning a new musical piece. You start with the basics and then weave in the complexities?"

Jamie smiled, appreciating the analogy. "Precisely, Casey. And today, we'll navigate these foundational notes, ensuring we're in tune with Git's symphony."

Dear reader, as you journey alongside Alex and Casey, remember we're in this together. Whether you're an enthusiastic newcomer like Alex, a hobbyist like Casey, or even someone with a bit more experience, this exploration is designed to resonate with all. As we traverse this path, picture yourself in that vibrant office space, soaking in the knowledge, and gearing up for the adventures in collaborative coding that lie ahead.

Git Workflow Visualization

As Jamie continued, she pointed to a detailed flow chart (Figure 3-3) pinned on the wall. "To understand the intricacies of Git, it's helpful to visualize its workflow," she started. The chart painted a clear picture, streamlining the relationship between repositories, commits, and branches.

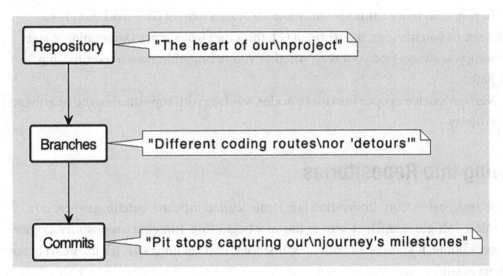

Figure 3-3. *Git workflow*

"Consider the flowchart as a map," Jamie suggested, seeing Alex and Casey's inquisitive eyes trace the routes. "Each stage or step is like a destination, guiding us through the Git journey."

The central box was labeled "Repository," illustrating its core role. Branching out were various arrows and pathways, leading to nodes titled "Commits" and "Branches."

"Every time we make changes to our code," Jamie explained, "we essentially journey from one node to the next. Starting at our repository—the heart of our project—we then branch out to explore different coding routes, making commits along the way to save our progress."

Casey, connecting the dots, remarked, "So when we create a branch, it's like taking a detour to experiment without affecting the main route?"

"Spot on, Casey," Jamie responded. "And when we're satisfied with our detour, we can merge it back into the main storyline, bringing our experiments to fruition."

Alex, always keen to break things down further, added, "And commits are our pit stops, capturing our journey's milestones?"

"Exactly, Alex," Jamie affirmed. "By marking these pit stops, we ensure we can always retrace our steps, revert changes if needed, or continue from where we left off."

To you, dear reader, this visualization isn't just a map of Git's workflow. It's a compass. As you navigate the world of Git, this chart will serve as your guiding star, ensuring you always find your way, whether you're branching out or committing to a path.

Next, let's delve deeper into these nodes, starting with repositories, the heartbeats of our projects.

Diving into Repositories

At the TechFusion Corp innovation lab, Jamie leaned forward, catching everyone's attention. "Alright team, let's start at the very beginning. Imagine a repository as your project's home. It's where all your files, histories, and versions live. It's the heart of your project in Git."

Understanding Repositories

A repository in Git, often termed a "repo," is essentially a directory or storage space where your projects can live. It can be local to a machine or hosted on a platform like GitHub or Azure DevOps. A repository doesn't just hold your codebase; it keeps track of the various versions, changes, and the entire commit history. Think of it as a living record of your project, offering insights into when, why, and how code has evolved over time.

Alex's eyes gleamed with curiosity, "So, how do we create this 'home' for our project?"

Jamie smiled and replied, "There are multiple ways, depending on where you want to house your repository. Let me break it down."

Creating a Repository

After explaining the importance of repositories, Jamie paused for a moment, letting the information sink in. She then declared with a hint of excitement, "Now that we understand the foundation, it's time to lay the first brick! Let's create our very first Git repository together."

CLI Approach

For those who like the command line, here's how you can set up a repository:

1. Navigate to the directory where you want to create the repository.

2. Type `git init` and press Enter.

3. This command initializes a new Git repository and begins tracking an existing directory. Voila! Your new local repository is ready.

Casey scribbled down notes as Jamie continued, "For those who prefer visual tools or are working in collaborative environments, platforms like Azure DevOps and GitHub offer intuitive interfaces."

Azure DevOps Approach

Azure DevOps, Microsoft's development collaboration tool, offers an integrated set of features for developers:

1. Sign in to your Azure DevOps account.

2. Create or choose an existing project.

3. Navigate to the **Repos** section.

4. Click on + **New repository**.

5. Fill in the necessary details and choose the desired settings.

6. Click on **Create**.

Your repository is now set up on Azure DevOps.

GitHub Approach

GitHub, a favorite for many developers globally, provides an easy way to host and manage repositories:

1. Log in to your GitHub account.

2. Click on the "+" icon at the top right corner, then select **"New repository."**

3. Fill in the repository name, description, and other settings.

4. Choose if you'd like to initialize the repository with a README, .gitignore, or license.

5. Click on **"Create repository."**

Alex, pointing to his laptop screen, remarked, "And there it is! Our project's new home on GitHub."

Jamie's methodical walk-through ensured that Alex, Casey, and the entire team felt comfortable with repositories. They now understood its central role in Git, setting the stage for the next integral component: Branches.

Exploring Branches

Jamie, seeing the team's growing confidence, decided to dive into another core Git concept. "Alright, team," she began, "Imagine you're writing a book. The main storyline is your master branch. But what if you wanted to explore an alternative ending or introduce a new character without affecting the main plot? That's where branches come in."

Understanding Branches

In Git, a branch represents an independent line of development. It's essentially a pointer to a specific commit. By default, Git calls this branch the "master" branch (though in many modern contexts, it's being renamed to "main").

When you make commits, you're adding to this main line. But creating a new branch means you diverge from the main line, providing an isolated environment to implement a feature, fix a bug, or even safely experiment without affecting the stable version.

Casey, drawing an analogy with her violin compositions, said, "So, it's like creating variations of a musical piece without altering the original score!"

"Exactly, Casey," Jamie replied with a nod.

Working with Branches

Jamie paused for a moment, observing the eagerness on the faces of Alex and Casey. "Alright," she said with a smile, "Let's not just discuss branches in theory. How about we create our first branch and explore the wonders it brings to our coding journey?"

CLI Approach

For the command-line enthusiasts:

- Creating a Branch

    - Use `git branch [branch-name]` to create a new branch.

- Switching Between Branches

    - Use `git checkout [branch-name]` to switch to the desired branch. For newer versions of Git, you can use git switch [branch-name].

- Viewing All Branches

    - Use `git branch` to see a list of all branches. The currently active branch will be highlighted.

As the team members tried out the commands on their systems, Jamie explained the visual tools' branch management aspects.

Azure DevOps Approach

Managing branches in Azure DevOps is quite straightforward:

- Go to your chosen repository within Azure DevOps.

- Navigate to the **Branches** section on the left sidebar.

- Click on **New branch** at the top. Fill in the name and base it on an existing branch if needed.

- You can also view, delete, or set security for branches from the same section.

GitHub Approach

Handling branches on GitHub:

- Go to your specific repository on GitHub.

- You'll see a dropdown labeled **Branch: master** (or **Branch: main**).

- Enter a new branch name in the textbox and select the option to create a new branch.

Alex, experimenting with creating branches on GitHub, remarked, "This is so intuitive! It's like having multiple playgrounds for different features."

With a deeper understanding of branches, the team was beginning to see the power of Git in project management and the flexibility it provided in software development. Jamie, sensing the team's anticipation, decided that it was the perfect time to discuss commits next.

The Art of Committing

Casey, adjusting her glasses, initiated the next discussion. "We've talked about the structure, the branches, but what about the content itself? How do we save our progress?" she inquired, with a note of curiosity.

Jamie nodded, "Great question, Casey. That brings us to commits."

What Are Commits?

In the world of Git, commits are like milestones on a journey. Imagine you're writing a book, and every chapter you complete is a significant achievement. Similarly, in coding, every feature or bug fix is crucial. To ensure you don't lose any of your progress, you would want to save these milestones. That's where commits come into play.

A commit in Git is essentially a snapshot of your code at a particular point in time. Every commit has a unique ID, allowing you to track changes, revert them if necessary, or switch between different stages of your code seamlessly.

Casey interjected, "So, every time I make a change and I'm satisfied with it, I should commit it to save that state?"

"Exactly," Jamie affirmed. "And the beauty of it is, every commit contains a message that describes what was done, allowing you and others to understand the evolution of the project."

Making Commits

Jamie emphasized, "Committing is a ritual every developer should master. It's the heartbeat of version control, capturing each pulse of progress. Now, let's dive into how this ritual unfolds across different platforms."

CLI Approach

For those working directly with the command line:

1. **Staging Changes**: Before committing, you need to stage your changes. Use the command

   a. `git add [filename]` for a specific file or,

   b. `git add .` to stage all changes in the directory.

2. **Committing Changes**: Once staged, you can commit your changes using

   a. `git commit -m "Your descriptive message here."`

Alex, practicing alongside, commented, "It's like setting checkpoints in a video game! You can always return to them if things go wrong."

Jamie smiled, "Exactly, Alex! And these checkpoints are visible and manageable on platforms like Azure DevOps and GitHub."

Azure DevOps and GitHub Approach

When you push your commits to platforms like Azure DevOps or GitHub

1. They appear as individual entries in the repository's commit history

2. Each commit showcases the author, the timestamp, and the associated message

3. You can view the changes made in each commit, comparing it with the previous state

4. It's also easy to revert to a previous commit or create a new branch from any commit point

Emma, always eager to visualize things, logged into the team's GitHub repository. She navigated to the commit history and saw the recent commits, each detailing the changes made. "This," she said, pointing to the screen, "is the beauty of version control. Every step, every decision is recorded."

Feeling empowered with their new understanding of commits, the team was ready to conclude their deep dive into Git's fundamental components. Jamie, with a sense of accomplishment, was prepared to wrap things up and give a teaser of what's next in their Git journey.

Concluding: Repositories, Commits, and Branches

Jamie gathered the team around, reflecting upon the journey they had undertaken. "We've traversed the foundational elements of Git today—from understanding the essence of repositories, diving deep into the realm of branches, to mastering the art of commits," she began.

Alex, with a glint of newfound confidence, responded, "It's like we've mapped the DNA of our projects, capturing every change, every decision, branching out with new ideas, and saving our progress as we go."

Casey nodded in agreement, "It's empowering to think of how these fundamentals give us so much control and clarity in our development process."

Charlie, always the voice of experience, chimed in, "And while these are the foundational blocks, there's so much more to explore. Especially when we begin collaborating with others."

Jamie smiled, her eyes shining with anticipation. "Precisely, Charlie. And that's where our next adventure leads us. We're about to dive into the world of Collaborative Coding with Git, exploring how multiple minds can seamlessly come together, shaping a project. Get ready, team; our journey is about to get even more exciting!"

Collaborative Coding with Git

The conference room buzzed with energy as developers settled into their chairs, steaming cups of coffee in hand. It was the subsequent session on mastering Git, and after the insightful discussion on repositories, commits, and branches, anticipation was high. Jamie entered the room, her vibrant energy immediately captivating everyone.

"Alright, team!" Jamie began with enthusiasm, "In our last session, we delved deep into the fundamentals of Git. But today, we're taking a step further into its collaborative aspects. Let's explore how Git doesn't just track our code but brings us together as developers. Are you all ready?"

Nods and murmurs of agreement echoed throughout the room. With a dramatic flourish, Jamie clicked a button, and a new flowchart illuminated the projector screen.

Collaboration Visualization

"Here we have a diagram showcasing how collaboration in Git works," Jamie pointed out, her laser pointer tracing the lines of the diagram (Figure 3-4). "This represents the crux of Git's collaborative prowess. Look at the two parallel roads—one symbolizing Alex's codebase and the other, our main project. And then, we have these bridges—the Pull Requests—that allow Alex to suggest his changes to the main project."

She continued, "And it's not just Alex. See this other road? That's Charlie's. He has his own bridge to the main project. This demonstrates the beauty of Git—it allows multiple developers to work independently, yet come together seamlessly."

With her pointer hovering over a fork in Alex's road, she added, "This fork here? That's when Alex decides to have his personal copy of the main project, allowing him to experiment without affecting the primary codebase."

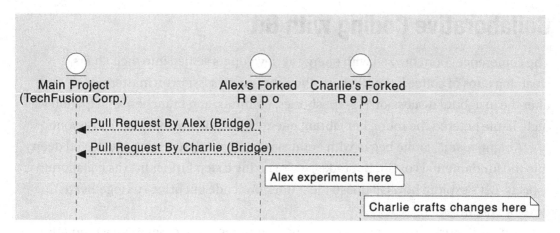

Figure 3-4. *Collaborative coding with Git*

As the flowchart faded, Casey whispered to Alex, "The visualization makes it so clear. Git truly is a game-changer for collaboration."

"We're just scratching the surface," Alex replied, eyes twinkling with anticipation, "I can't wait to dive deeper."

Jamie, catching the buzz in the room, grinned. "Hold on to that excitement. It's time to delve into the very heart of collaboration in Git."

The Heart of Collaboration

The room dimmed slightly, drawing everyone's attention to the large screen behind Jamie. An intricate image appeared: various individual puzzle pieces coming together to form a complete picture. Each piece was distinct, bearing unique patterns, yet when assembled, they transformed into a harmonious whole. "This," Jamie said, pointing to the puzzle, "is the essence of collaborative coding with Git."

"At its core, Git isn't just about managing code; it's about bringing developers together. Whether we're oceans apart or sitting right next to each other, Git allows us to stitch our individual contributions into a cohesive tapestry. Today, we're going to delve deep into this magic."

Understanding Pull Requests

Jamie continued, her cursor hovering over a button labeled "Pull Request" on the screen behind her. "Think of pull requests as the bridges of the coding world (As in Figure 3-5)" she began. "When a developer, says Alex, makes changes to a project, he doesn't directly send those changes to the main codebase. Instead, he requests the original project maintainers—like Casey—to review his contributions. It's a way to say, 'Hey, I've made these updates. Can you take a look and see if they fit into our project?'"

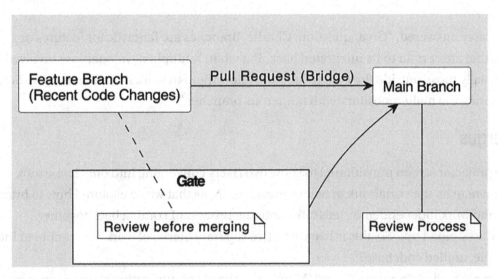

Figure 3-5. *Git branching*

She clicked, and an interface showed a list of changes, comments from different developers, and highlighted code differences. "This is where the magic happens. It's a platform for discussion, review, and feedback. Developers can comment on specific lines of code, suggest changes, or even commend good practices. Only after thorough review and discussion do changes get merged."

Casey chimed in, "It's a system of checks and balances. Before any code becomes part of the main project, it undergoes scrutiny. This ensures quality, avoids potential pitfalls, and maintains the integrity of our project."

Forks in the Road

Jamie shifted the projection to display a tree with its main trunk and several branches stemming out in different directions. "When working on a shared project, sometimes we don't want to make changes directly to the main repository, especially if those changes are experimental or uncertain. This is where 'forking' comes into play."

Alex nodded in understanding, "So, it's like taking a snapshot of the current project and having my own version to play around with?"

"Exactly," Jamie responded. "A fork is essentially your personal copy of the project. You can make any changes, add new features, or even fix bugs without affecting the original codebase. Once you're satisfied, you can then create a pull request, proposing your changes back to the main project."

Charlie, always curious, inquired, "But why not just create a new branch within the project?"

Casey answered, "Great question, Charlie. Branches are fantastic for features or fixes that are certain to be integrated back. But when multiple developers are involved, especially those outside the core team, forks allow them to work independently without cluttering the main repository with numerous branches."

Merges

The projector screen transitioned to show two rivers converging into one. Jamie took a moment to let the visual sink in before speaking. "Now that we've explored how to branch out and work independently, let's talk about the process of coming back together."

Casey piped up, "So, this is like when two separate pieces of work are combined into a single, unified codebase?"

Jamie smiled, "Spot on, Casey! 'Merging' is the act of integrating changes from one branch into another. When developers finish their individual tasks or features, they'll want to merge their code back into the main branch, ensuring the project remains up-to-date with everyone's contributions."

Alex, ever the skeptic, raised an eyebrow, "But what if two developers make conflicting changes? That must create chaos."

Jamie chuckled, "You're right, Alex. Conflicts can and do happen. But fear not, Git offers tools and techniques to help resolve these merge conflicts. And as we progress, we'll dive deep into resolving such intricacies."

Charlie, leaning forward with enthusiasm, added, "It's like two streams of thought flowing into a singular vision. It's incredible how Git manages to keep everything streamlined!"

Jamie took a deep breath, her excitement palpable. "Now that we've laid the foundation of collaboration in Git, it's time for us to roll up our sleeves and dive into a hands-on experience. Together, we'll walk through a simulated workflow with Alex and Casey, watching theory transform into practice. Are you all set, team? Our real adventure begins now!"

Hands-On: Team Workflow Simulation with CLI

While platforms like Azure DevOps and GitHub offer intuitive user interfaces, understanding the Command Line Interface (CLI) provides you with a fundamental grasp of Git operations. Let's dive into a simulated Git collaboration using just the CLI.

1. **Cloning the Project Locally**

   Start by cloning the repository to your local machine. Use the `git clone [repository_url]` command, where `[repository_url]` is the link to the repository you wish to work on.

2. **Making Changes and Committing Them**

   Navigate to the project directory and make the necessary changes. Once done, add the modified files using git `add.`, and commit the changes with a descriptive message using `git commit -m "Your descriptive message here."`

3. **Pushing Changes Back to the Repository**

   Push your updates back to the repository using the `git push origin master` command. This ensures the repository is updated with your local changes.

4. **Creating a Pull Request**

   While the actual creation of a pull request is platform-specific, the idea is to propose your changes to be reviewed. After pushing, go to the platform hosting the repository and initiate a pull request.

5. **Merging the Pull Request**

   Once reviewed and approved, the changes can be merged into the main project. A teammate or a repository administrator typically does this step.

With these steps, you've successfully simulated a Git collaborative workflow using the CLI.

Collaborative Coding with Git

Git's collaborative features have revolutionized the way developers work together. By understanding pull requests, forking, and merges, you're equipped to contribute to shared projects seamlessly.

As we progress, we'll explore the challenges that arise when multiple contributors work on the same project simultaneously—introducing the topic of "Conflicts, and Resolutions." But remember, every challenge in coding offers a learning opportunity. Ready to dive deeper?

Conflicts and Resolutions

The TechFusion Corp office was buzzing with the sound of keyboards and the occasional hum of a conversation. The latest release was on the horizon, and everyone was deep in their coding zones. The room's energy, however, shifted noticeably when Casey's surprised voice echoed, "Wait, what just happened? Why is my code not merging?"

Alex, sitting next to Casey, peered into her screen. "Oh, seems like a merge conflict," he mumbled, realizing he had just pushed changes to the same lines of code that Casey was working on.

Jamie, overhearing the conversation, decided this was an opportune moment to discuss an essential aspect of Git. With a reassuring smile, she addressed the team, "Merge conflicts can seem daunting, especially when you encounter them for the first time. But fear not, they're an integral part of collaborative coding, and with a little knowledge and patience, they're easily resolvable."

She then motioned toward the large screen, where a flowchart began to form, depicting a typical merge conflict scenario. The team leaned in, ready to dive deep into the intricacies of conflicts and their resolutions.

Understanding Merge Conflicts

In the world of collaborative coding, it's common for multiple developers to work on the same piece of code simultaneously. Merge conflicts arise when two or more developers change the same lines in a file or when one developer edits a file that another has deleted. Think of it as two trains racing toward each other on the same track. It's Git's way of saying, "Hey, I need some help deciding which change to keep!"

It was a crisp Monday morning at TechFusion Corp. Casey, eager to fix a bug she identified over the weekend, decided to make changes to a function in the project.py file. At the same time, Emma, having worked late last night, pushed her edits to the same function. Without realizing the overlapping efforts, they both attempted to push their changes.

The team's chat room was suddenly filled with messages from a puzzled Casey. Jamie, ever the guiding beacon, stepped in, "Merge conflicts are common, especially in bustling teams like ours. It happens when two or more changes target the same line of code. Git simply can't decide which one to take. It's like when two people try to talk at the same time; we can't understand either clearly." Jamie shared her screen, showing the side-by-side comparison of Casey's and Emma's code (Figure 3-6).

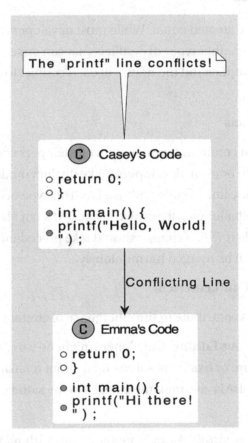

Figure 3-6. *Merge conflicts*

Jamie summed it up, "It's crucial for us to recognize and tackle these merge conflicts. Left unattended, they can lead to bugs in our code. Always communicate and be aware of what your team members are working on."

💡 **Quick Byte!**   "Always pull the latest changes from the main branch before you start coding. It'll help reduce the chances of running into a merge conflict. Think of it as checking the tracks before starting your train journey."

Types of Conflicts

Not all merge conflicts are created equal. While most developers might be familiar with content conflicts, there are other types of conflicts that can arise during the development process. It's essential to understand the nature of each conflict to address them appropriately.

- **Content Conflicts**

    This is the most common type of conflict developers encounter. It arises when two or more developers make distinct modifications to the exact same line of code within a file. This type of conflict is particularly challenging to resolve because it's not always immediately clear which change should take precedence or how the two changes can be merged harmoniously.

    Why Content Conflicts Occur

    Several reasons contribute to the emergence of content conflicts:

    1. **Simultaneous Editing:** Developers might be working on the same feature or fixing the same bug without realizing that someone else is also making changes to the same section of the code.

    2. **Lack of Communication:** In larger teams, without proper communication, multiple developers might end up working on the same part of the codebase.

3. **Delayed Merges:** If a developer works on a feature branch for an extended period and doesn't frequently merge changes from the main branch, the likelihood of conflicts increases when they finally decide to merge their changes.

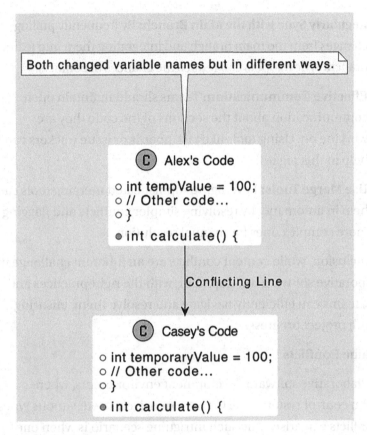

Figure 3-7a. *Content conflicts*

Scenario: As we can see in Figure 3-7a, Alex and Casey once had a tussle over changing a variable name. Alex changed it to tempValue, while Casey thought temporaryValue was more readable. When they tried merging, Git was at a crossroads.

Best Practices to Avoid Content Conflicts

While it's challenging to entirely prevent content conflicts, developers can adopt several best practices to minimize their occurrence:

1. **Regularly Sync with the Main Branch:** By frequently pulling changes from the main branch and integrating them into feature branches, developers can reduce the chances of conflicts.

2. **Effective Communication:** Teams should maintain open communication about the sections of the code they are working on. Using tools like task boards or issue trackers can help in this regard.

3. **Use Merge Tools:** Leveraging sophisticated merging tools can help in automatically resolving simpler conflicts and flagging more complex ones for manual resolution.

In conclusion, while content conflicts are an inherent challenge in collaborative software development, with the right practices and tools, teams can efficiently navigate and resolve them, ensuring smooth project progress.

- **Rename Conflicts**

  In collaborative software development environments, where version control systems like Git are extensively used, various types of conflicts can arise. One such intriguing scenario is when one developer renames a file, while another concurrently makes changes to the original file. This situation poses unique challenges for Git, and understanding it can aid developers in seamless collaboration.

Implications for Developers

This kind of conflict can lead to several issues:

1. **Data Loss:** If not resolved carefully, the changes made by Developer B might be overwritten or lost.

2. **Duplication:** If Git keeps both files, it can lead to redundancy in the codebase.

3. **Confusion:** For other team members, seeing two versions of
    what appears to be the same file can be bewildering.

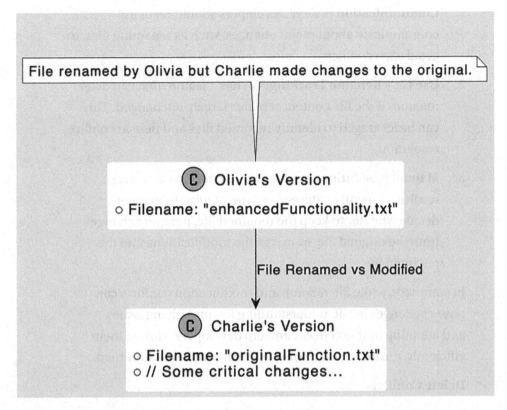

Figure 3-7b. *Rename conflicts*

Scenario: As we can see in Figure 3-7b, Olivia, our cloud expert,
decided to rename a file to better reflect its functionality, while at
the same time, Charlie made critical changes to the same file but
using its original name. A rename conflict ensued.

Resolving the Conflict

To effectively address this situation:

1. **Communication is Key:** Developers should regularly communicate about major changes, such as renaming files, to avoid such conflicts.

2. **Use Git's Rename Tracking:** Git has a feature that can detect renames if the file content remains largely unchanged. This can be leveraged to identify renamed files and help in conflict resolution.

3. **Manual Resolution:** In situations where Git can't auto-resolve the conflict, developers might need to manually decide whether to keep the renamed file, integrate changes from the original file, or merge the modifications into the renamed file.

In summary, while file rename and modification conflicts can pose challenges in Git, understanding the underlying issues and adopting best practices can help developers address them efficiently, ensuring a harmonious collaborative environment.

- **Delete Conflicts**

Version control systems, like Git, are indispensable tools in modern software development. They allow multiple developers to work on a project simultaneously, tracking changes and merging code seamlessly. However, there are instances where conflicts arise that can't be automatically resolved. One such type is the "Delete Conflict."

Challenges for the Development Team

Such a conflict presents multiple challenges:

1. **Data Integrity:** There's a risk of losing important changes if the conflict is not resolved with care.

2. **Workflow Disruption:** Until this conflict is addressed, other dependent features or fixes might be stalled.

3. **Potential Confusion:** For other team members, understanding why a file they're working on or referencing has been deleted can be perplexing.

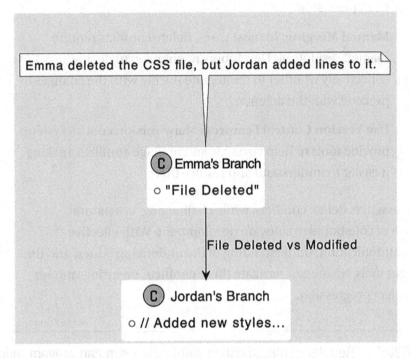

Figure 3-7c. Delete conflict

Scenario: As we can see in Figure 3-7c, Emma, with her eye for design, removed an obsolete CSS file. However, Jordan, trying to reuse some old styles, added a few lines to that very file. When they attempted to merge their changes, a delete conflict occurred.

Best Practices for Resolution

To handle delete conflicts effectively:

1. **Prioritize Communication:** Regular discussions about significant actions, like file deletions or major changes, can preempt many conflicts.

2. **Review the Changes:** Both developers should review the changes and the reason for deletion. Sometimes, the modifications might be critical, or the deletion might have been premature.

3. **Manual Merging:** In most cases, delete conflicts require manual resolution. Developers might need to decide collectively whether to reintegrate the file with the changes or proceed with the deletion.

4. **Use Version Control Features:** Many version control systems provide tools to help visualize and manage conflicts, making it easier to understand and resolve them.

In essence, delete conflicts, while challenging, is a natural part of collaborative software development. With effective communication, understanding of the underlying issues, and the right tools, teams can navigate these conflicts, ensuring smooth project progression.

💡 **Quick Byte!**   "Regular communication within the team can prevent many of these conflicts. Before renaming or deleting a file, always check with the team. A two-minute chat can save hours of resolution time."

Hands-On: Resolving a Merge Conflict with CLI

Merge conflicts can seem daunting, especially for developers newer to Git. The CLI provides tools to navigate and resolve these conflicts. Here, we'll guide you through a real-world example to make this process more approachable.

Setup

1. Both Alex and Casey clone the same repository.

2. Alex makes changes to `fileA.txt` and commits them.

3. Casey simultaneously makes different changes to the same lines in `fileA.txt` and commits them.

4. Casey pushes his changes to the repository.

5. Alex attempts to push his changes, leading to a merge conflict.

Step-by-Step Guide

1. **Detecting the Conflict**

    Command: `git push origin main`

    Output: Git informs Alex that his push has been rejected because there are changes on the remote that he doesn't have locally. It suggests a `git pull` first.

2. **Pulling and Viewing the Conflict**

    Command: `git pull origin main`

    Output: Git displays conflict markers within `fileA.txt`, showing both Alex's and Casey's changes.

3. **Resolving the Conflict**

    Alex needs to manually edit `fileA.txt`, deciding which changes to keep. After editing, the file should no longer contain the conflict markers (`<<<<<<<`, `=======`, `>>>>>>>`).

4. **Committing the Resolved File**

    After resolving the conflict, Alex adds the changes and commits them.

    Commands

    ```
    1. git add fileA.txt
    2. git commit -m "Resolved merge conflict in fileA.txt"
    ```

5. **Pushing the Resolved Changes**

    Now that the conflict is resolved, Alex can safely push his changes.

    Command: `git push origin main`

💡 **Quick Byte!**   "Always ensure you understand the changes you're merging when resolving a conflict. Don't rush the process; take your time to understand the context."

Conflicts and Resolution

The scene is set in TechFusion Corp's cozy conference room, with modern art pieces on the walls and a projector displaying the latest merged pull requests. The team, though a bit exhausted after the deep dive into merge conflicts, appears more confident in their collaborative coding journey.

Jordan, tapping a pen on the table, speaks up first, "Remember everyone, as developers, we're bound to come across merge conflicts. However, it's not just about resolving them—it's also about understanding the root cause. It's often a communication issue."

Jamie nods in agreement, "Absolutely, Jordan. Over the years, I've found that most merge conflicts arise from a lack of synchronization between team members. Make it a habit to pull the latest changes often and communicate about the parts of the codebase you're working on."

Emma, leaning back in her chair, adds, "In my experience, understanding the context of changes in a merge conflict is crucial. It's not just about code; it's about delivering value to our users."

Charlie chimes in, "And don't forget about our 'Buddy System'. When in doubt, review the code with a teammate. Two sets of eyes are always better than one."

Alex, reflecting on the hands-on exercise, comments, "I was initially nervous about resolving conflicts, especially on important branches. But with the CLI and the team's support, I feel more empowered."

Casey adds, "Plus, we've got documentation, best practices, and, most importantly, each other. We're all learning, growing, and facing challenges together."

Olivia, always the advocate for efficient workflows, concludes, "And as we move further, integrating Git with our CI/CD will make this process even smoother."

Jamie gives a final nod, "That's right. With patience, communication, and collaboration, there's no Git challenge we can't overcome."

PRACTICAL EXERCISE: PUTTING YOUR GIT KNOWLEDGE TO TEST

Before we delve into the intricacies of Git in modern workflows, let's put your newfound knowledge to the test. This exercise aims to provide you with hands-on experience, grounding your understanding of collaborative coding with Git and conflict resolutions in practical scenarios.

Exercise Overview

1. **Set Up a Repository**: Begin by creating a new repository on your platform of choice. Whether you're more familiar with GitHub or Azure DevOps, the fundamental concepts remain the same.

2. **Collaborate with Team Members**: Invite a few friends or colleagues to collaborate on your repository. Alternatively, create multiple accounts yourself to simulate a team environment.

3. **Branching and Coding**: Each "team member" should create their own branch and add some code to it. Remember the principles of Git branching discussed earlier.

4. **Simulate Conflicts**: To simulate merge conflicts, make sure two "team members" modify the same portion of the code in their respective branches.

5. **Merging and Resolving Conflicts**: Try merging the branches back into the main branch. Experience firsthand the conflicts that arise and employ the techniques we've discussed to resolve them.

6. **Review and Reflect**: After successfully resolving conflicts and merging all branches, review the final codebase. Reflect on the challenges faced and the steps taken to overcome them.

Resources

While we won't be providing a step-by-step guide, these official documentation links should aid you in navigating through the exercise:

1. **GitHub Documentation:** https://docs.github.com/en/repositories

2. **Azure DevOps Documentation:** https://learn.microsoft.com/en-us/azure/devops/repos/git/?view=azure-devops

---

Tip   While navigating through the documentation, try to relate back to the concepts we've covered in this chapter. Familiarize yourself with the platform's UI/UX, and don't hesitate to explore further!

Remember, practical application reinforces theoretical understanding. By the end of this exercise, you'll have a tangible grasp of Git's collaborative features and conflict resolution techniques. Once done, we'll journey forth into understanding how Git integrates seamlessly into modern development workflows.

Git in the Modern Development Workflow

In the buzzing environment of TechFusion Corp., Jamie gathered her team around. "Alright, team, now that we've got a good grasp on the intricacies of Git and how we collaborate, let's look at the bigger picture. Let's understand how Git is not just a version control system but a game-changer in our entire development workflow."

Alex leaned forward, intrigued, "I mean, I've always known Git to be super important for code management, but are you saying it's more than that?"

Jamie nodded, "Absolutely, Alex. In today's development landscape, Git is not just about managing versions of your code. It's become central to the very workflow of how modern software is built, tested, and deployed."

Evolution of Development Workflows

Back in the day, software development was a much more linear process. Developers would often wait for their turn to access the "main code." Integrations were less frequent, often leading to chaos and disruption.

Fast forward to today, and we have parallel development streams, with teams working concurrently and integrating their changes continuously. This is where Git shines. It streamlines these concurrent processes, ensuring that everyone's work aligns seamlessly.

Jordan jumped in, "And from my end of things, it's a blessing. With Git, project management becomes a breeze. We can integrate it with platforms like Azure DevOps and JIRA, allowing us to keep a close eye on project progress and ensuring that our deliverables are always on track."

Continuous Integration and Continuous Deployment (CI/CD)

The concept of CI/CD has revolutionized the way we build and deploy software. In Figure 3-8, we can see, after the trigger through repository, Continuous integration ensures that any code changes are automatically vetted and integrated, ensuring everything works harmoniously. Continuous deployment, on the other hand, ensures that our validated code gets into the hands of users without delay.

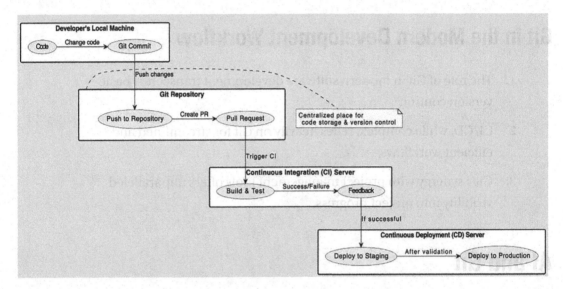

Figure 3-8. *CI/CD—general overview*

Charlie, ever the mentor, added, "It's crucial to understand that while we'll delve deeper into the intricacies of CI/CD in our Azure DevOps chapter, Git remains the beating heart of these processes. It's the foundation upon which our modern development practices are built."

Integration with Project Management Tools

Every code change, every commit, tells a story. When structured right, Git's commit messages can provide invaluable insights into the progress of tasks and user stories. Integrating Git with project management tools amplifies this, creating a two-way street of updates and insights.

Olivia, her eyes always on the cloud, remarked, "The beauty of this integration is its reciprocity. A change in the codebase can update your project management tool, and vice-versa. It's this seamless flow of information that ensures everyone's on the same page."

As Jamie wrapped up the discussion, she emphasized, "Git's not just a tool; it's an ecosystem. Understanding its broader role and integration points in the development world only magnifies its importance. It's about bringing efficiency, transparency, and harmony to our workflows."

Git in the Modern Development Workflow

1. The role of Git in modern software development transcends basic version control.

2. CI/CD, while complex, relies heavily on Git for streamlined and efficient workflows.

3. Git's synergy with project management tools offers unparalleled visibility into project progress.

AI and Git

At TechFusion Corp's conference room, the team gathered around the large projector screen. Jordan begins with a statement, "It's no surprise that Artificial Intelligence is revolutionizing the way we code. But how does this intertwine with Git? Let's dive deep."

Jamie nods, "AI isn't just about robots and self-driving cars. In the realm of software development, AI has made significant strides, enhancing our coding experience. When combined with Git, it's like having a smart assistant by your side, analyzing vast repositories and offering intelligent code suggestions."

Emma, with her design-oriented perspective, chimes in, "It's like having a spellchecker, but for coding! It's fascinating how it can predict code patterns and offer solutions."

Alex, always eager to learn, asks, "But how does AI understand our code in the Git repositories? Is it like it reads and comprehends our code?"

Olivia smiles, "In a way, yes. AI algorithms, especially machine learning models, are trained on massive datasets. They analyze patterns, structures, and even semantics in the code. Git repositories, being rich sources of diverse codebases, serve as excellent data points for these AI tools."

Jamie continues, "The synergy between AI and Git has paved the way for smarter coding practices. Predictive coding, real-time code reviews, and even personalized developer environments have become possible because of this integration."

Jordan concludes, "Today's session will be an exciting journey into the intersection of AI and Git, understanding the benefits it brings to our coding world and the challenges we should be aware of."

Historical Perspective

In the dim light of the conference room, Jamie projects a colorful timeline on the screen, showcasing significant milestones of AI in software development.

She begins, "To truly appreciate where we are today, we need to take a step back and look at the journey of AI in the world of coding."

- **Early 2000s—Rule-Based Systems:** "In the beginning, AI in software development was predominantly rule-based. Developers would define a set of rules, and the system would generate or analyze code based on these. It was a rigid system, and while it could handle specific tasks, it lacked flexibility."

- **Mid-2000s—Machine Learning Makes an Entry:** "Then came machine learning. Instead of relying solely on hardcoded rules, systems could now learn from examples. This was a game-changer. Tools started emerging that could predict possible code errors or even suggest code optimizations."

- **Late 2000s—Deep Learning Revolution:** "The emergence of deep learning architectures, especially neural networks, took AI capabilities in coding to a whole new level. Code became more than just syntax; it was about understanding context and semantics."

- **Early 2010s—Rise of Predictive Coding:** "With more sophisticated models, tools could now predict what a developer might type next, offering auto-completions and reducing the coding effort. It was like having a co-pilot guiding through the code."

Emma, intrigued, remarks, "It's almost like how design tools evolved to predict what designers might want next. From mere tools to intelligent assistants."

- **Mid 2010s—AI-Driven Code Reviews:** "By analyzing vast repositories, AI-driven tools could now review code in real-time, highlighting potential issues or suggesting better coding practices. It was no longer just about assisting developers but elevating the overall code quality."

- **Late 2010s—Integration with Version Control Systems:** "And that brings us to our current era. The integration of AI with Git and other version control systems. Using the historical data from repositories, AI tools provide insights, predict future issues, and even automate some mundane tasks."

Charlie, with his seasoned experience, nods in agreement, "The journey of AI in coding has been incredible. From simple rule-based systems to intelligent tools that understand context, it has truly transformed our coding experience."

Jordan concludes, "With this historical perspective, we can now delve deeper into how AI and Git together are setting the stage for the future of software development."

The AI-Git Synergy

In the main meeting room, Jamie switches slides to reveal a detailed flowchart illustrating the deep synergy between AI and Git.

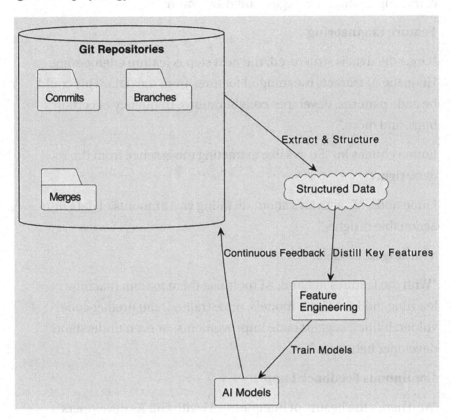

Figure 3-9. *AI in Git repositories*

She gestures toward the Figure 3-9, explaining, "To truly harness the capabilities of AI in software development, it's crucial to understand how it synergizes with Git."

1. **Data Collection from Git Repositories**

   "At the heart of AI's prowess is data. Git repositories are treasure troves of data. Every commit, merge, and branch contains rich information about coding patterns, developer behaviors, and even potential code vulnerabilities."

2. **Structured Data Extraction**

"However, raw Git data isn't directly usable. AI tools first structure this data. This involves parsing code, understanding file changes, extracting commit messages, and much more."

3. **Feature Engineering**

"Once the data is structured, the next step is feature engineering. Here, the AI extracts meaningful features from the data. This could be code patterns, developer collaborations, frequency of certain bugs, and more."

Emma chimes in, "So, it's like extracting the essence from the data, right?"

Jamie nods, "Exactly! It's about distilling vast amounts of data into actionable insights."

4. **Training AI Models**

"With the features in hand, AI tools use them to train machine learning models. These models, once trained, can predict code vulnerabilities, suggest code improvements, or even understand developer behaviors."

5. **Continuous Feedback Loop**

"And here's the beauty of integrating AI with Git. As developers continue to commit, push, and merge code, the AI models get a continuous stream of new data. This helps in refining the models, making them better over time."

Alex, trying to grasp the depth of it, asks, "So, the more we use Git, the smarter these AI tools become?"

Jamie smiles, "Precisely! It's a symbiotic relationship. Our coding practices feed the AI, and in return, the AI elevates our coding experience."

Jordan, pointing to the flowchart, adds, "This synergy doesn't just improve efficiency. It's reshaping how we approach software development. We're moving from a reactive approach to a proactive one, where issues are identified even before they manifest."

Benefits of AI in Git

At TechFusion Corp, the team always stays on top of the latest technological advances. Emma, being the frontend specialist, was intrigued by how AI could refine her coding process. Jamie, never one to miss a teachable moment, began discussing the various benefits that come with integrating AI in Git:

Predictive Coding

Jamie started with a fascinating point: "You know how we often type a few words on our smartphones, and it suggests the next word? Imagine something similar but for coding!"

How it works: As developers type out code, AI-driven tools analyze the patterns and, based on vast datasets and past code structures, predict the next lines or even entire code blocks. This not only speeds up the coding process but can also help prevent syntax errors and logical mistakes.

Emma's reaction: "It's like having a coding assistant whispering in your ear, making sure you're on the right track."

Code Review Assistance

Alex chimed in, recalling a recent error he had made, which could have been easily caught by an AI tool. Jamie nodded in agreement, highlighting how AI can be invaluable during code reviews.

How it works: By scanning the codebase, AI tools identify potential bugs, vulnerabilities, or areas of optimization. These tools understand code structures and can point out areas that might lead to future issues, ensuring a smoother development cycle.

Alex's reaction: "That would have saved me a couple of hours last week!"

Improved Code Search

Charlie, having been in the game for a while, remembered the days when finding a specific piece of code in large repositories felt like searching for a needle in a haystack. Jamie pointed out how AI has transformed this aspect.

How it works: Traditional search algorithms rely on exact matches. In contrast, AI-driven search algorithms understand the context and semantics behind code, fetching results that are contextually more relevant, even if they don't match the search query verbatim.

Charlie's reaction: "I wish we had this a decade ago!"

Personalized Coding Experience

Jamie left one of the most intriguing benefits for last. "Imagine your coding environment adapting to your habits, offering you tools and suggestions based on your past interactions."

How it works: By analyzing a developer's past coding patterns and preferences, AI can tailor the Integrated Development Environment (IDE) to individual needs. It might suggest commonly used functions, libraries, or even adjust the interface to better suit the developer's habits.

Casey's reaction: "That sounds like a dream! My IDE knows me better than I know myself."

Jordan, the project manager, summed up the conversation, "Harnessing the power of AI in our Git workflows is not just about convenience. It's about enhancing productivity, ensuring code quality, and fostering a more intuitive development environment."

Challenges and Limitations of Integrating AI with Git

Back at TechFusion Corp, while the team was excited about the prospects of AI in their Git workflows, they also wanted to be aware of the potential challenges. Being the voice of experience, Jamie decided to outline some of the challenges and limitations they might encounter.

Over-reliance on AI Tools

Jamie began, "It's easy to become dependent on AI-driven suggestions, especially when they often seem spot-on. However, this can lead to decreased problem-solving abilities over time."

How it works: While AI can predict code and suggest optimizations, over-relying on it might make developers complacent. They might stop challenging themselves to come up with unique solutions or overlook potential errors that AI didn't catch.

Charlie's reaction: "It's essential to remember that AI is a tool, not a replacement."

Misinterpretations and False Positives

Alex recalled a time when he used a grammar correction tool that misunderstood his intent. Jamie nodded, "Just like those tools, AI can sometimes misinterpret code context."

How it works: No AI is perfect. It can sometimes misinterpret the context or provide suggestions that might not be the most optimal for a specific scenario. Additionally, it might flag areas in the code that aren't actual issues, leading to wasted time.

Emma's reaction: "It's a good reminder to always double-check and not take every AI suggestion at face value."

Privacy and Data Security Concerns

Olivia, the cloud expert, raised an essential point about data security. "Many AI tools require access to our codebase. We need to ensure they handle our data with utmost confidentiality."

How it works: To provide accurate predictions and analyses, AI tools might need access to the entire codebase or parts of it. This can raise concerns about how the data is stored, processed, and whether it's shared with third parties.

Jordan's reaction: "Absolutely, data privacy is paramount. We must vet any tool we use."

Learning Curve and Integration Hiccups

While AI tools can simplify many processes, Jamie emphasized that "Like any new technology, there's a learning curve. Not every integration will be smooth."

How it works: Integrating AI tools with existing Git workflows might require changes in the way the team operates. There might be initial hiccups, compatibility issues, or the need for training sessions.

Casey's reaction: "A bit of initial struggle for long-term benefits seems fair!"

Jamie concluded, "Like any tool, AI has its strengths and weaknesses. It's up to us to leverage its advantages while being mindful of its limitations." The team nodded in agreement, appreciating the balanced perspective.

Pro Tips and Best Practices when Integrating AI with Git

Back at the TechFusion Corp's workspace, Jamie gathers the team for a knowledge-sharing session. With her years of experience, she has accumulated a wealth of tips and best practices when working with AI and Git.

Continuous Learning

Jamie starts, "The field of AI is ever-evolving. Keep yourself updated with the latest advancements and tool updates."

How it works: AI models and algorithms frequently undergo updates and optimizations. Staying updated ensures that you're leveraging the best capabilities of the tool.

Trust, but Verify

Charlie stresses, "While AI can be impressively accurate, always verify its suggestions, especially in critical code sections."

How it works: Blindly accepting AI's recommendations without understanding can lead to unintentional bugs or vulnerabilities.

Alex's input: "I remember accepting a code suggestion once without checking, only to spend hours debugging later."

Set Clear Boundaries

Olivia points out, "Ensure that your AI tools have clear permissions. Limit their access only to necessary parts of the codebase."

How it works: Setting permissions ensures data security and minimizes the risk of unintentional changes or breaches.

Jordan's reaction: "Protecting our IP is crucial. Clear boundaries are a must."

Use Feedback Loops

Jamie emphasizes the importance of feedback. "AI tools improve based on feedback. If a suggestion isn't right, report it."

How it works: Many AI-driven tools come with feedback options. Regular feedback helps train the AI for better accuracy over time.

Casey's input: "It's like training a puppy. The more feedback it gets, the better it becomes."

Collaborative Decision-Making

Emma suggests, "When unsure about an AI's recommendation, discuss it with the team."

How it works: A collective decision often leads to more informed choices, combining the best of AI and human intelligence.

Charlie's reaction: "Two heads are better than one, and with AI, it's like having an extra brain in the team."

Jamie wraps up the session, reminding the team that the marriage of AI and Git holds immense potential. "Let's harness its power judiciously and always prioritize the human touch in our coding endeavors."

The team departs, feeling empowered with a treasure trove of tips and best practices under their belt.

Git and AI Recap

The melding of AI with Git has reshaped coding practices. Through predictive coding, enhanced reviews, and a tailored developer environment, AI optimizes the coding process. However, it's vital for developers, like the team at TechFusion Corp, to balance reliance on AI tools with their expertise.

As AI's role in development grows, its synergy with Git promises further enhancements. It's an exciting frontier, and the key will be leveraging AI's strengths while maintaining the human touch in coding.

Conclusion

In this digital age, where coding is tantamount to creating worlds, a proper management system is the backbone of any successful software project. With Git at the helm, developers can travel through time, review historical changes, collaborate seamlessly, and even harness the power of Artificial Intelligence to optimize their workflows. From the fundamentals of repositories and commits to the complexities of merges and conflicts, we've journeyed through the vast universe of Git.

But, as with all tales of technology, the story never ends. We merely turn the page to a new chapter. From the abstract realm of code, we now move to a more tangible one—the world of data. Because what is code without data? They are two sides of the same coin, intertwined and indispensable.

Key Takeaways

- **Version Control Is Essential:** Git's importance in tracking changes, collaborating across teams, and safeguarding code against potential losses.

- **Collaboration and Efficiency:** Git enhances teamwork by streamlining workflows and reducing conflicts, making project management more efficient.

- **Adaptability and Future Readiness:** Understanding Git prepares developers for future technological advancements and integration with AI tools, ensuring they remain competitive and skilled.

- **Practical Skills:** Through hands-on examples and scenarios, readers gain practical skills in Git operations, reinforcing the theoretical knowledge with actionable insights.

Transitioning into Database Diaries

Having grasped the foundational aspects of Git, we now transition to Chapter 4, "Database Diaries: Chronicles of Structured Memories." This next chapter shifts our focus from the management and collaboration of code to the heart of data storage and manipulation. Understanding databases is critical for any software development, as it deals with efficiently storing, retrieving, and manipulating data. As we delve into databases, we'll explore their evolution, types, and the role they play in the broader context of software development, building on the foundational knowledge of Git to further equip our journey toward full-stack development proficiency.

Bonus Byte 2: Unleashing the Power of GitHub Pages

GitHub Pages is a streamlined static site hosting service designed to convert GitHub repositories into live websites. It's ideal for hosting personal blogs, project documentation, or organizational sites, primarily using HTML, CSS, and JavaScript. This service harnesses GitHub's robust infrastructure to offer reliable and integrated web hosting, directly linked with your GitHub projects.

One of the standout features of GitHub Pages is its free hosting, making it a perfect platform for developers, students, and creators to showcase their work without any additional costs. This cost-effectiveness, combined with ease of content updates through GitHub, makes it an attractive choice for those starting their online presence or looking to share projects and ideas with a broader audience.

How GitHub Pages Works

Setting up a repository for GitHub Pages is a straightforward process:

1. Personal or Organizational Pages:

    a. Create a new repository on your GitHub account named <username>.github.io, where <username> is your GitHub username.

    b. Example: If your GitHub username is johnDoe, the repository name should be johnDoe.github.io.

    c. This repository will host the HTML, CSS, and JavaScript files for your site.

2. Project Pages:

    a. Within your project's GitHub repository, you can use two methods to set up GitHub Pages:

- gh-pages Branch: Create a branch named gh-pages. GitHub Pages will serve the content from this branch.

- /docs Folder: Alternatively, you can store your website content in a /docs folder on the main branch.

3. Documentation Reference:

    a. For detailed steps on setting up your repository, GitHub provides comprehensive guides at GitHub Pages Documentation.

      `https://docs.github.com/en/pages`

GitHub Pages is optimized for hosting static content, primarily:

1. **HTML**: The backbone of your website, representing the structure and content.

2. **CSS**: Used for styling and layout of your web pages.

3. **JavaScript**: Adds interactivity and dynamic elements to your site.

In addition to these, GitHub Pages has excellent support for Jekyll, a static site generator:

1. **Jekyll**: It allows you to create more complex and sophisticated layouts. Jekyll processes your content and generates static HTML pages for your site.

2. Jekyll is natively supported by GitHub Pages, meaning you can directly use it without any additional setup.

Using Jekyll:

1. To use Jekyll, include a _config.yml file in your repository and organize your content accordingly.

2. GitHub Pages will automatically build and serve your Jekyll site.

Documentation for Jekyll:

For more information on using Jekyll with GitHub Pages, visit the Jekyll documentation at Jekyll Docs. `https://jekyllrb.com/docs/`

Setting Up a GitHub Pages Site

Setting up your GitHub Pages site starts with creating a new repository:

1. Log in to your GitHub account.

2. Click on the New repository button.

3. For a personal or organizational site, name your repository
   <username>.github.io. Replace <username> with your actual
   GitHub username.

   a. Example: If your GitHub username is janeDoe, your repository
      should be named janeDoe.github.io.

4. Initialize the repository with a README, if desired.

5. Click Create repository.

Once your repository is set up, it's time to add your website's content:

1. Clone the repository to your local machine using Git.

2. Add your HTML, CSS, and JavaScript files to the repository.

   a. Start with an index.html file, which will be the main page of
      your site.

   b. Include any additional assets (images, stylesheets, scripts, etc.)
      your site requires.

   c. Commit and push the changes back to GitHub.

   Example:

```sh code
git add index.html style.css script.js
git commit -m "Initial website files"
git push origin master
```

Finally, enable GitHub Pages for your repository:

1. Go to your repository on GitHub.

2. Navigate to Settings.

3. Scroll down to the Pages section.

4. Under the Source section, select the branch you want to deploy (usually master or main).

5. Choose the folder (root or /docs) containing your site.

6. Click Save, and GitHub Pages will automatically deploy your site.

Customizing Your Site

Using a custom domain with your GitHub Pages site adds a professional touch and enhances your brand identity:

1. **Acquire a Domain Name:** First, purchase a domain name from a domain registrar of your choice.

2. **Add a CNAME File:**

   a. In your GitHub repository, create a file named CNAME.

   b. Inside this file, write your custom domain name (e.g., www.example.com).

   c. Commit and push this CNAME file to your GitHub repository.

3. **Configure Your Domain's DNS Settings:**

   a. Go to your domain registrar's website.

   b. Navigate to the DNS management page.

   c. Add a CNAME record for www that points to <username>.github. io. Replace <username> with your GitHub username.

   d. If you want to use an apex domain (like example.com), add A records pointing to GitHub's IP addresses (found in GitHub's documentation).

4. **Enable HTTPS:** For security, ensure to enable HTTPS in your GitHub Pages settings, which is available once the custom domain is properly set and propagated.

For a detailed guide, refer to the GitHub documentation on custom domains: Setting up a custom domain—`https://docs.github.com/en/pages/configuring-a-custom-domain-for-your-github-pages-site`.

Enhance your GitHub Pages site with Jekyll themes:

1. **Choosing a Theme**

   a. Browse through Jekyll's theme directory or other theme repositories to find a theme that suits your site's purpose.

   b. Some themes are specifically designed for portfolios, blogs, or documentation.

2. **Applying the Theme**

   a. Once you select a theme, add the theme to your site's _config.yml file. For example: theme: `jekyll-theme-minimal`.

   b. Custom themes might require cloning or forking their repository.

3. **Customizing the Theme**

   a. Modify the theme's HTML, CSS, and JavaScript files to suit your style and needs.

   b. Update _config.yml with specific configurations like title, description, and navigation links.

4. **Creating Your Own Theme**

   a. If you're comfortable with HTML/CSS, consider creating your own Jekyll theme for a unique design.

   b. Follow Jekyll's documentation on creating and using custom themes. `https://jekyllrb.com/docs/themes/`.

Deploying Your Site on GitHub Pages

Deploying your site on GitHub Pages is a simple and automated process:

1. **Final Checks**

    a. Before deployment, ensure that all your website files (HTML, CSS, JavaScript, images, etc.) are correctly added, committed, and pushed to your GitHub repository.

    b. Verify that your index.html file is present and that all links and resources are correctly referenced.

2. **Deployment Process**

    a. Once your content is ready and pushed to GitHub, navigate to your repository's settings.

    b. In the Pages section, choose the branch you want to deploy (usually master or main).

    c. GitHub automatically builds your site from the selected branch. If you're using Jekyll, it will process your site and generate static HTML pages.

    d. After selecting your source, GitHub Pages will provide a URL where your site is published. It typically takes a few minutes for the site to go live.

3. **Monitoring Deployment**

    a. GitHub provides a deployment status on the Pages section of your repository settings. You can monitor the progress there.

    b. Once the deployment is successful, your site will be accessible at the provided URL (<username>.github.io or your custom domain).

4. **Updating Your Site**

    a. To update your site, simply make changes to your files, commit, and push them to your repository.

    b. GitHub Pages will automatically rebuild and redeploy your site with the new changes.

5. **Troubleshooting Deployment Issues**

   a. If you encounter any issues during deployment, check the GitHub Pages section for error messages.

   b. Common issues include file naming conflicts, incorrect paths, or missing files.

6. **Documentation Reference**

   a. For a detailed deployment guide and troubleshooting tips, visit the official GitHub Pages documentation: GitHub Pages Deployment Guide—https://docs.github.com/en/pages.

Conclusion

GitHub Pages stands out as a robust and user-friendly platform, perfect for hosting a variety of websites. From personal blogs and portfolios to project documentation, it offers a cost-effective, integrated, and straightforward solution for web hosting. Its compatibility with Jekyll further enhances its appeal, providing flexibility in design and content management.

Whether you're a student showcasing a project, a professional building a portfolio, or a hobbyist sharing your passions, GitHub Pages is an excellent choice for hosting your website. With its seamless GitHub integration, free hosting, and community support, it empowers users to create and maintain their online presence with ease and efficiency.

CHAPTER 4

Database Diaries: Chronicles of Structured Memories

In the previous chapter, you accompanied the TechFusion Corp team on a journey through the collaborative world of Git. Together with Jamie, Alex, Casey, and the rest, you navigated branches, merges, and even experienced the power of AI in coding.

Now, as the team settles down, ready for the next phase of their digital odyssey, Jamie gathers them for a new adventure. The room is abuzz with anticipation, and so should you be, as we delve deeper into the heart of software development.

"Data is everywhere," Jamie begins, addressing both her team and you, the reader. "It shapes our experiences and drives the logic of our applications. To build impactful software, we must understand how to efficiently store and retrieve this data. Today, we venture into the intricate world of databases."

Jamie introduces Charlie, a seasoned developer with deep knowledge of databases. "Charlie will lead us in this exploration," she announces. As Charlie steps forward, ready to unravel the mysteries of databases, you too are invited to join the team on this exploration.

"Databases are the silent guardians of data, ensuring it's stored, retrieved, and managed effectively," Charlie starts. "Whether it's the details of a user logging into an app or a complex transaction in a banking system, databases are at play."

As you read along, imagine yourself amidst the TechFusion Corp team, listening intently to Charlie. The stage is set for a new adventure, where bytes of data weave stories and tables form the tapestry of applications. Ready to dive into the Chronicles of Structured Memories?

© Arpit Dwivedi 2024
A. Dwivedi, *CodeMosaic*, https://doi.org/10.1007/979-8-8688-0276-8_4

The Essence of Data

In the bustling office of TechFusion Corp, the atmosphere was buzzing with anticipation. Fresh from their enlightening journey through Git, the team was eager to embark on their next adventure: understanding the world of data. Jamie, the seasoned lead developer, could sense the eagerness in the air. "Data," she began, addressing the team, "is the lifeblood of every application we create. Whether it's a user's login credentials or the intricate details of a transaction, data is pivotal. Today, we delve into understanding the essence of data and its omnipresence in our digital world."

As Jamie spoke, Alex, the enthusiastic new developer, couldn't help but recall the numerous times he had interacted with data, even without realizing it. The personalized playlists on his music app, the recommendations on his favorite shopping site, all were instances where data was silently at play.

Data in Applications: The Silent Facilitator

In the realm of software development, data silently facilitates every interaction, shaping user experiences and driving functionalities. Let's delve into understanding how this unsung hero navigates through applications:

- **Creation**

  Every action in an application leads to data creation. For instance, when you draft a message on a chat application, you're generating textual data.

- **Storage**

  This data doesn't vanish into thin air; it's stored meticulously in databases. These storage units ensure that your data remains intact and accessible.

- **Retrieval**

  The next time you log in, your chat history loads up seamlessly. This is the data retrieval process at work, fetching and displaying the stored data.

- **Manipulation**

  Often, data isn't displayed as-is. It may be sorted, filtered, or
  modified. For instance, your chat app may show the most recent
  messages first.

To visualize this cycle, consider a flowchart depicting the journey of a piece of data—
from creation to storage, retrieval, and manipulation.

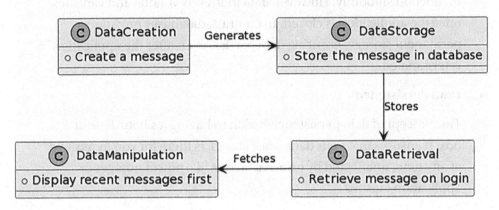

Figure 4-1. *Message handling system*

This flowchart in Figure 4-1 elucidates the cycle of data within an application,
making it easier to comprehend how a simple action translates into a series of data
operations.

In the TechFusion Corp office, Charlie elucidated this concept, using the analogy of
a social media post to explain the cycle. "Think of it like crafting a social media post," he
suggested to the team, including Alex and Casey. "Your post, be it text, images, or videos,
is data that gets stored and can be retrieved by others. It's an ongoing cycle: Create, Store,
Retrieve." Alex and Casey found themselves appreciating the depth of what seemed like
simple interactions on their favorite apps, realizing that there was much more happening
behind the scenes.

The Need for Storage: A Non-negotiable Necessity

Applications without data storage are like libraries without books—seemingly functional but fundamentally purposeless. Let's delve deeper into understanding why storing data is non-negotiable:

- **Temporary vs. Permanent Storage**

  Every application uses some form of temporary storage, like RAM, to function smoothly. However, data in RAM is volatile and vanishes once the application is closed. In contrast, databases provide permanent storage, ensuring data persists even after the application is terminated.

- **Data Persistence**

  The concept of data persistence is akin to having a safety deposit box. It ensures that your data, once stored, is there for you to retrieve at any time, unaffected by external factors like power outages or application crashes.

- **Security and Reliability**

  Databases don't just store data; they protect it. With features like encryption and backups, databases ensure that your data is secure and can be recovered even in case of system failures.

- **Scalability and Accessibility**

  Databases are designed to scale with growing data and user demands. They ensure data is accessible from anywhere, providing the backbone for applications to function seamlessly across different devices and geographies.

To illustrate this, consider a diagram comparing the benefits of permanent storage (databases) against temporary storage (RAM).

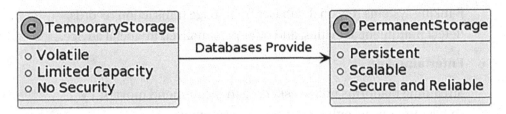

Figure 4-2. *Storage system overview*

This Figure 4-2 encapsulates the benefits of permanent storage, underscoring why databases are pivotal in ensuring data security, reliability, and scalability.

At TechFusion Corp, Charlie likened data storage to a superhero's utility belt. "Imagine you're a superhero," he said to the team, drawing a chuckle from Alex and Casey. "Your powers are your application's functionalities. But your utility belt, that's your data storage. It ensures you have what you need, when you need it, securely and reliably." The analogy resonated with the team, driving home the importance of data storage in application development.

Data and Real-World Applications: Transforming Industries

In today's digital age, data-centric applications are not just prevalent; they're transformative. Let's explore how data-driven applications are reshaping various industries:

- **Healthcare**

  Patient records, treatment histories, and diagnostic data are meticulously managed, allowing healthcare providers to offer personalized care. Data analytics aids in predicting outbreaks and enhancing preventative care.

- **E-Commerce**

  From tracking inventory and orders to understanding user preferences, data is pivotal. Real-time data analysis enables personalized recommendations and efficient supply chain management.

123

- **Finance**

  Banking systems rely on databases to manage transaction records, detect fraudulent activities, and offer personalized financial advice.

- **Entertainment**

  Streaming platforms utilize user data to recommend movies, TV shows, and music, enhancing user engagement.

- **Education**

  Learning platforms analyze data to tailor educational content to individual student needs, ensuring a more personalized learning experience.

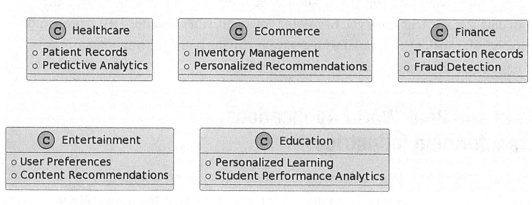

Figure 4-3. *Data applications*

Figure 4-3 illustrates the extensive use of data in modern applications across different industries.

At TechFusion Corp, Charlie highlighted how different sectors are harnessing the power of data. "Whether it's Alex's playlist recommendations or Casey's online shopping suggestions, data is working behind the scenes," he explained. The team nodded in understanding, recognizing the ubiquity of data in their daily lives.

The Transition from Git to Databases: Managing Code and Data

Understanding Git provides a solid foundation for grasping the principles of databases. Let's explore the parallels between version control and databases:

- **Storing Information**

  Just as Git stores and manages different versions of code, databases manage and store diverse sets of data.

- **Consistency and Integrity**

  Both Git and databases ensure that the stored information, whether code or data, remains consistent and uncorrupted.

- **Collaboration**

  Git facilitates collaborative coding, while databases enable multiple users to access and manipulate data concurrently, ensuring smooth workflow.

- **Retrieval and Updates**

  Git allows developers to retrieve past versions of code, while databases provide mechanisms to query and update stored data efficiently.

Charlie drew parallels between the team's experience with Git and databases. "Remember how Git helped us manage our code? Databases do the same for data," Charlie explained, bridging the gap between the two concepts for Alex, Casey, and the rest of the team.

Conclusion: The Essence of Data

The similarities between version control systems like Git and databases provide a seamless transition into understanding the intricacies of data management. As we delve deeper into the world of databases, we will explore the mechanisms that ensure efficient storage, retrieval, and manipulation of data.

Databases: The Keepers of Knowledge

Imagine a world without organization—a library with no catalogue system, a hospital with no patient records, or an online store with no inventory tracking. This would result in chaos. In the realm of software development, databases act as the organizers, efficiently managing and safeguarding data. They serve as the backbone of applications, ensuring seamless functionality and user experiences.

What Is a Database?

Databases are structured systems designed to collect, store, manage, and retrieve information. They ensure that data is easily accessible, manageable, and updated.

Role in Applications:

From social media platforms storing user profiles to e-commerce sites tracking orders, databases play a crucial role in almost every application. They ensure data integrity and facilitate quick retrieval and storage.

Types of Databases

- **Relational Databases (SQL)**

  Relational databases, often referred to as SQL databases, use a structure called a table to organize data into rows and columns. Examples include Microsoft SQL Server, MySQL, and PostgreSQL. These databases are known for their robustness and ACID compliance (Atomicity, Consistency, Isolation, Durability).

- **NoSQL Databases**

  NoSQL databases are designed to allow for more flexibility in storing data. They can store and process a large amount of unstructured data. Examples include MongoDB, Cassandra, and Redis.

- **Choosing the Right Database**

  The choice of database depends on the application's needs. While SQL databases are often chosen for transactions and data integrity, NoSQL databases can be preferred for scalability and flexibility.

Databases in Real-World Applications

- **Practical Usage**

  Databases find practical applications across various industries.
  For instance:

  - **Healthcare:** Medical applications use databases to manage
    patient records, prescriptions, and treatment histories. Quick
    retrieval of patient information can be life-saving.

  - **E-Commerce:** Platforms like Amazon and eBay use databases to
    track inventory, user preferences, and orders. This ensures that
    the customers see up-to-date product availability and receive
    personalized recommendations.

  - **Social Media:** Platforms like Facebook and Instagram use
    databases to store user profiles, posts, images, and interactions.
    Every like, comment, and share is recorded and retrieved from
    databases in real-time.

  - **Banking:** Banks heavily rely on databases to manage accounts,
    transactions, and customer data. The integrity and security of this
    data are paramount.

  - **Education:** Online learning platforms use databases to
    store course content, track student progress, and manage
    subscriptions.

- **Importance of Efficiency**

  The efficiency of these applications is often determined by how well
  they can store, retrieve, and manipulate data. Slow data retrieval can
  lead to poor user experiences, while data inconsistencies can lead to
  serious errors.

- **Diversity of Data**

  The diversity in the data types and structures managed by these
  applications underscores the need for different types of databases.
  While structured data fits well into SQL databases, unstructured or
  semi-structured data may find a better home in NoSQL databases.

Charlie continued his session, showcasing examples from healthcare, e-commerce, and social media to drive home the significance of databases. "Imagine logging into your favorite shopping site," he addressed the team, "and every time you visit, it forgets your preferences. Frustrating, right? That's where databases come in, ensuring seamless and personalized experiences."

Alex and Casey could see the light bulbs turning on in their heads as they realized the omnipresence and significance of databases in enhancing user experiences across different platforms.

Conclusion: Databases—The Keepers of Knowledge

Understanding databases as the keepers of knowledge sets the stage for delving deeper into the intricacies of data management. In the upcoming sections, we will explore SQL, the language that breathes life into relational databases, and understand how to harness its power effectively.

SQL: The Lingua Franca of Databases

Navigating the realms of databases, the TechFusion Corp team is set to explore the language that serves as the bridge between developers and databases—SQL. Jamie, recognizing Charlie's expertise in databases, hands him the mantle to guide the team through SQL. You, too, are about to delve into SQL, the Structured Query Language, understanding its indispensable role in managing databases.

Setting Up SQL Server

Charlie takes the lead to introduce everyone to SQL Server. SQL Server, he explains, is a relational database management system developed by Microsoft, and it's widely used in the industry. Understanding how to set it up is the first step in one's journey to mastering databases.

"Before we write any SQL queries, we need a place to run them," Charlie explains. He guides the team to download SQL Server Management Studio (SSMS), an integrated environment to manage the database server.

- Downloading and Installing SSMS:

  - You can download SSMS from the official Microsoft website.

    - Either you can follow this link: `https://learn.microsoft.com/en-us/sql/ssms/sql-server-management-studio-ssms?view=sql-server-ver16`

    - Or you can directly Google search for SSMS, and follow the steps.

  - The installation process is straightforward. Simply follow the on-screen instructions, selecting the default options where appropriate.

- Exploring the SSMS Interface:

  - Once installed, open SSMS to explore its interface:

    - **Object Explorer:** This is a tree-like structure that displays all your databases and their components. You can interact with databases, tables, views, and other database objects here.

    - **Query Window:** This is where you can write and execute your SQL queries.

    - **Results Pane:** The results of your executed queries will be displayed here.

Hands-On

Now that you're familiar with the SSMS interface, let's get our hands dirty. Here are some tasks you can perform:

1. Install SSMS.

2. Explore the Interface:

   a. Open SSMS and connect to a server instance.

   b. Navigate through the Object Explorer and identify databases, tables, and other objects.

      c. Open a Query Window and observe the layout.

      d. Execute a simple query like `SELECT 1`, and view the result in the Results Pane.

3. Familiarize with Menu Options:

      a. Explore the menu bar options like File, Edit, View, etc., to get a sense of the functionalities they offer.

4. Settings and Preferences:

      a. Navigate to the options (Tools ➤ Options) and explore the settings available to customize your SSMS experience.

With SSMS set up, you're now ready to delve into the world of databases and SQL queries. Next, we'll explore how to create databases and tables within SSMS.

Creating Databases and Tables

Charlie, known for his extensive knowledge in databases, began the session with a profound statement, "A well-structured database is like a well-organized library, where finding information is a breeze." Creating a database is your first step in the world of SQL. It's akin to setting up a new notebook where each page (table) holds different sets of information. Let's walk through how you can create a database and tables using SQL Server Management Studio (SSMS).

Creating a Database

A database is a structured set of data stored electronically. In SQL Server, a database holds tables, views, and other database objects.

1. SQL Syntax:

      a. `CREATE DATABASE YourDatabaseName;`

2. Task in SSMS:

      a. Open a new query window.

      b. Execute the `CREATE DATABASE` query.

      c. Refresh the Databases node in Object Explorer to see your new database.

Creating Tables

Tables are objects within a database that hold the data. Each table has columns (attributes) and rows (records).

1. SQL Syntax:

```
USE YourDatabaseName;
CREATE TABLE YourTableName (
    Column1 datatype,
    Column2 datatype,
    ...
);
```

2. Task in SSMS:

    a. Switch to your database using USE.

    b. Execute the CREATE TABLE query.

    c. Refresh your database node to see your new table under the Tables node.

Primary Key and Data Types

Each table usually has a primary key, a column that uniquely identifies each record. Data types define the kind of data each column can store.

1. SQL Syntax:

```
CREATE TABLE YourTableName (
    ID INT PRIMARY KEY,
    Name NVARCHAR(50),
    Age INT
);
```

2. Task in SSMS:

    a. Create a table specifying the primary key and data types for each column.

131

Viewing Tables

After creating tables, you can view their structure and data.

1. SQL Syntax:

   ```
   SELECT * FROM YourTableName;
   ```

2. Task in SSMS:

   a. Execute the SELECT query to view the data in your table.

Alex, with his eyes wide open, exclaimed, "Wow! It's incredible how we can set up and view a database so quickly!"

Hands-On

1. **Create a Database:** Create a database named TechFusionDB.

2. **Create a Table:** In TechFusionDB, create a table named Employees with columns ID, Name, Position, and Age.

3. **View Table:** View the structure and data of the Employees table.

By now, you've created a database and a table, laying the groundwork for storing data. Charlie smiled, seeing the team's enthusiasm, and said, "This is just the beginning. As we move forward, we will delve into how to populate this table with data and retrieve it when needed."

Basic SQL Queries: CRUD Operations

Charlie continued, emphasizing the foundational operations that make databases interactive and dynamic. "CRUD operations—Create, Read, Update, and Delete—are the essence of any data interaction," he explained.

CRUD Overview

CRUD stands for Create, Read, Update, and Delete—these are the basic operations performed on any database.

Importance: Understanding CRUD operations is crucial as they form the basis of data manipulation.

Create Operation

The Create operation refers to inserting new records into a table.

SQL Syntax:

```
INSERT INTO YourTableName (Column1, Column2, ...)
VALUES (Value1, Value2, ...);
```

Read Operation

The Read operation fetches and displays data from the tables.

SQL Syntax:

```
SELECT * FROM YourTableName;
```

Update Operation

The Update operation modifies existing records in a table.

SQL Syntax:

```
UPDATE YourTableName
SET Column1 = Value1, Column2 = Value2, ...
WHERE Condition;
```

Delete Operation

The Delete operation removes records from a table.

SQL Syntax:

```
DELETE FROM YourTableName WHERE Condition;
```

Hands-On

Perform CRUD Operations: Insert a new employee, retrieve all employees, update the age of an employee, and delete an employee record from the Employees table.

Wrapping up the session, Charlie remarked, "Mastering CRUD operations is fundamental for any developer working with databases." Casey, jotting down notes, realized how these operations are the building blocks of any application's data layer. "Next," Charlie continued, "let's delve into the art of selecting and filtering data to retrieve exactly what we need."

Data Selection, Filtering, and Functions

Charlie, having laid the foundation with CRUD operations, proceeded to introduce more advanced techniques. "Data selection and filtering is like fine-tuning your SQL queries to fetch exactly what you need," he began.

SELECT and WHERE Clause

The SELECT statement is used to select data from a database, and the WHERE clause filters the results to only those records that fulfill a specified condition.

SQL Syntax:

```
SELECT Column1, Column2, ...
FROM YourTableName
WHERE Condition;
```

ORDER BY and TOP Clauses

The ORDER BY clause sorts the result set in ascending or descending order, and the TOP clause is used to specify the number of records to return.

SQL Syntax:

```
SELECT TOP Number Column1, Column2, ...
FROM YourTableName
ORDER BY ColumnName ASC|DESC;
```

HAVING and GROUP BY Clauses

The GROUP BY statement groups rows that have the same values in specified columns into summary rows. The HAVING clause is like WHERE but operates on grouped records.

SQL Syntax:

```
SELECT ColumnName, aggregate_function(ColumnName)
FROM YourTableName
WHERE Condition
GROUP BY ColumnName
HAVING aggregate_function(ColumnName) Condition;
```

Functions: MIN, MAX, DISTINCT, etc.

SQL functions like MIN, MAX, and DISTINCT provide ways to perform operations on data.

SQL Syntax:

```
SELECT MIN(Column1), MAX(Column1), DISTINCT(Column1)
FROM YourTableName;
```

Hands-On

Filter and Select Data: Execute queries to fetch specific columns, filter and sort data, use functions like MIN, MAX, and DISTINCT, and group data using GROUP BY and HAVING clauses.

Charlie concluded, "These selection and filtering techniques allow you to interact with your data efficiently and fetch exactly what you need." Alex, impressed, thought about how these techniques would make data retrieval much simpler. "Now that we've explored data selection and filtering," Charlie said, transitioning to the next topic, "let's delve into the heart of relational databases: tables, relationships, and schemas."

Tables, Relationships, and Schemas

Diving deeper into the world of databases, Charlie began to unravel the complexities of tables, relationships, and schemas. "Think of these as the blueprint of a database," he explained, setting the stage for a deeper exploration.

Understanding Tables: Beyond the Basics

"Tables are more than just rows and columns," Charlie started, emphasizing that optimizing tables can significantly improve query performance.

- Indexes:
  - Charlie explained that indexes are like a table of contents for a database, speeding up data retrieval.
  - "By creating indexes, you enable SQL Server to find and retrieve data without scanning the entire table," he said.

- Alter Table:

  - He then delved into modifying tables after creation using the ALTER TABLE command.

    ```
    ALTER TABLE TableName

    ADD FOREIGN KEY (ColumnName) REFERENCES
    OtherTableName(ColumnName);
    ```

  - For instance, adding a new column or modifying existing ones ensures flexibility in managing data structures.

  - Alex noted, "So, we're not stuck with our initial design. That's helpful!"

Relationships

Charlie shifted focus to how tables interact with each other.

- **Types of Relationships**

  - He explained the one-to-one, one-to-many, and many-to-many relationships, illustrating with examples from an e-commerce application.

- **Referential Integrity**

  - "Ensuring referential integrity means keeping our relationships consistent," Charlie emphasized.

  - He demonstrated this by linking Customers, Orders, and Products tables.

Database Schemas

Moving on, Charlie introduced database schemas.

- He explained that schemas logically group tables, views, and other database objects.

- "Schemas can be used to categorize your data, making management and security more streamlined," Charlie noted.

Data Integrity

Finally, Charlie touched upon ensuring data integrity.

- Ensuring Consistency:

  - He discussed constraints like CHECK constraints that ensure data meets specific conditions.

  - "For instance, if we want to ensure that the Quantity in the Orders table is always positive, we can use a CHECK constraint," he explained.

Hands-On

1. **Exploring relationships:** Practice creating tables with different types of relationships and observe the interactions.

2. **Schema design:** Design a schema for an e-commerce platform, focusing on logical grouping and ease of data retrieval.

3. **Data integrity checks:** Implement CHECK constraints to ensure data integrity.

"Understanding the intricacies of tables, relationships, and schemas ensures our databases are efficient and reliable," Charlie concluded. Eager to continue the journey, he added, "Now, let's delve into further optimizing our data storage."

Optimized Queries

The quest for efficient data retrieval brings us to the doorstep of optimized queries. A well-crafted query not only ensures accurate data retrieval but also enhances the performance of applications. In this section, we delve into advanced SQL queries, the encapsulation of logic using stored procedures and functions, transactions, and best practices for query optimization.

Advanced SQL Queries

JOINs

SQL offers a powerful feature known as JOINs, allowing data retrieval from multiple tables in a single query. Different types of JOINs, such as INNER, LEFT, RIGHT, and FULL, cater to different data requirements.

```
-- Example of INNER JOIN
SELECT Orders.OrderID, Customers.CustomerName
FROM Orders
INNER JOIN Customers ON Orders.CustomerID = Customers.CustomerID;
```

Nested Queries

Nested queries or subqueries are queries embedded within another SQL query. They provide flexibility and can simplify complex queries.

```
-- Example of a nested query
SELECT CustomerName
FROM Customers
WHERE CustomerID IN (SELECT CustomerID FROM Orders WHERE Quantity > 5);
```

CASE and IF-ELSE Statements

Conditional logic like CASE and IF-ELSE statements allows for more dynamic and flexible queries.

```
-- Example of CASE statement
SELECT OrderID, Quantity,
CASE
    WHEN Quantity > 5 THEN 'High'
    ELSE 'Low'
END AS OrderVolume
FROM Orders;
```

Stored Procedures and Functions

Stored procedures and functions allow encapsulation of complex operations. While both can encapsulate a series of SQL statements, functions can return a value, whereas stored procedures cannot.

Stored Procedures

Stored procedures are precompiled collections of SQL statements that can be executed as a single call to the database server. They can accept parameters and don't return a value.

Here's an example of a stored procedure that retrieves all orders for a specific customer.

```
-- Creating a Stored Procedure
CREATE PROCEDURE GetCustomerOrders
    @CustomerID INT
AS
BEGIN
    SELECT * FROM Orders WHERE CustomerID = @CustomerID;
END;

-- Executing the Stored Procedure
EXEC GetCustomerOrders @CustomerID = 1;
```

Functions

Functions, on the other hand, are similar to stored procedures but can return a value. Functions can be used in SQL statements.

Here's an example of a function that calculates the total quantity of items ordered by a specific customer.

```
-- Creating a Function
CREATE FUNCTION TotalQuantityOrdered (@CustomerID INT)
RETURNS INT
AS
```

```
BEGIN
    DECLARE @TotalQuantity INT;
    SELECT @TotalQuantity = SUM(Quantity) FROM Orders WHERE CustomerID =
    @CustomerID;
    RETURN @TotalQuantity;
END;
-- Using the Function
SELECT dbo.TotalQuantityOrdered(1) AS TotalQuantity;
```

Use Cases

Stored procedures and functions encapsulate logic, making it easier to manage and modify. They can also enhance performance as they are precompiled.

Transactions

Transactions ensure that a series of SQL statements are executed completely or not at all, maintaining data consistency.

COMMIT and ROLLBACK

COMMIT saves all the transactions to the database, while ROLLBACK undoes the changes made during the current transaction.

```
-- Example of a transaction
BEGIN TRANSACTION;
UPDATE Account SET Balance = Balance - 100 WHERE AccountID = 1;
UPDATE Account SET Balance = Balance + 100 WHERE AccountID = 2;
COMMIT;
```

Query Optimization and Best Practices

Optimizing queries and adhering to best practices ensure that your database runs efficiently and your queries return results promptly.

Techniques for Query Optimization

1. **Indexing:** Create indexes on columns that are frequently used in WHERE, JOIN, and ORDER BY clauses to speed up query execution.

2. **Partitioning:** Break down a large table into smaller, more manageable pieces, called partitions.

3. **Denormalization:** Sometimes, selectively denormalizing a database can reduce the number of joins and enhance query performance.

4. **Query Caching:** Repeatedly running the same queries can be avoided by caching the results.

5. **Using Views:** Create views for complex queries that are run frequently.

6. **Analyzing Query Execution Plans:** SQL Server provides tools to analyze the execution plan of a query to understand its performance.

Best Practices in Design and Query Writing

1. **Consistent Naming Conventions:** Use a consistent naming convention for tables, columns, procedures, etc.

2. **Proper Use of Data Types:** Choose the most appropriate data type to save space and improve performance.

3. **Normalization:** Normalize data to eliminate redundancy.

4. ***Avoid SELECT:** Select only the columns you need.

5. **Commenting:** Comment your SQL scripts for better understanding and maintenance.

6. **Batch Operations:** Batch your SQL queries to reduce the number of calls to the database.

7. **Error Handling:** Implement proper error handling in your stored procedures and functions.

8. **Regular Maintenance:** Regularly update statistics, rebuild indexes, and perform other maintenance tasks.

By adopting these techniques and best practices, you can ensure that your database not only performs efficiently but is also easy to manage and maintain.

AI in Databases

Charlie, after summarizing SQL basics, advanced techniques, and optimizations, turned the team's attention toward an innovative and crucial topic: AI in databases. He emphasized that the future of database management lay in leveraging AI, and Microsoft's tools were at the forefront of this transformation.

Microsoft's Tools and Technologies in Databases

Microsoft offers a suite of tools and technologies designed to streamline database management while integrating AI capabilities.

- **Azure SQL Database:** Microsoft's cloud-based database service harnesses the power of AI to optimize performance and security. Features like automatic tuning and threat detection are driven by machine learning.

- **SQL Server 2019 Big Data Clusters:** This service allows for the integration of big data and AI with the traditional relational database management system. It provides functionalities such as data virtualization, data lakes, and scalable big data solutions.

- **Azure Machine Learning:** Developers can build, deploy, and manage machine learning models directly within their databases, streamlining the process of deriving insights from data.

AI's Role in Database Management

AI is playing a transformative role in database management, significantly impacting query optimization and storage predictions.

- **Query Optimization:** AI algorithms can learn from past query executions, optimizing plans for better performance.

- **Predictive Analysis for Storage:** AI can predict future storage requirements, ensuring that databases are scalable and cost-effective.

AI Tools like GPT in Database Work

Tools like GPT can be instrumental in easing database-related tasks for developers.

- **Natural Language Queries:** Developers can use GPT to convert natural language queries into SQL queries, simplifying the task of data retrieval.

- **Code Generation and Optimization:** GPT can assist in generating and optimizing SQL code, reducing the manual effort required in database management.

- **Documentation Assistance:** GPT can aid in auto-generating documentation for databases, making the process efficient and consistent.

The integration of AI in database management is not just a futuristic concept but a present-day reality. Tools and technologies offered by Microsoft, such as Azure SQL Database, SQL Server 2019, and Azure Machine Learning, have set the stage for a new era where databases are smarter, more efficient, and highly optimized (See Figure 4-4).

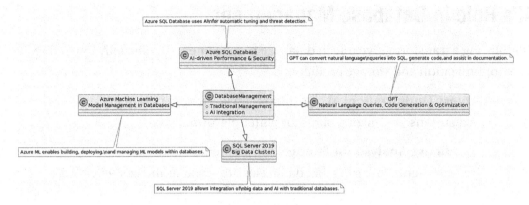

Figure 4-4. *AI integration in database*

Moreover, AI models like GPT can significantly ease the developer's workload by converting natural language queries into SQL, assisting in code generation, and even contributing to documentation and analysis. This seamless blend of traditional databases and AI promises a future of efficient storage, optimized queries, and predictive capabilities. We will delve deeper into the utilization of AI tools like GPT in database work in Chapter 10, "ChatGPT Charms: Wielding Words with AI."

Conclusion

In this chapter, we navigated through the intricacies of databases, starting from understanding the essence of data in applications, exploring various databases, and diving into SQL. We further explored the structural components of relational databases and delved into optimizing SQL queries. Toward the end, we touched upon the transformative role of AI in database management.

Key Takeaways

- Data is integral to applications, necessitating efficient storage and retrieval mechanisms.

- Databases, both SQL and NoSQL, are pivotal in managing and organizing this data.

- SQL is a powerful language for interacting with relational databases.

- Effective database design and optimized queries are crucial for performance.

- AI is progressively becoming an integral part of database management, promising optimizations and predictive capabilities.

Transitioning into Angular Adventures

Moving from the structured world of databases, Chapter 5, "Angular Adventures: Binding Data to Views," shifts our focus to the presentation layer of applications. This next chapter dives into how Angular enables developers to seamlessly connect their data (managed in databases) to user interfaces, creating dynamic and responsive web applications. As we progress, we'll explore Angular's powerful data-binding capabilities, which allow for the real-time display and interaction with data, marking another essential step in our journey toward full-stack development mastery.

CHAPTER 5

Angular Adventures: Crafting Smart User Interfaces

In this chapter, we'll delve into Angular, a framework that has redefined the standards of modern web development. Angular, with its comprehensive approach to building dynamic web applications, offers a blend of power and simplicity that appeals to both novice and seasoned developers.

As the TechFusion Corp team, led by Jamie, begins their exploration of Angular, they represent the journey many developers undertake when embracing this technology. Emma, with her expertise in frontend design, is particularly drawn to Angular's ability to create responsive and engaging user interfaces. Jamie, known for her emphasis on efficient and maintainable code, appreciates Angular's structured approach to application development.

Our focus will be on practical learning, starting with setting up the Angular environment. This foundational step is crucial for Alex and Casey, the new members of the TechFusion team, as it is for any developer stepping into the Angular world. We'll guide you through the process of creating your first Angular application, ensuring you understand each step of the journey.

Angular's core concepts, including components, services, and routing, will be our key areas of exploration. These concepts are not just theoretical; they are the building blocks of any Angular application. Understanding them is essential for creating sophisticated web applications that are both functional and visually appealing.

© Arpit Dwivedi 2024
A. Dwivedi, *CodeMosaic*, https://doi.org/10.1007/979-8-8688-0276-8_5

The journey through Angular is not just about learning a new technology; it's about adopting a mindset geared toward efficiency and innovation. As we progress, we'll also look at how Angular can be integrated with AI features, a step that TechFusion Corp is keen to explore. This integration represents the cutting edge of web development, where AI enhances user experience and application functionality.

Join us as we navigate the Angular landscape, where each concept we uncover will add to your toolkit as a web developer. By the end of this chapter, you'll have a solid understanding of Angular and how it can be used to create state-of-the-art web applications.

Getting Started with Angular

Before we dive into the technicalities, let's take a moment to understand why Angular stands out in the crowded space of web development tools. Angular is not just another framework; it's a platform that provides a cohesive solution for developing robust frontend applications. It's known for its ability to create single-page applications (SPAs) that offer a seamless user experience, akin to a desktop application.

One of Angular's key strengths is its two-way data binding feature, which ensures that changes in your application's user interface instantly influence the application's logic and vice versa. This feature alone significantly reduces the amount of boilerplate code you need to write and maintain.

Moreover, Angular's opinionated nature about how applications should be structured makes it an excellent choice for large-scale projects where consistency and maintainability are critical. It enforces good coding practices and offers a standardized way of developing web applications, which is particularly beneficial for teams.

With Angular, you're not just using a framework; you're adopting an ecosystem. Angular comes with a suite of tools and a rich set of libraries that cover a wide range of features, from form handling and routing to state management and internationalization. This comprehensive approach makes Angular a one-stop solution for all your frontend development needs.

Setting Up Your Angular Development Environment

Angular development requires Node.js and the Angular CLI. Here's how you can set up your environment on Windows, macOS, and Linux.

Windows Installation

1. Install Node.js:

    a. Download the Windows installer from the Node.js website.
        `https://nodejs.org/en/download`

    b. Run the installer and follow the prompts to install Node.js and
        npm (Node Package Manager).

2. Install Angular CLI:

    a. Open the Command Prompt and run "`npm install -g`
        `@angular/cli`."

    b. This installs the Angular CLI globally, making it available from any
        directory in the Command Prompt.

💡 **Pro Tip for Windows Users**   Run your Command Prompt as an administrator
to avoid permission issues during installation.

---

macOS Installation

1. Install Node.js:

    a. Download the macOS installer from the Node.js website.
        `https://nodejs.org/en/download`

    b. Open the downloaded file and follow the instructions to install
        Node.js and npm.

2. Install Angular CLI:

    a. Open the Terminal and run "`sudo npm install -g`
        `@angular/cli`."

    b. Using sudo may be required to avoid permission issues.

💡 **Did You Know?**   On macOS, you can also use Homebrew, a package manager for macOS, to install Node.js by running brew install node.

Linux Installation

1. Install Node.js:

   a. For Debian-based distributions like Ubuntu, use "sudo apt-get install nodejs" and "sudo apt-get install npm."

   b. For Red Hat-based distributions like Fedora, use "sudo dnf install nodejs" and "sudo dnf install npm."

2. Install Angular CLI:

   a. Run "sudo npm install -g @angular/cli" in the Terminal.

💡 **Note for Linux Users**   The exact commands for installing Node.js may vary depending on your Linux distribution. Always refer to your distribution's package manager documentation for the most accurate instructions.

Verifying the Installation

After installation, you can verify that Node.js and Angular CLI are correctly installed:

- Run "node -v" and "npm -v" to check the versions of Node.js and npm.

- Run the "ng version" to verify that the Angular CLI is installed.

💡 **Quote to Reflect**   "Setting up your development environment is the first step in your journey as an Angular developer. It's the foundation upon which all your applications will be built."

Creating Your First Angular Application

With the environment setup, it's time to create your first Angular application. In your command line, navigate to the folder where you want your project to be and run "ng new my-first-angular-app." This command scaffolds a new Angular application named "my-first-angular-app."

Navigate into your project folder ("cd my-first-angular-app") and start the development server with "ng serve." Open your browser and go to "http://localhost:4200/" to see your new app running something like Figure 5-1.

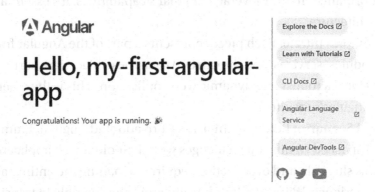

Figure 5-1. *This is an image showing the default first page of Angular App*

💡 **Did You Know?**   The default port for Angular's development server is 4200, but you can change it using the --port flag, like ng serve --port 4300.

Understanding the Project Structure

When you create a new Angular application, the CLI sets up a specific project structure. This structure includes several folders and files, each with a specific purpose:

- **src/app:** Contains the components, services, and other files related to your application logic.

- **src/assets:** For static assets like images, icons, etc.

- **src/environments:** Environment-specific configuration files.

- **angular.json:** Configuration file for Angular CLI.

💡 **Quote to Ponder**   "The structure of your Angular application reflects your approach to coding: organized, modular, and efficient."

Understanding Angular Architecture

Angular's architecture is a roadmap for building scalable and maintainable web applications. It's designed not just for coding simplicity, but also for enhancing application performance. To fully leverage Angular's capabilities, it's essential to grasp its fundamental architecture.

Imagine a complex puzzle. Each piece represents a part of the Angular framework—components, modules, services, and directives. When these pieces are correctly assembled, they form a robust and dynamic web application. This is the essence of understanding Angular's architecture.

A Real-World Scenario: Before TechFusion Corp adopted Angular, Emma, the frontend specialist, faced significant challenges with their older web applications. The user interface was sluggish, and every action required reloading the entire page, leading to a poor user experience. With Angular's introduction, she was able to transition the application to an **SPA**, dramatically enhancing the user experience by allowing for seamless interactions without page reloads.

This example underscores the transformative impact of Angular's architecture. It not only simplifies development but also elevates the end-user experience. Now, let's delve into the core components of Angular to see how each contributes to building powerful web applications.

Figure 5-2 outlines the fundamental architecture of Angular, focusing on key elements like Components, Services, Dependency Injection (DI), Directives, Data Binding, and Routing.

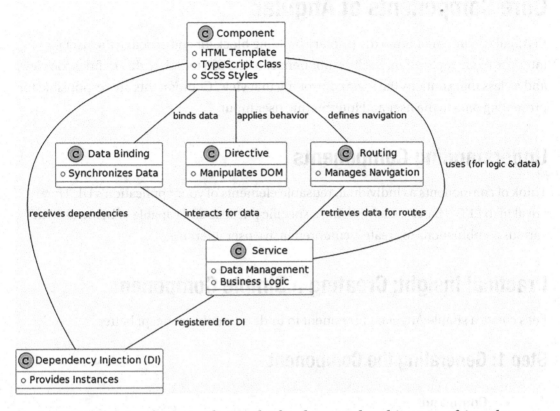

Figure 5-2. *This is a figure outlining the fundamental architecture of Angular*

Figure 5-2 illustrates the interconnected nature of Angular's core architectural components. It shows how components, the primary elements of the UI, interact with services for data and logic. Dependency Injection (DI) is crucial in supplying dependencies to both components and services. Directives are used to enhance and manipulate the DOM within components, while Data Binding synchronizes data between the components and the model. Lastly, Routing manages the navigation between different views, facilitating the Single Page Application experience.

With this visual overview of Angular's architecture, we have a solid foundation for understanding how the framework operates. Now, let's dive into each section one by one to explore their functionalities and roles in building Angular applications in greater detail.

Core Components of Angular

In Angular, components are the primary building block for constructing the user interface of an application. Each component consists of a template that defines the view, and a class that contains the logic controlling that view. Components are responsible for presenting data to the user and interpreting user input.

Understanding Components

Think of components as individual, reusable elements of your application's UI. They are akin to LEGO blocks, each serving a specific purpose and capable of being used in various combinations to create a comprehensive user interface.

Practical Insight: Creating a Simple Component

Let's create a simple Angular component to understand this concept better:

Step 1: Generating the Component

- **Command**

  Use Angular CLI to generate a new component. Open your terminal or command prompt and navigate to your Angular project directory.

  Run the command: "`ng generate component UserProfile`."

- **Result**

  This command creates a new directory `src/app/user-profile` with four files:

  - user-profile.component.ts (TypeScript class)

  - user-profile.component.html (template)

  - user-profile.component.spec.ts (test file)

  - user-profile.component.scss (styling)

Step 2: Understanding the Component Files

Template File (user-profile.component.html)

1. **Purpose:** Defines the HTML template associated with the component.

2. **Content:** Add HTML to display user details. For example, use tags like `<h1>`, `<p>` to show the user's name and bio.

3. **Data Binding:** Use Angular's data binding syntax to dynamically display data from the TypeScript class.

Class File (user-profile.component.ts)

1. **Structure:** Includes a TypeScript class decorated with @Component, which includes metadata like the selector and the path to the template and SCSS files.

2. **Properties:** Declare properties like userName and userBio that you'll display in the template.

3. **Methods:** Write any methods needed for the component's functionality.

Test File (user-profile.component.spec.ts)

1. **Purpose:** Used for writing unit tests for the component.

2. **Testing Framework:** Angular uses **Jasmine** and **Karma** for testing. Familiarize yourself with basic testing concepts to test component behavior.

Styling File (user-profile.component.scss)

1. **Usage:** Write SCSS/CSS styles specific to this component. These styles will apply only to this component's template, thanks to Angular's view encapsulation.

2. **Example:** Style the user profile details, like font size for the user's name and bio.

By following these steps, you've created a user profile component in Angular. This helps you understand the structure of an Angular component and the role of each file within it. Experiment by adding more properties, styles, and even methods to enhance the component's functionality and presentation.

Remember, the key to mastering Angular lies in understanding these building blocks and how they work together to create dynamic web applications.

Linking to Emma's Experience: When Emma needed to create a dynamic user info section on the TechFusion Corp website, she utilized an Angular component for this task. The component was responsible for fetching and displaying user data dynamically, leading to a more interactive and personalized user experience.

Angular Component Lifecycle Hooks

After understanding how components are integral to Angular applications, as seen in Emma's experience at TechFusion Corp, it's important to delve into the concept of component lifecycle hooks in Angular. These hooks provide visibility into key moments in the lifecycle of components and directives, allowing you to execute custom logic at specific times.

Understanding Lifecycle Hooks

Lifecycle hooks are specialized methods provided by Angular that offer a way to tap into specific moments in the life of a component or directive. They are essential for managing tasks like initializing data, cleaning up resources, or reacting to changes in input properties.

Common Lifecycle Hooks:

- **ngOnInit**
  - Triggered after Angular has initialized all data-bound properties of a component.
  - **Usage:** Ideal for initializing data in a component.
- **ngOnChanges**
  - Called whenever Angular detects changes to input properties of the component.

- **Usage:** Useful for responding to changes in properties provided by parent components.

- **ngDoCheck**

  - Invoked with every change detection run, providing a way to detect and act upon changes that Angular can't or won't detect on its own.

  - **Usage:** Custom change detection or update operations.

- **ngAfterViewInit**

  - Called after Angular initializes the component's views and child views.

  - **Usage:** Interacting with the template's DOM elements.

- **ngOnDestroy**

  - Executed just before Angular destroys the component.

  - **Usage:** Useful for cleaning up resources like subscriptions or timers to prevent memory leaks.

Practical Application:

In the case of the UserProfileComponent created for TechFusion Corp, Emma might use

- ngOnInit to fetch user data when the component initializes

- ngOnDestroy to unsubscribe from any Observables to prevent memory leaks

Understanding and correctly utilizing Angular's lifecycle hooks allows for more precise and efficient control over component behavior. They play a crucial role in managing resources, responding to changes, and ensuring optimal performance of your Angular applications.

Components form the heart of Angular applications, driving both the look and functionality of the user interface. As we've seen, they are highly versatile and can be tailored to suit the specific needs of your application.

Next, we'll explore Angular modules. While components are about individual UI elements, modules are about how these elements and other parts of an application are organized and grouped together. Understanding modules is key to mastering Angular's architecture and building more complex applications.

Modules in Angular

Modules in Angular play a pivotal role in organizing and grouping together components, services, directives, and pipes. They provide a way to encapsulate and manage related parts of your application. Every Angular application has at least one module, the root module, typically named "AppModule," which serves as the entry point for the application.

Modular Approach

Angular's modular approach allows for a more organized and maintainable codebase, especially beneficial in large-scale applications. It's similar to organizing a book into chapters; each module in Angular is like a chapter that encapsulates a specific functionality or set of related features.

Application: Structure of Angular Modules

An Angular module is a class marked by the @NgModule decorator, which includes

1. **Declarations:** The view classes (components, directives, and pipes) that belong to this module

2. **Imports:** Other modules whose exported classes are needed by component templates declared in this module

3. **Providers:** Creators of services that this module contributes to the global collection of services

4. **Bootstrap:** The main application view, called the root component, which hosts all other app views

Example: In the case of the TechFusion Corp application, Emma structured the AppModule to include essential components like the navigation bar and user profile, and imported modules like FormsModule for handling forms and HttpClientModule for making HTTP requests.

💡 **Pro Tip**   When building an Angular application, carefully plan your modules to ensure that they are cohesive, encapsulating related functionalities. This makes your application more scalable and easier to maintain.

Modules are the backbone of any Angular application, providing the necessary structure and organization. They ensure that the application is modular, scalable, and easy to maintain.

Moving forward, we'll delve into services and dependency injection, another cornerstone of Angular. These concepts are crucial for managing business logic and data in an Angular application, allowing for more efficient and reusable code.

Services and Dependency Injection in Angular

Services in Angular are fundamental for managing business logic and data. They are singleton objects that can be injected into components and other services, making them a central place to manage application-wide functionalities like data fetching, logging, or user authentication.

Creating a Service via Angular CLI

To create a service in Angular:

1. **Generate the Service:** Open your terminal and navigate to your Angular project directory.

   Run the command: "ng generate service userData."

2. **Service File Created:** This command creates a new file named userData.service.ts in your project's src/app folder.

Implementing the UserDataService

In the `userData.service.ts` file, define a service to fetch user data:

```Typescript
``` Typescript code
import { Injectable } from '@angular/core';
import { HttpClient } from '@angular/common/http';
import { Observable } from 'rxjs';

@Injectable({
  providedIn: 'root'
})
export class UserDataService {

  constructor(private http: HttpClient) { }

  getUserData(): Observable<any> {
    // Replace with the actual API URL
    const apiUrl = 'https://example.com/api/users';
    return this.http.get(apiUrl);
  }
}
```

This service uses Angular's HttpClient to make a GET request to an API. The getUserData() method fetches user data from a specified URL.

Injecting the Service into a Component

Now, integrate this service into the UserProfileComponent:

1. **Modify UserProfileComponent:** Open the user-profile. component.ts file.

2. Inject UserDataService:

   ```Typescript
   ``` Typescript Code
   import { Component, OnInit } from '@angular/core';
   import { UserDataService } from '../user-data.service';
   ```

```
@Component({
  selector: 'app-user-profile',
  templateUrl: './user-profile.component.html',
  styleUrls: ['./user-profile.component.scss']
})
export class UserProfileComponent implements OnInit {
  userData: any;

  constructor(private userDataService: UserDataService) { }

  ngOnInit(): void {
    this.userDataService.getUserData().subscribe(data => {
      this.userData = data;
    });
  }
}
```

In this component, **UserDataService** is injected via the constructor. The **ngOnInit**
lifecycle hook calls the **getUserData()** method to retrieve user data and assign it to the
userData property.

Practical Scenario at TechFusion Corp: At TechFusion Corp, Emma integrates the
UserDataService into the **UserProfileComponent**. This service fetches user details (like
Alex and Casey's information) from an API and displays them based on user selection in
the dropdown menu of the component.

Understanding Observables and Promises: Introduction to Asynchronous Operations in Angular

In Angular development, managing asynchronous operations is essential, particularly
when dealing with tasks like HTTP requests. This is where Observables and Promises
come into play. Both offer ways to handle asynchronous operations, but they have
distinct characteristics and use cases.

Observables in Angular

What Are Observables?

- Part of the RxJS library in Angular.

- Handle multiple asynchronous events over time.

- They represent a stream of data that can be observed and manipulated over time.

Usage in Angular

- Angular extensively uses Observables in its HTTP service and for handling events like form submissions.

- Observables are ideal for dealing with multiple asynchronous events and complex data transformations.

Working with Observables

- A service makes an HTTP request and returns an Observable.

- Components or services subscribe to the Observable to receive data asynchronously.

- Example:

```
``` TypeScript Code
this.myService.getData().subscribe(data => {
  // Handle the asynchronous data here
});
```
```

Promises in Angular

What Are Promises?

- Native to JavaScript.

- Deal with single asynchronous events, resolving to a value or rejecting with an error.

Promises in Angular Services

- Angular can work with Promises, especially when dealing with APIs that return them or in scenarios requiring a single, one-time asynchronous operation.

- Observables can be converted to Promises using the `.toPromise()` method.

- Example:

  Converting an Observable to a Promise using `.toPromise()` method.

  ```Typescript
  async function fetchData() {
  const data = await this.myService.getData().toPromise();
    // Use the data from the Promise
  }
  ```

Comparing Observables with Promises

- **Multiplicity:** Observables can handle multiple values over time, making them suitable for ongoing data streams. Promises deal with a single asynchronous event.

- **Cancellation:** Observables can be unsubscribed from, providing the ability to cancel ongoing operations. Promises, once started, cannot be cancelled.

- **Use Cases**
  - **Observables:** Best suited for handling HTTP requests in Angular, event handling, and situations where the data stream is continuous or complex.

  - **Promises:** Ideal for simpler, one-time asynchronous operations that resolve to a single value.

Conclusion and Best Practices: Observables with Promises

In Angular development, choosing between Observables and Promises depends on the nature of the asynchronous operation. Observables are generally preferred for their flexibility and control, particularly in complex scenarios involving multiple events or data streams. Promises, being simpler and more straightforward, are suitable for one-time, straightforward asynchronous tasks. Understanding both concepts and their appropriate usage is crucial for effective asynchronous data management in Angular applications.

Implementing services and dependency injection in Angular streamlines the management of business logic and data across different parts of an application. It not only simplifies code but also enhances application efficiency and maintainability.

Key Angular Concepts: Directives, Data Binding, and Routing

Angular, a powerful framework for building dynamic web applications, offers a suite of tools and features that empower developers to create highly interactive and user-friendly interfaces. Among these tools are Directives, Data Binding, and Routing—each playing a pivotal role in how Angular applications function and how users interact with them. In this section, we'll delve into these key concepts, understanding their functionalities and how they contribute to making Angular a preferred choice for modern web application development.

Angular Directives

Directives in Angular are powerful tools that modify and manipulate the DOM in your application templates. They come in two main varieties:

- **Structural Directives**, like *ngIf and *ngFor, alter the layout by adding, removing, or manipulating DOM elements.

- **Attribute Directives**, like ngStyle and ngClass, change the appearance or behavior of an element or component.

Practical Use: In TechFusion Corp's projects, Emma often uses *ngFor for iterating over data arrays to display user profiles efficiently.

Data Binding in Angular

Data binding is a crucial Angular feature that connects the component's logic to its template, enabling dynamic data exchange between them. There are several types of data binding:

- **Interpolation ({{ }}):** Displays component properties in the template.

- **Property Binding ([ ]):** Binds element properties to component properties.

- **Event Binding (( )):** Responds to user events in the component.

- **Two-Way Binding ([( )]):** Combines property and event binding for two-way data exchange.

Example: Emma uses two-way binding ([(ngModel)]) to bind form inputs to component properties, allowing real-time UI updates.

Routing and Navigation in Angular

Angular's routing enables navigation between different views or components without reloading the page, essential for Single Page Applications (SPAs).

- **Configuring Routes:** Define routes in AppRoutingModule, associating URL paths with components.

- **Router Outlet (<router-outlet>):** A placeholder in the template where the routed component's view is displayed.

- **Navigation Links:** Use the routerLink directive for in-app navigation.

Practical Application: Emma implemented lazy-loading routes in the TechFusion Corp dashboard, enhancing performance by loading components only when needed.

Efficient Angular Applications

Understanding and effectively using directives, data binding, and routing are key to creating efficient, dynamic, and user-friendly Angular applications. These concepts form the backbone of Angular's approach to building modern web applications, enabling developers to create sophisticated user interfaces and navigation flows.

Next, we'll delve into performance optimization strategies for Angular applications, ensuring they not only function well but also deliver a smooth and responsive user experience.

Optimizing Angular Applications for Performance

Optimizing Angular applications is crucial in the fast-paced world of web development. Performance not only impacts user experience but also affects how your application ranks in search engines and retains users. Angular provides a robust set of tools and methodologies for enhancing performance. In this section, we will explore key techniques and best practices to optimize Angular applications effectively.

Techniques for Performance Optimization

- **Lazy Loading of Modules**
  - **Concept:** Lazy loading involves loading feature modules only when they are necessary, typically upon navigation to a route that requires the module.
  - **Benefit:** This reduces the initial load time and the size of the application bundle.
  - **Pro Tip:** Use Angular's built-in router to easily implement lazy loading for different application routes.

- **Change Detection Strategies**
  - **Strategy:** Utilize ChangeDetectionStrategy. OnPush to minimize Angular's change detection cycles.
  - **Application:** This strategy is particularly effective for components that rely on input properties or observable subscriptions, as it limits change detection to explicit component state changes.
  - **Pro Tip:** Combine OnPush strategy with immutable data structures to ensure efficient change detection.

- **Ahead-of-Time (AOT) Compilation**

  - **Mechanism:** AOT compilation converts Angular HTML templates and TypeScript code into efficient JavaScript during the build process, rather than at runtime.

  - **Advantage:** This approach significantly reduces the application's load time and runtime compiler's overhead.

  - **Pro Tip:** Always use AOT compilation for production builds to leverage performance benefits.

- **Optimizing Dependencies**

  - **Maintenance:** Keep Angular and its dependencies up-to-date for performance improvements and security patches.

  - **Code Auditing:** Regularly review and remove unused libraries and code segments to reduce the overall application size.

  - **Pro Tip:** Use tools like Webpack Bundle Analyzer to identify and eliminate unnecessary code from your bundles.

Best Practices for Angular Performance

- **Efficient Use of Observables**

  Unsubscribe from observables in components using lifecycle hooks to prevent memory leaks.

- **Optimize Template Expressions**

  Avoid complex logic in template expressions, which can lead to performance issues during change detection.

- **Server-side Rendering (SSR)**

  Use Angular Universal for server-side rendering to improve the initial loading time and SEO of your application.

- **Pro Tip**

  Implement service workers for caching and offline capabilities, enhancing the perceived performance of your application.

167

Profiling and Benchmarking

- Use **Chrome DevTools** for profiling Angular applications to identify bottlenecks, such as memory leaks or slow JavaScript execution.

- **Performance Testing:** Regularly conduct performance testing as part of your development process to catch and rectify performance issues early.

- **Pro Tip:** Leverage Angular's built-in profiling tools and hooks to gain insights into performance at runtime.

By implementing these optimization techniques and adhering to best practices, you can significantly enhance the performance of your Angular applications. Remember, a performant application is key to providing a smooth and enjoyable user experience.

AI Integration in Angular Applications

Incorporating Artificial Intelligence (AI) into Angular applications is more than a trend; it's a transformative approach to creating smart, user-centric web applications. AI opens up exciting possibilities such as enhancing user experiences, automating tasks, and implementing advanced features like personalization and analytics.

Benefits of AI Integration

- **Enhanced User Experience:** AI can bring a new level of interactivity and responsiveness.

- **Automation**: Frees up developers' time by automating routine tasks.

- **Advanced Functionalities:** AI enables features like personalized user experiences and predictive systems.

Implementing AI in Angular

- **Chatbots and Virtual Assistants**

  Integrating AI-powered chatbots can revolutionize user interaction. Tools like Dialogflow offer easy-to-integrate APIs for building chatbots that can guide users, answer queries, and provide instant support.

- **Personalization Engines**

  Use AI to tailor user experiences, such as customizing content feeds or product recommendations. Machine learning algorithms can analyze user behavior and preferences to deliver a personalized experience.

Utilizing AI APIs in Angular

Choose an AI platform like Google Cloud AI, IBM Watson, or Azure AI, and follow these steps:

1. **Obtain API Keys:** Register on the chosen AI platform and get the necessary credentials.

2. **API Integration:** Use Angular services to call AI APIs, handling the asynchronous responses using Observables or Promises.

3. **Integrate into Components:** Process and present the AI-driven data or interactions within your Angular components.

Practical AI Implementation Examples

- **Simple AI Chatbot Integration**

  - **Tool:** Use Dialog Flow to create a chatbot.

  - **Integration:** Implement the chatbot in an Angular application using Dialogflow's API. Utilize Angular services to send user inputs to the chatbot and display the responses in the UI.

- **AI-Based Recommendation Engine**

  - **Concept:** Develop a recommendation engine for an e-commerce site.

  - **Approach:** Use a machine learning API to analyze user data and provide personalized product recommendations. Integrate this API into an Angular service and use it to fetch and display recommendations on the product pages.

Best Practices and Ethical Considerations

- **Performance:** Ensure AI integrations are efficient and don't negatively impact app performance.

- **Scalability:** AI solutions should be scalable with your application.

- **User Privacy:** Adhere to data privacy laws and be transparent about how user data is used.

- **Ethical AI Use:** Implement AI responsibly, ensuring fairness and avoiding bias.

Future Trends and Challenges

- **Advancements:** Expect continued growth in AI capabilities, including more sophisticated natural language processing and augmented reality integrations.

- **Challenges:** The biggest challenge might be integrating complex AI features while maintaining app performance and user privacy.

Integrating AI into Angular applications is a powerful way to enhance functionality and user experience. By following these guidelines and experimenting with AI features, developers can create more intelligent and responsive applications.

PRACTICAL EXERCISE: BUILDING AN EMPLOYEE DATA DISPLAY APPLICATION IN ANGULAR

Before we move forward to the next chapters, let's apply what you've learned in a hands-on exercise. This practical task will solidify your understanding of Angular services, components, data binding, and directives.

Exercise Overview

This exercise involves creating an Angular application that displays employee details. You'll be building a service to fetch employee data and a component to display it based on user selection from a dropdown menu.

Steps for the Exercise:

1. Set Up a New Angular Project:

   a. Use Angular CLI to initialize a new project.

   b. Navigate to your project directory.

2. Generate an Angular Service:

   a. Create a service named `EmployeeDataService`.

   b. Hardcode an array of employee objects within this service, each with properties like `id, name, role,` and `department`.

3. Create an Angular Component:

   a. Generate a component named `EmployeeDetails`.

   b. This component will be responsible for displaying the employee information.

4. Implement Service Logic:

   a. In `EmployeeDataService`, write methods to retrieve all employees and an individual employee by ID.

   b. This simulates fetching data from a server or database.

5. Update the Component:

   a. Inject EmployeeDataService into your EmployeeDetails component.

   b. Implement logic to handle user selection from a dropdown and to display the corresponding employee details.

6. Design the Component's Template:

   a. Include a dropdown list populated with employee names using Angular's `*ngFor` directive.

   b. Display the selected employee's details (name, role, department) using Angular's `*ngIf` directive.

7. Test Your Application:

   a. Run your Angular application.

   b. Test the functionality of the dropdown and the display of employee details.

Additional Challenge

Try adding a feature that allows adding new employees to the list. This could involve creating a simple form and updating the service logic to include the new employee data.

Resources and Tips

1. **Angular Documentation:** Official Angular Docs—`https://angular.io/docs`

2. **Angular CLI Guide:** Familiarize yourself with Angular CLI commands for generating services and components.

3. **Stack Overflow:** A great resource for specific issues or errors you might encounter.

4. **Angular Community:** Join forums or communities for support and new perspectives.

Tip   While navigating through the documentation, try to relate back to the concepts we've covered in this chapter. Familiarize yourself with the platform's UI/UX, and don't hesitate to explore further!

Reflection and Next Steps

Once you complete the exercise, reflect on the process. Consider the challenges you faced and how you overcame them. Understanding how to create and manipulate services and components is fundamental in Angular development.

This exercise is designed to be a bridge between theoretical knowledge and practical application, giving you a clearer understanding of Angular's capabilities in building dynamic applications.

Solution Code

The complete solution code for this exercise is available in a Git repository. You are encouraged to try the exercise on your own first and use the solution as a reference or for verification.

Conclusion

In this chapter, we've journeyed through the dynamic world of Angular, uncovering its architecture, capabilities, and the exciting realm of AI integration. From the foundational concepts of components and services to the advanced implementation of AI-driven features, we've seen how Angular can be leveraged to create sophisticated, efficient, and intelligent web applications.

As we close this chapter, remember that the skills and knowledge acquired here are not just about Angular; they are stepping stones toward becoming a versatile web developer. The principles of modular design, responsive UIs, and AI integration extend beyond the boundaries of any single framework.

Key Takeaways

- **Angular's Framework:** An in-depth understanding of Angular's architecture, including components, services, directives, data binding, and routing, essential for building modern web applications.

- **Practical Application:** Hands-on examples demonstrate Angular's power in creating responsive and engaging user interfaces, emphasizing the framework's efficiency and innovation.

- **AI Integration:** Exploration of incorporating AI into Angular applications, highlighting the transformative potential of AI for automating tasks, personalizing user experiences, and implementing advanced functionalities.

- **Performance Optimization:** Strategies for optimizing Angular applications to ensure they are performant, maintainable, and scalable.

Transitioning into .NET Narratives

As we conclude our journey through Angular, the stage is set for Chapter 6, ".NET Narratives: Weaving the Backend Tapestry." Building on the frontend techniques and AI integration explored in Angular, the next chapter will delve into the robust and versatile .NET framework. Here, we will explore how backend development complements the frontend, completing the picture of full-stack development. This transition signifies a shift from the client-side focus to integrating and developing server-side logic, further enriching your toolkit as a versatile developer.

CHAPTER 6

.NET Narratives: Weaving the Backend Tapestry

In the dynamic world of TechFusion Corp, a new dawn heralds a shift in focus. From the client-facing intricacies of Angular, we pivot to the robust backbone of application development—the backend. Here, we meet Charlie, a seasoned .NET Core developer, whose journey with .NET is as rich and varied as the framework itself. Let us have a look at the evolution of .NET:

- **The Birth of .NET:** Launched by Microsoft in 2002, .NET started as a proprietary software framework aimed at simplifying application development across various Windows platforms. It was a bold move by Microsoft to unify the development experience under a single programming model.

- **Growing with the Industry:** As technology advanced, so did .NET. It expanded to support web services, mobile apps, and game development, ensuring developers always had a robust, scalable, and versatile framework at their disposal.

- **Community Involvement:** Microsoft encouraged a vibrant community around .NET. This community, teeming with developers, contributors, and enthusiasts, has been a cornerstone of .NET's evolution, driving innovations and improvements through open-source contributions.

- **.NET Core—a Game Changer:** The release of .NET Core in 2016 marked a new era. It was a leap toward modern development needs, prioritizing cross-platform compatibility, open source development, and cloud integration. This strategic shift made .NET Core not just a successor to .NET but a beacon of modern backend technologies.

© Arpit Dwivedi 2024
A. Dwivedi, *CodeMosaic*, https://doi.org/10.1007/979-8-8688-0276-8_6

- **Today's .NET Ecosystem:** The current .NET ecosystem, with .NET 5 and beyond, continues to evolve, embracing global trends and technologies. It's not just about Windows anymore; .NET now caters to a myriad of platforms, offering tools for building everything from lightweight web apps to sophisticated cloud solutions.

💡 **Insight**   .NET Core's open source approach has not only broadened its appeal but has also led to a surge in community-driven enhancements, making it one of the most progressive frameworks in today's software development landscape.

In the corridors of TechFusion Corp, Charlie, with his profound experience in .NET, is set to unravel the intricacies of this versatile framework, guiding us through its capabilities and how it forms the cornerstone of robust backend development.

The World of .NET: A Comprehensive Overview

As Charlie addresses the team, his enthusiasm for .NET is palpable. He's about to guide them through the diverse landscape of .NET's capabilities and the multitude of applications it supports, showcasing why it remains a powerhouse in the world of software development.

Capabilities and Advantages of .NET

.NET isn't just known for its versatility; it's also lauded for its robust performance and developer-friendly environment. Here, Charlie highlights the key strengths that make .NET a preferred choice for developers and enterprises alike.

- **Unified Development Experience:** .NET's consistency across various platforms streamlines the development process, reducing the learning curve and increasing developer productivity.

- **Performance and Scalability:** High performance and scalability are hallmarks of .NET, making it suitable for everything from small-scale applications to enterprise-level solutions.

- **Comprehensive Tooling and Libraries:** With a rich set of tools like Visual Studio and an extensive library ecosystem, .NET simplifies building, testing, and deploying applications.

The Versatility of .NET in Application Development

Delving into the practical applications of .NET, Charlie brings to light how .NET's flexibility spans across various domains, making it a versatile tool in a developer's toolkit.

- **Desktop Development Prowess:** Through frameworks like WPF and Windows Forms, .NET offers a robust platform for crafting sophisticated desktop applications.

- **Web Development with MVC:** The ASP.NET MVC framework is a testament to .NET's prowess in web development, enabling the creation of dynamic, scalable websites.

- **RESTful Services with WebAPI:** .NET's WebAPI is a powerful framework for building RESTful services, crucial for modern web applications' backend development.

- **Cross-Platform Mobile Apps:** Xamarin extends .NET's capabilities to mobile app development, enabling the creation of native applications for Android and iOS.

- **Cloud-Ready with Azure:** .NET's seamless integration with Azure exemplifies its readiness for cloud-based application development, further broadening its scope.

💡 **Pro Tip**   To truly appreciate .NET's capabilities, start with a project that leverages its diverse frameworks, like a web service using WebAPI or a desktop application with WPF.

Charlie's presentation leaves the team, especially Alex, inspired by the potential of .NET. They begin to see it not just as a framework but as a comprehensive platform for modern software development.

Preparing the Development Environment

In the world of software development, the right tools and setup are as crucial as coding skills. Alex is ready to take his first step into .NET Core development, and Charlie is there to guide him through the process of setting up an efficient and effective development environment.

Installing Visual Studio

Before diving into the world of .NET Core development, the first essential tool is Visual Studio. This powerful Integrated Development Environment (IDE) is the cornerstone for .NET developers.

- **Selecting the Right Edition**

  - For .NET Core development, Visual Studio 2019 or later is recommended.

  - The Community Edition is free and fully featured, ideal for individual developers or small teams.

  - Download Visual Studio Community Edition.

- **Installation Process**

  - From your Downloads folder, double-click the bootstrapper named `VisualStudioSetup.exe` or named something like `vs_community.exe` to start the installation.

  - If you receive a User Account Control notice, choose Yes. It'll ask you to acknowledge the Microsoft License Terms and the Microsoft Privacy Statement. Choose Continue.

  - After the Visual Studio Installer is installed, you can use it to customize your installation by selecting the feature sets—or workloads—that you want.

  - Select the ".NET Core cross-platform development" workload.

- This includes all necessary components for .NET Core development, such as the .NET Core SDK, runtime, and project templates for creating WebAPIs.

- After you choose the workload(s) you want, select **Install**.

Configuring .NET Core

With Visual Studio installed, the next step is to ensure that the .NET Core Software Development Kit (SDK) is properly configured. This SDK is the toolkit that allows developers to build and run .NET Core applications.

- **Verifying the .NET Core SDK**

  - Open a command prompt or terminal and run "`dotnet --version`" to check the installed SDK version.

  - This ensures that the setup is correct and the SDK is ready for use.

- **IDE Setup**

  - Get to know Visual Studio's interface.

  - Pay special attention to the Solution Explorer for project management and the code editor, where most development work happens.

Initial Setup for .NET Core WebAPIs

The final step in the preparation phase is to create and configure a new WebAPI project. This process lays the groundwork for all future development work on .NET Core WebAPIs.

- **Creating a New WebAPI Project**

  - Go to **File ➤ New ➤ Project** in Visual Studio.

  - Choose the "`ASP.NET Core Web Application`" template.

  - This step is crucial in defining the basic structure of your WebAPI project.

- **Configuring the WebAPI Project**

  - In the new project dialog, select the "API" template and make sure the framework version is set to "ASP.NET Core 3.1" or later.

  - This action sets up the foundational elements of a WebAPI project, including dependencies and configuration files.

💡 **Tip**   Spend some time exploring the generated files in your new project. Understanding the purpose and function of files like Startup.cs and appsettings. json is key to mastering .NET Core WebAPI development.

With these steps, Alex has successfully set up his .NET Core development environment. He's now equipped with the tools and configurations needed to start building robust and scalable WebAPIs.

WebAPI Architecture: The Backbone of Backend Development

As Alex and the team gather around, Charlie prepares to delve into the essence of WebAPI architecture. His aim is to provide a foundational understanding of how WebAPIs operate within .NET Core, using diagrams to illustrate the flow and structure.

General WebAPI Architecture Flow

Charlie begins by explaining the general architecture of a WebAPI using a sequence diagram (Figure 6-1). "Think of this as the blueprint of our backend services," he says.

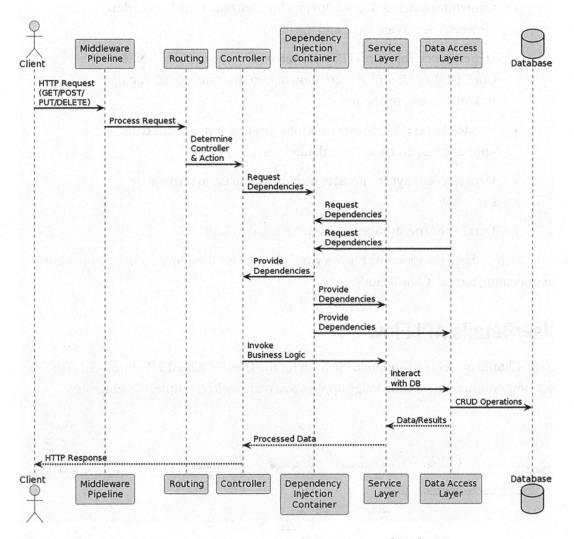

Figure 6-1. *This is a sequence diagram outlining General WebAPI Architecture Flow*

- **Middleware Pipeline:** Middleware handles every HTTP request and response. It's like the gatekeeper, managing tasks such as authentication and logging.

- **Routing:** Determines which controller and action to invoke based on the request URL and method.

- **Controllers:** Act as the conductors, orchestrating the flow of data between the service layer and the client.

- **Dependency Injection (DI) Container:** A central part of .NET Core, DI simplifies object creation and management, enhancing modularity and testability.

- **Service Layer:** Where business logic resides. It processes data, applies rules, and handles calculations.

- **Data Access Layer:** Interacts with the database to retrieve or save data.

- **Database:** The storage system where data is kept.

"Each of these components plays a vital role, and we'll explore them in more depth in upcoming topics," Charlie adds.

UserDetails API Flow

Next, Charlie presents a sequence diagram for the UserDetails API (Figure 6-2). "Let's see how our theoretical knowledge applies to a real-world example," he suggests.

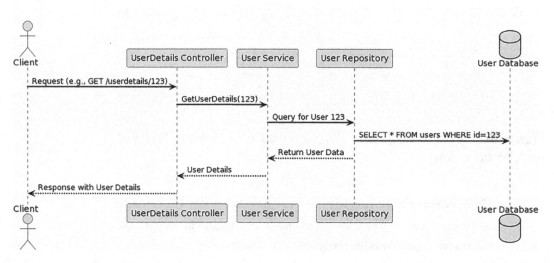

Figure 6-2. *This is a sequence diagram outlining General WebAPI Architecture Flow*

- **Client Request:** Begins with the client sending a request to fetch user details (e.g., GET /userdetails/123).

- **UserDetails Controller:** Receives the request and calls the User Service to fetch the required data.

- **User Service:** The business logic layer, where the request is processed.

- **User Repository:** Interacts with the User Database to retrieve the user's data.

- **Database Interaction:** A query is made to the database to fetch the user's details.

- **Data Flow Back:** The retrieved data flows back from the database to the client, providing the requested information.

"This flow represents a basic operation in our UserDetails component," explains Charlie. "In the coming chapters, we will guide you through creating an API like this, step by step."

As the session concludes, the team, especially Alex, feels a growing sense of excitement. The upcoming chapters promise to transform this theoretical framework into practical, hands-on experience, marking another milestone in their journey through the world of .NET Core WebAPIs.

.NET Core Architectural Layers Explained

After laying the groundwork with an overview of WebAPI architecture, Charlie steers the team into a deeper exploration of .NET Core's architectural layers. Alex, with his newfound understanding of WebAPIs, is eager to see how these abstract concepts translate into actual code.

Understanding the Architectural Layers

- **Presentation Layer**

    - **Role**

        This layer, primarily composed of Controllers in a WebAPI, handles user interaction.

        It receives user input, processes it (with the help of the Business Logic layer), and returns the output.

    - **Controllers in Context**

        Controllers in .NET Core serve as the entry point for HTTP requests. They interpret user inputs and determine the appropriate response or action to take.

- **Business Logic Layer (Service Layer)**

    - **Role**

        - This is where the core functionality of the application resides.

        - It processes data, applies business rules, and ensures that the correct business model is employed.

    - **Integration with Controllers**

        - Controllers call upon services provided by this layer to perform operations

        - This ensures that the presentation layer remains separate from the business rules and logic.

- **Data Access Layer**

    - **Role**

        - This layer interacts with the database or any data source.

        - It includes code for accessing data stores, CRUD (Create, Read, Update, Delete) operations, and managing connections.

- **Connection to Business Logic**

  - The Data Access Layer provides the necessary data to the
    Business Logic Layer, allowing it to make informed decisions and
    perform operations.

Setting Up a .NET Core WebAPI Project

With the conceptual understanding in place, Charlie guides the team in setting up a
.NET Core WebAPI project. "Let's put theory into practice," he suggests.

- Creating a New WebAPI Project in Visual Studio

  - Open Visual Studio and select **File ➤ New ➤ Project.**

  - Choose "ASP.NET Core Web Application" and click **"Next."**

  - Name the project (e.g., UserDetailsAPI) and select a location.

  - Choose "API" as the project template and ensure the target
    framework is set to .NET Core 3.1 or later.

- Exploring the Project Structure

  - **Controllers Folder:** This is where the presentation layer lives.
    The team explores the default WeatherForecastController as an
    example.

  - **Models and Services:** Charlie explains that models will define
    the data structure, and services will contain business logic,
    though these are not explicitly set up in the template.

Crafting the First API Controller

Charlie, recognizing the importance of practical application, decides to lead the team
through the process of coding a GET controller for retrieving user details. "Let's turn
theory into reality," he announces, opening the newly created .NET Core WebAPI project.

Steps for building the UserDetails API Controller:

- **Setting Up the Controller**

  - In Visual Studio, navigate to the "Controllers" folder in your project.

  - Right-click and choose Add ➤ Controller. Select API Controller— Empty and name it UserDetailsController.

- **Coding the GET Method**

  - Charlie starts by explaining the structure of a controller method:

```Csharp code
[ApiController]
[Route("[controller]")]
public class UserDetailsController : ControllerBase
{
    [HttpGet("{id}")]
    public IActionResult GetUserDetails(int id)
    {
        // Logic to retrieve user details will go here
    }
}
```

  - Explanation:

    - ApiController attribute denotes a WebAPI controller.

    - Route("[controller]") sets the route to this controller. For UserDetailsController, the route will be /userdetails.

    - [HttpGet("{id}")] indicates that this method responds to HTTP GET requests. The {id} is a placeholder for the user ID.

    - GetUserDetails(int id) is the action method that gets called when the API route /userdetails/{id} is accessed.

- **Implementing the Logic**

  - For now, Charlie adds a simple logic to return a mock user detail:

```Csharp Code
public IActionResult GetUserDetails(int id)
{
    var userDetails = new { Id = id, Name = "John Doe",
Email = "john.doe@example.com" };
    return Ok(userDetails);
}
```

- Explanation:

  - This method creates a mock user object and returns it. In a real scenario, this method would interact with the service layer to fetch data from a database.

  - Ok(userDetails) sends the user details back to the client with an HTTP 200 status code.

Charlie concludes, "This simple controller is our first functional piece in the UserDetails API. As we progress, we'll replace the mock data with actual database interactions and business logic."

Deep Dive into Controllers and HTTP Methods

Having established the basics of setting up a GET controller, Charlie decides to broaden the team's understanding of controllers and HTTP methods, which are integral to WebAPI development.

Controllers: The Traffic Controllers of WebAPI

Controllers in .NET Core WebAPIs are classes that handle HTTP requests and responses. Each controller can contain multiple actions (methods) to respond to different types of HTTP requests.

A controller is typically associated with a specific resource, like UserDetailsController for user-related operations.

Understanding HTTP Methods

Types of HTTP methods:

- **GET**
  - Used to retrieve data from the server.
  - For example, fetching user details.
- **POST**
  - For creating new resources.
  - For instance, adding a new user.
- **PUT**
  - Used for updating existing resources.
  - For example, modifying user details.
- **DELETE**
  - For removing resources.
  - Such as deleting a user.

Each of these methods corresponds to standard CRUD (Create, Read, Update, Delete) operations in database terminology.

Hands-On: Expanding the UserDetails API

Charlie encourages the team, especially Alex, to try implementing other methods in the UserDetailsController.

Task

Create actions for POST, PUT, and DELETE methods in the UserDetailsController. These should handle creating a new user, updating an existing user's details, and deleting a user, respectively.

Example Template for POST Method

```Csharp code
[HttpPost]
public IActionResult CreateUser(UserDetails userDetails)
{
    // Logic to add a new user
    return CreatedAtAction(nameof(GetUserDetails), new { id = userDetails.
Id }, userDetails);
}
```

Explanation

- The [HttpPost] attribute marks this action for handling POST requests.

- The CreateUser method takes a UserDetails object, processes it, and ideally, adds it to the database.

- The method returns a CreatedAtAction response, which includes the new resource's URI.

"Understanding these methods and their appropriate use is crucial for effective API development," Charlie remarks. "Experimenting with these methods will give you a real feel for building a functional API."

As the session wraps up, the team feels a growing sense of confidence. They're not just learning about WebAPIs; they're actively building one, piece by piece. Alex, in particular, is eager to take on the task, ready to apply his newfound knowledge to create a more comprehensive API.

Business and Data Layer: Beyond the Basics

Charlie gathers the team for a hands-on session, focused on bringing the UserDetails API to life by integrating business logic and data access layers. "The real power of an API lies in its ability to process and manage data efficiently," he explains.

Creating a Service Layer

With a solid understanding of controllers and HTTP methods, Charlie guides the team into the next critical aspect of WebAPI development: implementing business logic. "Business logic is the brain of our application," he explains. "It's where the real rules and operations of our API are defined and executed."

- It encompasses the rules, calculations, and algorithms that define the operations of the application.

- In .NET Core, business logic is often placed in a service layer, separate from the controller, to maintain a clean architecture.

Setting Up the UserService

Charlie leads the team in adding a new Services folder to the project. This folder will house the business logic.

They create a UserService class within this folder. "This class will encapsulate all our user-related business operations," Charlie notes.

Implementing Business Operations

In the UserService, they define a method named GetUserDetails which takes a user ID and returns user details.

Charlie highlights the importance of validation and processing in this method before it interacts with the database. "This is where we ensure our data is correct and secure," he remarks.

```Csharp code
public class UserService
{
    public UserDetails GetUserDetails(int id)
    {
        // Add business logic here (e.g., validation)
        // Placeholder for database interaction
```

```
    return new UserDetails { Id = id, Name = "John Doe", Email = "john.
    doe@example.com" };
  }
}
```

Connecting to the Controller

Injecting UserService

Back in the **UserDetailsController**, they inject the **UserService** via the constructor, a practice that aligns with the Dependency Injection pattern in .NET Core.

"This allows our controller to focus on handling requests and sending responses, while UserService handles the business logic," Charlie explains.

```Csharp code
public class UserDetailsController : ControllerBase
{
    private readonly UserService _userService;

    public UserDetailsController(UserService userService)
    {
        _userService = userService;
    }

    [HttpGet("{id}")]
    public IActionResult GetUserDetails(int id)
    {
        var userDetails = _userService.GetUserDetails(id);
        return Ok(userDetails);
    }
}
```

Setting Up the Data Access Layer

The data layer is responsible for all direct interactions with the database. It includes CRUD operations, database connections, and query handling.

Utilizing Entity Framework Core, a popular ORM in .NET Core, simplifies these interactions.

Creating UserRepository

The next step is setting up the UserRepository. This class will directly interact with the database.

They add a **UserRepository** class in a new **Repositories** folder. "This class will handle all our database queries," says Charlie.

Implementing Database Operations

The UserRepository is implemented with methods to interact with the database. Initially, they use placeholder implementations.

"Eventually, we'll use Entity Framework Core here to handle our database interactions," he adds.

```Csharp Code
public class UserRepository
{
    public UserDetails GetUserById(int id)
    {
        // Placeholder for actual database interaction
        return new UserDetails { Id = id, Name = "John Doe", Email = "john.
        doe@example.com" };
    }
}
```

Connecting UserRepository with UserService

The UserService is then updated to use UserRepository, establishing a clear flow from the controller to the database.

```csharp code
public class UserService
{
    private readonly UserRepository _userRepository;

    public UserService(UserRepository userRepository)
    {
        _userRepository = userRepository;
    }

    // Business logic methods...
}
```

Charlie concludes the session with a sense of accomplishment. "You now have the foundational knowledge to build a layered WebAPI," he says. "Each layer has its distinct role, ensuring our application is organized, maintainable, and scalable."

The team, now more confident in their understanding of .NET Core's architecture, looks forward to enhancing the UserDetails API with real database interactions and more complex business logic.

Fortifying Your API: Security Essentials

As the UserDetails API development progresses, it's crucial to integrate robust security measures. Implementing authorization not only protects the API from unauthorized access but also ensures data integrity and privacy.

The Importance of API Security

Security as a Priority: In the world of WebAPIs, security is not an afterthought. It's a fundamental design aspect that safeguards your application against threats like unauthorized access and data breaches.

Layers of Security: From authentication (verifying who you are) to authorization (verifying what you can do), each layer adds a crucial barrier against potential vulnerabilities.

Implementing Authorization in UserDetails API

- **Integrating JWT Authentication**

  - JSON Web Tokens (JWT) are a popular method for secure authorization in WebAPIs. They are compact, self-contained tokens that encode user information.

  - The UserDetails API incorporates JWT to manage user authentication and authorization.

- **Authorization Flow**

  - **User Authentication:** When a user logs in, the client application sends the credentials to an authorization server.

  - **Token Issuance:** Upon successful authentication, the authorization server issues a JWT, which the client application then uses for subsequent requests.

  - **Token Validation:** Each request to the UserDetails API includes the JWT. The API validates this token, ensuring it's legitimate and current before processing the request.

Understanding Authorization with a Sequence Diagram

To illustrate how authorization operates within the API, let's look at a sequence diagram (Figure 6-3).

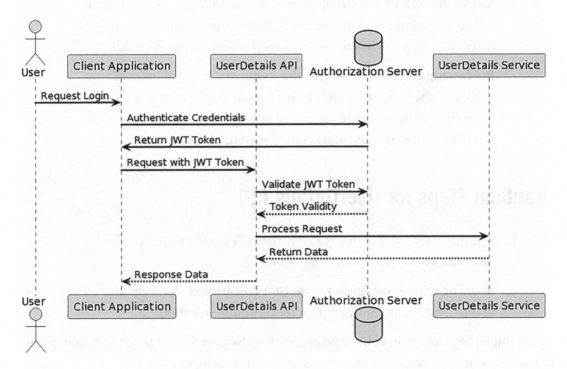

Figure 6-3. *This showcases the interaction between the user, client application, UserDetails API, and authorization server, providing a clear visual understanding of the authorization process*

Explanation of the Authorization Sequence Diagram (Figure 6-3) Flow:

- **User Requests Login:** The process begins with the user initiating a login request through the client application.

- **Authentication by Authorization Server:** The client sends the user's credentials to an authorization server. This server is responsible for verifying the user's identity.

- **Issuance of JWT Token:** Upon successful authentication, the authorization server issues a JWT token. This token encapsulates the user's identity and any claims or roles.

- **Client Requests UserDetails API with JWT:** The client then makes a request to the UserDetails API, attaching the JWT token for authorization.

- **API Validates JWT Token:** Upon receiving the request, the UserDetails API communicates with the authorization server to validate the JWT token. This step ensures the token is valid and not tampered with.

- **Processing and Responding to the Request:** Once the token is validated, the UserDetails API processes the request. If the user is authorized to perform the requested operation, the API retrieves or modifies data as needed and sends a response back to the client.

Practical Steps for UserDetails API

1. Setting Up JWT Middleware: Configure JWT middleware in **Startup.cs** to validate incoming tokens.

2. Securing Endpoints: Apply the [Authorize] attribute to endpoints in the UserDetailsController that require authentication.

By implementing these security measures, the UserDetails API is not only functional but also secure, instilling confidence in its users and developers alike.

Securing an API is a critical aspect of modern web development. In this section, we addressed the importance of implementing robust security measures, particularly focusing on authorization techniques. By integrating JWT-based authorization into the UserDetails API, we have taken a significant step toward ensuring that only authenticated and authorized users can access or modify data. This not only safeguards sensitive information but also fortifies the API against potential security threats.

The sequence diagram provided a visual understanding of how JWT tokens are used in securing API requests, illustrating the flow from user authentication to data retrieval or modification. It's crucial to remember that security is an ongoing process. As developers, staying vigilant, updating security protocols regularly, and adhering to best practices are key to maintaining a secure and reliable API.

With the UserDetails API now equipped with basic security mechanisms, it stands as a more complete and secure example of a WebAPI, ready to handle real-world data and user interactions securely and efficiently.

Mastering .NET Core: Advanced Techniques, Tools, and Best Practices

In this section, we blend essential techniques, tools, and advanced concepts to provide a comprehensive guide on mastering .NET Core WebAPIs. This approach not only revisits and builds upon Dependency Injection (DI) and Middleware but also introduces additional elements like filters, best practices, and productivity tools in Visual Studio.

As we delve deeper into the .NET Core framework, it's essential to understand and utilize the array of tools and advanced concepts available. These elements are critical in crafting efficient, scalable, and maintainable WebAPIs. Let's explore these advanced techniques and tools that can elevate our WebAPI development to new heights.

Revisiting Dependency Injection (DI)

DI in Varied Scenarios: We've seen DI in action within controllers, but its utility extends to scenarios like injecting a caching service into a repository for optimized data retrieval, or providing a custom logging service to track application behavior across different layers.

DI Best Practices in Action: A scenario where a singleton service, such as a configuration reader, is injected into transient services like controllers, ensuring consistent and efficient access to configuration settings throughout the application lifecycle.

Middleware: Orchestrating Requests and Responses

Middleware in Depth: Consider a use case where middleware authenticates API keys in each request, ensuring that only requests with valid keys proceed further in the pipeline, thus securing the API against unauthorized access.

Custom Middleware Use Case: Creating a custom middleware to handle cross-origin requests, allowing the API to specify which domains can access its resources and under what conditions, enhancing both security and flexibility.

Filters: Fine-Tuning WebAPI Behavior

Action Filters for Data Validation: In a scenario where user input must meet specific criteria before proceeding, an action filter can pre-validate this data, preventing invalid or harmful requests from reaching business logic.

Exception Filters for Centralized Error Handling: Utilizing exception filters to handle exceptions thrown across various API actions. This unified approach allows for consistent error logging and response formatting, improving the API's reliability and maintainability.

Leveraging Visual Studio's Productivity Tools

IntelliSense for Rapid Development: Imagine a scenario where developers need to implement a new feature quickly. IntelliSense speeds up this process by suggesting relevant methods and properties, reducing the time spent searching through documentation.

Debugger in Complex Scenarios: A complex debugging scenario where a developer needs to trace the execution flow across various components of the API. Visual Studio's debugger allows setting breakpoints, examining variable values, and stepping through code to identify and resolve issues efficiently.

By integrating these advanced techniques and tools, developers are better equipped to handle a wide array of scenarios in WebAPI development, from securing endpoints to optimizing performance and ensuring maintainability. These practices don't just address immediate development needs; they lay the foundation for building APIs that stand the test of time in an ever-evolving technological landscape.

AI and .NET: A Modern Approach

As the tech world rapidly embraces the transformative power of artificial intelligence (AI), .NET Core developers have a unique opportunity to integrate cutting-edge AI capabilities into their applications. In this chapter, we explore various AI features and tools that can be synergized with .NET Core, extending beyond Azure Cognitive Services to encompass a broader range of AI functionalities.

Exploring the Landscape of AI in .NET

1. **Azure Cognitive Services:** These services offer a suite of pre-built AI models that cover a wide range of functionalities, from natural language processing and speech recognition to computer vision and decision-making. They provide an easy entry point for .NET developers to incorporate AI without needing deep machine learning expertise.

2. **OpenAI API:** OpenAI's offerings, including powerful models like GPT (Generative Pre-trained Transformer), can be integrated into .NET applications. This allows for advanced natural language understanding and generation, enabling scenarios like automated customer support, content creation, and more.

3. **ML.NET:** Microsoft's own machine learning framework, ML.NET, allows developers to create custom AI models directly within the .NET ecosystem. This framework is particularly useful for scenarios where specific data patterns or behaviors need to be learned and predicted.

Practical AI Integration Scenarios in .NET Core

- **Sentiment Analysis and User Feedback:** Integrating sentiment analysis to understand user feedback sentiment, enhancing user experience by adapting responses or content based on user emotions.

- **Chatbots and Virtual Assistants:** Leveraging AI models like GPT for creating sophisticated chatbots and virtual assistants that can handle complex user queries, automate responses, and provide a dynamic interaction experience.

- **Image and Speech Recognition:** Utilizing computer vision and speech recognition services to develop applications that can interact with users in more natural and intuitive ways, such as voice commands or image-based searches.

- **Predictive Analytics:** Employing ML.NET to build predictive models that can forecast trends based on historical data, applicable in areas like inventory management, sales forecasting, and user behavior prediction.

Ethical and Practical Considerations

- **Ethical AI Use:** It's vital to use AI responsibly, ensuring user privacy and avoiding biases in AI models. Transparent communication about how AI is used and ensuring fairness in AI-driven decisions is key.

- **Performance and Scalability:** When integrating AI into WebAPIs, consider the impact on performance. Efficient handling of AI service calls, caching strategies, and asynchronous programming are critical to maintaining optimal application performance.

This topic emphasizes the vast potential of AI integration in .NET Core applications, highlighting various tools and services available to developers. It illustrates a future where .NET Core applications are not just functionally rich but also intelligent, adaptable, and more aligned with user needs and behaviors.

PRACTICAL EXERCISE: THE EMPLOYEEDETAIL COMPONENT API

Building upon the Angular application that displays employee details, this hands-on exercise focuses on developing the backend part of the EmployeeDetail component using .NET Core WebAPI. We'll create an API that interacts with a simulated database to fetch and display employee data, mirroring the frontend functionality developed in Angular.

Exercise Overview

This exercise involves constructing a WebAPI in .NET Core that serves the data required by the EmployeeDetails Angular component. You will create endpoints to fetch employee data, which will be displayed in the Angular application.

Steps for the Exercise:

1. Set Up a New .NET Core WebAPI Project:

   a. Use .NET CLI or Visual Studio to create a new WebAPI project.

   b. Name the project appropriately, for example, EmployeeDetailAPI.

2. Create a Model for Employee Data:

   a. Define an Employee model in the Models folder with properties like Id, Name, Role, and Department.

3. Generate a Controller for Employee Data:

   a. Create an EmployeeController within the Controllers folder.

   b. This controller will handle requests related to employee data.

4. Simulate Database Logic:

   a. For simplicity, simulate a database using a static list of employees in the controller or a separate service class.

   b. Implement methods to retrieve all employees and individual employee details.

5. Implement Controller Methods:

   a. Define HttpGet methods in EmployeeController to fetch all employees and a specific employee by ID.

   b. These methods will utilize your simulated database logic to return employee data.

6. Test the API:

   a. Run the API project and test the endpoints using a tool like Postman or a browser.

   b. Ensure that the endpoints return the correct employee data in response to requests.

7. Connect the Angular Frontend with .NET Core Backend:

    a. Update the Angular EmployeeDataService to fetch data from your .NET Core WebAPI instead of using hardcoded data.

    b. Modify the Angular service to make HTTP GET requests to the endpoints you created in the WebAPI.

Resources and Tips

- **.NET Core Documentation**: Explore the official .NET Core documentation for in-depth guides and tutorials. `https://docs.microsoft.com/en-us/dotnet/core/`

- **.NET CLI Guide:** Familiarize yourself with .NET CLI commands for creating projects, models, and controllers.

- **Community Forums:** Platforms like Stack Overflow offer a wealth of information for troubleshooting and best practices.

Reflection and Next Steps

After completing the exercise, take some time to review the integration between the Angular frontend and the .NET Core backend. Consider how data flows from the server to the client and the role of WebAPI in facilitating this interaction. This exercise serves as a practical application of your .NET Core knowledge, solidifying your understanding of building and connecting backend services with frontend applications.

Solution Code

The complete solution code for this exercise is available in a Git repository. You are encouraged to try the exercise on your own first and use the solution as a reference or for verification.

Conclusion

As we reach the conclusion of this chapter, we reflect on the intricate journey through the world of .NET Core backend development. From the fundamentals of setting up a WebAPI project to the integration of advanced features like security and AI, this chapter has been a deep dive into the essential skills and techniques required for modern backend development in .NET Core.

Key Takeaways

- **Understanding WebAPI Architecture:** We explored the architectural layers of a WebAPI, understanding the role of controllers, services, and data access layers.

- **Practical Application:** The hands-on exercises, including building the UserDetails and EmployeeDetail components, provided practical experience in implementing API endpoints and integrating business logic.

- **Security and AI Integration:** We learned the importance of securing our APIs and the exciting possibilities opened up by integrating AI features using tools like Azure Cognitive Services.

- **Advanced Techniques:** The chapter delved into advanced concepts like middleware, dependency injection, and filters, highlighting their significance in building scalable and maintainable WebAPIs.

What's Next?

With a solid grasp of .NET Core's backend development explored in Chapter 6, we now transition to Chapter 7, "Data Vistas: Painting with Numbers," which will focus on expanding our development horizon further into the realm of client-side development. This next chapter promises to immerse us in the world of data visualization and frontend development, exploring the use of Angular alongside external libraries for crafting compelling user interfaces and narratives from raw data. As we transition, the emphasis is on leveraging the power of Angular to transform complex data into visually intuitive stories, bridging the gap between backend processes and frontend presentation to provide a holistic full-stack development experience. This journey will not only enhance our understanding of Angular's capabilities but also underscore the importance of data visualization in today's data-driven decision-making landscape.

CHAPTER 7

Data Vistas: Painting with Numbers

In the bustling offices of TechFusion Corp, a shift in focus was palpable. The company, having successfully navigated the complexities of backend development with .NET Core, was now steering toward a new challenge—transforming raw data into compelling visual narratives. This pivotal transition marked the beginning of a journey into the vibrant world of frontend development and data visualization, crucial in today's data-driven decision-making landscape.

At the forefront of this new endeavor was Emma, a Frontend Specialist renowned for her keen eye for design and user experience. Emma's journey in TechFusion Corp had been one of continual growth and adaptation. With a background steeped in UI/UX design and a deep understanding of Angular, she was perfectly poised to lead this phase. Her expertise in leveraging external libraries for Angular was not just a skill but an art form, a craft she had honed over years of experience.

Chapter 7, "Data Vistas: Painting with Numbers," unfolds with Emma at its core, delving into the realms of user interface design and data representation through the lens of external libraries and tools. This chapter promises a journey through various landscapes of technology—from the aesthetic finesse of Angular Material to the intricate data storytelling capabilities of Chart.js and the robust, feature-rich UI possibilities offered by DevExtreme. Additionally, the chapter will explore the cutting-edge frontier where data visualization meets Artificial Intelligence, revealing how AI is reshaping the way we interpret and present data.

💡 The right UI can make or break your application—it's where function meets form.

© Arpit Dwivedi 2024
A. Dwivedi, *CodeMosaic*, https://doi.org/10.1007/979-8-8688-0276-8_7

The importance of data visualization in the current corporate and technological world cannot be understated. It has become a pivotal skill, turning abstract numbers into understandable stories, influencing decisions, and enhancing user engagement. This chapter will contrast the crafting of custom visualizations using libraries like Chart.js against the utilization of powerful tools like Power BI and Tableau, providing a comprehensive understanding of the options available to developers and data scientists alike.

Leveraging External Libraries for UI Components

As the digital canvas of web development broadens, the art of crafting user interfaces demands both creativity and efficiency. In this realm, Angular emerges as a masterful painter, with its palette rich in external libraries, each offering unique hues and textures to the UI landscape. This section explores how these libraries, far more than mere tools, become integral to sculpting user experiences that are both functional and visually captivating.

Unboxing Angular's External Library Treasures

In the world of Angular development, external libraries are akin to hidden treasures, offering a wealth of functionalities that transform the way developers approach frontend design. These libraries, brimming with pre-built components and tools, not only streamline the development process but also open doors to innovative design possibilities. They are pivotal in achieving efficiency, scalability, and superior user experience.

UI Renaissance: Meeting Modern Needs

The requirements for user interfaces in modern web applications are constantly evolving. Developers like Emma, adept in the Angular ecosystem, strategically choose a combination of external libraries to meet these needs. Angular Material, with its comprehensive design system, Chart.js for its dynamic data visualization capabilities, and DevExtreme for advanced UI components, are among the key libraries that Emma integrates into her projects, preparing for a deep dive into their functionalities later in the chapter.

Toolkit Exploration: Enterprise and Responsive Design

Emma's toolkit is diverse, each tool serving a specific purpose:

NG-ZORRO for Enterprise Applications

NG-ZORRO is particularly suited for enterprise-level applications, offering a rich set of components that blend functionality with aesthetic appeal. To integrate NG-ZORRO in an Angular project, you start by

1. **Installation:** Run `npm install ng-zorro-antd`.

2. **Integration:** Import **NgZorroAntdModule** into the Angular module.

3. **Practical Application:** Create a sleek and interactive data table using `<nz-table>`, demonstrating NG-ZORRO's capability to handle complex data structures.

Responsive Design with Ngx-Bootstrap

Ngx-Bootstrap is another gem in Angular's library collection, renowned for its responsiveness and ease of use.

1. Integrating Ngx-Bootstrap into an Angular project begins with installing it via npm (`npm install ngx-bootstrap`).

2. And then importing the necessary modules (like **BsDropdownModule**) into your Angular module.

3. A typical use case is creating a responsive navigation bar. This involves using the `<nav>` element combined with directives provided by Ngx-Bootstrap, such as `[isAnimated]` and `[autoClose]`, to create a navigation bar that adapts to various screen sizes and enhances the user experience.

Crafting Superior Interfaces with Ngx-Bootstrap

A practical application of Ngx-Bootstrap can be seen in creating a responsive layout. Utilizing the grid system (`<div class="row">` and `<div class="col-xs| sm|md|lg|xl">`), you can effectively organize content on different screen sizes.

This system allows you to specify how many columns each element should span on different devices, ensuring that the layout remains coherent and aesthetically pleasing across all platforms.

💡Did you know?   Using Angular libraries like NG-ZORRO can significantly reduce development time by providing ready-to-use components.

Transformative Impact: Beyond Aesthetics

The adoption of these external libraries has a transformative effect on TechFusion Corp's project. It results in a significant reduction in development time and an enhanced user experience. Feedback from end users and stakeholders underscores the improvement, with particular praise for the intuitive design and responsive nature of the new interface.

Preview of Deep Dives

While NG-ZORRO and Ngx-Bootstrap have set the stage for UI excellence, there is much more to explore. In the following sections, we will dive into the specifics of Angular Material, unravel the dynamics of data representation with Chart.js, and explore the advanced capabilities of DevExtreme. Each library will be dissected to reveal its core strengths and practical applications in real-world scenarios, continuing the journey of innovation and efficiency in UI design.

Angular Material

Angular Material stands as a cornerstone in the Angular ecosystem, offering a suite of high-quality UI components grounded in Material Design principles. This section delves into the world of Angular Material, exploring its components, design principles, and customization options. We'll also compare it with similar libraries, like PrimeNG, to provide a broader perspective on UI toolkit options in Angular.

In-Depth on Angular Material

Angular Material brings a touch of elegance and functionality to Angular applications. It's built on Material Design principles, which focus on crafting beautiful, intuitive, and consistent user interfaces. Key components of Angular Material include

- **Navigation Elements**
  Such as **MatToolbar**, **MatSidenav**, and **MatMenu**, which help in creating responsive navigation bars and menus.

- **Form Controls**
  Including **MatFormField**, **MatInput**, and **MatSelect**, offering various options for user input.

- **Layout Components**
  Like **MatGridList** and **MatCard**, enabling developers to create structured and attractive layouts.

- **Buttons and Indicators**
  With elements like **MatButton** and **MatProgressBar**, adding interactive and dynamic feedback to user actions.

Customization is one of Angular Material's strengths, allowing developers to modify the default themes or create new ones to align with their application's branding. This involves using Angular's theming system, where you can define custom colors and styles in SCSS files.

Building an Interface with Angular Material

To integrate Angular Material in your project:

- **Installation**
  Run ng add @angular/material in your project directory.

- **Importing Modules**
  - Import the necessary Angular Material modules in your app. module.ts.
  - For example, MatButtonModule for buttons and MatToolbarModule for the toolbar.

- **Creating a Navigation Bar**

  - Use `<mat-toolbar>` to create a top navigation bar.

  - Include navigation items using `<mat-button>`.

  - Implement responsive design by adding `<mat-sidenav-container>` and `<mat-sidenav>` for a collapsible side navigation.

- **Building a Form**

  - Utilize `<mat-form-field>` along with `<input matInput>` for text inputs.

  - Add options like `<mat-select>` and `<mat-option>` for dropdowns.

- **Styling**

  - Customize the appearance using Angular's theming system in your SCSS files, setting your primary, accent, and warn palettes.

Comparison with Other Libraries: PrimeNG

While Angular Material excels in Material Design compliance, libraries like PrimeNG offer a diverse array of components with different design philosophies. PrimeNG is known for its vast component library, flexibility, and ease of customization. Unlike Angular Material, which adheres strictly to Material Design, PrimeNG provides a more eclectic mix of styles and components, catering to a wider range of design requirements. This makes PrimeNG a suitable choice for projects seeking design variety and customization beyond the Material Design framework.

Angular Material and libraries like PrimeNG each offer unique advantages, catering to different aspects of UI development. Angular Material's adherence to Material Design principles suits projects looking for a consistent and tested design language, while PrimeNG offers more variety in design and customization. Understanding the strengths and use-cases of each library is crucial in making an informed decision that aligns with the project's design goals and requirements. The next sections will further expand on data visualization tools, diving deeper into libraries like Chart.js and DevExtreme.

The Art of Data Visualization

In the rapidly evolving domain of web development, data visualization emerges as a key player. It's not just about presenting data; it's about telling a story, making complex information accessible and actionable. For businesses and clients, this translates into data-driven decisions made clearer and faster.

Custom Visualization vs. Specialized Tools

In the arena of data visualization, developers often face a choice between leveraging custom visualization libraries and utilizing specialized tools. This decision hinges on various factors such as project requirements, time constraints, and desired levels of customization. Let's explore these two paths in more detail.

Exploring Custom Visualization Libraries

Custom libraries like Chart.js and DevExtreme present a world of possibilities for tailor-made visualizations.

- **Flexibility and Integration**
  These libraries shine when it comes to customization. They allow developers to create visualizations that align precisely with the project's design and functional requirements. Their seamless integration into web applications ensures consistency in user experience.

- **Development Time and Expertise**
  However, this flexibility comes with its challenges. Creating complex visualizations often demands more development time and a deeper understanding of the library's capabilities.

Navigating Specialized Tools

On the other side of the spectrum, specialized tools such as Power BI and Tableau offer a different approach.

- **Rapid Development and Data Handling**
  These tools are designed for speed and efficiency. They provide pre-built templates and intuitive interfaces that allow for quick creation of visualizations, even with large datasets.

- **Customization and Integration Limits**
  The trade-off, however, is in customization and integration. While they offer some customization options, they typically cannot match the level of tailor-made solutions provided by libraries. Additionally, integrating these tools into existing web applications can sometimes lead to design and experience inconsistencies.

Contextual Application

The choice between custom libraries and specialized tools often depends on the specific context of a project:

- **Short-Term and Rapid Projects**
  For projects with tight deadlines or the need for quick turnaround, specialized tools can be the go-to option.

- **Brand-Centric and Unique Visualizations**
  Projects requiring unique visualizations that closely align with brand identity may benefit more from the flexibility of custom libraries.

- **Handling Complex Data**
  When projects involve complex data processing and analysis, specialized tools with their robust data handling capabilities become invaluable.

Insight   "Choosing between custom libraries and specialized tools? It's like picking the right brush for your canvas—each has its unique stroke."

Emma's Strategies at TechFusion Corp

At TechFusion Corp, Emma faced a scenario where the client demanded quick turnaround times for complex data visualization tasks. Balancing efficiency with effectiveness was key.

- **Rapid Development with Specialized Tools**
  For one urgent project, Emma chose Power BI. The client needed complex data visualizations within a tight deadline, and Power BI's ready-to-use templates allowed Emma to deliver high-quality results quickly, even though customization options were limited.

- **Customized Visualization for Specific Needs**
  In another instance, the project demanded highly customized data visualizations that aligned with the company's branding. Here, Emma opted for Chart.js. Though it required more development time, it offered the flexibility to tailor every aspect of the visualization to the client's specific needs.

Through these scenarios, the value of choosing the right tool for data visualization becomes evident. Emma's ability to discern which method best suited each project phase at TechFusion Corp was crucial. This versatility in handling data visualization— knowing when to opt for speed and when to focus on customization—is an invaluable skill in modern web development.

💡 **Pro Tip**   To make your data tell a story, choose your visualization tool wisely— Chart.js for customization, Power BI for analytics.

The Palette of Charts

In the world of data visualization, charts are the canvas on which data tells its story. Each chart type offers a unique perspective, revealing different insights and narratives embedded within the data. This section explores the diverse array of chart types available and provides guidance on selecting the most suitable one for various data scenarios.

Overview of Chart Types

Data visualization encompasses a wide range of chart types, each suited for specific kinds of data and insights:

- **Bar Charts**
  Ideal for comparing quantities across categories. They are straightforward and effective for showing differences between discrete groups.

- **Line Charts**
  Best for illustrating trends over time. They are commonly used for time-series data where continuity and change are the focal points.

- **Pie Charts**
  Useful for showing proportional or percentage relationships within a dataset. They provide a quick visual comparison of parts to the whole.

- **Scatter Plots**
  Excellent for identifying correlations and patterns between two variables. They help in revealing the relationship and distribution of data points.

- **Heatmaps**
  Effective in displaying complex data patterns through variations in coloring. They are particularly useful for visualizing data density or intensity over a map or matrix.

- **Pivot Grids**
  Pivot grids are powerful for summarizing and analyzing large datasets, allowing for the exploration of data along multiple dimensions.

Selecting the Right Chart for Your Data

Choosing the appropriate chart type is crucial for effective data visualization:

- **Data Nature and Storytelling**
  The nature of your data (categorical, continuous, comparative, etc.)
  and the story you want to tell should guide your chart selection. For
  example, line charts are fitting for continuous data where trends and
  changes over time are important.

- **Data Scenarios and Chart Suitability**

  - For comparative data analysis among different categories, bar
    charts are often the most effective.

  - When dealing with relationships between numerical values,
    scatter plots can provide clarity.

  - To display parts of a whole or percentages, pie charts offer an
    immediate visual impact.

- **Clarity and Impact Considerations**
  It's vital to choose chart types that present data clearly and
  compellingly. Avoid overly complex or cluttered visuals that might
  lead to misinterpretation. The goal is to make the data as accessible
  and insightful as possible.

The variety of chart types at our disposal is a testament to the diverse ways we can
represent data. The key lies in matching the right chart type with the right dataset and
narrative. Effective use of charts not only brings data to life but also makes it engaging
and insightful, turning numbers into stories that can inform and persuade.

Implementing Charting Libraries

In the quest to make data more comprehensible and visually engaging, charting libraries
play a pivotal role. They are the tools that transform raw numbers into insightful,
interactive visual narratives. This section delves into the implementation of two
prominent charting libraries in the Angular ecosystem: Chart.js and DevExtreme. Chart.
js offers simplicity and ease of use for basic visualizations, making it an ideal choice

for straightforward graphical representations. On the other hand, DevExtreme caters to more complex UI requirements, providing a robust suite of features for advanced data visualization challenges. Whether it's a simple line chart to depict a trend or a comprehensive data grid for detailed analysis, these libraries equip developers with the necessary tools to bring data to life in an Angular application.

Chart.js for Basic Visualizations

Chart.js is renowned for its simplicity and power in creating engaging charts. It's a perfect tool for developers looking to add basic but visually striking charts to their Angular applications.

Installation and Setup in Angular

- **Installation**

  - Install Chart.js via npm with `npm install chart.js`.

  - For detailed installation instructions, visit the Chart.js Installation Guide.

    `www.chartjs.org/docs/latest/getting-started/installation.html`

- **Angular Module Integration**

  - Import Chart.js into your Angular project. Add `import { ChartsModule } from "ng2-charts";` to your main app module.

  - Include `ChartsModule` in the imports array of your `@NgModule` decorator.

Creating a Bar Chart in an Angular Component

The creation of a bar chart involves several steps, each contributing to the final visualization:

Component Configuration

In your TypeScript file, set up the chart configuration. This includes the type of chart, the data it will display, and any options to customize its appearance.

Example configuration:

```typescript
``` Typescript code
public barChartOptions = {
  scaleShowVerticalLines: false,
  responsive: true
};
public barChartLabels = ['2006', '2007', '2008', '2009', '2010', '2011', '2012'];
public barChartType = 'bar';
public barChartLegend = true;
public barChartData = [
  {data: [65, 59, 80, 81, 56, 55, 40], label: 'Series A'},
  {data: [28, 48, 40, 19, 86, 27, 90], label: 'Series B'}
];
```

In the example variables define

- **barChartOptions:** Defines chart options like whether vertical lines are shown and if the chart is responsive

- **barChartLabels:** Labels for the x-axis, typically representing categories or time intervals

- **barChartType:** Specifies the type of chart, which is "bar" in this case

- **barChartLegend:** Determines if a legend is displayed

- **barChartData:** The data for the chart, with each object representing a series of data points

HTML Template Setup

In your component's HTML template, add the <canvas> element where the chart will render.

Use the baseChart directive to bind your chart data:

```html
```HTML code
<canvas baseChart
    [chartData]="barChartData"
```

```
    [chartOptions]="barChartOptions"
    [chartType]="barChartType">
</canvas>
```

The baseChart directive binds your Angular component's chart configuration to the Chart.js chart in your template.

Data and Options: Bind the barChartData and barChartOptions to your chart in the HTML. This will display the bar chart based on the data and options you've configured.

For a detailed guide on creating a bar chart, refer to the Chart.js Bar Chart Documentation: www.chartjs.org/docs/latest/charts/bar.html.

Best Practices for Chart.js

- **Ensure Responsiveness:** Set responsive: true in your chart options to make sure your chart adapts to different screen sizes.

- **Accessibility Considerations:** Provide alternative content for those who may not be able to visually interpret the chart.

- **Performance Optimization:** For larger datasets, reduce redraws and limit animations to enhance performance.

DevExtreme for Complex UIs

DevExtreme, with its comprehensive suite of UI components, is a powerhouse in the Angular ecosystem, offering advanced capabilities for creating intricate and responsive user interfaces. This segment will guide you through the process of integrating DevExtreme into an Angular application, focusing specifically on creating a bar chart.

Integration of DevExtreme in Angular

The journey with DevExtreme begins with its integration into your Angular project:

- **Installation**
  - Install DevExtreme by running npm install devextreme devextreme-angular.

- This command adds both DevExtreme and its Angular integration module to your project.

- For detailed installation instructions, check the DevExtreme Installation Guide.

- **Module Setup**

- After installation, import DevExtreme modules into your Angular project.

- For a bar chart, you would import DxChartModule:

```Typescript
```Typescript code
import { DxChartModule } from 'devextreme-angular';
@NgModule({
  // ...
  imports: [
    // ...
    DxChartModule
    // ...
  ]
})
export class AppModule { }
```
```

Creating a Bar Chart with DevExtreme

Here's how you can create a bar chart in your Angular component:

Component Configuration

Define the data and configuration for your bar chart in the component TypeScript file:

```Typescript
```Typescript code
import { Component } from '@angular/core';
@Component({
  selector: 'app-bar-chart',
  templateUrl: './bar-chart.component.html'
})
```
```

```
export class BarChartComponent {
  chartData = [
    { argument: 'Category1', value: 10 },
    { argument: 'Category2', value: 20 }
    // ... more data points
  ];
}
```

HTML Template Setup

In the component's HTML template, add the DevExtreme chart component:

```HTML code
<dx-chart [dataSource]="chartData">
  <dxi-series argumentField="argument" valueField="value" type="bar"></
  dxi-series>
</dx-chart>
```

This snippet creates a bar chart bound to the chartData array. The dxi-series directive specifies the chart type and the fields for the chart's arguments and values.

Best Practices for DevExtreme Charts

When working with DevExtreme charts:

- **Responsive Design:** Make sure your chart is responsive to different screen sizes.

- **Data Binding:** Use Angular's data binding features to dynamically update your charts.

- **Performance:** For large datasets, consider optimizing data processing and rendering to enhance performance.

Implementing DevExtreme in Angular projects opens up a world of possibilities for creating complex and dynamic UI components. A bar chart is just a starting point; DevExtreme's library is filled with numerous widgets and tools that can cater to a variety of advanced UI requirements, significantly elevating the user experience of any web application.

♥Quick Trick   Remember, the key to effective data visualization is not just in the data, but in how you present it. Libraries like DevExtreme can be your secret tool.

In this section of "Implementing Charting Libraries," we explored how Chart.js and DevExtreme enhance data visualization in Angular applications. Chart.js offers simplicity and ease for basic charts, making it suitable for straightforward visual needs. DevExtreme, with its advanced capabilities, is ideal for more complex and interactive UI components. The choice between these libraries should align with your project's requirements—Chart.js for simplicity and quick implementation, and DevExtreme for comprehensive and intricate UI designs. Understanding and leveraging these libraries effectively can transform how data is presented and interacted with in your applications.

AI in Data Visualization

In the evolving landscape of data analysis, Artificial Intelligence (AI) is playing an increasingly pivotal role in data visualization. AI technologies are not just enhancing but revolutionizing the way we interpret and represent data. They bring the power to automatically uncover deeper insights, predict trends, and facilitate the creation of sophisticated visualizations that would be challenging to construct manually.

Automated Insight Generation: AI algorithms can sift through vast datasets to identify patterns and correlations, presenting these findings through intuitive visualizations. This capability is particularly valuable in sectors like finance, healthcare, and marketing, where understanding complex data patterns is crucial for decision-making.

AI Tools and Techniques for Visualization

The market offers a variety of AI-driven visualization tools, each bringing unique capabilities to the table.

- **TensorFlow for Advanced Analysis**
  TensorFlow, an open source platform, is widely used for machine learning and neural network-based visualizations. It can process large volumes of data to produce predictive models, which can then be visualized to forecast trends and outcomes.

- **Tableau and Microsoft Power BI with AI Integration**
  Tools like Tableau and Microsoft Power BI have integrated AI capabilities to enhance their visualization power. These platforms use AI to offer predictive analytics, trend identification, and even natural language processing to transform complex datasets into understandable visual narratives.

- **Natural Language Processing (NLP)**
  AI's NLP capabilities allow these tools to generate textual descriptions and summaries of visual data, making the data more accessible to a broader audience.

Practical Applications

AI-driven visualization tools are being used in various industries to provide deeper insights:

- In marketing, these tools can analyze customer data to identify buying patterns and preferences, which can then be visualized for targeted marketing strategies.

- In healthcare, AI can help visualize patient data trends, aiding in predictive diagnostics and treatment planning.

The integration of AI in data visualization marks a significant leap forward in how we interact with and understand data. As AI technologies continue to advance, we can expect even more innovative and intuitive ways to visualize complex datasets. The future of data visualization with AI holds immense potential, promising to transform raw data into actionable insights more efficiently and effectively than ever before.

> 💡 **Interesting Fact**   AI isn't just for number crunching; it can transform data into captivating visual narratives.

Conclusion

In this chapter, we journeyed through the multifaceted world of data visualization and UI components in Angular, guided by the expert hands of Emma at TechFusion Corp. We explored how external libraries, both for UI components and charting, can significantly elevate the quality and effectiveness of web applications.

Key Takeaways

Here are the key takeaways:

- **Integration of External Libraries:** The integration of libraries like Ngx-Bootstrap, NG-ZORRO, and Angular Material offers immense benefits in UI design, providing both efficiency and aesthetic appeal.

- **Angular Material and Its Alternatives:** We delved into Angular Material's capabilities and compared it with other libraries like PrimeNG, emphasizing the importance of selecting the right tool for specific project requirements.

- **The Art and Science of Data Visualization:** The chapter highlighted the critical role of data visualization in modern web development. Through Emma's experience at TechFusion Corp, we saw the practical applications of both custom visualization techniques and specialized tools like Power BI and Tableau.

- **Diverse Palette of Charts**: We examined a variety of chart types available through Chart.js, discussing how to choose the appropriate chart type based on the data and the story it needs to tell.

- **Implementing Charting Libraries:** The chapter provided detailed guidance on implementing Chart.js for basic visualizations and DevExtreme for more complex UI scenarios, demonstrating their distinct applications.

- **AI in Data Visualization:** Finally, we touched on the role of AI in enhancing data visualization, exploring AI-driven tools and techniques that are reshaping how we interpret complex data sets.

What's Next?

As we transition to Chapter 8, "Designing Dreams and Solving Schemes," we move from the realm of data visualization to the broader landscape of software design and problem-solving. This chapter aims to explore the structured approach to software challenges, turning ideas into reality. It will cover various facets of software architecture, design patterns, teamwork in design, and the role of AI in this process.

Designing Dreams and Solving Schemes

Welcome to the dynamic and thought-provoking world of software design. In this chapter, we embark on an insightful journey into the heart of designing software. While software design is a vast and ever-evolving field, our focus here will be to present you with a foundational understanding of key design principles. These principles form the backbone of both high-level and low-level designs, integral to the creation of efficient, scalable, and user-friendly software applications.

This chapter is not just about theories and abstract concepts; it's also about seeing these principles come to life. To achieve this, we will be walking alongside Jamie, a seasoned lead developer at TechFusion Corp. Jamie faces a challenging task: to develop a feature rich in user interaction and demanding in data processing. Her journey through this challenge will serve as a practical case study, demonstrating how theoretical design principles are applied in real-world scenarios.

As we delve into Jamie's story, remember, software design is more than just writing code. It's about problem-solving, innovation, and thinking ahead. It requires a delicate balance of technical acumen, creativity, and foresight. Whether you're a budding developer or an experienced coder, the insights from this chapter will empower you to design software that's not just functional, but also impactful and sustainable.

Our exploration will cover essential topics such as software architecture, load balancing, design patterns, and much more. Each of these areas plays a critical role in the development process, and understanding them will equip you with the tools to craft effective software solutions.

So, let's turn the page and begin our journey into the world of software design, guided by the practical experiences of Jamie and her team at TechFusion Corp. Prepare to be engaged, enlightened, and inspired!

© Arpit Dwivedi 2024
A. Dwivedi, *CodeMosaic*, https://doi.org/10.1007/979-8-8688-0276-8_8

Jamie's Challenge: Setting the Stage

At TechFusion Corp, Jamie has encountered a particularly intricate feature request from a client, one that will test the team's ingenuity and technical acumen. This request is not just a test of their coding skills but a challenge that necessitates a deep dive into the principles of software design and architecture.

Detailed Feature Request: An Interactive Data Visualization Tool

Client's Requirement:

- Development of an interactive data visualization tool.
- The tool must handle large datasets and provide real-time, interactive data visualizations.
- Features:
  - Customizable charts
  - Live data feeds
  - User-driven data manipulation

The Complexity of the Request

Technical Intricacies:

- Managing large data sets without compromising performance.
- Ensuring smooth and real-time user interactions with complex data.

Potential Risks:

- System lag or crashes during high data load.
- Poor user experience due to delayed data rendering or non-intuitive interfaces.

Jamie's Initial Reaction and Strategic Approach

Analyzing the Challenge:

- Jamie understands the need for a robust backend capable of fast data processing.

- Recognizing the importance of an intuitive, responsive frontend for user interaction.

Preliminary Strategy:

- Planning to leverage advanced data caching and efficient data retrieval methods.

- Considering the use of modern frontend frameworks for a seamless user experience.

Preparing for a Structured Solution

Importance of Proper Design and Analysis:

- Jamie acknowledges that a haphazard approach could lead to significant issues, such as system inefficiency or user dissatisfaction.

- Emphasizes the need for a carefully thought-out design, balancing both backend efficiency and frontend usability.

Referring to the Feature Request Process

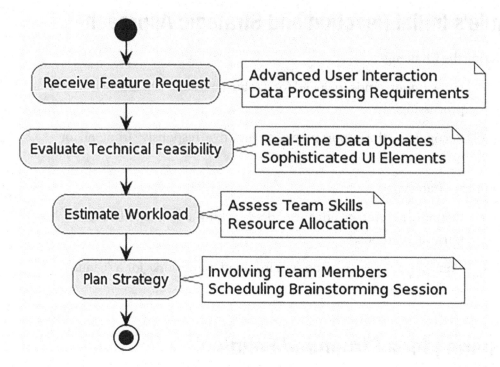

Figure 8-1. *A visual breakdown of Jamie's initial response to the feature request*

For a visual overview of Jamie's initial approach to this complex request, see Figure 8-1. This flowchart outlines the steps from understanding the client's needs to formulating a strategic plan.

To ensure a successful outcome, Jamie plans to delve into some fundamental software design concepts. This exploration will provide clarity and a solid foundation for approaching this complex project.

Foundations of Software Architecture

In the realm of software development, architecture is not just about the foundational structure; it's about envisioning a system that is robust, scalable, and efficient. For Jamie and her team at TechFusion Corp, embarking on the interactive data visualization tool project, a well-thought-out software architecture is indispensable. This project, with its demands for handling large datasets and ensuring real-time user interaction, hinges on the strength of its architectural design.

Jamie's Architectural Considerations

Software architecture in application development is akin to the blueprint in building construction. It lays out the framework for system design, addressing key concerns like scalability, performance, and maintainability. In Jamie's project—developing an interactive data visualization tool—selecting the right software architecture is critical for handling large datasets and ensuring seamless real-time user interaction.

Understanding Client-Server Models

In a client-server model, software architecture is divided into two parts: the client, which interacts with the user, and the server, which handles data processing and storage. To understand it better, have a look at Figure 8-2, which explains flow of Client-Server model:

- Client Role:

  - Interacts directly with the user, focusing on UI processing for real-time data presentation.

- Server Role:

  - Handles the heavy lifting of data processing and storage.

- Interaction:

  - The client sends data requests to the server, which processes these requests and responds back with the required data.

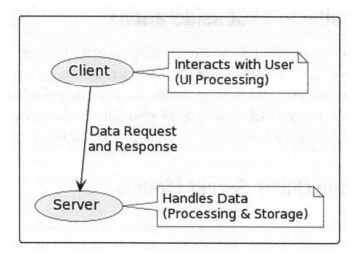

Figure 8-2. *Client-server model*

For Jamie's project, this model allows efficient data handling, with the server managing heavy data processing, while the client focuses on presenting data interactively to users.

Exploring Microservices Architecture

Microservices architecture involves developing a single application as a suite of small, independently deployable services. Each service runs its own process and communicates through lightweight mechanisms, often an HTTP-based API. To understand it better, have a look at Figure 8-3, which explains flow of Microservices Architecture:

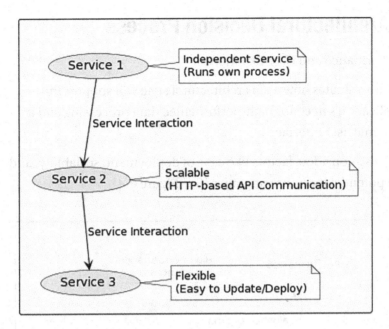

Figure 8-3. *Microservices architecture*

- Independent Services:

  - Each service (Service 1, Service 2, Service 3) runs its own process, contributing to different aspects of the application.

- Scalability and Communication:

  - Services are scalable and communicate with each other via HTTP-based APIs, allowing for flexibility in development and deployment.

- Flexibility:

  - Each microservice can be updated or deployed independently, facilitating ease of maintenance and adaptability.

This approach offers Jamie flexibility in scaling and updating different parts of the application independently, making it ideal for a complex project like the data visualization tool.

Jamie's Architectural Decision Process

Balancing Performance and User Experience:

- Jamie evaluates how each architectural style will support the application's need for high-performance data processing and a dynamic user interface.

- She also considers factors like ease of deployment, scalability, and the potential for future upgrades (See Figure 8-4).

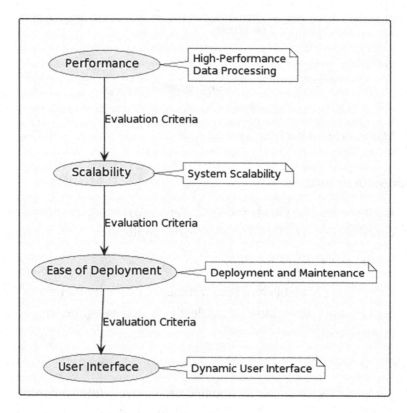

Figure 8-4. *Jamie's architectural decision process*

The choice of software architecture sets the foundational stage for Jamie's project, influencing how well the application meets its performance goals and user expectations. Whether it's a client-server model for efficient data handling or a microservices architecture for flexibility and scalability, the decision will shape the project's development path and its ultimate success.

Balancing the Load: A Critical Component

In the complex landscape of software development, load balancing plays a pivotal role in managing system resources efficiently. It involves distributing network or application traffic across multiple servers to ensure no single server bears too much load. For Jamie's ambitious data visualization tool, which demands high responsiveness and robust data processing, load balancing is not just an enhancement; it's a necessity.

The Importance of Load Balancing in Jamie's Project

Critical for Performance

Jamie's tool, designed to handle large, dynamic datasets and provide real-time visualizations, relies heavily on the server's ability to process data swiftly and efficiently. Load balancing is key to achieving this.

Consequences of Neglect

Without effective load balancing, the system could face significant challenges: server overloads leading to crashes or slowdowns, and a detrimental impact on user experience due to delayed data rendering (See Figure 8-5).

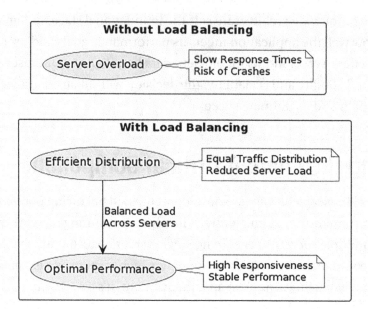

Figure 8-5. *Illustrating the impact of load balancing in Jamie's project, showing the system's performance with and without it*

Exploring Types of Load Balancers

Diverse Load Balancing Techniques—Jamie considers various load balancing techniques:

- **Round-Robin**

  Simple and efficient, distributing requests equally across servers.

- **Least Connections**

  Directing new requests to the server with the fewest active connections.

- **IP Hash**

  Allocating requests based on the IP address of the client, ensuring user session persistence.

For her data visualization tool, Jamie leans toward a combination of the Least Connections and IP Hash methods to balance efficiency and user session continuity.

Jamie's Implementation Strategy

Jamie plans to integrate load balancing into the system architecture, ensuring that it complements the client-server interaction and microservices setup—**Strategically Implementing Load Balancing**.

♥ Pro Tip   When implementing load balancing in a data-intensive application, it's crucial to consider factors like session persistence, server capacity, and the nature of the client requests to choose the most suitable load balancing method.

Load balancing emerges as a fundamental component in Jamie's data visualization tool project. It's a testament to her foresight and understanding of the system's needs, ensuring that the application not only functions efficiently but also delivers a seamless user experience.

Designing Blueprints: Jamie's Guide

In software development, a design blueprint serves as the architectural plan, guiding the construction and evolution of an application. For complex projects like Jamie's interactive data visualization tool, a well-crafted blueprint is vital. It outlines how various components interact, ensuring that the final product is both efficient and aligned with the project's objectives.

Jamie's Blueprint Creation for the Data Visualization Tool

Jamie starts by defining the tool's core functionality, envisioning how it will handle large datasets and enable user interactions. She then sketches out the major components, such as data processing modules, user interface elements, and interaction handlers—**Jamie's Methodical Approach**.

Her blueprint, shown in Figure 8-6, is particularly focused on managing large data loads efficiently while providing a smooth and responsive user experience—**Addressing Project-Specific Needs**.

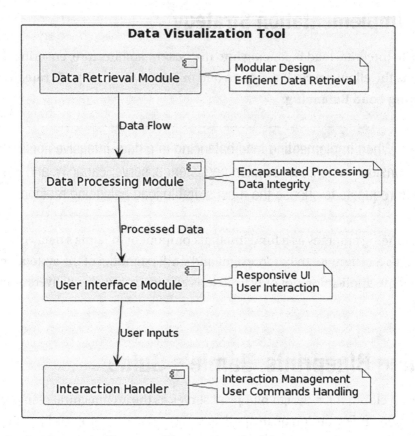

Figure 8-6. *A schematic diagram illustrating the blueprint, showing key components and their interactions within the tool*

Core Design Principles in Blueprinting

Modularity

Jamie incorporates modularity into her design, structuring the tool into distinct, interchangeable modules. This approach not only simplifies development but also enhances the tool's adaptability to changing requirements.

Encapsulation

She also emphasizes encapsulation, ensuring that each module's internal workings are hidden from the others. This principle is crucial for maintaining data integrity and system security, especially when handling sensitive or large-scale data.

Integrating Principles into the Blueprint

In her blueprint, Jamie delineates clear boundaries between different modules, such as data retrieval, processing, and visualization. Encapsulation is employed to protect data and functionalities from unauthorized access and to maintain a clean separation of concerns.

♥ Pro Tip   When designing complex software systems, applying principles like modularity and encapsulation from the blueprint stage can significantly enhance the system's maintainability and scalability.

Jamie's approach to creating a design blueprint for the data visualization tool showcases the critical role of planning and applying fundamental design principles. Her meticulous blueprint not only sets the stage for efficient development but also ensures that the final product meets the high standards of performance and usability required for such a complex application.

Patterns and Anti-Patterns: Jamie's Reference

In the complex world of software development, design patterns are proven solutions to common problems, while anti-patterns are common pitfalls that can lead to ineffective and problematic designs. Jamie, well-versed in both, knows that the right patterns can enhance her data visualization tool's functionality, and being aware of anti-patterns is crucial to avoid development traps.

Identifying and Applying Design Patterns

Jamie's Method for Identifying Patterns: Jamie assesses the needs of her project and matches them with appropriate design patterns. For instance, she opts for the Observer pattern to handle real-time data updates, ensuring that any data change is automatically reflected in the user interface.

Suitable Patterns for Data Visualization: Other patterns like Factory for creating different visualization components and Singleton for managing a single data source are also considered.

Figure 8-7 is a diagram showing the integration of the Observer pattern in the data visualization tool, demonstrating how data changes propagate to the UI. It visually represents how Jamie integrates the Observer design pattern into her data visualization tool, ensuring real-time UI updates in response to data changes.

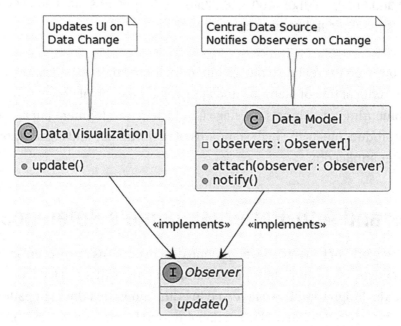

Figure 8-7. *Integration of observer pattern in data visualization tool*

Recognizing and Avoiding Anti-Patterns

Common Anti-Patterns in Software Development: Jamie is cautious of pitfalls like the God Object, which centralizes functionality in a single class, and Spaghetti Code, which results from lack of structure and can make maintenance a nightmare.

Jamie's Experience with Anti-Patterns: Drawing from past experiences, Jamie actively works to avoid these anti-patterns, ensuring her code is modular and maintainable.

💡 **Pro Tip**   Regular code reviews and refactoring are essential practices to identify and address anti-patterns early in the development process.

Balancing Patterns and Anti-Patterns in Design

Strategic Use of Patterns: Jamie's design approach is a balance—leveraging the strengths of design patterns while being vigilant about not falling into anti-pattern traps.

Case Study Example: In her current project, Jamie effectively uses the Observer pattern to update visualizations dynamically, avoiding the God Object anti-pattern by distributing responsibilities across multiple modules.

Understanding and applying design patterns, coupled with an awareness of anti-patterns, is key to creating a successful and sustainable software application. Jamie's strategic approach in her data visualization tool project serves as a testament to the power of well-applied design principles and the pitfalls of common mistakes in software design.

Iterative Collaboration: Merging Jamie's Development Cycle and Team Synergy

In the fast-paced world of software development, merging the iterative development process with effective team collaboration can be the key to success. This approach not only addresses the evolving complexity of projects but also harnesses the diverse skills within a team. Jamie's journey in creating the data visualization tool at TechFusion Corp exemplifies this harmonious blend of iterative development and collaborative design.

The Iterative Development Approach in Jamie's Project

Implementing Iterative Development: Jamie adopts an iterative development model, allowing her team to build the feature in phases, evaluating and refining at each step.
Benefits for Complex Projects: This approach proves invaluable in managing the complexity of the data visualization tool, as it evolves to incorporate new insights and user feedback.

Insights from Jamie's Iterative Process

Navigating Challenges: Jamie encounters and addresses several challenges, such as integrating complex data processing features and adapting to changing user requirements.
Lessons Learned: Each iteration brings valuable lessons, enhancing the team's ability to respond to technical hurdles and user needs efficiently.

Jamie's Team Synergy in Collaborative Design

Fostering Team Collaboration: Jamie leverages the diverse expertise of her team members, including Emma's UI/UX skills and Alex's innovative coding capabilities.
Dynamic Teamwork: The team's collaborative efforts are coordinated through regular meetings, shared documentation, and joint problem-solving sessions.

Tools and Techniques for Enhanced Collaboration

Utilizing Collaboration Tools: Jamie's team employs various tools and techniques, such as version control systems, shared code repositories, and collaborative platforms, to streamline their workflow.
Importance in Teamwork: These tools play a crucial role in maintaining clear communication, tracking progress, and ensuring that everyone is aligned with the project's goals.

The fusion of iterative development with collaborative design in Jamie's project underscores the importance of flexibility, continuous learning, and team synergy in modern software development. This approach not only led to the successful creation of the data visualization tool but also set a precedent for how complex projects can be effectively managed through iterative collaboration.

AI in Software Design: Aiding Jamie's Process

In the realm of software design, AI tools are revolutionizing the way developers approach the creation and refinement of applications. These tools offer innovative solutions, automate repetitive tasks, and provide insights that significantly enhance the design process. Jamie, in her data visualization project, leverages several AI tools to optimize design and tackle complex challenges. Here are some key AI Tools Benefiting Software Design:

- **Sketch2Code by Microsoft**

  - **Functionality:** Converts hand-drawn sketches into HTML code.

  - **Impact on Design:** Assists Jamie in rapidly prototyping UI designs from initial sketches, speeding up the design process.

- **Adobe Sensei**

  - **Functionality:** Uses AI and machine learning to automate design tasks in Adobe's suite of tools.

  - **Impact on Design:** Enhances Jamie's ability to create visually appealing UI elements with intelligent image handling and layout optimization.

- **Figma's Auto Layout**

  - **Functionality:** An AI-powered feature in Figma that automatically adjusts the layout based on content changes.

  - **Impact on Design:** Streamlines Jamie's UI/UX design process, making it easier to maintain consistency and responsiveness in her visualizations.

- **Autodesk's Generative Design**

  - **Functionality:** Uses AI to generate design alternatives based on specific input parameters and constraints.

  - **Impact on Design:** Helps Jamie explore a broader range of design possibilities for certain components of her project, ensuring optimal functionality and aesthetics.

- **Canva's Design Suggestions**

  - **Functionality:** Offers AI-driven design recommendations for graphics and layouts.

  - **Impact on Design:** Provides Jamie with creative suggestions for marketing materials and user guides related to her data visualization tool.

- **Runway ML**

  - **Functionality:** Brings machine learning models to creative media applications, allowing non-experts to use advanced algorithms.

  - **Impact on Design:** Empowers Jamie's team to incorporate machine learning features into their UI, enhancing interactivity and user engagement.

Each of these tools contributes uniquely to the design process, enabling Jamie and her team to push creative boundaries, automate routine tasks, and explore innovative design solutions. Their incorporation into the project workflow leads to enhanced efficiency, creativity, and overall design quality.

Resolving Jamie's Challenge

In this case study, we embark on a journey with Jamie as she tackles the development of a data visualization tool at TechFusion Corp. The focus here is on the step-by-step application of various software design principles, which played a pivotal role in shaping the tool's development:

- **Architectural Choices**

  Jamie's first step involves selecting the right architecture. She opts for a microservices architecture, recognizing its suitability for handling large datasets and facilitating scalability. Each microservice is designed to handle a specific aspect of data processing or visualization, enabling a more manageable and efficient development process.

- **Implementing Load Balancing**

  To ensure the system remains responsive despite heavy data loads, Jamie integrates load balancing. She carefully selects a load balancing strategy that distributes incoming data requests evenly across multiple servers, thereby avoiding potential bottlenecks.

- **Modular UI Design**

  In designing the user interface, Jamie applies the principle of modularity. She breaks down the UI into smaller, manageable components, each responsible for specific functionalities like data input, visualization rendering, or user interaction. This approach allows for easier updates and scalability of the interface.

- **Applying Design Patterns and AI Tools**

  Jamie leverages AI tools like GitHub Copilot to streamline the coding process and generate efficient code structures. She also implements the Observer design pattern, allowing real-time updating of visualizations as new data is processed. This pattern ensures that any change in the dataset is immediately reflected in the user interface, enhancing the tool's interactivity.

Throughout the development, Jamie faces challenges such as integrating disparate data sources and optimizing data processing for real-time updates. By iteratively applying the chosen design principles and continuously refining her approach, she addresses these challenges effectively. Her iterative approach, coupled with team collaboration, leads to a robust and user-friendly data visualization tool.

Jamie's experience in developing the data visualization tool is a clear demonstration of the practical application of theoretical design principles. The step-by-step application of architecture, load balancing, modularity, and AI tools not only resolves the initial challenge but also provides a framework for future projects. This case study highlights the importance of a thoughtful and integrated approach to software design, essential for tackling complex and evolving project requirements.

Conclusion

Jamie's journey through the development of the data visualization tool at TechFusion Corp has been a tale of innovation, challenge, and triumph. It stands as a testament to the power of integrating a range of software design principles and tools in a cohesive and effective manner. This journey not only shaped a successful project but also paved the way for future explorations in software development.

Key Takeaways

- **The Value of Architectural Planning:** Jamie's choice of a microservices architecture underlines the importance of foundational planning in handling complex projects.

- **Efficiency of Load Balancing:** The implementation of load balancing techniques was crucial in managing high data volumes and maintaining system responsiveness.

- **Significance of Modular Design:** Adopting a modular approach in UI design enhanced flexibility and ease of updates.

- **Leveraging AI Tools:** The integration of AI tools like GitHub Copilot proved instrumental in optimizing coding processes and sparking innovative solutions.

- **Practical Application of Design Patterns:** The use of design patterns like Observer facilitated real-time data updates, enhancing user engagement.

- **Iterative Development and Team Collaboration:** Jamie's iterative approach, combined with effective team collaboration, was key in refining the tool and adapting to evolving requirements.

What's Next?

As we close this chapter on Jamie's insightful journey, we turn our gaze to the horizon, where a new chapter awaits. Chapter 9, "Copilot Chronicles: Coding with a Digital Companion," promises to delve into the world of AI-powered development,

244

with a special focus on GitHub Copilot. We will explore how this digital muse is revolutionizing the coding process, offering insights into its strengths, limitations, and ethical considerations. This upcoming chapter is not just about understanding a tool; it's about envisioning the future of coding, where AI companions become integral to our development workflow. Get ready to embark on an exciting exploration of coding alongside an AI-powered ally, discovering how it can enhance your coding experience, challenge your creativity, and shape the future of software development.

Bonus Byte 3: Leveraging GPT for Automated PlantUML Diagrams

In the rapidly evolving landscape of software development and documentation, the integration of artificial intelligence (AI) with automated tools presents a groundbreaking opportunity for efficiency and innovation. One such integration is the use of Generative Pre-trained Transformer (GPT) models, like OpenAI's GPT-3, in the automatic generation of PlantUML diagrams. This chapter aims to explore this synergy, focusing on how GPT models can interpret natural language descriptions and translate them into PlantUML code.

PlantUML stands out as a powerful tool for creating a wide array of diagrams such as sequence diagrams, class diagrams, and more, which are essential in documenting software architectures and processes. The ability of GPT models to understand and convert complex software concepts and user stories into PlantUML code not only streamlines the process of creating these diagrams but also opens doors to higher accuracy and consistency in software documentation.

The following sections will delve into the intricacies of PlantUML, the types of diagrams it can create, and how GPT models can be effectively utilized to generate PlantUML code for various scenarios. Additionally, we will explore the practical aspects of visualizing this code into diagrams using online tools or setting up a local environment for diagram conversion. This chapter aims to provide a comprehensive guide for leveraging AI in enhancing the efficiency and quality of diagrammatic representations in software development.

Introduction to PlantUML

PlantUML is an open source tool that allows users to create diagrams from a plain text language. It's particularly popular in the software development community for its simplicity and ease of integration with various documentation tools.

The tool is designed to facilitate quick and easy diagram creation, making it an indispensable resource for developers, project managers, and documentation professionals.

Types of Diagrams Created with PlantUML:

1. **Sequence Diagrams:** Used to depict the flow of operations, messages, or events between objects or components in a system.

2. **Class Diagrams:** These diagrams illustrate the structure of a system by showing its classes, attributes, operations, and the relationships between objects.

3. **Use Case Diagrams:** Ideal for representing the functionality of a system from an end-user perspective.

4. **Activity Diagrams:** Used to model the workflow of a system or a process, showing the sequence of activities and decisions.

5. **Component Diagrams:** Focus on the organization and wiring of the various components of a system.

6. **State Diagrams:** Describe the states and transitions of a system or an object over time.

Each of these diagrams serves a unique purpose in representing different aspects of a system, contributing significantly to the understanding and communication of complex software architectures and processes.

Utilizing GPT for PlantUML Code Generation

GPT (Generative Pre-trained Transformer) models have revolutionized various aspects of natural language processing. One of their remarkable capabilities is generating code from natural language descriptions.

In the context of PlantUML, GPT models can interpret software concepts, user stories, or task descriptions and translate them into the PlantUML language. This allows for the automated generation of diagrams from textual descriptions, significantly simplifying the process of visual documentation in software development.

Generating PlantUML Code for Different Scenarios:

- **From Descriptions to Code:** Developers can input descriptions like "Display the interaction between the user interface and the database in a login system" into a GPT model. The model then generates the corresponding PlantUML code for a sequence diagram depicting this interaction.

- **Handling Complexity:** GPT's advanced language understanding enables it to handle complex scenarios, generating code for intricate diagrams such as detailed class diagrams or comprehensive activity diagrams.

- **Refinement and Customization:** While the initial output from GPT provides a solid foundation, developers may refine and tailor the generated PlantUML code to suit specific documentation requirements or to add more detail.

The integration of GPT models into the process of creating PlantUML diagrams not only saves time but also ensures a higher level of accuracy and standardization in documentation. This topic demonstrates the potential of AI in automating and enhancing technical documentation tasks.

From Code to Diagram: Tools and Execution

Online Tools for PlantUML Visualization:

- Once PlantUML code is generated, it can be visualized using various online tools. These platforms allow users to paste the generated code and instantly view the resulting diagram.

- Popular online tools include PlantUML's official website, which features an online server for immediate diagram rendering, and other integrated web services like Creately or Lucidchart that support PlantUML code.

- These tools are particularly useful for quick visualization and are accessible without the need for any local environment setup.

Setting Up a Local Environment for PlantUML:

- For those who prefer or require offline access, setting up a local environment for PlantUML visualization is a viable option.

- **Installation**: This involves installing PlantUML, which typically requires Java Runtime Environment (JRE) as a prerequisite. Detailed installation instructions can be found on the PlantUML website.

- **Usage**: After installation, PlantUML diagrams can be created by running the tool with the generated code as input. This can be done through various methods such as command line, integrated development environments (IDEs), or text editors with PlantUML plugins.

- **Flexibility and Control**: A local setup offers more control over the diagram generation process, including customization of output formats and integration with other software development tools.

Whether using online platforms for convenience and accessibility or setting up a local environment for greater control and offline access, these tools and methods provide flexible options for turning PlantUML code into clear, visual diagrams.

Practical Example: GPT-Generated PlantUML Diagram

To demonstrate the practical application of GPT for PlantUML diagram generation, let's consider a realistic software development scenario.

Scenario Description: Imagine we need to document the workflow of a user authentication system. Our description of the GPT model might be, "Create a sequence diagram for a user logging into a system, including steps from entering credentials to receiving a success or failure response."

Upon receiving this description, the GPT model generates the following PlantUML code:

```
```
@startuml
actor User
participant "Login Interface" as UI
database "User Database" as DB

User -> UI : Enter credentials
UI -> DB : Validate credentials
alt successful login
    DB -> UI : Success response
    UI -> User : Display dashboard
else failed login
    DB -> UI : Failure response
    UI -> User : Show error message
end
@enduml
```
```

This code represents the sequence of interactions in the user authentication process.

Using an online PlantUML tool or a local environment, we input the above code to generate the diagram.

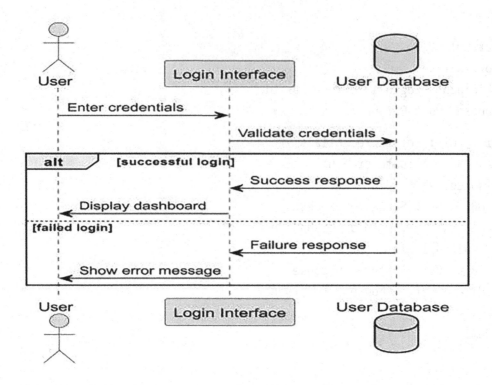

The generated diagram accurately reflects the described process, showcasing how GPT can effectively translate natural language into a structured visual representation.

This example illustrates the potential of AI in automating and enhancing the documentation process, especially in complex software development scenarios.

Conclusion

The use of GPT models for automated PlantUML diagram generation marks a significant advancement in the field of software documentation. This technology not only simplifies the process of creating diagrams but also ensures a higher level of precision and standardization. As AI continues to evolve, its integration into various aspects of software development promises to bring further efficiency and innovation. The future of technical documentation and design could see a greater reliance on AI-powered tools, transforming the way we visualize and understand complex systems.

CHAPTER 9

Copilot Chronicles: Coding with a Digital Companion

Welcome to the era of AI-Assisted. Have you ever been deep in coding, meticulously piecing together logic and functions, and then, out of nowhere, you hit a snag? It's in moments like these where having a knowledgeable coding companion can make a world of difference. This is where GitHub Copilot comes into play, not just as a tool, but as a partner in your coding journey.

In the vibrant tech halls of TechFusion Corp, Jordan, the project manager, is always on the lookout for tools that can propel the team forward. His latest find, GitHub Copilot, is like a breath of fresh air, bringing a wave of AI-powered coding assistance. It doesn't matter if you're a fresh-faced coder like Alex, full of curiosity and questions, or a seasoned expert like Charlie; Copilot has something for everyone, enhancing your coding process with its intuitive suggestions and insights.

This chapter is more than just an introduction to GitHub Copilot; it's an immersive experience. You'll uncover the mechanics behind Copilot, its ingenious capabilities, and even grapple with the ethical implications of AI in software development. Alongside the team at TechFusion Corp, these concepts will be brought to life, showcasing how Copilot can seamlessly integrate into your everyday coding tasks.

© Arpit Dwivedi 2024
A. Dwivedi, *CodeMosaic*, https://doi.org/10.1007/979-8-8688-0276-8_9

The Dawn of AI-Powered Development

As we segue from Jordan's strategic vision to a more granular look at AI in coding, let's explore how this innovation is taking shape at TechFusion Corp. The incorporation of GitHub Copilot is not just about new technology; it's about a new way of thinking and solving problems in software development.

Navigating Through AI's Impact in Coding

When Jordan proposed the exploration of GitHub Copilot, he wasn't just introducing a new tool; he was opening the door to a realm where coding meets artificial intelligence. This marked a significant shift at TechFusion Corp, one that Charlie, with his years of experience, was about to navigate.

Note   AI-driven tools like GitHub Copilot are not just coding assistants. They are trained on vast repositories of code, enabling them to provide contextually relevant suggestions, transforming how developers approach problem-solving.

Exploration into AI-Assisted Coding

Charlie's initial exploration into GitHub Copilot was filled with a mix of curiosity and skepticism. However, as he delved deeper:

- **From Skepticism to Awe:** Charlie began to see the potential of Copilot, not just as a coding assistant but as a learning companion that could offer intelligent code suggestions and insights.

- **Inspiring the Team:** His journey soon sparked interest among other team members, including Alex and Casey. They were intrigued by how Copilot could streamline complex coding tasks, making development more intuitive.

Tip   Embrace AI tools like GitHub Copilot with an open mind. Spend time understanding its suggestions to enhance not just your coding speed but also your coding intellect.

The Evolution from Traditional to AI-Driven Tools

The transition from traditional coding practices to AI-assisted development marks a significant evolution in the field. We're witnessing:

- **A Historical Shift:** The leap from basic compilers to sophisticated AI-driven tools like Copilot represents a fundamental change in the approach to software development.

- **Transforming Developer Roles:** These AI tools are reshaping the developer's role from purely writing code to collaborating with intelligent systems for innovative solutions.

Copilot's Integral Role in Modern Development

As Charlie integrated Copilot into his daily workflow, he discovered:

- **More Than Just Autocomplete:** Copilot's ability to suggest entire code blocks and adapt to his coding style was a game-changer, offering not just efficiency but also enhanced problem-solving strategies.

- **A New Collaboration Paradigm:** The team found that Copilot augmented their skills, leading to a more dynamic and innovative coding process.

You can see in Figure 9-1 that contrasts the traditional coding process with the process enhanced by GitHub Copilot. The diagram is designed to highlight differences in efficiency and code quality between these two approaches.

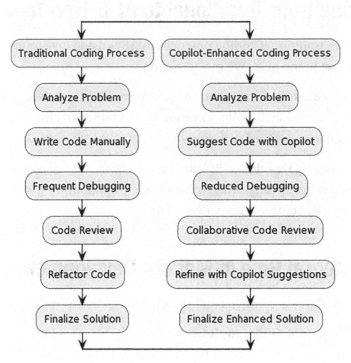

Figure 9-1. *A visual that contrasts the traditional coding process with the process enhanced by GitHub Copilot*

- **Left Side—Traditional Coding Process**

  - **Analyze Problem:** The process begins with a thorough analysis of the coding problem.

  - **Write Code Manually:** Developers write all code manually, relying on their expertise and knowledge.

  - **Frequent Debugging:** This approach often leads to frequent debugging due to manual errors or oversights.

  - **Code Review:** The code undergoes a review process, which can be time-consuming.

- **Refactor Code:** Based on the review, the code is often refactored for optimization or to fix issues.

- **Finalize Solution:** The final step is to finalize the solution after thorough testing and refinement.

- **Right Side—Copilot-Enhanced Coding Process**

  - **Analyze Problem:** Similar to traditional coding, it starts with problem analysis.

  - **Suggest Code with Copilot:** GitHub Copilot suggests code snippets and solutions, reducing the manual coding load.

  - **Reduced Debugging:** The AI assistance leads to fewer errors, thereby reducing debugging time.

  - **Collaborative Code Review:** Code review becomes more collaborative, as Copilot's suggestions are also reviewed.

  - **Refine with Copilot Suggestions:** Further refinements are made using Copilot's intelligent suggestions.

  - **Finalize Enhanced Solution:** The final solution is enhanced by the AI's insights, leading to potentially higher-quality code.

Concluding this section, it's evident that the integration of AI tools like GitHub Copilot at TechFusion Corp is a testament to a broader shift in the software development world. This transition to AI-enhanced coding practices is not just a fleeting trend but a new chapter in the story of software development.

GitHub Copilot: The Digital Muse

As we move from the broader impacts of AI in development, let's zoom in on GitHub Copilot, a tool that's reshaping the coding experience. It's not just a utility; it's a source of inspiration, a digital muse that's transforming the way developers write code.

The Magic Behind Copilot's Abilities

Imagine a tool that not only understands your code but also predicts and enhances it. That's GitHub Copilot for you. Developed from a vast repository of coding languages and frameworks, Copilot is like a wise sage in the world of coding, offering context-aware suggestions and solutions.

- **Contextual Understanding:** When Charlie, our seasoned developer, works on Python, Copilot seamlessly provides snippets that fit right into his project's narrative.

- **Language Agility:** Whether it's JavaScript intricacies or SQL queries, Copilot is adept at a wide range of languages, making it a versatile tool for any developer.

Copilot in Real-World Application

Let's dive into how GitHub Copilot operates in real coding situations. We'll follow Charlie as he tackles two distinct coding challenges, demonstrating Copilot's capabilities in enhancing both efficiency and creativity.

Scenario 1: Streamlining Complex Code

Challenge Description: Charlie is tasked with writing a complex data sorting algorithm in Python.

Copilot's Role: As Charlie types the initial function, Copilot suggests an optimized sorting algorithm, reducing his development time significantly.

Real-World Impact: What could have been hours of coding and testing is transformed into a collaborative session where Copilot provides not just code but also best practices and efficient approaches.

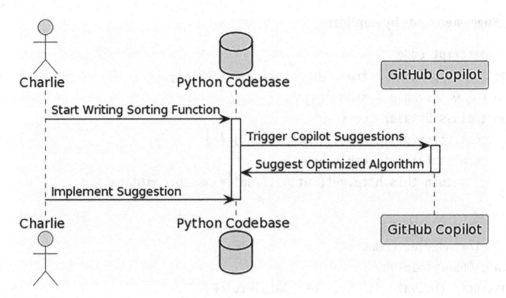

Figure 9-2. *A visual that illustrates the interaction between Charlie, GitHub Copilot, and the Python codebase*

Figure 9-2 illustrates the interaction between Charlie, GitHub Copilot, and the Python codebase. It starts with Charlie initiating the coding of a sorting function. As he types, Copilot is activated, suggesting an optimized algorithm. Charlie then implements this suggestion, streamlining the coding process.

Scenario 2: Enhancing Creative Problem-Solving in .NET and Angular

Challenge Description: Charlie is tasked with developing an interactive user interface for a .NET application with an Angular frontend. The objective is to create a responsive and user-friendly interface that dynamically updates based on backend data.

Copilot's Contribution: While working on the Angular component, Charlie contemplates how to efficiently fetch and display data from the .NET backend. GitHub Copilot, recognizing the context, suggests an innovative approach using Angular's HttpClient and RxJS for reactive data handling.

Suggested Code by Copilot:

```typescript
```Typescript code
import { HttpClient } from '@angular/common/http';
import { Observable } from 'rxjs';
export class DataService {
    constructor(private http: HttpClient) { }
    fetchData(): Observable<any> {
        return this.http.get('https://api.example.com/data');
    }
}
// In the Angular Component
data$: Observable<any>;
constructor(private dataService: DataService) {
    this.data$ = this.dataService.fetchData();
}
```
```

The suggested approach uses Angular's HttpClient to make asynchronous HTTP requests to the .NET backend. By returning an Observable, it allows the Angular component to reactively update the UI as new data arrives or changes, enhancing the interactivity and responsiveness of the user interface.

This method, recommended by Copilot, not only aligns with modern best practices in Angular development but also introduces Charlie to a more efficient way of handling data in a reactive programming paradigm.

This real-world application of GitHub Copilot in a .NET and Angular project showcases its ability to not just assist in coding but to guide developers toward more efficient and modern development patterns. Charlie's experience reflects how AI-assisted tools can enhance both the efficiency and creativity of software development, leading to superior user experiences and more effective code.

Beyond a Tool: A Partner in Code

GitHub Copilot is more than a coding assistant; it's a partner that understands and adapts to your unique coding style.

- **Personalized Coding Experience:** Copilot tailors its suggestions to match Charlie's coding habits, evolving from a tool to a personalized coding companion.

- **Learning Curve:** The more Charlie codes with Copilot, the more attuned it becomes to his preferences and techniques.

💡 **Tip**   Use Copilot for a week and watch how it adapts to your coding style, turning your coding sessions into a duo of human intelligence and AI efficiency.

Shaping the Future of Coding

It's clear that this tool is a game-changer. It's not just about faster coding; it's about smarter, more creative, and collaborative coding.

- **Redefining Coding Tools:** Copilot is pushing the boundaries, transforming the way we think about coding assistance.

- **A Future of Collaboration:** Envision a future where AI tools like Copilot are integral to every coding project, enhancing creativity and efficiency.

- **Looking Ahead:** With a deeper understanding of Copilot's capabilities, we now venture into how to effectively integrate this digital muse into your daily coding practice, moving to our next topic: "Access, Setup, and Integration of GitHub Copilot."

Access, Setup, and Integration of GitHub Copilot

In the bustling world of TechFusion Corp, a new chapter unfolds as the team, led by the insightful Jordan and the seasoned developer Charlie, embarks on integrating a powerful ally into their workflow: GitHub Copilot. This section is dedicated to guiding you, alongside Charlie and his colleagues, through the vital steps of accessing and setting up GitHub Copilot in your development environment.

Here, we will unravel the pathways to obtaining Copilot, exploring its subscription models and special offers for the curious minds in academia. Charlie will demonstrate how to seamlessly integrate Copilot into popular IDEs, like Visual Studio Code, reflecting the diverse coding preferences at TechFusion Corp. From understanding the nuances of its installation to maximizing its potential in various coding scenarios, this journey with Charlie and the team promises to arm you with the knowledge to transform GitHub Copilot into an indispensable tool in your coding arsenal.

Availability and Subscription Models

In the digital corridors of TechFusion Corp, Jordan and Charlie are leading a new initiative: introducing GitHub Copilot to their development team. If you, like Charlie and his team, are considering bringing this AI-powered assistant into your coding journey, the first step is understanding how to access it. GitHub Copilot is designed for both individual developers and larger organizations, offering a range of subscription plans to suit diverse needs and scales.

Subscription Options Unveiled

GitHub Copilot's subscription models cater to various users, from solo developers to multinational corporations. Let's break down these options:

- **Individual Subscription:** Perfect for independent developers or small teams. This plan provides complete access to all of Copilot's features, allowing you to enhance your coding efficiency on a personal or small team level. It's a straightforward, per-user subscription, making it easy to get started.

- **Enterprise Subscription:** Tailored for larger teams and organizations like TechFusion Corp. This model includes everything in the Individual plan, plus additional features for administrative control and team collaboration.

Explore GitHub Copilot Subscription Plans: `https://github.com/features/copilot`

Choosing the right model is crucial. Consider your project's size, the nature of your team's collaboration, and budget constraints to make an informed decision.

Integrating Copilot in Organizations

For organizations considering Copilot, there are additional factors to weigh in:

- **Licensing for Teams:** Managing multiple licenses is straightforward with GitHub's enterprise solutions. It offers flexibility and control for team leaders and IT administrators.

- **Security and Compliance:** GitHub Copilot is designed to align with corporate security standards and compliance requirements, ensuring your code remains secure and private.

Learn About GitHub Copilot for Enterprises: `https://docs.github.com/en/copilot/github-copilot-enterprise/overview/about-github-copilot-enterprise`.

At TechFusion Corp, Jordan and Charlie weigh these aspects, ensuring their choice aligns with the company's coding practices and security standards.

In summary, GitHub Copilot offers a range of subscription options to suit different coding environments. Whether you're a solo developer or part of a large organization, there's a plan that fits your needs.

As Charlie and the TechFusion team finalize their subscription choice, they set an example for a strategic approach to adopting new technology. It's your turn now to explore these options and see how GitHub Copilot can transform your coding experience.

GitHub Scholar Program for Students

With TechFusion Corp's decision to adopt GitHub Copilot, it's clear that cutting-edge tools can significantly enhance coding capabilities. If you're a student, you have a unique opportunity to access these tools without cost through the GitHub Scholar Program. This program is tailored to support your educational journey in software development.

Benefits of the GitHub Scholar Program

The GitHub Scholar Program offers more than just free access to GitHub Copilot; it's a comprehensive package designed to empower your learning and development in the coding world.

- **Wide Range of Tools:** Gain access to a plethora of GitHub resources, including Copilot, to enhance your coding skills and project work.

- **No Cost Access:** The program is available at no cost to students enrolled in accredited educational institutions.

Steps to Enrol in the Program

Enrolling in the GitHub Scholar Program is a straightforward process. Here's how you can get started:

- **Verify Academic Status:** Use your academic email to sign up on the GitHub Education website. You'll need to provide proof of enrollment, such as a valid school ID or enrollment verification document.

- **Complete the Enrollment:** Follow the instructions for verification. Once your student status is confirmed, you'll gain access to the suite of tools offered by GitHub.

- **Start Exploring:** With enrollment complete, dive into the world of GitHub Copilot and other GitHub tools. Use these resources to boost your learning and practical coding experience.

Enrol in the GitHub Scholar Program: `https://education.github.com/pack`.

For students embarking on a technology career, the GitHub Scholar Program is an invaluable resource. It not only provides access to tools like GitHub Copilot but also opens up a world of possibilities for learning and innovation in software development. I encourage you to take advantage of this opportunity to elevate your coding journey.

Setting Up GitHub Copilot in IDEs

Now that you've chosen the right GitHub Copilot subscription, the next exciting step is to bring this AI-powered assistant into your coding world. Integrating Copilot into your preferred Integrated Development Environment (IDE) is straightforward. Here, you'll get to know about setting up Copilot in Visual Studio Code (VS Code) and touch on its integration in other development environments.

Integrating Copilot in Visual Studio Code

VS Code, known for its versatility and wide usage among developers, offers an easy way to integrate GitHub Copilot. Let's walk through the steps:

- **Open Visual Studio Code:** Launch your VS Code application.

- **Navigate to Extensions:** Click on the Extensions icon in the Activity Bar on the side of the window to open the Extensions view.

- **Find GitHub Copilot:** In the Extensions view, type "GitHub Copilot" in the search bar.

- **Install the Copilot Extension:** Locate the GitHub Copilot extension in the search results and click on the "Install" button.

- **Reload if Required:** After installation, you might need to reload VS Code to activate the extension fully.

Once installed, GitHub Copilot starts offering suggestions as you type code. These suggestions can be accepted by simply pressing the "Tab" key, seamlessly integrating Copilot's intelligence into your coding process.

Expanding Beyond Visual Studio Code

While VS Code is a common choice for many, GitHub Copilot's flexibility extends to other environments:

- **Other IDEs:** If you're using an IDE other than VS Code, GitHub Copilot may still be available. Check Copilot's documentation for specific instructions on integration with your IDE.

- **Adaptable to Various Setups:** Copilot is designed to adapt to different coding environments, including cloud-based development platforms and other code editors.

Explore GitHub Copilot's Documentation for Other IDEs: `https://docs.github.com/en/copilot/using-github-copilot/getting-started-with-github-copilot`.

Integrating GitHub Copilot into your IDE is like unlocking a new level of coding proficiency. Whether it's through the familiar interface of VS Code or another IDE of your choice, Copilot's capabilities can significantly streamline your development process, making coding more efficient, enjoyable, and creative.

Maximizing Copilot's Potential in Development

Embracing GitHub Copilot isn't just about installing it; it's about integrating its capabilities into your daily coding tasks effectively. Here are some tips and best practices to help you make the most out of Copilot's potential:

- **Understand Copilot's Suggestions:** Spend time familiarizing yourself with the types of suggestions Copilot offers. It's important to understand why a particular piece of code is suggested and how it fits into your overall coding objective.

- **Refine Your Comments:** Copilot responds to the context in your code, including comments. Writing clear and descriptive comments can guide Copilot to provide more accurate and useful code suggestions.

- **Iterative Coding Approach:** Use Copilot as part of an iterative coding process. Start with a rough draft of your code and then refine it with Copilot's suggestions, allowing for a collaborative coding experience.

- **Customize to Fit Your Style:** Copilot learns from your interactions. Regularly accepting or declining its suggestions helps it adapt to your coding style and preferences over time.

GitHub Copilot is more than a tool for basic code completion; it offers advanced features that can significantly aid in complex coding scenarios:

- **Autocomplete for Entire Functions:** Copilot can generate entire functions or classes based on your initial input, providing a robust starting point for complex coding tasks.

- **Support for Multiple Languages and Frameworks:** Whether you're working in Python, JavaScript, TypeScript, or even less common languages, Copilot can provide relevant suggestions. Its understanding of different frameworks and libraries also aids in more specific development tasks.

- **Code Refactoring Assistance:** Copilot can assist in refactoring existing code, suggesting more efficient or cleaner ways to achieve the same functionality.

- **Test Generation:** For developers focusing on test-driven development, Copilot can suggest appropriate unit tests for your code, streamlining the testing process.

By effectively utilizing GitHub Copilot, you can elevate your coding from routine task execution to creative problem-solving. Whether you're tackling everyday code or diving into complex development challenges, Copilot stands as a versatile and powerful ally, ready to enhance your coding efficiency and creativity.

Beyond IDEs: Copilot's Broader Integrations

GitHub Copilot's versatility extends beyond traditional IDEs, making it a valuable tool in a variety of coding environments. Let's explore how Copilot adapts to different settings, enhancing your development process wherever you code.

- **Cloud-Based Development:** Copilot thrives in cloud-based development environments. It integrates seamlessly with cloud IDEs, bringing its intelligent coding assistance to platforms like GitHub Codespaces or other web-based editors.

- **Non-traditional Environments:** Even in less conventional coding environments, such as local text editors or bespoke development setups, Copilot can offer valuable insights and code suggestions, ensuring that your development process remains efficient and innovative.

- **Team Projects:** Copilot shines in team environments. Its suggestions can spark new ideas and solutions during collaborative coding sessions, making it a valuable asset for brainstorming and problem-solving in group projects.

- **Code Consistency:** For teams, maintaining code consistency is crucial. Copilot can help standardize coding practices across team members, ensuring a unified approach to project development.

From choosing the right subscription model to installing Copilot in your favorite IDE and adapting it to various environments, these steps are your gateway to a more intelligent coding process.

Whether you're coding in a traditional IDE, a cloud-based environment, or collaboratively with a team, Copilot has the potential to significantly enhance your development experience. It's not just about writing code; it's about innovating and evolving with the changing landscape of software development.

Explore the possibilities with GitHub Copilot and witness how it can elevate your coding journey to new heights.

Strengths and Limitations of GitHub Copilot

As GitHub Copilot increasingly becomes a staple in the developer's toolkit, it's vital to paint a complete picture of what it offers and where it needs human partnership. This tool, while transformative, comes with its own set of strengths and limitations. Our aim here is to delve into these aspects, providing you with a comprehensive understanding to use Copilot most effectively in your development journey.

Unveiling the Strengths of GitHub Copilot

GitHub Copilot has garnered attention for its ability to significantly enhance the development process. Let's explore its key strengths:

- **Accelerating Development:** Copilot stands out for its ability to offer real-time coding suggestions, drastically reducing the time spent on routine coding tasks. This acceleration allows you to focus on more complex aspects of your projects.

- **Enhancing Code Quality:** Often, Copilot suggests optimized and efficient coding practices. These suggestions can lead to improved code quality, incorporating best practices and modern coding standards.

- **Learning and Adaptability:** One of Copilot's unique features is its ability to learn from your coding patterns. Over time, it becomes a more personalized assistant, adapting its suggestions to better align with your style and preferences.

- **Diverse Language Support:** Copilot's proficiency spans a wide array of programming languages and frameworks. Whether you're working on a web application in JavaScript or managing data in Python, Copilot provides relevant and intelligent suggestions.

Recognizing the Limitations of GitHub Copilot

While GitHub Copilot offers numerous benefits, it's equally important to recognize its limitations:

- **Dependency and Overreliance:** There's a risk of becoming overly reliant on Copilot for coding solutions. It's crucial to understand the logic behind its suggestions and not use them blindly, maintaining your coding skills and intuition.

- **Areas Requiring Human Judgment:** Copilot cannot replace the nuanced understanding and decision-making that human developers bring to complex problems, unique project requirements, and ethical considerations.

- **Learning Curve and Misinterpretations:** New users may experience a learning curve in interpreting Copilot's suggestions. Additionally, Copilot might not always accurately interpret your coding intentions, requiring a discerning eye to select the most appropriate solutions.

In sum, GitHub Copilot is a powerful tool that can significantly enhance your coding process, provided its use is balanced with an understanding of its limitations. Embrace its strengths to accelerate development and improve code quality, but remain vigilant and engaged in your coding decisions. Use Copilot as an assistant, not a replacement, to ensure that your development work remains innovative, ethical, and uniquely yours.

Ethical Considerations in AI-Powered Coding

In the rapidly evolving world of software development, the integration of AI tools like GitHub Copilot presents not just opportunities for innovation but also raises important ethical considerations. As developers, it's crucial to navigate this new terrain with an awareness of the potential ethical implications these tools bring to our coding practices.

Code Originality: One of the foremost concerns with AI-assisted coding is the blurring lines around code originality. GitHub Copilot, while an efficient assistant, might suggest code that closely resembles its training data. It becomes vital for developers to use these suggestions as a starting point, transforming them with original thought and creativity to ensure the integrity of the code remains intact.

Potential Biases in AI: AI algorithms, including those powering Copilot, are trained on vast datasets that may contain inherent biases. These biases can inadvertently influence the code suggestions provided, potentially leading to skewed or unfair outcomes. As developers, recognizing and actively working to counteract these biases is essential in ensuring fair and unbiased software solutions.

Dependency and Decision-Making: Over Reliance on tools like Copilot could impact a developer's ability to grow and refine problem-solving skills. While Copilot can significantly speed up coding, it's important to maintain a balance, ensuring that critical thinking and personal coding expertise continue to develop.

The Role of Developer Insight: Despite the advanced capabilities of AI tools, the unique insights and intuition that human developers bring to the table remain invaluable. While Copilot can suggest, it doesn't understand the broader context or the specific goals of a project like a human developer does.

Maintaining Ethical Standards: Using GitHub Copilot responsibly involves applying your own judgment to its suggestions. This means critically evaluating the code it generates, understanding its purpose, and modifying it as necessary to align with ethical coding practices.

While tools like GitHub Copilot can revolutionize the way we code, they also bring responsibilities. As developers, it's up to us to use these tools wisely, ensuring that our software not only excels in functionality but also upholds the highest ethical standards.

The Future of AI in Software Development

As we stand at the forefront of a technological revolution, the role of AI in software development is not just growing; it's transforming the very fabric of how we create, analyze, and deploy software. With tools like GitHub Copilot leading the charge, the future of AI in this field is both exciting and profound. Here, we'll explore some predictions and possibilities for AI's evolving role and its implications for developers.

- **Automated Code Generation:** AI is expected to advance in automating routine coding tasks, allowing developers to focus more on strategic and creative aspects of software projects.

- **Enhanced Predictive Algorithms:** Future AI developments may offer more advanced predictive capabilities, foreseeing potential issues and optimizations in software design before they even arise.

- **AI in Quality Assurance:** AI's role in software testing and quality assurance is poised to expand, potentially offering more thorough and efficient validation processes.

- **Customized Development Environments:** AI could lead to more personalized and adaptive development environments, tailoring the coding experience to individual developer's styles and preferences.

- **Ethical and Responsible AI Usage:** As AI becomes more integral to software development, a greater emphasis will be placed on ethical considerations and responsible use of AI tools.

- **New Developer Skill Sets:** Developers might need to adapt their skills to include a deeper understanding of AI principles and ethics, as well as learning to effectively collaborate with AI-powered tools.

As we speculate on the future of AI in software development, it's clear that the landscape is set for significant change. These advancements promise to not only streamline the development process but also open up new horizons for innovation and creativity. For developers, staying abreast of these changes and proactively adapting skills will be key to thriving in this AI-driven future. Embracing AI tools like GitHub Copilot today is a step toward becoming an integral part of this exciting and evolving journey in software development.

Conclusion

As we wrap up our exploration of GitHub Copilot, we've traversed its capabilities, ethical considerations, and glimpsed into its promising future. This journey has not only highlighted Copilot's role in enhancing coding efficiency and creativity but also underscored the importance of balancing AI assistance with human insight.

Key Takeaways

- **GitHub Copilot as a Revolutionary Tool:** Emphasizes Copilot's role in changing the development process by providing real-time, contextually relevant code suggestions.

- **Enhanced Coding Efficiency and Creativity:** Illustrates how Copilot accelerates coding tasks and fosters innovative solutions.

- **Ethical Considerations and Best Practices:** Discusses the importance of balancing AI assistance with human insight, ensuring ethical use and maintaining code integrity.

- **Future of AI in Development:** Speculates on the expanding role of AI in software development, highlighting the need for developers to adapt to AI-driven tools like Copilot.

Beyond Code and into Natural Language

Looking ahead, the software development landscape continues to evolve with AI's growing influence. Our next chapter pivots to another groundbreaking AI advancement: ChatGPT. As we transition from the coding-focused assistance of GitHub Copilot to the conversational AI of ChatGPT, we are entering a domain where AI's potential extends beyond code into the realm of natural language processing and interaction. This next chapter promises to delve into how ChatGPT is redefining interactions and functionalities in the digital world, marking another step forward in our ongoing journey through the ever-expanding universe of AI technology.

CHAPTER 10

ChatGPT Charms: Wielding Words with AI

Welcome to the enthralling world of ChatGPT in "ChatGPT Charms: Wielding Words with AI." This chapter is a deep dive into the art of prompt engineering using ChatGPT, particularly focusing on its version 3.5. Here, you'll discover not just how to communicate with an AI but how to make it an invaluable ally in your development projects.

Why ChatGPT? Imagine an AI that not only understands your queries but also provides responses that can transform your approach to coding and problem-solving. That's the essence of ChatGPT. It's about harnessing a tool that thinks and assists like a developer. In this chapter you will

- **Explore:** The subtleties of prompting an AI to achieve desired outcomes
- **Learn:** How ChatGPT can elevate your coding efficiency and creativity

We will also touch upon the ethical use of AI in development, ensuring that innovation goes hand-in-hand with responsibility. And while our main focus is ChatGPT 3.5, we'll briefly venture into the realm of ChatGPT 4.5 to see what the future holds. So, gear up to learn, innovate, and transform your development workflow with the magic of AI. Let's begin this journey of learning and discovery together!

© Arpit Dwivedi 2024
A. Dwivedi, *CodeMosaic*, https://doi.org/10.1007/979-8-8688-0276-8_10

Prompt Powerplay

In the realm of AI-driven development, the power of communication cannot be overstated. The first step to unlocking ChatGPT's potential is mastering the art of prompt crafting. This skill is essential for developers seeking to leverage AI for innovative solutions.

Understanding Prompt Dynamics

Clarity and Specificity: The key to effective prompts is clarity. The more specific your prompt, the more precise ChatGPT's response.

Context Matters: Providing context in your prompts helps ChatGPT understand the exact nature of your request, leading to more relevant responses.

Crafting Prompts: A Developer's Approach

Define Your Objective: Start by clearly defining what you want to achieve with your prompt. Are you seeking a solution to a coding problem, ideas for debugging, or creative input for a project?

Use Clear, Concise Language: Avoid ambiguity. Be direct and to the point to ensure that ChatGPT grasps your request accurately.

Real-World Scenario: Alex's Challenge

Alex encounters a challenging bug in his Angular application. The application is not updating the user interface in response to changes in the underlying data model, a critical feature for the project's success.

Crafting the Prompt for ChatGPT

In search of a solution, Alex turns to ChatGPT. He crafts a detailed prompt that not only describes the issue but also provides context about his project.

Alex's Prompt to ChatGPT

"Hello ChatGPT, I'm working on an Angular project where I'm facing a UI update issue. My application is supposed to dynamically update a list on the user interface whenever the data model changes. However, the UI isn't reflecting these changes. I'm using Angular's ngOnChanges lifecycle hook to detect changes, but it seems to be ineffective. Can you suggest a solution or an alternative approach to ensure the UI updates as expected?"

ChatGPT's Insightful Response

ChatGPT processes Alex's prompt and provides a comprehensive response.

ChatGPT's Response

"Hi, from your description, it seems the issue might be related to Angular's change detection mechanism. While ngOnChanges is useful for detecting changes to input properties, it might not be the best fit for your scenario. Instead, consider using Angular's BehaviorSubject and Observable from RxJS for a more reactive approach. Here's a simplified example:

```typescript
```Typescript Code
import { BehaviorSubject } from 'rxjs';

export class YourService {
  private dataSource = new BehaviorSubject<any[]>([]);
  data = this.dataSource.asObservable();

  updateData(newData: any[]) {
    this.dataSource.next(newData);
  }
}
// In your component
export class YourComponent {
  listData$: Observable<any[]>;
  constructor(private yourService: YourService) {
    this.listData$ = this.yourService.data;
  }
```
```

```
  // Method to update data
  updateList() {
    // Update the data model and the UI will reactively update
    this.yourService.updateData(newData);
  }
}
```

This approach utilizes BehaviorSubject to create a data stream that your component can subscribe to. Whenever updateData is called with new data, the BehaviorSubject emits this data, and your component's UI will update reactively."

Implementing the Solution

Intrigued by ChatGPT's response, Alex implements the suggested approach. By integrating BehaviorSubject and subscribing to the data stream in his component, he successfully resolves the UI update issue. The application now dynamically reflects changes in the data model, enhancing the user experience significantly.

Tips for Advanced Prompt Crafting

Iterative Approach: Don't hesitate to refine your prompts based on initial responses. It's a learning curve for both you and ChatGPT.

Leverage Examples: Sometimes, providing an example within your prompt can guide ChatGPT to better understand and respond to your needs.

By mastering prompt crafting, you unlock a world where ChatGPT becomes more than an AI—it becomes a reliable partner in your development journey. In the following sections, we'll explore how these skills can be applied in various development scenarios, enhancing both efficiency and creativity.

Developer's Digital Djinn

ChatGPT is more than just a question-answer machine; it's a versatile tool that can revolutionize your development work. Here, we dive into its diverse roles, offering practical ways to integrate ChatGPT into your daily coding tasks.

Beyond Basic Questions: ChatGPT's Role in Coding

Think of ChatGPT as your coding assistant. It can help you write code, find errors, and even give advice on best practices. For instance, if you're stuck on a function, ChatGPT can suggest improvements or different ways to write it.

Interactive Exercise: Script Writing with ChatGPT

Task: Let's create a Python script to sort a list of names.

Step-by-Step

1. **Start with a Prompt:** Ask ChatGPT to help write a Python script for sorting a list of names alphabetically.

2. **Review ChatGPT's Response:** It might give you a basic script. Let's say it suggests using Python's sorted() function.

3. **Refine the Script:** Test the script. If it doesn't work as expected, tweak it based on ChatGPT's suggestions or ask for alternative methods.

Result: You'll have a working script and a better understanding of how to collaborate with AI in coding.

Real-World Application: Charlie's Challenge at TechFusion Corp

Scenario: Charlie is integrating a new API and faces some issues.

Using ChatGPT

1. **Describing the Problem:** Charlie explains to ChatGPT that he's getting an error when calling the API.

2. **ChatGPT's Suggestions:** ChatGPT proposes checking the API key and the data format being sent.

3. **Implementation:** Charlie realizes he forgot to update the API key. After fixing it, the integration works smoothly.

Learning: This experience shows how ChatGPT can help pinpoint issues quickly, saving time and effort.

Tips for Working with ChatGPT

Keep Learning: The more you use ChatGPT, the better it gets at understanding your coding style and needs. Keep refining your prompts for more tailored assistance.

Creative Collaboration: Use ChatGPT for more than just solving problems. It can help brainstorm new features or improve existing code.

ChatGPT can be a game-changer in your development work. It's not just about getting answers; it's about creating a collaborative workflow where AI complements your coding skills.

Mastering the Prompt Palette

In the journey with ChatGPT, one of the most crucial skills is mastering the art of prompt crafting. This skill determines how well ChatGPT understands and responds to your development needs. Here, we'll explore techniques to refine your prompts for better, more targeted responses.

The Essence of Effective Prompting

Be Specific: The more detailed your prompt, the more accurate ChatGPT's response. For example, instead of asking, "How do I fix this code?" provide the specific error message or describe the code's intended function.

Context Is Key: Include relevant context. If you're working on a web application using React, mention it. This helps ChatGPT tailor its responses to your specific environment and requirements.

Interactive Example: Crafting the Perfect Prompt

Scenario: You need to optimize a database query in a SQL Server environment.

   Step-by-Step Prompt Refinement

1. **Initial Prompt:** "How to optimize a database query?"

2. **Improved Prompt:** "I'm working with SQL Server and need to optimize a query that retrieves customer data based on purchase history. Here's the current query: [Your Query]. How can I make it faster?"

3. **Response Analysis:** Review ChatGPT's suggestions, such as indexing certain columns or rewriting the query. Implement and test these suggestions in your environment.

4. **Outcome:** Through this iterative process, you not only refine your prompting skill but also enhance your understanding of query optimization in SQL Server.

See Figure 10-1, guiding you through the prompt crafting process. It starts with your objective, branches out based on the complexity of your task, and guides you on including necessary details and context, leading to a well-structured prompt.

Explanation of the Decision Tree in Figure 10-1

1. **Identify Objective:** Start by defining the main goal of your prompt. This sets the direction for your interaction with ChatGPT.

2. **Complexity Assessment:** Determine if the task at hand is complex.

   a. If Yes, break down the task into smaller, more manageable components.

   b. If No, proceed with the task as it is.

3. **Specify Context:** Add relevant technical details to your prompt, providing necessary background information to ChatGPT.

4. **Detailing Components:** If your task has multiple components,

   a. Detail each component separately, ensuring each part is clearly described.

   b. If not, describe the task as a whole.

5. **Include Examples:** If applicable, include examples such as code snippets or error messages to give ChatGPT a clearer understanding.

6. **Formulate Prompt:** Combine all the gathered information into a clear and concise prompt.

7. **Review and Refine:** After receiving an initial response, review and refine your prompt based on ChatGPT's feedback, aiming for a more targeted interaction.

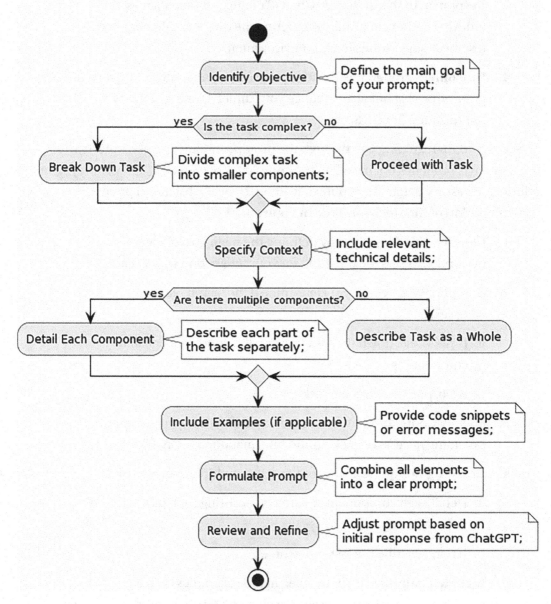

Figure 10-1. *ChatGPT prompt crafting decision tree*

This decision tree serves as a guide to systematically craft effective prompts, leading to more accurate and helpful responses from ChatGPT.

Scripting Sorcery with ChatGPT

In the toolkit of a modern developer, automation is key. ChatGPT can be a powerful ally in this realm, helping to conjure scripts, automate routine tasks, and create boilerplates that save time and reduce errors. This section explores how to effectively use ChatGPT for these purposes.

Automating with Precision and Creativity

Script Generation: Use ChatGPT to generate basic scripts or boilerplates. For instance, ask it to create a script for data retrieval from a database, and then modify it to fit your specific needs.

Custom Automations: ChatGPT can assist in automating tasks like sending regular reports, processing data, or even managing routine server maintenance tasks.

Example: Automated Testing Script

Objective: Create an automated testing script for a web application.

    Process

1. **Define the Task:** Clearly state your requirement to ChatGPT—you need a script to automate the testing of specific functionalities of a web application.

2. **ChatGPT's Input:** ChatGPT might provide a basic structure or even a complete script using a popular testing framework like Selenium or Jest.

3. **Refinement:** Take ChatGPT's script as a starting point and refine it. Add specific test cases, customize commands, or integrate it into your existing test suite.

Outcome: You'll have a custom automated testing script tailored to your application, significantly speeding up your testing process.

Real-World Scenario: Efficiency at TechFusion Corp

Challenge: The development team at TechFusion Corp needs to automate their testing process for a new feature in their application.

Using ChatGPT

1. **Initial Script:** They ask ChatGPT to create a basic automated test script for their user login functionality.

2. **Customization:** The team then adds more test cases to the script, such as checking for failed logins and testing password reset functionality.

3. **Integration:** Finally, they integrate this script into their continuous integration/continuous deployment (CI/CD) pipeline.

Impact: This approach reduces the time spent on manual testing and ensures more consistent, reliable test results.

Embracing ChatGPT for Development Magic

By incorporating ChatGPT into your scripting and automation tasks, you can focus more on complex and creative aspects of development. It's about blending AI efficiency with human ingenuity to elevate your coding practice.

In the next section, we'll explore how ChatGPT can be used to develop plugins and integrations, further expanding its role in the development workflow.

Plugin Potions and ChatGPT

In the world of software development, plugins and integrations form the backbone of many applications, extending their capabilities and enhancing user experience. ChatGPT, with its deep understanding of code and algorithms, can play a pivotal role in this area. This section delves into how ChatGPT can be used to develop and refine plugins and integrations.

AI-Driven Development of Plugins

Conceptualization: Utilize ChatGPT to brainstorm ideas for plugins. Whether you need a tool to improve workflow, manage data, or enhance user interaction, ChatGPT can help you outline the basic concept and functionality.

Code Generation: Once you have a concept, ChatGPT can assist in generating the foundational code for your plugin. This can be especially useful for standard functionalities like user authentication, data processing, or API integration.

Practical Application: Integrating a ChatGPT Plugin

Objective: Develop a plugin that integrates ChatGPT into an existing application, enhancing its interactive capabilities.

Step-by-Step Implementation

1. **Define Functionality:** Decide what you want the plugin to achieve. For example, enabling ChatGPT to answer user queries directly within the app.

2. **ChatGPT's Contribution:** Ask ChatGPT to generate a basic structure or code snippets for the plugin, focusing on the integration points and key functionalities.

3. **Customization and Refinement:** Modify the generated code to fit into your application's architecture and meet specific requirements.

Outcome: A functional ChatGPT-powered plugin that adds a new dimension of interactivity and utility to your application.

Real-World Example: TechFusion Corp's Integration Project

Scenario: TechFusion Corp wants to enhance its customer service portal with AI capabilities.

Approach

1. **Initial Idea:** The team conceptualizes a ChatGPT plugin that can provide instant, AI-driven responses to customer inquiries.

2. **Development:** Using ChatGPT, they create a prototype that integrates seamlessly with their existing portal.

3. **Deployment and Feedback:** After testing and refining, the plugin is deployed. It significantly improves response time and customer satisfaction.

Impact: This project demonstrates the practical benefits of integrating AI into existing systems, showcasing improved efficiency and enhanced user experience.

The development of plugins and integrations with ChatGPT not only streamlines the process but also opens up new possibilities for innovation. It allows developers to focus more on creative solutions and less on repetitive coding tasks.

Architectural Alchemy

In the world of software development, the ability to translate ideas into tangible designs and diagrams is crucial. ChatGPT can play a significant role in this "Architectural Alchemy," assisting developers in conceptualizing and visualizing system architectures.

ChatGPT: A Partner in Design

Idea Generation: Begin by discussing your project idea with ChatGPT. It can help brainstorm and refine concepts, suggesting possible features or improvements.
Structural Guidance: ChatGPT can provide insights on system architecture, offering advice on best practices and potential design patterns.

Interactive Exercise: Designing with AI

Objective: Create a system architecture for a new web application.

Process

1. **Initial Discussion:** Share your application idea with ChatGPT, including key features and functionalities.

2. **ChatGPT's Input:** Ask ChatGPT for suggestions on structuring your application. It might propose a microservices architecture, a monolithic design, or other relevant structures.

3. **Visualization:** Use ChatGPT's suggestions to sketch out a basic architecture diagram, detailing how different components of your application will interact.

Outcome: A preliminary system design that serves as a blueprint for your development process.

Real-World Scenario: TechFusion Corp's Design Challenge

Challenge: TechFusion Corp needs to design a scalable system for their new data analytics platform.

Using ChatGPT

1. **Collaborative Brainstorming:** The development team collaborates with ChatGPT to explore various architectural approaches, considering scalability and performance.

2. **Design Formation:** Based on the discussion, ChatGPT helps outline a modular architecture that can handle large-scale data processing efficiently.

3. **Refinement:** The team refines the design, incorporating their specific business logic and technical requirements.

Impact: This approach allows TechFusion Corp to quickly arrive at a robust and scalable system architecture, reducing the time typically spent in the design phase.

Leveraging AI for Architectural Innovation

ChatGPT's ability to assist in system design not only accelerates the design process but also brings a fresh perspective to architectural challenges. It's about combining human creativity with AI's computational power to create innovative and efficient systems.

Automation Artistry

Automation in software development is not just about saving time; it's about enhancing accuracy, consistency, and enabling developers to focus on more complex and creative tasks. ChatGPT can be a maestro in this domain, helping to orchestrate automated workflows that transform the way development teams operate.

Streamlining Development with AI

Workflow Optimization: ChatGPT can assist in identifying tasks within your development process that are ripe for automation, such as data entry, report generation, or even certain aspects of code testing.

Custom Scripting: Use ChatGPT's insights to develop scripts that automate these tasks. The AI can provide a starting point for the script, which you can then refine to suit your specific needs.

Hands-On Example: Creating an Automated Workflow

Objective: Create a script to automatically organize files in a project directory.

Step-by-Step Guide

1. **Define the Task:** Specify the types of files you want to organize (e.g., .jpg, .txt) and the desired structure.

2. **Consult ChatGPT:** Describe your requirements to ChatGPT and ask for a basic Python or Bash script that can handle this file organization.

3. **Script Customization:** Receive a basic script from ChatGPT, then modify and test it in your environment to ensure it meets your specific needs.

Outcome: An efficient script that automatically sorts files, reducing the clutter in your project directory and saving you the time and effort of doing it manually.

The Power of AI in Everyday Tasks

Embracing ChatGPT for automation in development isn't just about tackling complex challenges; it's also about simplifying everyday tasks. This approach allows developers to spend more time on creative problem-solving and less on routine work.

Tuning the Digital Harp

In the symphony of software development, each tool plays a crucial role, and ChatGPT is no exception. This section focuses on fine-tuning your interactions with ChatGPT to achieve the most harmonious and effective outcomes, particularly in the context of development projects.

Optimizing ChatGPT for Your Needs

Understanding ChatGPT's Responses: Learn to interpret ChatGPT's responses and how they can be applied in your specific development context.

Customizing Interactions: Tailor your prompts to align with your development goals, whether it's for coding, debugging, or brainstorming new ideas.

Customizing a Debugging Assistant

Objective: Create a ChatGPT-based tool to assist with debugging JavaScript code.

   Process

1. **Identify Common Issues:** Start by listing common errors you encounter in your projects.

2. **Interaction with ChatGPT:** Craft prompts for ChatGPT that describe these errors and ask for suggestions on resolving them.

3. **Tool Creation:** Based on ChatGPT's responses, develop a simple tool that aggregates common errors and ChatGPT's suggested solutions.

Outcome: A personalized debugging assistant powered by ChatGPT, tailored to your specific coding environment and challenges.

Streamlining Project Management at TechFusion Corp

Challenge: TechFusion Corp's project management team struggles with efficiently allocating resources across multiple projects.

Unique Application of ChatGPT

1. **Initial Consultation:** The team consults ChatGPT for insights on optimizing resource allocation.

2. **Innovative Solution:** ChatGPT suggests a framework for evaluating project demands based on historical data and current team strengths.

3. **Implementation:** The team develops a new resource allocation strategy, informed by ChatGPT's suggestions, leading to more balanced project management.

Impact: This strategic approach results in more efficient use of resources and higher team productivity.

Maximizing the Potential of AI in Development

By fine-tuning your interaction with ChatGPT, you transform it from a general AI tool into a specialized asset for your development needs. It's about creating a synergy between AI capabilities and your unique project requirements.

Guardians of Ethics and Originality

As we weave AI technologies like ChatGPT into the fabric of software development, it becomes imperative to pause and consider the ethical landscape that surrounds these advancements. This section aims to shed light on the ethical considerations and the importance of maintaining originality when employing AI tools in development projects.

A Journey Through Ethical Considerations

Before delving into specific examples and best practices, let's understand why ethical considerations are not just an optional part of AI development, but a cornerstone of responsible innovation.

- **Data Privacy and Security:** In an era where data is abundant, protecting user privacy is paramount. How we handle and secure data within AI-driven applications speaks volumes about our commitment to user trust.

- **Bias and Fairness:** The algorithms powering AI are only as unbiased as the data they learn from. Recognizing and correcting biases is a step toward fair and equitable technological solutions.

Ethical Scenarios in Development

Navigating through ethical dilemmas requires a blend of awareness, action, and continuous learning. Let's explore some real-world challenges and how they can be addressed.

Respecting User Privacy

Challenge: An AI-powered analytics tool inadvertently risks exposing user data.
Solution: Implement robust encryption, anonymize user data, and maintain transparency with users regarding how their data is used.

Combating Bias in AI Systems

Challenge: A recruitment tool, assisted by ChatGPT, displays bias in candidate selection.
Solution: Regularly audit the tool for biases, diversify training datasets, and ensure human oversight in critical decision-making processes.

Originality in AI-Created Content

In the sphere of content creation, AI tools can be both a boon and a challenge. Ensuring that the content is original and retains the creator's unique voice is crucial.

- **Plagiarism and AI:** With AI's ability to generate text, the risk of creating content that mirrors existing sources is real. Developers must employ strategies to ensure the uniqueness of AI-generated content.

- **Creative Integrity:** Balancing AI assistance with human creativity is the key to maintaining the authenticity and integrity of the work.

Embracing Ethical AI

Ethical considerations in AI are not static; they evolve as technology advances. Staying informed, embracing best practices, and fostering an environment of ethical awareness are essential steps in leveraging AI responsibly.

In this ever-changing technological landscape, being guardians of ethics and originality is not just a role but a commitment to shaping a future where AI is used with conscience and integrity.

Exploring ChatGPT 4.5 (GPT Plus)

In the ever-evolving realm of artificial intelligence, ChatGPT 4.5, also known as GPT Plus, stands at the forefront of innovation. This advanced iteration of ChatGPT offers a suite of enhanced features, setting new benchmarks in AI's capabilities. Let's embark on an exploratory journey to understand what GPT Plus brings to the table and how it differs from its predecessor, ChatGPT-3.

GPT Plus: A New Era in AI Development

GPT Plus is not just an incremental update; it represents a significant leap in AI technology. With its improved understanding of complex queries and enhanced customization options, GPT Plus is poised to revolutionize how developers interact with AI. It brings forth a nuanced approach to language processing, opening up possibilities for more sophisticated applications in software development.

Delving into the Advanced Features of GPT Plus

Transitioning from ChatGPT-3, GPT Plus offers a range of advancements:

1. **Enhanced Comprehension and Response Accuracy:** GPT Plus demonstrates a deeper understanding of user prompts, providing more accurate and contextually relevant responses. This improvement is particularly beneficial for developers who rely on precise information for their coding and software design tasks.

2. **Customization at Its Core:** One of the standout features of GPT Plus is the ability to tailor the AI model to specific needs. This customization extends the tool's utility across various development scenarios, allowing for more targeted and effective AI assistance.

Real-World Application: Leveraging GPT Plus

In a scenario where a developer is tasked with creating a sophisticated content generation tool for a marketing platform, GPT Plus offers an array of advanced functionalities that can significantly elevate the project's outcome.

- Training a Custom Model for Targeted Content
  - **Adapting GPT Plus:** The developer begins by tuning GPT Plus to the specific language and style of the marketing platform. This involves feeding the AI with data that reflects the brand's tone, audience preferences, and marketing goals.
  - **Custom Content Generation:** The trained model is then capable of producing content that is not just relevant but also resonates with the target audience, maintaining the brand's voice and meeting specific marketing objectives.
- Integrating Advanced Features for Enhanced Interactivity
  - **Image and File Processing:** Unlike its predecessors, GPT Plus can interact with images and other file types.
  - **Using Plugins for Expanded Functionality:** The developer can integrate various plugins with GPT Plus, further enhancing its

capabilities. For instance, a plugin might enable the AI to pull in real-time data from social media platforms, ensuring that the content is not only relevant but also timely and trend-aware.

- Seamless Integration and Performance Evaluation

  - **Incorporating into the Marketing Platform:** Once the custom model is trained and the additional features are integrated, the tool is seamlessly embedded into the marketing platform's workflow.

  - **Evaluating the Impact:** The effectiveness of the GPT Plus-powered tool is measured by analyzing user engagement, content relevance, and the overall impact on marketing campaigns. The developer monitors metrics such as click-through rates, audience engagement, and content reach to assess the performance.

Outcome: A Revolutionized Marketing Approach

The content generation tool powered by GPT Plus marks a significant upgrade from traditional methods. Not only does it produce high-quality, relevant content, but it also brings a level of interactivity and personalization that was previously unattainable. This results in a marketing strategy that is more dynamic, responsive, and effective, ultimately driving higher engagement and better campaign results.

In this real-world application, GPT Plus stands out as a versatile and powerful tool that can transform the landscape of content creation, making it an invaluable asset in modern marketing and development strategies.

Beyond Text: GPT Plus and DALL-E Integration

GPT Plus's capabilities are not limited to text generation. Its compatibility with models like DALL-E introduces a new dimension to AI applications, where textual inputs can be transformed into visually compelling content. This integration paves the way for innovative uses in fields that require a combination of textual and visual creativity.

As we navigate through the capabilities and potential of GPT Plus, it becomes clear that this advanced AI model is not just a tool but a catalyst for innovation and efficiency in software development. It marks a significant milestone in the AI journey, heralding a future where the boundaries of AI's capabilities are continually expanding.

Conclusion

As we wrap up our journey through the world of ChatGPT, it's evident that this AI tool is reshaping the way we approach software development. We've explored a range of uses, from crafting effective prompts to implementing advanced AI features in real-world projects.

Key Takeaways

- **Crafting the Perfect Prompt**: The ability to communicate effectively with ChatGPT is fundamental. Fine-tuning our prompts helps us get the most relevant and useful responses, making our development tasks more manageable.

- **A Versatile Development Companion:** Whether it's automating mundane tasks, generating code, or brainstorming new ideas, ChatGPT proves to be an invaluable ally in a developer's toolkit.

- **Navigating Ethical AI Use:** The power of ChatGPT comes with the responsibility to use it ethically. Ensuring data privacy, avoiding bias, and maintaining content originality are essential in AI-assisted projects.

- **Looking Ahead with GPT Plus:** With the advent of ChatGPT 4.5, we're entering a new realm of possibilities. Its enhanced features, including image and file processing capabilities, open doors to even more creative and efficient applications.

Onward

As developers, we're at the forefront of an exciting era where AI tools like ChatGPT aren't just aids but partners in our creative process. It's a field ripe with opportunities for innovation, efficiency, and growth. Let's continue to embrace these tools with a spirit of curiosity, responsibility, and forward-thinking.

CHAPTER 11

Agile Aesthetics and Azure DevOps Dynamics

Welcome to Chapter 11, where we dive into the dynamic world of Agile methodologies and discover how they come to life in Azure DevOps. This chapter is tailored for new developers, offering a comprehensive introduction to Agile principles and practices, and how they can be effectively implemented using Azure DevOps tools.

Agile—a Developer's New Paradigm: Agile methodologies represent a significant shift from traditional, rigid project management approaches. They emphasize flexibility, collaboration, and customer satisfaction. For developers, this means more adaptive planning, evolutionary development, early delivery, and continual improvement.

♥ Fact   The Agile Manifesto, comprising four foundational values and twelve principles, was conceived in 2001 by seventeen software developers. It has since revolutionized software development processes worldwide.

Azure DevOps—Bringing Agile to Life: Azure DevOps provides a suite of tools that align perfectly with Agile principles, offering an integrated environment for planning, developing, testing, and deploying software. Its features, such as Azure Boards, Repositories, and Pipelines, are designed to support and enhance the Agile workflow.

In this chapter, you'll gain insights into Scrum and Kanban methodologies, learn about sprints, stories, and tasks, and explore how Azure DevOps can be a powerful ally in your Agile journey. Whether you're managing complex software projects or just starting in software development, understanding Agile and Azure DevOps is key to succeeding in today's fast-paced development landscape.

© Arpit Dwivedi 2024
A. Dwivedi, *CodeMosaic*, https://doi.org/10.1007/979-8-8688-0276-8_11

Agile Manifesto

As we step into the Agile world, it's essential to start at the foundation: the Agile Manifesto. This manifesto isn't just a document; it's a mindset that has reshaped the landscape of software development. Understanding its principles is crucial for any developer embarking on an Agile journey. It's more than a methodology; it's a paradigm shift in managing and participating in software projects.

Unpacking the Agile Manifesto

The Agile Manifesto emerged from a desire to find better ways of developing software—a response to the limitations of traditional, rigid project management methods. At its heart, the manifesto is about valuing:

1. **Individuals and Interactions** over processes and tools. It's about people-driven development, where collaboration and communication take precedence.

2. **Working Software** over comprehensive documentation. Agile prioritizes delivering functional software to customers over extensive paperwork.

3. **Customer Collaboration** over contract negotiation. This value emphasizes working closely with customers to meet their needs effectively.

4. **Responding to Change** over following a plan. Agile is synonymous with flexibility, adapting to changes rather than adhering strictly to initial plans.

The Manifesto in Action

For developers, the Agile Manifesto means embracing change, focusing on delivering value, and continuously seeking feedback to improve. It's a move away from the "waterfall" method of rigidly structured development phases to a more fluid, iterative process.

Practical Example: Imagine you're working on a software feature. Instead of waiting to complete the entire project before receiving feedback, Agile encourages incremental development. You build a part of the feature, review it with your team and stakeholders, adjust based on feedback, and continue. This iterative cycle is visualized as loops in the tree diagram, where each loop represents a stage of development, review, and adaptation.

In essence, the Agile Manifesto is about creating software in a human-centered, responsive, and collaborative way. As we move further into Agile methodologies, these principles will guide our understanding and implementation of Agile practices.

Scrum vs. Kanban

In the Agile universe, Scrum and Kanban stand out as two widely adopted methodologies. Both of these have a unique approach to managing software development projects. For the developers who are new to Agile, understanding the differences between Agile and Kanban is the key.

Scrum: Structured Agility

Overview: Scrum is known for its structured approach to managing projects. It divides the work into time-boxed iterations known as "sprints," typically lasting two to four weeks.

Key Components: The Scrum framework includes roles like the Scrum Master and Product Owner, and artifacts like the Product Backlog and Sprint Backlog.

Developer's Perspective: For developers, Scrum provides a clear structure with regular planning and review sessions. This can help developers in managing complex projects and achieving incremental progress.

Kanban: Continuous Flow

Overview: In contrast, Kanban is less structured. For improving efficiency, Kanban focuses on visualizing the workflow and limiting work-in-progress (WIP).

Key Components: Kanban utilizes a Kanban board, divided into columns representing different stages of the workflow. Tasks are represented as cards that move from left to right as they progress.

Developer's Perspective: Kanban offers flexibility and continuous delivery. It's ideal for teams that require a high degree of adaptability and for projects with frequently changing priorities.

Choosing the Right Approach

The decision between Scrum and Kanban often depends on the project's nature and the team's working style. Scrum's structured sprints are suitable for projects with clearly defined stages, while Kanban's fluid approach works well in environments where priorities shift frequently.

💡 **Practical Tip**   Teams new to Agile might start with Scrum due to its defined roles and processes, which provide a clear framework. However, as teams mature and processes evolve, integrating Kanban principles can enhance flexibility and responsiveness.

As we continue, it's important to remember that Agile is not a one-size-fits-all solution. The choice between Scrum and Kanban should align with the team's needs and the project's demands.

Sprints, Stories, and Tasks

Agile project management is a modular and iterative approach, which makes complex projects more manageable and responsive to change. For developers new to Agile, understanding the breakdown of work into sprints, stories, and tasks is crucial for navigating daily work within Agile teams.

Sprints: The Heartbeat of Agile Projects

Definition: Sprints are short, consistent development cycles that allow teams to deliver incremental value regularly. They typically last between one to four weeks and culminate in a review and planning for the next cycle.

Developer's View: For developers, sprints provide a structured yet flexible framework for focusing on a set amount of work, encouraging frequent reassessment and adjustment as needed.

User Stories: Building Blocks of Functionality

Purpose: User stories are short, simple descriptions of a feature told from the perspective of the end user. They help keep the team focused on delivering value to users.

Crafting Stories: Developers contribute by defining the technical details needed to implement the functionality described in a user story, ensuring that the user's needs are met.

Tasks: The Nuts and Bolts

Granularity: Tasks are the smallest units of work and involve detailed activities that need to be completed to fulfill a user story. They are often technical and specific to the developer's area of expertise.

Organization: Tasks are often tracked on a board or list within the sprint, allowing developers to see progress and what needs to be done next.

The Agile Workflow: An Example

Scenario: A new feature is being developed for an application. The sprint begins with planning, where the team decides on the user stories they will tackle. Each story is then broken down into tasks, such as writing code, creating tests, or updating documentation.

Developer's Role: As a developer, you would pick up tasks, work on them during the sprint, and update their status as you progress. The sprint concludes with a review of what was accomplished and what could be improved.

Understanding sprints, stories, and tasks is fundamental for developers as they engage with Agile methodologies. These components structure the workflow, ensuring that the team can adapt to changes while systematically advancing toward project goals.

Azure DevOps Introduction

Azure DevOps stands as a robust suite of development tools that support a variety of software development practices, including Agile methodologies. As a new developer, familiarizing yourself with Azure DevOps is pivotal for modern software delivery. This introduction will walk you through the platform's capabilities and illustrate how it can streamline your development process.

Overview of Azure DevOps

Azure DevOps is a platform that offers end-to-end DevOps toolchain for developing and deploying software. It comprises several services that cover the full development lifecycle, from planning work with Agile tools to source code management, building, testing, and deployment.

Key Components of Azure DevOps

Azure Boards: Agile project management service that supports planning and tracking work, code defects, and general issues using Kanban and Scrum methodologies.

Azure Repos: A source code management service hosting private Git repositories for version control of code.

Azure Pipelines: A CI/CD service that automates building, testing, and deploying applications to any cloud or on-premises.

Azure Test Plans: Offers a suite of tools for testing applications, including manual and exploratory testing tools.

Azure Artifacts: Allows teams to share packages such as Maven, npm, NuGet, and more, and integrate package sharing into their CI/CD pipelines.

Developers' Perspective on Azure DevOps

For developers, Azure DevOps is a one-stop-shop that facilitates collaboration, enhances productivity, and allows teams to deliver higher-quality software faster. It's a platform that scales with the team's needs and integrates with a wide ecosystem of development tools.

The Agile Edge with Azure DevOps

Embracing Azure DevOps means embracing a culture of continuous improvement and innovation. Its integration with Agile practices helps teams respond to market changes faster, aligns development work with business needs, and builds the right product through iterative development.

As we delve deeper into each component of Azure DevOps, you'll gain a better understanding of how to leverage this powerful platform in your Agile development journey.

Project Management with Azure Boards

Azure Boards is an essential component of Azure DevOps that provides a suite of Agile tools to support project management. It offers rich functionalities for planning, tracking, and discussing work among teams. For a developer new to Agile, understanding how to navigate and utilize Azure Boards is key to managing and contributing to projects efficiently.

The Agile Hub in Azure DevOps

Azure Boards is designed to be the hub where all project planning and management activities converge. It allows you to create and track work items, manage backlogs, and visualize team progress with Kanban boards, dashboards, and custom reporting tools.

Breaking Down Work into Manageable Items

User Stories: In Azure Boards, you can create user stories that articulate what the end user wants and why. This is essential for keeping the team's work focused on delivering value.

Tasks and Bugs: User stories are then broken down into tasks, which represent the individual work units necessary to achieve a story. Bugs can also be tracked and prioritized alongside these tasks.

Sprint Planning and Execution

Iteration Planning: Use Azure Boards to plan iterations or sprints by assigning user stories and tasks to each iteration, ensuring a balanced workload and clear objectives for what needs to be accomplished.

Daily Stand-ups: Azure Boards' dashboards can facilitate daily stand-ups by providing a clear view of what each team member is working on and highlighting any blockers.

Collaboration and Transparency

Collaboration is at the core of Azure Boards. The tool allows every team member to have visibility into the project's progress, fostering an environment of transparency and collective responsibility.

Harnessing Azure Boards for Agile Success

With Azure Boards, you can effectively manage your Agile projects by aligning activities with Agile principles and practices. It supports continuous delivery by enabling teams to plan, measure, and adjust their efforts in a coherent and collaborative manner.

Repositories in Azure DevOps

Azure Repos provides a secure and integrated environment for version control, making it a natural extension of the Git knowledge you acquired in Chapter 3. Here, we'll focus on how Azure Repos, as part of the broader Azure DevOps suite, facilitates and streamlines code management for Agile teams.

Building on Git's Strengths

Azure Repos harnesses the power of Git, which you're already familiar with from "Chapter 3: Git Going." It takes Git's distributed version control capabilities and enhances them with a user-friendly interface and additional features tailored for team collaboration.

A Unified Environment for Code Management

Integration with Azure Boards: Azure Repos connects directly to Azure Boards, linking commits and pull requests to work items, providing full traceability from a task or bug to the actual changes in code.

Pull Requests and Code Reviews: Strengthening team collaboration, Azure Repos offers comprehensive tools for pull requests and code reviews, essential practices for maintaining code quality in an Agile environment.

Leveraging Azure Repos for Agile Development

Code Sharing and Collaboration: Azure Repos is designed to support Agile teams, where collaboration and rapid iterations are the norm. It enables developers to share code, review each other's work, and merge changes with confidence.

Branch Policies and Build Validation: Protect your main branches with policies and build validation features in Azure Repos. These ensure that code meets quality standards before it's merged, aligning with Agile's emphasis on delivering working software.

In the subsequent section, we will explore Continuous Integration and Continuous Deployment (CI/CD) practices and how Azure Pipelines enable these practices to flourish within Azure DevOps.

Continuous Integration and Continuous Deployment (CI/CD)

Continuous Integration (CI) and Continuous Deployment (CD) are pivotal practices in Agile development that facilitate automated testing and deployment. Azure Pipelines, a prominent service within Azure DevOps, is designed to simplify and automate these practices, allowing Agile teams to maintain a steady pace of software delivery.

Understanding CI/CD in the Agile Context

Continuous Integration: CI is the practice of automating the integration of code changes, allowing teams to detect issues early by running tests against each change.

Continuous Deployment: CD extends CI by automatically deploying the code changes after successful tests, ensuring that new features and fixes are delivered to users quickly and reliably.

Implementing CI/CD with Azure Pipelines

Creating a pipeline in Azure DevOps is a straightforward process that can be summarized in the following steps:

1. **Create a New Pipeline:** Start by navigating to Azure Pipelines in your Azure DevOps project and select "Create Pipeline."

2. **Select Your Repository:** Azure Pipelines works with various Git repositories. Choose the repository where your code is located.

3. **Configure the Pipeline:** Use the classic editor for a GUI-based setup or the YAML editor for code-based pipeline configuration. The YAML editor allows more customization and can be version-controlled along with your code.

4. **Define Build Tasks:** Set up tasks to restore dependencies, build your application, and run tests. Azure Pipelines provides predefined tasks for common actions or custom scripts.

5. **Set Triggers:** Configure triggers to determine when the pipeline should run. Triggers can be set for events like code commits or pull requests.

6. **Define Deployment:** For CD, define the deployment process, including the environments (dev, test, production) and any approval steps required before the deployment is finalized.

7. **Run and Monitor:** Run the pipeline manually or through a trigger to test the configuration. Monitor the build and deployment through the Azure DevOps interface, which provides logs and status updates.

Practical Example: Setting up a Pipeline

Scenario: Charlie, at TechFusion Corp, is tasked with setting up a deployment pipeline for their Angular-.NET web application.

Step-by-Step Example

1. **Initiating Pipeline Creation:** Charlie navigates to the Azure DevOps portal, selects the "Pipelines" section, and clicks on "Create Pipeline."

2. **Repository Selection:** He then chooses the Git repository hosting the Angular-.NET application code.

3. **Pipeline Configuration:** Charlie opts to use the YAML editor for its versatility and checks in the YAML file to the repository, allowing for version control of the pipeline configuration.

4. **Defining Build Tasks:** He includes tasks for restoring dependencies, building the .NET backend, building the Angular frontend, and running unit tests.

5. **Triggering Mechanism:** Charlie configures the pipeline to trigger on commits to the main branch, ensuring that every change is automatically built and tested.

6. **Deployment Definition:** He then sets up stages for deploying to testing and production environments post successful build and test execution.

7. **Notification Setup:** Finally, Charlie adds a step to send email notifications to the team on build success or failure.

YAML Example for an Angular-.NET Application:

```yaml
````yaml code
trigger:
- main

pool:
  vmImage: 'windows-latest'
```
```

```
steps:
- task: NuGetToolInstaller@1

- task: NuGetCommand@2
  inputs:
    restoreSolution: '**/*.sln'

- script: 'dotnet build $(solution)'
  displayName: 'Build .NET'

- script: 'npm install -g @angular/cli'
  displayName: 'Install Angular CLI'

- script: 'cd AngularApp && npm install && ng build --prod'
  displayName: 'Build Angular App'

- task: DotNetCoreCLI@2
  inputs:
    command: 'test'
    projects: '**/*Tests/*.csproj'
    arguments: '--configuration Release'

- task: CopyFiles@2
  inputs:
    SourceFolder: 'AngularApp/dist'
    Contents: '**'
    TargetFolder: '$(build.artifactstagingdirectory)'

- task: PublishBuildArtifacts@1

- task: SendEmail@1
  inputs:
    To: 'devteam@techfusioncorp.com'
    Subject: 'Build $(Build.BuildNumber) - $(Build.SourceBranch)'
    Body: 'The build pipeline execution is complete. Status:
    $(Build.Status)'
    Attachments: '$(build.artifactstagingdirectory)/**'
```

Pipeline Execution and Monitoring: Once the pipeline is configured, Charlie commits the YAML file to the repository. This triggers the first build, and the pipeline executes according to the defined steps. The team receives an email notification with the build status, allowing them to quickly address any issues or proceed with deployment.

Through Azure Pipelines, Charlie has established a robust CI/CD process that enhances the team's ability to deliver high-quality software consistently. It exemplifies how Agile teams can leverage automation to align with the principles of iterative development and continuous delivery.

CI/CD as Agile Enablers

In the Agile methodology, the ability to adapt and respond to change is paramount. CI/CD practices are the embodiment of this principle, providing a framework for consistent and reliable software delivery that keeps pace with the Agile cycle of iteration and incremental improvement.

The Agile Rhythm with CI/CD

Rapid Iterations: CI/CD aligns perfectly with the Agile rhythm of rapid iterations. Continuous Integration ensures that each code commit is tested and merged regularly, allowing for quick detection and resolution of issues.

Feedback Loops: Agile is all about feedback loops, and CI/CD amplifies this by providing immediate feedback on the integration and deployment status, enabling teams to adapt and evolve their product with real-time insights.

Quality Assurance: With automated testing in the CI/CD pipeline, code quality is constantly evaluated, ensuring that the increments produced are of high quality and ready for deployment.

Reduced Time to Market: CD, whether it's Continuous Deployment or Continuous Delivery, ensures that once the code is tested, it's ready to be delivered to customers, significantly reducing the time to market.

Empowering Teams with Automation

Focus on Value: Automation of the integration and deployment process allows Agile teams to focus on creating value rather than on repetitive tasks. This maximizes the team's efficiency and keeps them aligned with the Agile goal of delivering value to the end user.

Risk Mitigation: By automating the build and deployment processes, teams can mitigate the risks associated with manual release processes, leading to more stable and predictable releases.

Scalable Practices: As the team grows and the project scales, CI/CD practices supported by Azure Pipelines ensure that the processes can scale too, without a proportional increase in overhead or complexity.

CI/CD: Agile's Technical Backbone

The technical practices of CI/CD are crucial for supporting Agile's adaptive project management and product development philosophies. They are not just tools or practices but are integral to the Agile way of working, enabling teams to deliver working software frequently and with high efficiency.

By integrating CI/CD practices with Azure Pipelines, Agile teams ensure that they can reliably and consistently deliver software that meets the evolving needs of their customers and stakeholders. It's a strategic capability that underpins the Agile commitment to continual improvement and customer satisfaction.

Conclusion

As we conclude this chapter on Agile methodologies and Azure DevOps, we've established a solid foundation of knowledge that is essential for modern software development. This chapter has equipped you with an understanding of Agile principles, the functionalities of Azure DevOps, and the critical practices of CI/CD, all through the lens of Azure Pipelines.

Key Takeaways

- **Embracing Agile:** The insights into Agile principles, including Scrum and Kanban, provide you with the flexibility to choose and adapt methodologies that best suit your project's needs.

- **Mastering Azure DevOps:** The exploration of Azure Boards, Repos, and Pipelines illustrates how these tools collectively enhance Agile project management and collaborative development.

- **CI/CD Efficiency:** Understanding CI/CD within the realm of Azure Pipelines underscores the importance of automation in ensuring a steady and quality-driven software delivery process.

As we conclude this chapter, we arrive at a significant juncture in "Codemosaic." The journey through the first 11 chapters has laid a comprehensive foundation, equipping you with a deep understanding of diverse yet interconnected pieces—from Agile and Azure DevOps to Git, Angular, databases, .NET, and innovative AI tools like GPT and Copilot.

- **Transitioning from Understanding to Application**

  - The journey thus far has been about understanding the individual pieces of the software development puzzle. We've delved into the principles of Agile methodologies, the multifaceted nature of Azure DevOps, and the transformative power of CI/CD practices. These chapters have been the building blocks, each one a critical piece of our larger mosaic.

  - As we step beyond these foundational chapters, we embark on an exciting new phase. The next eight chapters, "MosaicTile 1" through "MosaicTile 8," represent a shift from theoretical understanding to hands-on application. Here, we'll interweave the knowledge gained with practical AI tools, bringing to life a comprehensive development process.

- **Envisioning the Complete Mosaic**

  - Imagine each of the upcoming chapters as a vital tile in our Code Mosaic. Individually, they explore specific applications of AI in software development. Collectively, they form a complete picture, showcasing a seamless and integrated approach to analyzing, designing, developing, and deploying software, with AI as a central enabler.

  - These chapters will not only reinforce the concepts learned but will introduce you to advanced applications of AI. We'll explore how AI can be intricately integrated into every facet of development, enhancing efficiency, fostering creativity, and driving innovation.

- **Embarking on a Transformative Journey**

  - This next phase in "Codemosaic" is where theoretical concepts are actualized and brought to life. It's an invitation to dive into a world where AI is not just a supplementary tool but a transformative force, reshaping the landscape of modern software development.

  - Prepare to embark on this transformative journey through "MosaicTile 1" to "MosaicTile 8," each step revealing more of the immense potential and capability that AI brings to software development.

As we move forward, let's embrace the intricate process of building our Code Mosaic, where each new chapter, each "MosaicTile," adds depth and clarity to the complete picture of innovative, AI-enhanced software development.

PART II

Crafting the Mosaic

CHAPTER 12

Mosaic Tile 1: Setting Up the Stage—Ideation and Boards

As we embark on this practical journey in "Code Mosaic," remember the enthusiasm and curiosity of Alex, the fresh energy of Casey, the wisdom of Jamie, the leadership of Jordan, the cloud expertise of Olivia, and the backend mastery of Charlie. You've seen them evolve, and now it's your turn. Imagine yourself stepping into Tech Fusion Corp, armed with the knowledge from the first 11 chapters, ready to tackle a new challenge— the AI and Software Development Dashboard. This is more than just a project; it's your canvas to paint the future of software development.

In this chapter, we'll not just reiterate what Agile and Azure DevOps are, as we've done that in "Agile Aesthetics and Azure DevOps Dynamics." Instead, we'll dive into the practicalities, exploring the Azure DevOps boards, breaking down user stories, tasks, and more. Imagine Alex navigating through these, and now, it's your turn. From ideation to deployment, this is where your theoretical knowledge meets practical application. It's not just about learning; it's about evolving into a developer who can seamlessly integrate AI insights into software solutions.

Practical Guide to Azure Board Setup

Setting up Azure Boards is a pivotal step in managing your AI and Software Development Dashboard project effectively. Here's a detailed guide to get you started:

1. Sign Up for Azure DevOps

    a. Visit the Azure DevOps page and click "Start free with GitHub" or "Start free."

        https://dev.azure.com/

    b. Follow the prompts to either create a new Microsoft account or sign in with an existing one.

        You'll find something like Figure 12-1 after following the above steps.

Figure 12-1. *Login page Azure Devops*

Click Continue.

2. Create an Organization:

    a. After Step1, you'll be prompted to create a new organization as in Figure 12-2.

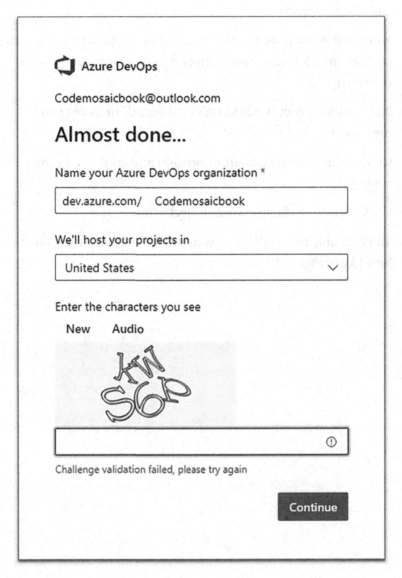

Figure 12-2. *Create a new organization*

    b. Enter "CodeMosaicOrg" or a name of your choice, select the region closest to you, fill captcha, and click "Continue."

    c. You'll be directed to the organization's dashboard. Bookmark this URL for easy access.

3. Create a New Project:

    a. You will then be prompted to create a new project, or you can click on "New project" at the top right corner of your organization's dashboard.

    b. Name your project "CodeMosaicDashboard" or as per your preference.

    c. Choose the visibility (public or private) and additional project settings.

    d. Click "Create" to finalize your project setup.

    e. You'll be able to see all the information related to your project here like in Figure 12-3.

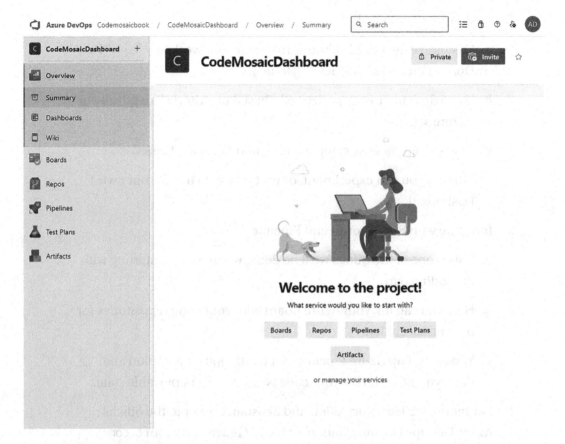

Figure 12-3. *Create a new project*

4. Configure Azure Boards:

   a. In your new project, you can navigate to the "Boards" section in the sidebar.

   b. You can start by creating new work items. You can choose from different types such as "User Stories," "Tasks," or "Bugs."

   c. Organize your work items into sprints for better iteration planning.

   d. We'll be setting this up in subsequent topics of this chapter.

5. Customize Your Board:

   a. Customize the board columns to mirror your workflow (e.g., "To Do," "In Progress," "Review," "Done").

   b. Use swimlanes to categorize tasks based on criteria like priority or feature set.

   c. Employ tags for easy categorization and filtering of tasks.

   d. This too you can experiment, or wait till we do this for our own Dashboard.

6. Integrate with Repositories and Pipelines:

   a. This is one of the things we'll be doing when we'll be starting with the coding part.

   b. Here you can ink your Azure Board with your code repositories for better traceability.

   c. You can set up Azure Pipelines for continuous integration and deployment, ensuring your code is always in a deployable state.

7. For more detailed information and assistance, refer to the official Azure DevOps Documentation: `https://learn.microsoft.com/en-us/azure/devops/?view=azure-devops`.

By following these steps, you'll have a fully set up Azure Board, ready to manage the development of your AI and Software Development Dashboard. Remember, while the project and organization names are given as "CodeMosaicOrg" and "CodeMosaicDashboard" for illustration, you're free to choose names that resonate with your project's identity you are experimenting with.

Introduction to the AI Dashboard

Embark on a journey to create the AI and Software Development Dashboard, a single-page application that's not just a tool, but a narrative of AI's transformative role in software development. This dashboard, a marvel of modern technology, will vividly visualize critical metrics like AI tool adoption rates, enhancements in coding efficiency, and the latest trends in AI-driven software innovations.

In the chapters ahead, we'll meticulously navigate through each phase of the development process, from initial design to final deployment, ensuring every aspect of this SPA exemplifies top-tier development standards. Leveraging Angular's dynamic frontend capabilities and .NET's robust backend framework, the dashboard will stand as a testament to efficient data processing, seamless API integration, and captivating data visualization.

As we prepare to translate this ambitious concept into a tangible reality, our journey will be enriched by AI-driven brainstorming. This approach promises not just to adhere to best practices but to redefine them, infusing our development pathway with groundbreaking insights and innovative solutions. Let's harness the potential of AI to refine and elevate our vision for the AI Dashboard, setting the stage for a development journey that's as enlightening as it is technical.

Ready for this immersive experience? Let's dive in and let AI guide our path to innovation.

Brainstorming with AI: Crafting the AI Dashboard

In this section, we'll harness the power of AI to brainstorm and structure the AI and Software Development Dashboard project effectively. AI-driven tools like GPT can offer insightful suggestions, answer complex queries, and help in high-level planning. Here's how you can engage AI in the brainstorming process:

1. Defining the Scope and Vision:

   a. Interact with AI to refine your vision for the dashboard. Ask questions like, "What features are essential for a software development dashboard?" or "How can AI enhance data visualization in software development metrics?"

2. Module Segregation and High-Level Planning:

   a. Use AI to help segregate the dashboard into logical modules. For example, "What would be the primary modules of an AI-driven software development dashboard?"

   b. Discuss the feasibility and dependencies of each module, ensuring a structured approach.

3. Crafting User Stories:

   a. Engage with AI to draft User Stories for each module. Ask, "What would be the key tasks for developing the data visualization module in the AI dashboard?"

   b. Ensure each User Story is comprehensive, covering aspects like feature descriptions, acceptance criteria, and estimated efforts.

4. Refining and Prioritizing:

   a. Utilize AI to prioritize User Stories based on factors such as business value, technical complexity, and dependencies.

   b. Seek AI's input on refining User Stories, ensuring they align perfectly with the project's goals and timeline.

Adopting Best Practices in AI-Driven Development

Adopting best practices in AI-driven development ensures that the AI and Software Development Dashboard not only meets but exceeds modern development standards. This involves an iterative approach where AI insights are leveraged to optimize every phase of the development process. Here's how you can ensure best practices are ingrained in your development lifecycle:

1. Code Quality and Review:

   a. Utilize AI to enforce coding standards and perform automated code reviews. This ensures high code quality and reduces manual review efforts.

2. Efficient Testing and Debugging:

   a. Integrate AI tools to automate testing processes, identify potential bugs, and suggest fixes, speeding up the development cycle and ensuring a robust product.

3. Smart Project Management:

   a. Leverage AI for predictive project analytics, risk assessment, and resource allocation, ensuring the project stays on track and within budget.

4. Seamless Integration and Continuous Deployment:

   a. Employ AI-driven CI/CD pipelines to automate build, test, and deployment processes, ensuring that your application is always in a releasable state.

By embracing these practices, you can ensure that the development of your AI and Software Development Dashboard is not just cutting-edge but also adheres to the highest standards of software excellence.

From Ideation to Action: Creating User Stories

As we transition from the theoretical foundations laid in the earlier chapters to the dynamic, hands-on development of the AI and Software Development Dashboard, it's crucial to align our approach with the principles of agility and innovation. This phase marks the practical application of concepts, ideas, and technologies we've discussed, encapsulating them into a cohesive, actionable development plan. The upcoming sections will guide you through this transformative journey, ensuring each step is clear, practical, and aligned with the best practices in AI-driven development.

Brainstorming AI Dashboard Idea

In this phase, we'll engage in a simulated conversation with GPT to demonstrate how AI can assist in refining the AI Dashboard concept. The goal is to showcase an effective brainstorming process, leveraging AI to crystallize our project vision and technical strategy.

Example Dialogue

Developer: "I'm planning an AI Dashboard as a single-page application. What technologies should I consider for a robust and scalable application?"
GPT: "For a scalable and responsive front-end, Angular is a great choice. It's well-suited for building single-page applications. For the backend, .NET provides a robust framework that integrates well with Angular. SQL can serve as a reliable database solution. For deployment and project management, consider Azure web slots and Azure DevOps."

Developer: "How can I ensure the dashboard effectively visualizes AI's impact on software development?"

GPT: "Incorporate dynamic data visualization components like Angular Material tables for structured data display and DevExtreme for interactive charts. These tools can help you represent complex data like AI tool adoption rates and coding efficiency improvements in a user-friendly manner."

Developer: "I want to tap into AI's potential to revolutionize software development. How can I represent this impact in the dashboard?"

GPT: "To truly showcase AI's empowerment in software development, consider tables that track AI tool adoption across different teams or projects. For APIs, you might create endpoints that aggregate data on AI-driven bug fixes or feature implementations. Charts can then visualize trends over time, like the increasing speed of development cycles or the growing complexity of tasks being automated."

Developer: "Can you suggest specific tables and charts that would effectively demonstrate these trends?"

GPT: "Certainly. A "Projects vs. AI Tools" table can show the correlation between tool usage and project metrics. For charts, a line chart could depict the evolution of coding efficiency, while a stacked bar chart might illustrate various AI tools' contributions to different phases of the software development lifecycle. API-wise, consider endpoints that serve real-time data on AI tool performance metrics and coding efficiency improvements."

This interaction demonstrates the brainstorming phase's importance, providing clarity on technology choices and feature implementation. Next, we'll utilize AI's guidance to divide the project into focused, manageable sections, outlining the User Stories for each development phase.

Dividing the Work with AI's Guidance

In this section, we will engage in a detailed conversation with AI to strategically divide the AI Dashboard project into manageable and focused User Stories. This conversation aims to outline the structure of the project and create a clear development roadmap.

Example Dialogue

Developer: "We have our AI Dashboard concept ready. Can you guide me on how to divide the project into manageable parts (User Stories) for efficient development and tracking?"

GPT: "Certainly. To ensure a structured approach, consider dividing your project into these key development phases, each representing a User Story.

1. User Story for Architectural Blueprint (Blueprint Bonanza):

   a. Focus on the architectural design. Define database tables, API contracts, and UI components, laying down a complete blueprint of the application.

2. User Story for Data Infrastructure (Data Strategies):

   a. Construct the database, define tables, and populate data. This User Story involves actual creation and setup of the database, preparing the foundation for API development and data visualization.

3. User Story for API Development (.NET API Artistry):

   a. Develop the required APIs, ensuring they are robust, secure, and efficiently serve the required data to the frontend.

4. User Story for Frontend Development (Frontend Fitness with Angular):

   a. Translate the architectural blueprint into a functional UI, integrating it seamlessly with the backend APIs.

5. User Story for Data Visualization (Data Visualization Delight):

   a. Implement interactive data visualization components, ensuring insightful and intuitive data presentation.

6. User Story for AI Tool Exploration (Integration Ingenuity with Smart Tools):

   a. Analyze, explore, and evaluate potential external AI tools and APIs that could be integrated, documenting how these integrations can be achieved.

7. User Story for Deployment and Hosting (Smart Deployment Delight):

   a. Focus on hosting and deployment strategies, investigating direct deployment via VS or setting up CI/CD pipelines for continuous deployment."

Developer: "That's a comprehensive breakdown. How do I ensure these User Stories are well-documented and tracked?"

GPT: "Each User Story should have a clear description, acceptance criteria, and estimated effort. Use Azure DevOps to track progress, assign tasks, and manage sprints. Regularly review and adjust your User Stories as the project evolves."

This structured conversation provides a clear roadmap for developing the AI Dashboard, dividing the work into focused, manageable User Stories, and ensuring each aspect of the project is meticulously planned and tracked.

Practical Agile Implementation

Embarking on the AI Dashboard project, it's crucial to not just have a vision, but also a concrete, structured plan to bring it to life. In this section, we'll adopt a hands-on, practical Agile approach, meticulously setting up sprints, crafting User Stories, and ensuring every task is clear, actionable, and aligned with our project goals. You'll be guided through each step, from organizing sprints in Azure DevOps to interacting with AI to draft User Stories with precision. Screenshots from an actual sprint setup will be shared, offering a visual, step-by-step guide to ensure you can replicate the process smoothly.

Setting Up Sprints in Azure DevOps

Setting up sprints in Azure DevOps is a pivotal step in Agile project management. This process involves organizing your development cycle into manageable time frames, aligning them with your project goals. Here's a guide to help you set up sprints effectively:

1. Access Your Azure DevOps Project:

    a. Log into your Azure DevOps account and select your "CodeMosaicDashboard" project.

2. Navigate to Sprints:

    a. In your project dashboard, go to the "Sprints" section.

    b. You can find it as highlighted in Figure 12-4, 4th option under boards.

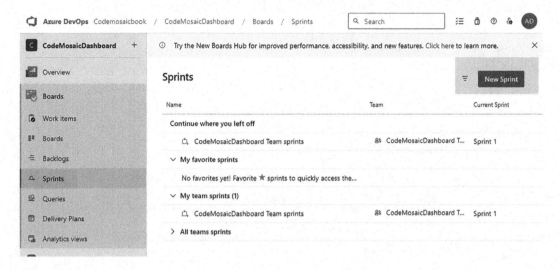

Figure 12-4. *Setting up the sprint*

3. Create a New Sprint:

   a. Click on "New Sprint" and set the time frame (usually two to four weeks).

   b. Name your sprint thoughtfully to reflect the goals or the main User Story it addresses as in Figure 12-5.

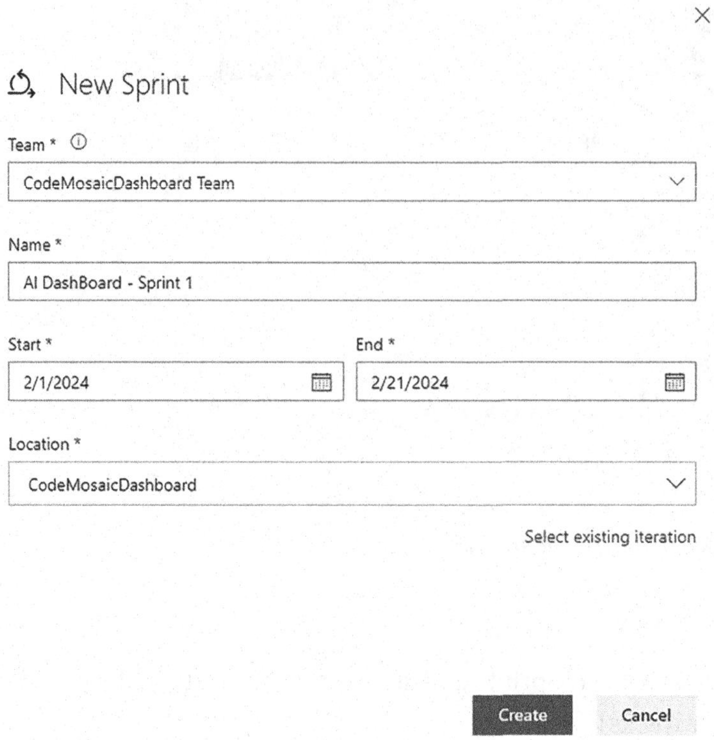

Figure 12-5. *New sprint*

    c. As per our project, I've named the Sprint "AI DashBoard - Sprint 1," and have made it a 3-week sprint. Sprints are generally 2–3 weeks, but here you can change it as per your pace you are planning to complete the project, or you can even create multiple sprints and divide your User Stories accordingly.

You can follow these steps while setting up your sprints in Azure DevOps, ensuring a well-structured and efficient workflow for the AI Dashboard project. Remember, the key to successful Agile implementation lies in flexibility and continuous improvement.

Creating and Detailing User Stories in Azure DevOps

Creating detailed and actionable User Stories is essential for a clear and efficient development process. Here are the steps how you can craft and detail your User Stories in Azure DevOps.

Access and Setup in Azure DevOps for User Story 1

To kickstart the development of the AI Dashboard, it's essential to set up your workspace properly in Azure DevOps. Here's how you can access your project and prepare for creating your first User Story:

1. Log into Azure DevOps:

   a. Visit the Azure DevOps site and sign in with your credentials.

2. Select Your Project:

   a. From the dashboard, choose the "CodeMosaicDashboard" project.

3. Navigate to Backlogs:

   a. In the project dashboard, locate and click on the Backlogs section to access the area where you'll manage your User Stories.

4. Prepare for User Story Creation:

   a. Familiarize yourself with the interface. Ensure you're comfortable with the layout and know where to find the "New Work Item" button as shown in Figure 12-6.

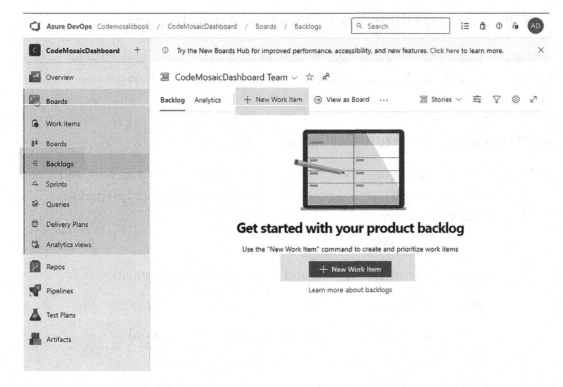

Figure 12-6. *New Work Item*

This initial setup is crucial as it ensures you have a solid and organized starting point for managing your project's User Stories effectively.

User Story Creation and Initial Drafting in Azure DevOps for User Story 1

Creating your first User Story effectively sets the tone for your project's development. Here's how you can draft User Story 1—"Architectural Blueprint for AI Dashboard":

1.   Initiate User Story Creation:

     a.   In the "Backlogs" section, click on "New Work Item" and select "User Story" to start creating your User Story.

2.   Naming Your User Story:

     a.   Title your User Story "Architectural Blueprint for AI Dashboard" as shown in Figure 12-7. This title should reflect the essence and primary focus of the User Story.

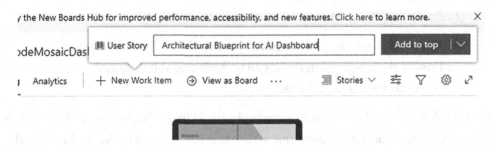

Figure 12-7. *User Story*

3. Initial Description:

   a. Begin drafting a description that outlines the primary goal of
      the User Story. Mention that this User Story aims to define the
      structural layout of the application, including database schema,
      API contracts, and UI components.

This initial drafting phase is vital as it provides a clear, concise overview of what the
User Story aims to achieve, setting a focused direction for the development work ahead.

AI-Enhanced Brainstorming for User Story 1

To ensure User Story 1 is comprehensive and sets a solid foundation for the AI
Dashboard, a detailed description and AI-assisted brainstorming are pivotal:

1. Enhancing the Description:

   a. Elaborate on the User Story's description. Detail the importance
      of each component (database schema, API contracts, UI
      components) and how they collectively form the backbone of the
      AI Dashboard.

2. Incorporating AI Insights:

   a. Engage with AI to brainstorm innovative ideas or solutions for the
      architectural blueprint. Pose questions like, "How can we ensure
      our database schema supports future scalability?" or "What are
      the best practices for API contracts in a .NET environment?"

3. Refining the Blueprint:

    a. Use the insights from AI to refine your architectural blueprint. Ensure the description covers all technical and functional requirements comprehensively.

A well-crafted detailed description, enriched with AI insights, will ensure that User Story 1 lays a robust foundation for the subsequent development phases of the AI Dashboard.

Drafting Acceptance Criteria with AI Assistance for User Story 1

Defining clear and measurable acceptance criteria is key to ensuring the successful completion of User Story 1. Let's engage in a detailed conversation with AI to draft these criteria:

Example GPT Conversation

Developer: "I'm detailing User Story 1, focused on creating an Architectural Blueprint for our AI Dashboard. What should be the key acceptance criteria to ensure a comprehensive and robust design?"

GPT

"For a robust Architectural Blueprint, your acceptance criteria should include

Database Schema Clarity: The schema should be fully defined, normalized, and support efficient querying. All relationships must be accurately represented and properly indexed.

API Contract Precision: API endpoints must adhere to RESTful standards, ensuring clear and consistent communication between the front- and backend. Documentation should be versioned and comprehensive.

UI Component Detailing: UI components need to be meticulously listed, with clear interaction models and adherence to the design system. Ensure components are scalable and align with the project's performance and usability goals.

Scalability and Performance Consideration: The blueprint should facilitate future scalability and maintain optimal performance standards across all components."

Developer: "That's insightful. How do I ensure these criteria are effectively communicated and adhered to by the development team?"

GPT: "Document each criterion clearly in the User Story and discuss them in your sprint planning meetings. Ensure each team member understands their importance and how they contribute to the project's success. Regularly review these criteria during your development process to ensure compliance and address any deviations promptly."

By having this detailed conversation with AI, you can draft precise and actionable acceptance criteria for User Story 1, ensuring a solid and clear foundation for your AI Dashboard project.

After drafting the Description and acceptance criteria, Your User Story will look like Figure 12-8.

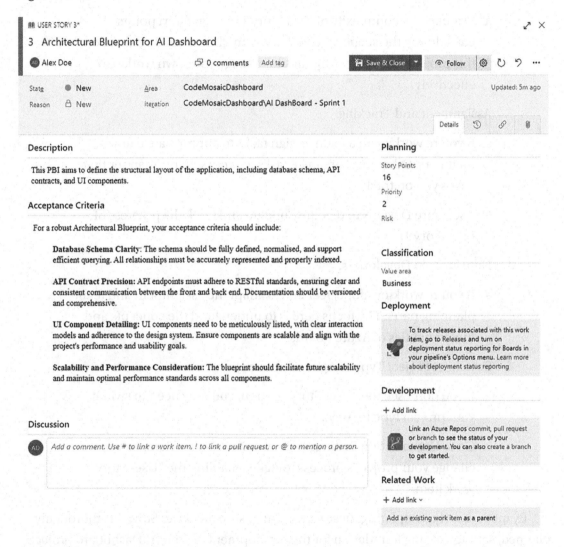

Figure 12-8. Describing the User Story

Finalizing User Story 1: Effort Estimation, Assignment, and Tracking

Concluding the setup for User Story 1 involves estimating efforts, assigning tasks, and ensuring proper tracking:

1. Effort Estimation:

   a. Evaluate the complexity of User Story 1. Assign effort points considering the scope of work. As you might be working alone on this project, use these estimates to manage your own workload effectively.

2. Assignment and Tracking:

   a. If you're working in a team, assign tasks to appropriate team members. Otherwise, organize tasks for yourself in a manner that keeps you on track.

   b. Use Azure DevOps to regularly update and track the progress of User Story 1.

3. Note for Solo Developers:

   a. If you're working alone, feel free to adapt the assignment and team planning parts. The focus here is to understand the concepts and functionalities of Azure Boards.

4. Switching Project Type to Agile (if needed):

   a. If you don't see the "User Story" option, you may need to switch your project type to Agile.

   b. Go to Organization Settings ➤ Boards ➤ Process. Here, you can change your project's process to Agile, enabling the "User Story" work item.

By meticulously completing these steps, you ensure that User Story 1 is thoroughly planned, setting a strong foundation for the development of your AI Dashboard project.

Detailing Remaining User Stories

Following the structured approach used for detailing the first User Story, you can similarly articulate the remaining User Stories for the AI Dashboard project. Each User Story should be crafted with a clear title, a comprehensive description, and well-defined acceptance criteria. Here's an overview of the remaining 6 User Stories:

1. **User Story: Data Infrastructure (Data Strategies)**

   a. **Title:** "Database Design and Data Management"

   b. **Description:** Establish the project's data infrastructure, focusing on database creation, table setup, and data insertion for API and visualization purposes.

   c. **Acceptance Criteria:** Database and tables are created as per schema, with data accurately inserted, ready for API integration and data visualization.

2. **User Story: API Development (.NET API Artistry)**

   a. **Title:** "API Development for Data Access"

   b. **Description:** Develop and document RESTful APIs to facilitate seamless data flow between the database and the frontend application.

   c. **Acceptance Criteria:** APIs are fully functional, documented, and adhere to RESTful standards, ensuring smooth data retrieval and submission.

3. **User Story: Frontend Development (Frontend Fitness with Angular)**

   a. **Title:** "Frontend UI/UX Implementation"

   b. **Description:** Translate the design blueprint into a functional and interactive frontend, ensuring a seamless user experience.

   c. **Acceptance Criteria:** The frontend is responsive, interactive, and accurately reflects the design blueprint, with all components functioning as intended.

4. **User Story: Data Visualization (Data Visualization Delight)**

   a. **Title:** "Implementing Data Visualization Components"

   b. **Description:** Integrate dynamic data visualization components to represent project metrics and AI tool impacts effectively.

   c. **Acceptance Criteria:** Charts and graphs are interactive, insightful, and accurately represent the underlying data, enhancing the dashboard's analytical capabilities.

5. **User Story: AI Tool Exploration (Integration Ingenuity with Smart Tools)**

   a. **Title:** "Evaluation and Planning for AI Tool Integration"

   b. **Description:** Analyze and plan the integration of external AI tools and APIs, documenting potential use cases and integration strategies.

   c. **Acceptance Criteria:** A comprehensive evaluation is done, with a clear plan for potential AI tool integrations, enhancing the dashboard's functionality.

6. **User Story: Deployment and Hosting (Smart Deployment Delight)**

   a. **Title:** "Deployment and Hosting Strategy"

   b. **Description:** Focus on planning and executing the deployment strategy, ensuring the application is hosted and accessible.

   c. **Acceptance Criteria:** The application is successfully deployed, hosted, and accessible, with a strategy in place for continuous deployment and integration.

You can follow similar steps to create and detail these User Stories, assigning effort based on your understanding and capacity. A screenshot of how your Azure DevOps backlog and sprint view might look is provided to illustrate how these user stories may appear after creation (Figure 12-9).

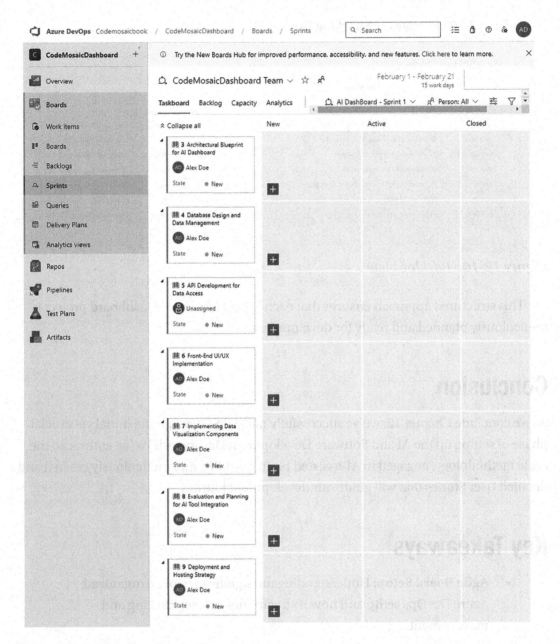

Figure 12-9. *Sprint view*

Figure 12-10 illustrates the backlog view.

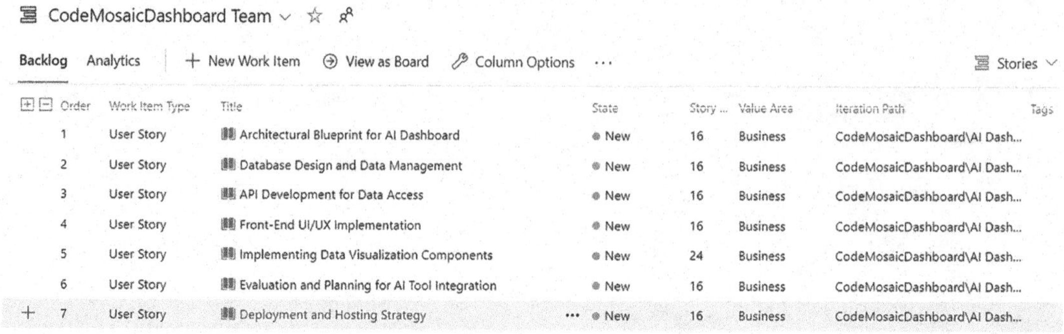
CodeMosaicDashboard Team
Backlog
Analytics
New Work Item
View as Board
Column Options
Stories
Order
Work Item Type
Title
State
Story ...
Value Area
Iteration Path
Tags
1 User Story Architectural Blueprint for AI Dashboard New 16 Business CodeMosaicDashboard\AI Dash...
2 User Story Database Design and Data Management New 16 Business CodeMosaicDashboard\AI Dash...
3 User Story API Development for Data Access New 16 Business CodeMosaicDashboard\AI Dash...
4 User Story Front-End UI/UX Implementation New 16 Business CodeMosaicDashboard\AI Dash...
5 User Story Implementing Data Visualization Components New 24 Business CodeMosaicDashboard\AI Dash...
6 User Story Evaluation and Planning for AI Tool Integration New 16 Business CodeMosaicDashboard\AI Dash...
7 User Story Deployment and Hosting Strategy New 16 Business CodeMosaicDashboard\AI Dash...

***Figure 12-10.** Backlog view*

This structured approach ensures that each aspect of your AI Dashboard project is meticulously planned and ready for development.

Conclusion

As we conclude Chapter 12, we've successfully navigated through the initial yet crucial phase of setting up the AI and Software Development Dashboard. We've embraced the Agile methodology, engaged in AI-assisted brainstorming, and meticulously created and detailed User Stories that will guide our development journey.

Key Takeaways

- **Agile Board Setup:** Understanding the significance of an organized Azure DevOps setup and how it streamlines project tracking and management.
- **AI-Assisted Brainstorming:** Leveraging AI for refining ideas, planning the project scope, and ensuring a comprehensive understanding of each User Story.
- **User Story Crafting:** Creating detailed User Stories, setting clear acceptance criteria, and ensuring a structured approach to the AI Dashboard's development.

Onward

As we transition to Chapter 13, "Mosaic Tile 2: Blueprint Bonanza—Designing with AI Tools," we'll delve deeper into the art and science of designing an AI and Software Development Dashboard. We'll explore

- **Designing the Dashboard:** Principles of creating an informative and user-friendly dashboard, ensuring that every element serves a purpose.

- **AI in UI/UX Design:** Harnessing AI's potential to create innovative design prototypes, layouts, and enhancing user experience.

- **Creating Interactive Prototypes:** Utilizing AI tools for prototyping, user experience testing, and ensuring that the dashboard is not only functional but also intuitive and engaging.

Get ready to transform your ideas into visually compelling and functionally robust designs in the next chapter of our AI-driven development journey!

CHAPTER 13

Mosaic Tile 2: Blueprint Bonanza—Designing with AI Tools

With our User Stories meticulously planned and our Agile board set, we now embark on the first leg of our practical journey in "Blueprint Bonanza." Here, we delve deep into designing the foundational structure of our AI Dashboard. This isn't just about building; it's about architecting a system that embodies efficiency, scalability, and innovation.

In this chapter, we not only explore the technical intricacies of design but also how AI can become our ally in this creative process. As we craft the blueprint of our AI Dashboard, it serves as a tangible example to elucidate design principles, AI integration, and best practices. Our objective is clear: to equip you with the knowledge to not just understand design concepts but to implement them, leveraging AI to navigate the complexities of crafting a sophisticated software solution. Ready to unfold the blueprint of success?

Architectural Design with AI Assistance

As we venture into the heart of our AI Dashboard project, the architectural design emerges as a cornerstone, shaping the future of our application. This segment, "Architectural Design with AI Assistance," is not just about laying down the blueprint; it's about revolutionizing it with the power of AI.

Here, we will navigate through the intricate maze of database structures, API frameworks, and UI components, with AI as our guide. Each step is deliberate, each decision data-driven, ensuring that our architectural design isn't just robust—it's

© Arpit Dwivedi 2024
A. Dwivedi, *CodeMosaic*, https://doi.org/10.1007/979-8-8688-0276-8_13

futuristic. Ready to witness how AI transforms the traditional design process into an intelligent, dynamic creation journey? Let's dive into the detailed discussions, one component at a time.

Database Design Discussion with AI

In the realm of software development, the database is not just a storage compartment; it's the bedrock upon which dynamic, data-driven applications stand. As we embrace the era of AI-enhanced development, understanding and optimizing database design becomes not just a necessity but a strategic advantage. AI's prowess in pattern recognition, predictive analysis, and automated optimization introduces a new paradigm in database architecture. Let's embark on this journey, where AI doesn't just assist but elevates our approach to database design, making our systems more efficient, scalable, and intelligent.

Next, we'll delve into the significance of database design and how engaging AI can refine this crucial phase, culminating in a simulated, insightful dialogue between a developer and AI.

The Importance of Database Design

A well-designed database is the cornerstone of any robust software application. It's not just about storing data; it's about retrieving it efficiently, maintaining data integrity, and ensuring scalability as your application grows.

AI can revolutionize traditional database design by

- **Optimizing Data Structures:** AI algorithms can analyze data access patterns and suggest optimal table structures, indexing strategies, and query optimizations.

- **Ensuring Data Integrity:** AI can predict potential data anomalies and suggest constraints and validation rules to maintain data integrity.

- **Scalability Projections:** AI can forecast future data growth and recommend scaling strategies, ensuring your database design is future-proof.

Next, we'll explore an example conversation between a developer and AI, showcasing how AI can assist in making these crucial database design decisions.

Example GPT Conversation: Enhancing Database Design

Developer: "As a database architect, I'm seeking to optimize our database for an AI-driven dashboard. What schema design would ensure efficient querying and scalability?"

GPT (AI Database Architect): "For optimal performance, consider a schema that supports indexing on frequently queried columns. Ensure tables are normalized to reduce redundancy. For scalability, design your schema to accommodate sharding, allowing your database to distribute loads and grow seamlessly."

Developer: "How can I maintain data integrity and predict anomalies?"

GPT (AI Database Architect): "Implement strict data validation rules and constraints at the schema level. Utilize AI-driven anomaly detection systems to monitor data patterns and flag inconsistencies or unexpected behaviors."

Developer: "What strategies should I adopt for future data growth?"

GPT (AI Database Architect): "Forecast data growth using predictive analytics. Plan for horizontal scaling strategies, like database sharding, and consider implementing flexible, cloud-based storage solutions to handle increased data loads efficiently."

This conversation exemplifies how AI can guide and enhance database design, ensuring a robust, scalable, and intelligent backend for your application.

In sum, the intersection of AI and database design opens new vistas for efficiency, integrity, and scalability. The dialogue between developers and AI architects reveals the potential for AI to refine schema structures, anticipate growth, and ensure robustness. This intelligent approach lays a solid foundation for the data-driven backbone of our AI Dashboard, setting the stage for seamless integration with other system components. Ready to explore how AI similarly revolutionizes API design and structuring? Let's proceed to the next subtopic.

API Design and Structuring with AI

The design and structuring of APIs are pivotal in shaping how different components of an application interact and communicate. In this segment, we dive into the realm of API design, not just to structure these crucial pathways but to refine them with the acumen of AI. The intricate dance of requests and responses, the art of defining endpoints, and the science of securing data transactions—all these aspects of API architecture are about to be enhanced by AI's analytical prowess and predictive capabilities.

In the realm of API design and structuring, the focus is not just on creating pathways for data flow but on architecting these pathways intelligently to enhance security, scalability, and maintainability. Here's how we approach this intricate task:

- **Layered Architecture**

  - Emphasize the significance of a layered architecture (Controller, Business, and Data layers) for clear segregation of concerns, making the API easier to manage and scale.

- **RESTful Principles**

  - Discuss the importance of adhering to RESTful principles for API design, ensuring stateless communication and intuitive endpoint structuring.

- **Security Best Practices**

  - Highlight the paramount importance of security in API design, discussing strategies for secure data transmission, authentication, and authorization.

- **Database Connectivity**

  - Outline best practices for database connectivity, ensuring efficient and secure data access and manipulation.

Leveraging AI in API Design and Structuring

AI transforms API development by offering data-driven insights and automation, leading to more efficient and secure APIs. Here's how AI can assist:

- **Automated Code Generation**

  - AI can generate boilerplate code for standard API functions, speeding up the development process.

- **Security Enhancement**

  - AI tools can analyze code for vulnerabilities, suggesting improvements and automating the implementation of security best practices.

- **Performance Optimization**

  - AI can analyze usage patterns to suggest optimizations, ensuring APIs handle requests efficiently.

- **Intelligent Error Handling**

  - AI can predict potential failure points, allowing developers to proactively implement robust error handling.

Next, we'll showcase an example GPT conversation demonstrating Enhancing API Design with AI Insights:

Developer: "I need to design a data layer function in **C#** to retrieve data from SQL Server. How should I structure it for optimal performance and security?"

GPT (AI Backend Expert): "Start by using parameterized queries to protect against SQL injection. For performance, consider using async methods like **ReadAsync** for non-blocking data retrieval. Ensure you're using **using** statements for proper disposal of SQL connections."

Developer: "Can you suggest a pattern for handling errors effectively in this context?"

GPT (AI Backend Expert): "Implement a robust exception handling strategy. Use try-catch blocks to capture specific SQL exceptions. Log detailed error information for debugging, but avoid exposing sensitive details to the client. Consider custom exception classes for more granular control."

Developer: "How can AI assist in further optimisation of this function?"

GPT (AI Backend Expert): "AI can analyze execution patterns and suggest index optimizations in your database. It can also recommend caching strategies for frequently queried data to reduce database load and improve response times."

Developer: "What about automating code generation for standard API functions?"

GPT (AI Backend Expert): "AI-powered tools can generate boilerplate code for CRUD operations, ensuring consistency and freeing you to focus on complex business logic. They adhere to best practices and can be customized to fit your specific requirements."

The dialogue between the developer and AI showcases the immense potential of integrating AI in API development. AI's ability to offer advanced insights for code optimization, error handling, and performance enhancement is invaluable. As we conclude this segment on API design and structuring, it's evident that AI is not just a tool, but a partner in crafting efficient, secure, and robust APIs.

UI Component Planning with AI

Navigating the landscape of UI design requires not just a keen eye for aesthetics but also a deep understanding of user interaction and experience. As we step into the realm of "UI Component Planning with AI," we embrace the synergy of design principles and AI-driven insights. This segment is dedicated to transforming our UI design approach, making it not only visually appealing but also intuitively functional. AI's role in this transformation is not just supportive but pivotal, offering a fresh perspective on how components can be crafted, structured, and optimized. Ready to explore how AI can elevate our UI components to new heights? Let's delve into the best practices and AI enhancements that will shape our dashboard's user interface.

Best Practices for UI Component Planning in Angular

When designing UI components in Angular, it's crucial to adopt a structured and strategic approach. A well-planned component structure enhances maintainability, scalability, and user experience. Here are some best practices:

- **Component Modularity**

  - Design components to be modular and reusable. Each component should have a single responsibility, making the application easier to manage and scale.

- **State Management**

  - Implement efficient state management strategies to ensure smooth data flow and component interaction, enhancing the user experience.

- **Responsive Design**

  - Ensure your components are responsive, providing an optimal user experience across different devices and screen sizes.

- **Performance Optimization**

  - Pay attention to performance bottlenecks. Use strategies like lazy loading and change detection strategies to optimize your application's performance.

- **Consistent Styling**

  - Maintain consistency in styling and theming across your components to ensure a cohesive look and feel.

Next, we'll explore how AI can assist in achieving these best practices, offering insights and automation to refine our UI design process.

Leveraging AI for Enhanced UI Design in Angular

AI has the potential to significantly enhance the UI design process, offering insights that lead to more intuitive and efficient user interfaces. Here's how AI can contribute:

- **Automated Layout Design**

  - AI can analyze user interaction data to suggest optimal component placement, ensuring an intuitive layout that enhances user experience.

- **Personalization**

  - AI can tailor the UI by learning individual user preferences and behaviors, offering a personalized experience for each user.

- **Accessibility Enhancements**

  - AI can ensure that UI components meet accessibility standards, making the application usable for people with a wide range of abilities.

- **Predictive UI Adjustments**

  - AI can predict user actions and preload resources or data, making the application feel faster and more responsive.

- **Visual Consistency Analysis**

  - AI can analyze the UI for visual consistency, ensuring that the styling is coherent across the application.

Next, we'll demonstrate these AI capabilities in a practical setting through a simulated technical conversation between a developer and GPT:

Developer: "I'm facing performance issues with my Angular app, particularly when rendering complex data-bound components. How can I optimize this?"

GPT (AI Angular Expert): "Consider implementing trackBy in your *ngFor to prevent unnecessary DOM manipulations. Also, evaluate your change detection strategy; OnPush can significantly reduce the number of checks performed."

Developer: "I've tried that, but I'm still seeing delays. Could there be an issue with data retrieval?"

GPT (AI Angular Expert): "It's possible. Ensure your data retrieval methods are optimized. Use RxJS operators like debounceTime or distinctUntilChanged to manage rapid user inputs effectively. Also, consider server-side pagination or virtual scrolling for large datasets to reduce front-end load."

Developer: "Great advice! How about ensuring the UI components are responsive and accessible?"

GPT (AI Angular Expert): "For responsiveness, use Angular Flex Layout for a flexible and responsive design. For accessibility, ensure you're using ARIA roles and attributes correctly. Testing with tools like Lighthouse can provide insights into potential accessibility issues."

This conversation provides a glimpse into how AI can offer practical, technical solutions to improve performance, responsiveness, and accessibility in Angular UI component design.

As we wrap up the segment on Architectural Design with AI Assistance, it's clear that AI's role is transformative. From shaping robust database designs to structuring APIs and planning UI components, AI has proven to be an invaluable ally. This journey has not only enriched our understanding but has also laid a solid foundation for our AI Dashboard. Ready to transition from the realm of planning to actualizing these designs? Let's venture into the next crucial phase: Database Designing, where our structures and relationships come to life.

Creating Tasks Under the User Story 1: Architectural Blueprint for AI Dashboard

As we pivot from the architectural design discussions to practical implementation, it's time to translate our blueprint into actionable tasks. Under the User Story titled "Architectural Blueprint for AI Dashboard," let's create four distinct tasks, each dedicated to a pivotal aspect of our dashboard's architecture:

- **Task: Database Architecture Design**

  - **Description**: Outline the architectural structure of the database, focusing on how data will be organized and accessed for the AI Dashboard.

- **Task: API Architecture Planning**

  - **Description**: Plan the architecture of the APIs, defining how they will interact with the database and UI components, ensuring efficient and secure data communication.

- **Task: UI Architecture Design**

  - **Description**: Design the architectural framework of the UI components, detailing how they will render data and interact with backend services.

- **Task: Architectural Integration**

  - **Description**: Plan the integration of the database, APIs, and UI components, ensuring they function cohesively and align with the overall architectural blueprint.

As these tasks are set into motion, let's move them into the "Active" state and mark our User Story as "Active" too, solidifying our commitment to transforming our architectural blueprint into a functional AI Dashboard. After this your board might look like Figure 13-1.

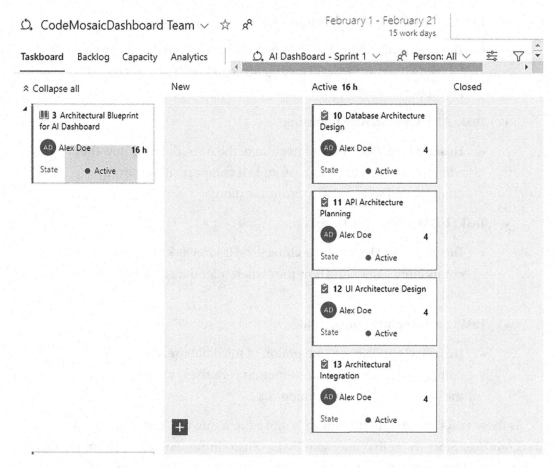

Figure 13-1. *Create tasks*

Database Designing

In the fabric of a data-driven application like our AI Dashboard, the database is not merely a storage unit but the core that holds and reflects the intricate patterns of AI's impact on software development. This segment on Database Designing is dedicated to meticulously structuring our database to effectively encapsulate and represent the vast array of data, ensuring not only the integrity of data storage but also its seamless flow and accessibility. As we embark on this crucial phase, we leverage both our understanding of data relationships and the prowess of AI to architect a database that's not just functional but insightful and future-ready.

Preparing the Database Design for the AI Dashboard

As we lay the groundwork for our AI Dashboard's database, our focus is on clarity, efficiency, and relevance. The goal is to craft a database that not only stores our data but also mirrors the intricate dynamics of AI in software development. Here's how we envision structuring our database:

1. **Database Name: AIDashboardDB**—A central repository encapsulating the impact of AI on software development projects.

2. **Primary Table—ProjectMetrics:**

   a. This table will be the heartbeat of our dashboard, holding key metrics that reflect AI's influence on various projects.

3. Columns and Data Types:

   a. **ProjectID** (INT, Primary Key): Unique identifier for each project.

   b. **ProjectName** (VARCHAR): Name of the software project.

   c. **AIIntegrationLevel** (VARCHAR): Categorizes the level of AI integration (e.g., None, Partial, Full).

   d. **EfficiencyImprovement** (FLOAT): Percentage improvement in development efficiency due to AI.

   e. **FeatureCount** (INT): Total number of features in the project.

   f. **AIDrivenFeatureCount** (INT): Number of features developed or enhanced by AI.

   g. **BugCountBeforeAI** (INT): Number of bugs before AI integration.

   h. **BugCountAfterAI** (INT): Number of bugs after AI integration.

   i. **DevelopmentTimeBeforeAI** (INT): Development time in days before AI integration.

   j. **DevelopmentTimeAfterAI** (INT): Development time in days after AI integration.

k. **AI_Technology_Used** (VARCHAR): Specific AI tools or technologies implemented.

l. **AI_Impact_Area** (VARCHAR): Area of software development impacted by AI (e.g., Code Quality, Project Management).

4. Key Considerations:

a. **Primary Key:** Ensures each project's data remains unique and identifiable.

b. **Data Types:** Carefully chosen to reflect the nature of the data and optimize storage.

c. **Normalization:** The table is designed to minimize redundancy and ensure data integrity.

Next, we'll discuss how AI can assist in determining the optimal column types and data structures to further refine our database design.

AI in Database Design

Incorporating AI in database design can lead to significant enhancements and optimizations. Here's how AI can assist, along with potential prompts for AI interaction:

1. Schema Optimization

a. **Detail:** AI can analyze data patterns to suggest an optimal database schema, ensuring efficient data storage and retrieval.

b. **AI Prompt:** "Suggest an optimal schema for a software project database focusing on AI impact metrics."

2. Data Integrity Enhancement

a. **Detail:** AI can predict data anomalies and recommend constraints to maintain data integrity.

b. **AI Prompt:** "Identify potential data anomalies in software development metrics and suggest database constraints to prevent them."

3. Scalability Planning

   a. **Detail:** AI can forecast data growth and recommend scalable database structures like sharding or partitioning.

   b. **AI Prompt:** "Based on projected growth, recommend a scalable structure for the AI Dashboard database."

4. Automated Data Type Recommendations

   a. **Detail:** AI can analyze data characteristics and suggest appropriate data types for each column to optimize performance and storage.

   b. **AI Prompt:** "Analyze the dataset and recommend data types for each column in the AI Dashboard database."

5. Visualization Assistance

   a. **Detail:** AI can assist in planning the database structure by suggesting a visualization approach, like ER diagrams or data flow diagrams.

   b. **AI Prompt:** "Suggest a visualization approach for representing the relationships and flow in the AI Dashboard database."

6. Performance Tuning

   a. **Detail:** AI can assess query performance and suggest indexing or query optimization techniques.

   b. **AI Prompt:** "Analyze query patterns and suggest optimization techniques for the AI Dashboard database."

These prompts and AI's capabilities can be leveraged to ensure that the database design is not only robust and efficient but also intelligently aligned with the specific needs of the AI Dashboard.

Visualization

Creating a visual representation of our database structure is crucial for understanding the relationships and the overall design. A diagram can provide a clear, concise view of our tables, their fields, and the primary key, aiding in comprehending the database's role in our AI Dashboard.

For the AIDashboardDB with the ProjectMetrics table, your PlantUML code might look something like Figure 13-2:

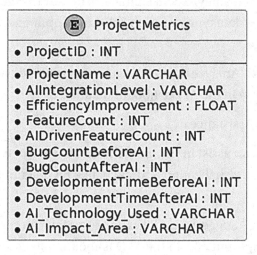

Figure 13-2. *Project metrics table structure*

Visualizing our database structure provides a clear, intuitive understanding of the data we're working with. It's a foundational step in ensuring that our AI Dashboard is built on a robust, well-organized database, setting the stage for the dynamic and insightful data presentation we aim to achieve. With this structured visualization, we're ready to move forward confidently, knowing that our database design aligns perfectly with our project's goals.

API Architecture Planning

As we embark on the meticulous journey of API design for our AI Dashboard, it's imperative to reflect on the insights garnered from our previous AI-assisted brainstorming sessions. These discussions have not only illuminated the path to crafting APIs that resonate with our dashboard's dynamic requirements but also underscored the importance of a design that speaks the language of efficiency, security, and user-centricity. Our APIs, DataGridAPI, PieChartAPI, and StackedBarChartAPI, are set to become the lifelines of our dashboard, each responsible for orchestrating the flow of data to its destined visual component. This section is dedicated to transforming these conceptual blueprints into detailed, structured, and well-orchestrated API designs, ensuring that every data interaction is a step toward insightful and interactive user experiences.

DataGridAPI Design: Detailed View

- **Purpose and Business Logic**

    - DataGridAPI serves as the primary conduit for detailed project data, essential for the grid component in our AI Dashboard. It meticulously retrieves project metrics, ensuring users can interact with a rich, informative dataset. This API is engineered to deliver precision and speed, embodying the principle of bringing data to life.

- **API Structure and Interaction**

    - Rooted in robust business logic, DataGridAPI meticulously structures requests, ensuring optimal data retrieval. It's a harmonious blend of technology and strategy, reflecting our commitment to a seamless user experience.

- **Design Diagram**

    - Here's an enriched sequence diagram, offering a deeper insight into the API's operational narrative, including business logic layers.

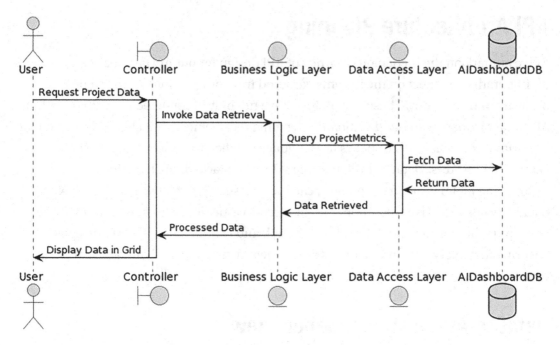

Figure 13-3. *Sequence diagram—API—DataGrid*

Figure 13-3 intricately illustrates the journey of a data request through the layers of DataGridAPI. From the user's request to the final presentation in the grid, each interaction is carefully choreographed. The Business Logic Layer and Data Access Layer encapsulate the core operations, ensuring that data retrieval is not just a transaction but a testament to our system's efficiency and intelligence.

PieChartAPI Design: Detailed View

- **Purpose and Business Logic**

  - The PieChartAPI is intricately designed to extract and process data for visual representation in a pie chart. It aims to offer insights into the distribution of AI integration levels across various projects. By aggregating and categorizing data, this API paints a vivid picture of AI's role in enhancing software development practices.

- **API Structure and Interaction**

  - The PieChartAPI is adept at handling complex data aggregation and transformation, ensuring that the end result is not just data but actionable insights, presented in an engaging, visually appealing pie chart format.

- **Design Diagram**

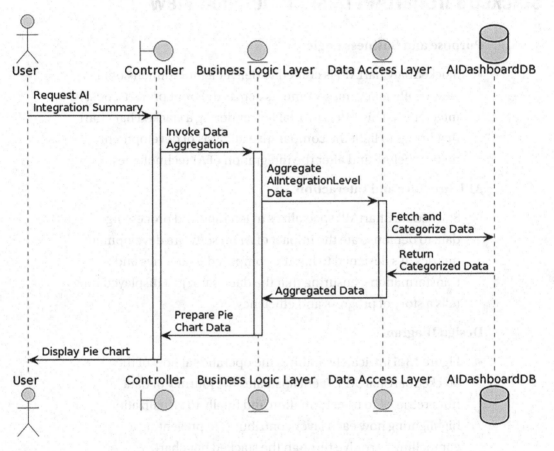

Figure 13-4. *Sequence diagram—API—pie chart*

- Figure 13-4 meticulously captures the flow from user request to pie chart visualization. It highlights the layers involved in data aggregation and processing, ensuring that the PieChartAPI not only serves data but also enhances the interpretability and visual appeal of the information presented.

- PieChartAPI, with its strategic design and visualization, reinforces the narrative that our AI Dashboard is not just about data presentation; it's about storytelling through data. It exemplifies our commitment to providing a platform where data is not merely seen but experienced and understood.

StackedBarChartAPI Design: Detailed View

- **Purpose and Business Logic**

  - StackedBarChartAPI is crafted to deliver a multidimensional view of efficiency improvements across different projects, post AI integration. This API is pivotal for rendering a stacked bar chart that brings to light the comparative analysis of development metrics before and after the integration of AI technologies.

- **API Structure and Interaction**

  - StackedBarChartAPI specializes in fetching and processing data to demonstrate the impact of AI on software development metrics. It's designed to handle complex data queries and transformations, ensuring that the data is not just displayed but tells a story of progress and efficiency.

- **Design Diagram**

  - Figure 13-5 intricately outlines the operational flow of the StackedBarChartAPI. It encapsulates the journey of data from retrieval to transformation and finally to visualization, highlighting how each layer contributes to presenting a compelling narrative through the stacked bar chart.

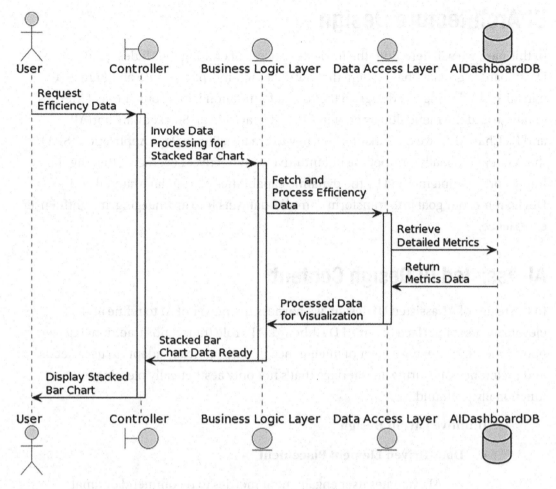

Figure 13-5. *Sequence diagram—API—StackedChart*

StackedBarChartAPI is a testament to our commitment to not just present data but to narrate the transformative power of AI in software development. It ensures that every bar in the chart is a story of progress, a marker of efficiency, and a testament to AI's role in shaping the future of software development.

UI Architecture Design

In this part, we will delve into the intricate process of crafting the UI design for our AI Dashboard, a crucial phase where the raw data metamorphoses into an interactive narrative. Anchoring our design in the robust foundation laid by our "Project Metrics" database and the meticulously crafted APIs—DataGridAPI, StackedBarChartAPI, and PieChartAPI—we embark on a journey to create a Single Page Application (SPA) that's not just visually compelling but intuitively interactive. Leveraging the Angular framework, complemented by the dynamic capabilities of Angular Material and DevExtreme, our goal is to transform complex datasets into an engaging, insightful user experience.

AI-Assisted UI Design Content

In the realm of AI-assisted UI design, we harness the power of AI to refine and elevate the user interface of our AI Dashboard. AI's role transcends traditional design boundaries, introducing a layer of intelligence that dynamically adapts to user needs and preferences, ensuring an interface that's not only aesthetically pleasing but also functionally profound.

- **Intuitive Layout Design**

  - **Data-Driven Element Placement**

    - AI evaluates user engagement metrics to recommend optimal placement for interactive elements like buttons or charts.

    - **Example GPT Prompt:** "Given user interaction heatmaps, suggest a layout that maximizes visibility for key components."

  - **User Flow Optimization**

    - AI assesses navigation patterns to streamline user journeys, minimizing clicks and enhancing the overall flow.

    - **Example GPT Prompt:** "Analyze user navigation logs and propose a layout that simplifies the user journey."

- **Dynamic Content Personalization**

  - **Behavior-Based Content Adjustment**

    - AI customizes content presentation based on individual user behaviors, ensuring relevance and engagement.

    - **Example GPT Prompt:** "How can I tailor content display based on a user's past interactions and preferences?"

  - **Real-Time Content Adaptation**

    - AI modifies content in real-time, responding to user actions for a personalized, dynamic experience.

    - **Example GPT Prompt:** "Suggest a method to dynamically adjust dashboard content based on ongoing user interactions."

- **Responsive and Adaptive Interface**

  - **Cross-Device Consistency**

    - AI ensures the interface maintains functionality and aesthetic across different devices and screen sizes.

    - **Example GPT Prompt:** "Recommend best practices for maintaining UI consistency across various devices."

  - **Adaptive Layouts:**

    - AI facilitates the creation of layouts that adapt to different orientations and resolutions without losing coherence.

    - **Example GPT Prompt:** "What are some AI-driven strategies for crafting adaptive UI layouts?"

- **Predictive User Experience Enhancements**

  - **Anticipatory Design Elements**

    - AI predicts user needs and pre-loads resources or adjusts the interface to streamline the experience.

    - **Example GPT Prompt:** "How can AI anticipate user needs to preload resources and enhance responsiveness?"

- **Proactive Interaction Suggestions**

  - AI suggests interactions or content based on predictive analysis, making the experience feel intuitive and natural.

    - **Example GPT Prompt:** "Can AI suggest user interactions proactively based on their behavior patterns?"

- **Automated Aesthetic and Functional Adjustments**

  - **Continuous Design Improvement**

    - AI monitors UI performance and user feedback to suggest iterative design enhancements.

      - **Example GPT Prompt:** "How can AI analyze user feedback to suggest UI improvements?"

  - **Aesthetic Harmony and Functional Efficiency**

    - AI ensures that UI changes uphold aesthetic harmony and improve functional efficiency simultaneously.

      - **Example GPT Prompt:** "Propose a method for AI to balance aesthetic and functional aspects in UI design."

These detailed points and example prompts should guide the conversation with AI effectively, ensuring a rich, insightful dialogue on AI-assisted UI design.

Example GPT Conversation for UI Design

Developer: "I'm finalizing the UI for our AI Dashboard SPA. I plan to display data using a DataGrid from Angular Material and charts from DevExtreme. How should I structure the components for optimal integration and user experience?"

GPT (AI Design Expert): "A master component approach can be effective for your SPA. You can have a single parent component housing the grid and charts. This centralizes your API calls and data processing, ensuring a cohesive flow of information."

Developer: "Sounds efficient. Should I be aware of any considerations when using DevExtreme for the charts?"

GPT (AI Design Expert): "DevExtreme offers rich charting capabilities, perfect for your needs. However, keep in mind that it's a premium tool, so plan for potential costs in commercial projects. For the grid, Angular Material is a robust, free alternative that integrates well with Angular."

Developer: "Great! And how can I ensure the SPA remains responsive and user-friendly across different devices?"

GPT (AI Design Expert): "Ensure your master component is responsive by using flexible layouts and media queries. Test the SPA across different devices and screen sizes. Also, optimize data handling in your API interactions to maintain smooth performance."

This conversation guides the efficient structuring of UI components and the thoughtful integration of tools like Angular Material and DevExtreme, balancing functionality, aesthetics, and cost considerations.

Visualization of UI Structure

Figure 13-6 represents the UI structure of our AI Dashboard SPA. The **MasterComponent** is the central element, integrating the Angular Material DataGrid, DevExtreme PieChart, and DevExtreme StackedBarChart. Each chart and grid component is fueled by its respective API, ensuring a data-driven, interactive experience. The **DataGridAPI**, **PieChartAPI**, and **StackedBarChartAPI** are visually represented as feeding data directly into the **MasterComponent**, illustrating the seamless data flow and cohesive component interaction within the SPA.

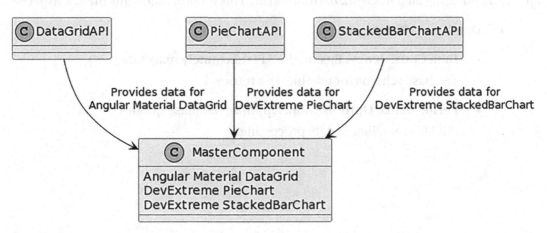

Figure 13-6. *UI component interaction*

In this section, we've navigated the intricate landscape of UI design, ensuring our AI Dashboard is not just functional but visually engaging. Leveraging AI insights, we've crafted a master component that harmoniously integrates Angular Material and DevExtreme, showcasing data through a grid and dynamic charts. The detailed visualization encapsulates this synergy, illustrating a design that's intuitive, responsive, and tailored to deliver an unparalleled user experience. This meticulous approach sets a new standard for UI design, highlighting the transformative power of AI in crafting user-centric interfaces.

Integrating Design Components

In the realm of creating an AI Dashboard, integrating design components is paramount. This stage is about bringing together the meticulously crafted database, APIs, and UI components into a seamless, efficient whole. It's crucial to view these components not as isolated entities but as interconnected parts of a unified system. This holistic approach ensures that every data interaction and user experience is coherent, fluid, and in harmony with the overarching goal of the dashboard: to provide insightful, interactive visual narratives based on AI-driven data.

Integration of Design Components

Integrating the design components of our AI Dashboard requires a comprehensive approach, ensuring all parts work harmoniously. This section highlights the key aspects:

- **Database-API Integration**

  - **Data Consistency:** Ensure the APIs accurately reflect the database schema for reliable data retrieval.

  - **Performance Optimization:** Optimize database queries within the APIs for efficient data processing.

- **API-UI Integration**

  - **Data Representation:** APIs should deliver data in a format readily consumable by the UI components, facilitating smooth data rendering.

  - Responsiveness: Design APIs to respond swiftly, ensuring UI components update dynamically without lag.

- **Unified System Overview**

  - **Seamless Interaction:** All components should interact seamlessly, presenting a unified frontend experience backed by robust API and database designs.

  - **Error Handling:** Implement comprehensive error handling mechanisms across the layers to maintain system integrity during unexpected scenarios.

Understanding and implementing these integration aspects ensure a fluid, responsive, and user-friendly AI Dashboard.

Visualization of the Entire Application

We can see in Figure 13-7 a detailed design that represents the high-level architecture of your AI Dashboard application. This image illustrates the integration between the database, the three APIs (DataGridAPI, PieChartAPI, StackedBarChartAPI), the Angular services, and the master Angular component along with the interactions with Angular Material and DevExtreme components.

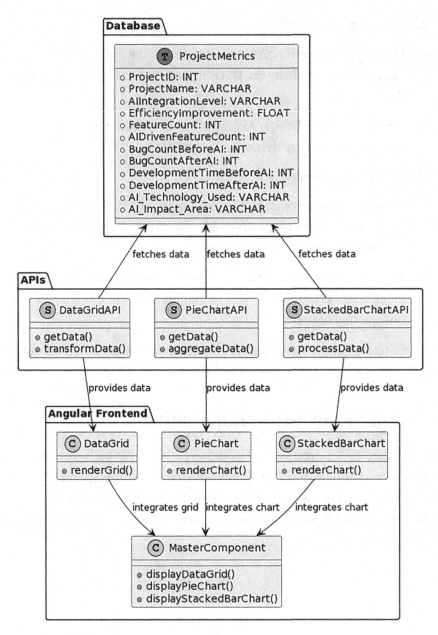

Figure 13-7. *Complete high-level visualization*

Figure 13-7 represents the high-level architecture of your AI Dashboard, where

- **ProjectMetrics** is the main table in your database.

- **DataGridAPI**, **PieChartAPI**, and **StackedBarChartAPI** are the services that fetch and process data from **ProjectMetrics**.

- **MasterComponent** is the main Angular component that integrates the data grid, pie chart, and stacked bar chart.

- **DataGrid**, **PieChart**, and **StackedBarChart** are individual components responsible for rendering the respective UI elements. They receive data from their respective APIs and are integrated into the **MasterComponent**.

Please note that this is a high-level representation and may require adjustments based on the specific details of your implementation.

Note   This diagram offers a basic representation of the AI Dashboard's architecture. When working on actual projects, the specific design may vary significantly. Factors influencing these variations include the architectural pattern adopted, visual standards of the project, and technology stack differences. This visualization serves as a foundational guideline, and adaptations may be necessary to align with the unique requirements of each project. Always consider project-specific contexts when interpreting or utilizing this diagram.

Conclusion

As we conclude this chapter, we reflect on the intricate journey of designing the AI Dashboard. From the initial sketches of our database structure to the fine-tuning of API designs and the thoughtful crafting of the UI, each step was pivotal. Integrating AI into our design process didn't just add a layer of intelligence; it transformed our approach, making it more data-driven, efficient, and user-centric.

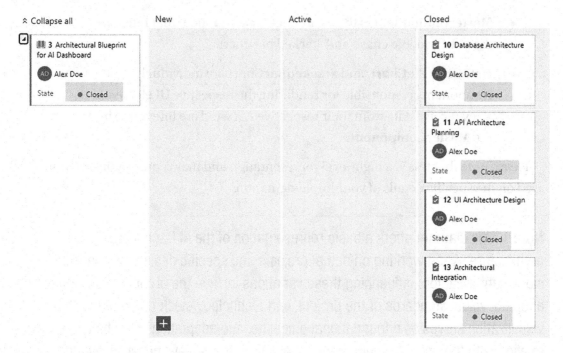

Figure 13-8. *Completed tasks*

The successful completion of the tasks under our first user story, "Architectural Blueprint for AI Dashboard" as in Figure 13-8, signifies more than just checked boxes. It represents a comprehensive understanding and a solid foundation upon which we will build our application. The visualization of the completed tasks and the closed user story in our Agile board is not just a testament to the work done but a reaffirmation of the methodical and strategic approach we've adopted.

Key Takeaways

- **AI as a Design Partner:** The seamless integration of AI in the design process, from database structuring to UI crafting, exemplifies the transformative potential of AI in software development.

- **Holistic Approach:** The journey underscored the importance of viewing the database, APIs, and UI components not as isolated entities but as integral parts of a cohesive system.

- **Efficiency and Scalability:** The discussions and designs reiterated the need for efficiency in data management and scalability in application architecture.

As we move forward, the tasks accomplished here lay a robust groundwork for the subsequent phases of our project. The insights gained, the structures created, and the integration achieved set a precedent for the chapters to come.

Onward

As we conclude our journey through the meticulous design process of our AI Dashboard, we stand at the threshold of our next venture: "Mosaic Tile 3: Data Dynamics." This chapter, which aligns with our subsequent user story, will navigate the nuanced terrains of data collection strategies, database design refined by AI insights, and the pivotal practices of ethical data handling.

Embarking on this next chapter means not just theorizing but actualizing our database structure within Azure SQL. We'll transform our blueprint into reality, meticulously crafting our "ProjectMetrics" table and ensuring our data is not just stored but poised to tell a compelling story of AI's impact in software development. Let's dive deep into the realms of data dynamics, where each byte holds the potential to drive innovation and efficiency in our AI Dashboard.

CHAPTER 14

Mosaic Tile 3: Data Dynamics

As we progress on our journey through CodeMosaic, we approach a pivotal phase: Data Dynamics. This chapter, dedicated to Database Design and Data Management, marks the commencement of our second user story. Our focus is not just on the mechanics of database creation but on establishing a robust data infrastructure that resonates with the needs of our AI Dashboard. Here, we don't just handle data; we sculpt it, ensuring it's structured, meaningful, and ready to empower our APIs and visualization components. The user story ahead, "Database Design and Data Management," aims to craft a solid foundation, setting the stage for seamless API integration and insightful data visualization.

Setting Up Tasks for User Story: Database Design and Data Management

To ensure a structured approach to our user story, let's outline the tasks that will guide our journey through database design and data management:

- **Setting Up with Azure**
    - **Description:** Initialize our journey by leveraging Azure's free trial, ensuring we have the necessary environment set up for our database creation and management.
- **Database Creation and Management in Azure SQL**
    - **Description:** Create and configure our database within Azure SQL, setting the stage for a robust and scalable data management system.

367

© Arpit Dwivedi 2024
A. Dwivedi, *CodeMosaic*, https://doi.org/10.1007/979-8-8688-0276-8_14

- **Crafting the Database Structure**

  - **Description:** Design the structure of our primary database, focusing on creating a schema that accurately reflects the needs of our AI Dashboard.

- **Data Insertion and Manipulation**

  - **Description:** Populate our database with relevant data, ensuring it's ready for interaction with our upcoming APIs.

- **Creating Stored Procedures**

  - **Description:** Establish efficient and secure procedures for data retrieval, aligning our database operations with best practices and performance standards.

After setting it all up, you can move the story to "Active," and your board should look like Figure 14-1.

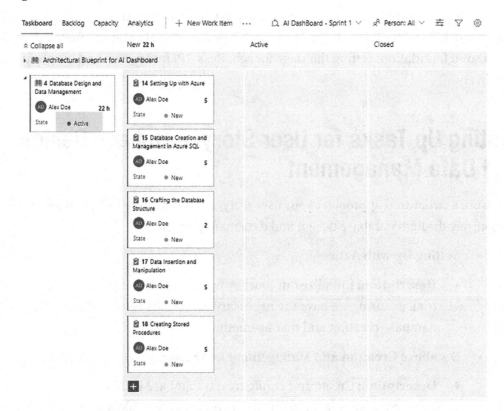

Figure 14-1. *User story 2—tasks*

Each task is a step toward realizing our user story, ensuring that every aspect of database design and management is executed with precision and foresight, you can keep on moving the tasks to Active and Closed when you are starting with it, similar to the User Story. Let's embark on this detailed journey, where every task brings us closer to a data infrastructure that's not just functional but insightful and aligned with our AI Dashboard's vision.

Best Practices in Data Management

In this pivotal segment of our journey, we delve into the essence of effective data management, specifically focusing on structured databases like SQL. As we navigate through the complex landscape of data dynamics, our emphasis lies on establishing practices that uphold data integrity, fortify security, and optimize data retrieval. These best practices are not just guidelines but the keystones that ensure our database's robustness and reliability, especially within the Azure SQL environment. Let's explore these practices, understanding their significance, the common pitfalls they help avoid, and how AI can aid us in adhering to these standards.

- **Regular Database Backups**
  - **Description:** Maintaining frequent backups to prevent data loss.
  - **Common Problem:** Risk of data loss due to unexpected incidents.
  - **Solution:** Implement automated backup routines in Azure SQL.
  - **AI Prompt:** "Suggest a schedule and strategy for database backups in Azure SQL."
- **Proper Indexing**
  - **Description:** Utilizing indexes to speed up data retrieval.
  - **Common Problem:** Slow query responses, impacting application performance.
  - **Solution:** Analyze query patterns and create efficient indexes.
  - **AI Prompt:** "Identify which tables and columns in the database would benefit most from indexing."

- **Data Validation**

  - **Description:** Ensuring data integrity through validation checks.

  - **Common Problem:** Inaccurate data leading to unreliable analytics.

  - **Solution:** Implement validation rules at both database and application levels.

  - **AI Prompt:** "Generate a list of essential validation rules for maintaining data integrity."

- **Secure Connection Strings**

  - **Description:** Protecting database credentials and connection strings.

  - **Common Problem:** Exposure of sensitive data, leading to security breaches.

  - **Solution:** Use Azure Key Vault to securely manage connection strings and credentials.

  - **AI Prompt:** "Outline best practices for managing database connection strings securely in Azure."

- **Efficient Query Design**

  - **Description:** Crafting queries that maximize performance and minimize load.

  - **Common Problem:** Inefficient queries that strain database resources.

  - **Solution:** Optimize query structure and consider using stored procedures for complex operations.

  - **AI Prompt:** "Analyze the current query patterns and suggest optimizations for efficiency."

- **Monitoring and Performance Tuning**

  - **Description:** Continuously monitoring database performance and tuning configurations.

  - **Common Problem:** Unaddressed performance bottlenecks leading to suboptimal operations.

  - **Solution:** Utilize Azure SQL's performance insights and adjust configurations as needed.

  - **AI Prompt:** "Provide a monitoring strategy to identify performance bottlenecks in real-time."

- **Scalability Considerations**

  - **Description:** Designing the database with future growth and scalability in mind.

  - **Common Problem:** Inability to handle increased load or data volume efficiently.

  - **Solution:** Plan for scalability using Azure SQL's elastic pool and other scalable features.

  - **AI Prompt:** "Recommend strategies to ensure the database remains scalable as the project grows."

- **Data Encryption and Security**

  - **Description:** Implementing measures to secure data at rest and in transit.

  - **Common Problem:** Vulnerability to data breaches and unauthorized access.

  - **Solution:** Use Azure's built-in encryption capabilities to secure data.

  - **AI Prompt:** "Suggest comprehensive data encryption strategies for data at rest and in transit."

These practices, complemented by AI's analytical prowess, form the bedrock of a secure, efficient, and reliable database structure. As we meticulously integrate these practices into our database design and management, we fortify our AI Dashboard's data infrastructure, ensuring it's not just robust but also intelligent and forward-thinking.

AI's Role in Data Management

In the rapidly evolving realm of data management, Artificial Intelligence (AI) emerges as a transformative force, streamlining complex tasks, injecting efficiency, and ushering in a new era of automated database maintenance and optimization. From crafting intricate SQL scripts to refining stored procedures, AI's role is pivotal, ensuring data integrity, enhancing performance, and facilitating insightful decision-making processes. Some Key Areas and AI Prompts for them:

- **Scripting and Query Optimization**

  - **Detail:** AI can scrutinize query patterns, suggest optimization strategies, and automate script generation for routine tasks, ensuring performance and accuracy.

  - **AI Prompt:** "Provide optimization suggestions for this SQL query to enhance performance and reduce execution time."

- **Automated Query Writing**

  - **Detail:** AI can convert high-level requirements or data schemas into precise SQL queries, bridging the gap between conceptual design and database interaction.

  - **AI Prompt:** "Generate a SQL query to retrieve data based on this schema and specified conditions."

- **Sheet-to-SQL Conversion**

  - **Detail:** AI effortlessly transforms data sheets into SQL insertion queries, streamlining the data migration process.

  - **AI Prompt:** "Convert this data sheet into a series of SQL insertion queries, ensuring data integrity and proper formatting."

- **Stored Procedure Creation and Refinement**

  - **Detail:** AI can dissect complex stored procedures, offering insights for refinement, modularization, and performance enhancement.

  - **AI Prompt:** "Analyze and suggest improvements for this stored procedure to enhance efficiency and maintainability."

- **Query Performance Tuning**

  - **Detail:** AI evaluates query performance, recommending indexing strategies and structural adjustments for optimal database interaction.

  - **AI Prompt:** "Assess this query's performance and suggest indexing or structural changes for optimization."

- **Legacy Code Interpretation**

  - **Detail:** AI navigates through legacy stored procedures, elucidating the logic, and proposing modernization strategies for contemporary database environments.

  - **AI Prompt:** "Interpret and suggest modernization strategies for this legacy stored procedure."

- **Database Design Visualization**

  - **Detail:** AI assists in visualizing database structures, offering intuitive representations like ER diagrams or data flow diagrams for better understanding and analysis.

  - **AI Prompt:** "Generate a visual representation for this database schema to illustrate table relationships and data flow."

- **Intelligent Data Anomaly Detection**

  - **Detail:** AI proactively monitors data patterns, identifying anomalies or inconsistencies, and suggesting corrective actions to uphold data quality.

  - **AI Prompt:** "Identify potential data anomalies in this dataset and suggest preventive measures."

- **Automated Data Validation**

  - **Detail:** AI enforces data validation rules, ensuring data entered into the database meets predefined standards and formats.

  - **AI Prompt:** "Suggest data validation rules for this table schema to ensure data quality and consistency."

- **Adaptive Query Caching**

  - **Detail:** AI predicts data access patterns, recommending adaptive caching strategies to expedite data retrieval and reduce load on the database.

  - **AI Prompt:** "Recommend caching strategies for frequently accessed data in this database to improve retrieval times and reduce server load."

Through these strategic interventions, AI not only simplifies the data management landscape but also ensures that database systems are more intelligent, responsive, and aligned with organizational objectives. By harnessing AI's capabilities, database administrators and developers can expect a shift toward more proactive, predictive, and automated data management practices.

Setting Up with Azure

Azure, Microsoft's cloud platform, offers a comprehensive suite of services to build, deploy, and manage applications. For our AI Dashboard project, Azure's SQL Database service will be instrumental. In this section, we guide you through the initial steps of setting up with Azure, leveraging the free trial, and navigating potential pitfalls.

- Accessing Azure:

  - Navigate to **portal.azure.com**.

  - Use the same Microsoft account as you did for Azure DevOps (dev.azure.com) to ensure seamless integration and management.

- Understanding Azure's Free Trial:

  - Azure offers a generous $200 credit for the first 30 days and 12 months of popular free services.

  - This trial is an excellent opportunity to explore and utilize Azure services without upfront costs.

- Activating Your Azure Free Trial:

  - Locate the "Start with an Azure free trial" section upon logging in. It could look something like Figure 14-2.

Start with an Azure free trial

Get $200 free credit toward Azure products and services, plus 12 months of popular free services.

Figure 14-2. *Azure free trial*

  - Click on Start and follow the prompts to activate your trial, which includes entering payment details for account verification. Once done, you'll see a page like Figure 14-3.

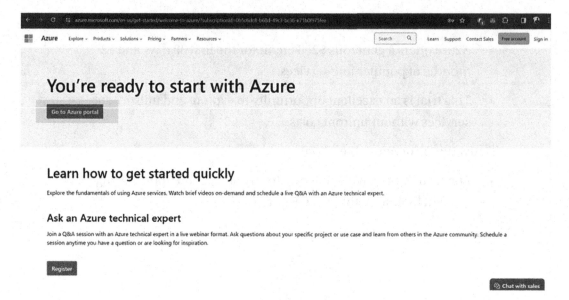

Figure 14-3. *Start with Azure*

Click on "Go to Azure Portal."

- **Note:** Be vigilant with service usage. Ensure you understand the billing and usage policies to avoid unintended charges.

- Navigating to SQL Databases:

- Once in the Azure portal, search for "SQL databases" in the marketplace or navigate through the resource categories as in Figure 14-4.

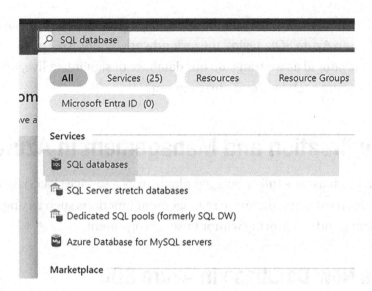

Figure 14-4. *Search SQL*

- Familiarize yourself with the interface and options available for SQL database services.

- Note: It could happen that after selecting SQL Database, you still see the Start for free Page; in this case, please sign out and sign in again.

Cautions and Best Practices

- While the Azure free trial is an excellent resource, it's essential to monitor your service usage.

- Regularly check the usage and cost estimates in the Azure portal to avoid surpassing the free credit limit.

- Be proactive in shutting down or deallocating resources when not in use, as some services might incur costs even when idle.

- Remember, the free trial is your sandbox. Explore, learn, and experiment, but do so with an awareness of the trial's terms and conditions.

In the next section, we'll delve into the specifics of database creation and management within Azure SQL, laying the groundwork for our AI Dashboard's data infrastructure. Stay tuned as we translate our database design into a live, operational structure within Azure's robust cloud environment.

Database Creation and Management in Azure SQL

The Azure SQL Database is a fully managed platform as a service (PaaS) database engine. It handles most of the database management functions such as upgrading, patching, backups, and monitoring without user involvement.

Creating a New Database in Azure SQL

- **Navigate to the Azure Portal:** Log in to your Azure account and go to the SQL databases service.

- **Create a New Database**

  - Click on "Add" to create a new database as in Figure 14-5.

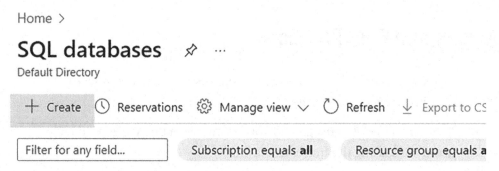

Figure 14-5. *Create new database*

- You'll be prompted to fill in details such as database name, server, and pricing tier.

- Since you might be logging in for first time, and might not have a server and resource group, so you might get error as in Figure 14-6.

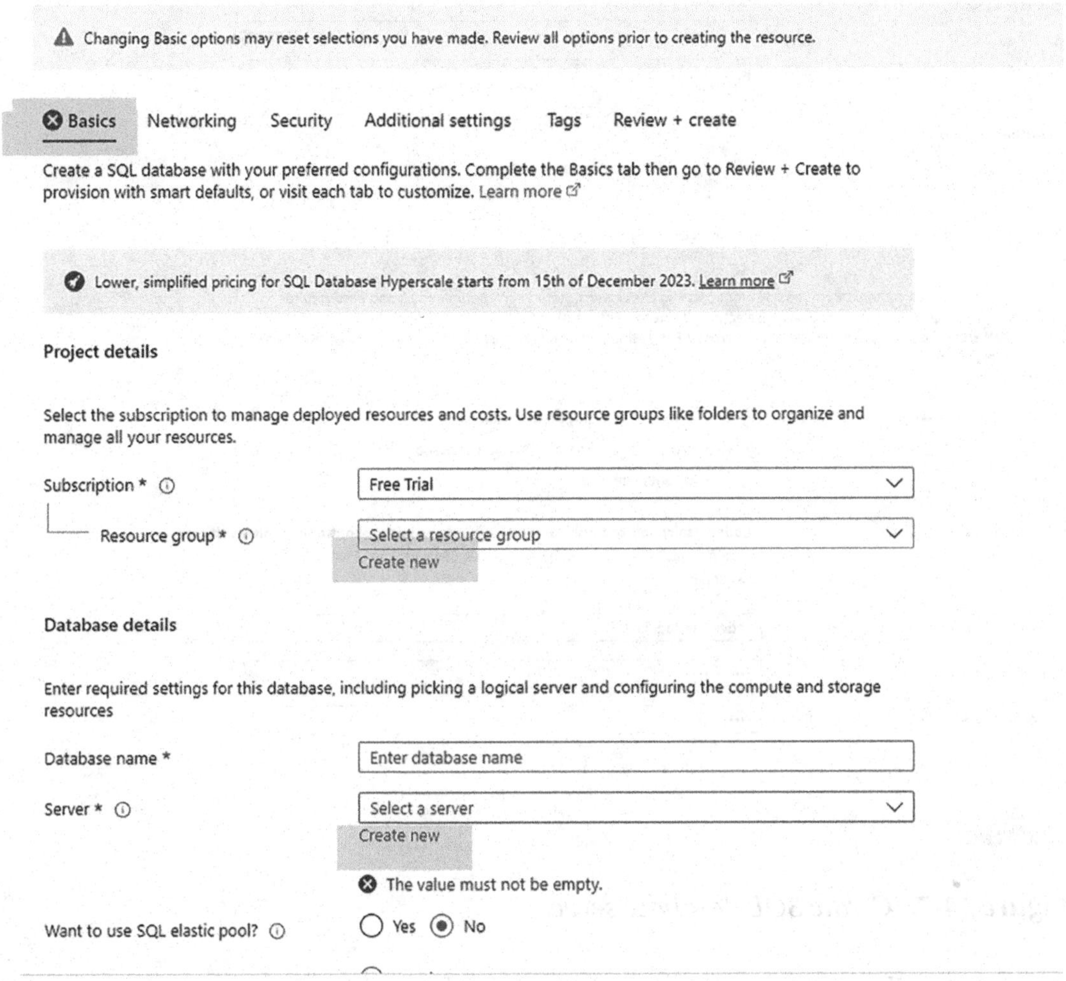

⚠ Changing Basic options may reset selections you have made. Review all options prior to creating the resource.

❌ **Basics**   Networking   Security   Additional settings   Tags   Review + create

Create a SQL database with your preferred configurations. Complete the Basics tab then go to Review + Create to provision with smart defaults, or visit each tab to customize. Learn more ☐

✅ Lower, simplified pricing for SQL Database Hyperscale starts from 15th of December 2023. Learn more ☐

Project details

Select the subscription to manage deployed resources and costs. Use resource groups like folders to organize and manage all your resources.

Subscription * ⓘ	Free Trial ∨
└── Resource group * ⓘ	Select a resource group ∨
	Create new

Database details

Enter required settings for this database, including picking a logical server and configuring the compute and storage resources

Database name *	Enter database name
Server * ⓘ	Select a server ∨
	Create new
	❌ The value must not be empty.
Want to use SQL elastic pool? ⓘ	○ Yes ● No

Figure 14-6. *Initial errors*

- In this case firstly you can create a server.

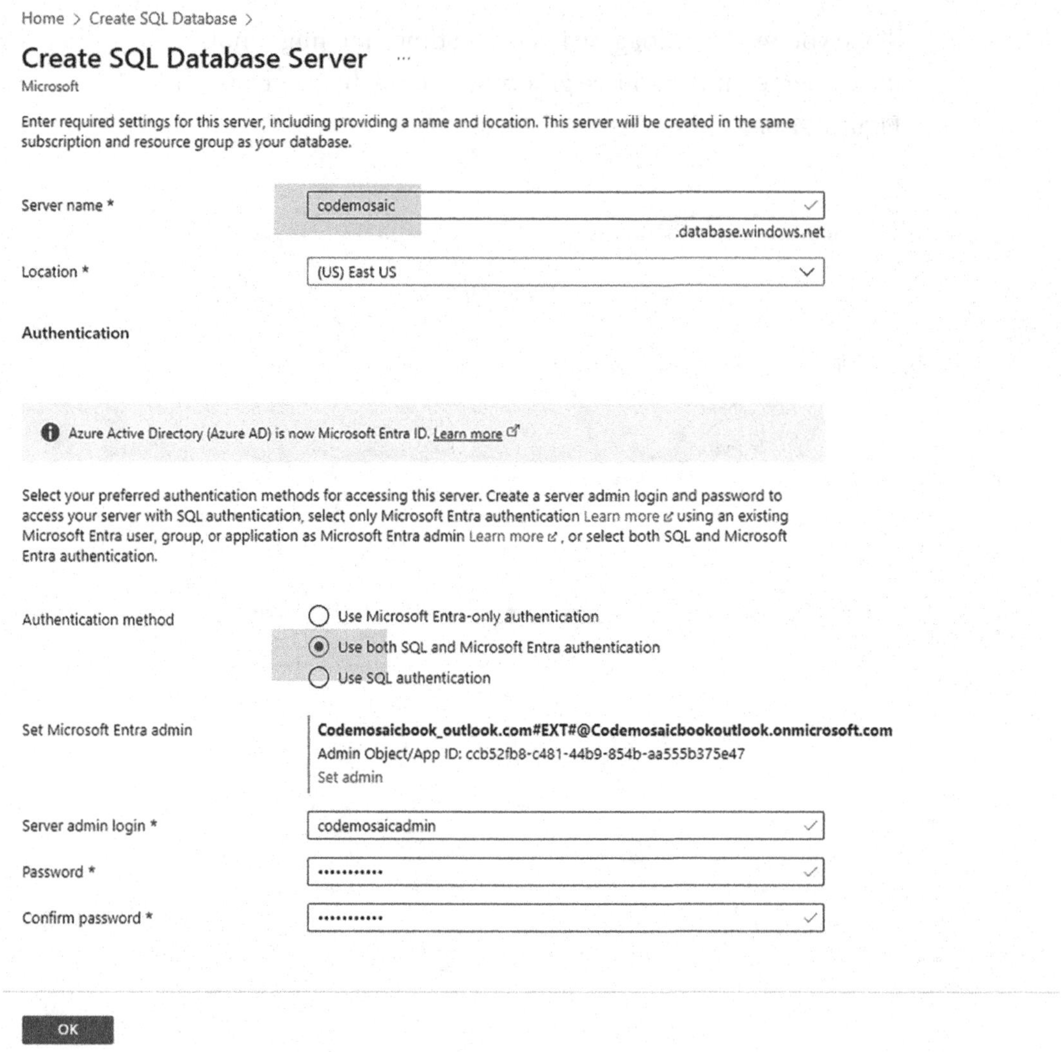

Home > Create SQL Database >

Create SQL Database Server   ···
Microsoft

Enter required settings for this server, including providing a name and location. This server will be created in the same subscription and resource group as your database.

Server name *	codemosaic ✓
	.database.windows.net
Location *	(US) East US ∨

Authentication

ⓘ Azure Active Directory (Azure AD) is now Microsoft Entra ID. Learn more ⌐

Select your preferred authentication methods for accessing this server. Create a server admin login and password to access your server with SQL authentication, select only Microsoft Entra authentication Learn more ⌐ using an existing Microsoft Entra user, group, or application as Microsoft Entra admin Learn more ⌐ , or select both SQL and Microsoft Entra authentication.

Authentication method	○ Use Microsoft Entra-only authentication
	● Use both SQL and Microsoft Entra authentication
	○ Use SQL authentication
Set Microsoft Entra admin	**Codemosaicbook_outlook.com#EXT#@Codemosaicbookoutlook.onmicrosoft.com**
	Admin Object/App ID: ccb52fb8-c481-44b9-854b-aa555b375e47
	Set admin
Server admin login *	codemosaicadmin ✓
Password *	············ ✓
Confirm password *	············ ✓

OK

Figure 14-7. *Create SQL database server*

You can give any server name you prefer, and an Authentication method as well similar to Figure 14-7.

- Then you can create a resource group as in Figure 14-8.

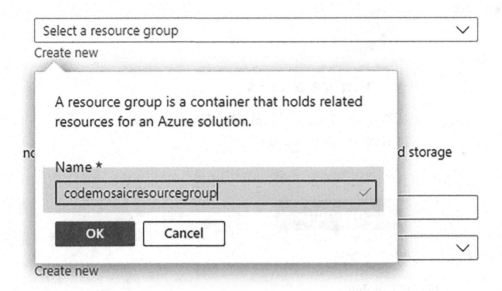

Figure 14-8. *Create resource group*

- **Configure Database Settings:** Choose your desired compute and storage resources. Azure offers a range of options to fit various needs and budgets.

- **Review and Create:** Double-check your settings and click "Create" to provision your new database.

Connecting Azure Database with MSSQL Server

Once your Azure SQL database is deployed, it's time to connect it with MSSQL Server; do do that you can firstly download SSMS from here: `https://learn.microsoft.com/en-us/sql/ssms/download-sql-server-management-studio-ssms?view=sql-server-ver16#download-ssms`.

Once done with this, you can follow these steps to connect with your database:

- **Configure Access**

  - Go to your SQL Database, and configure access. For that you will see this option (Figure 14-9) when you navigate to your SQL database.

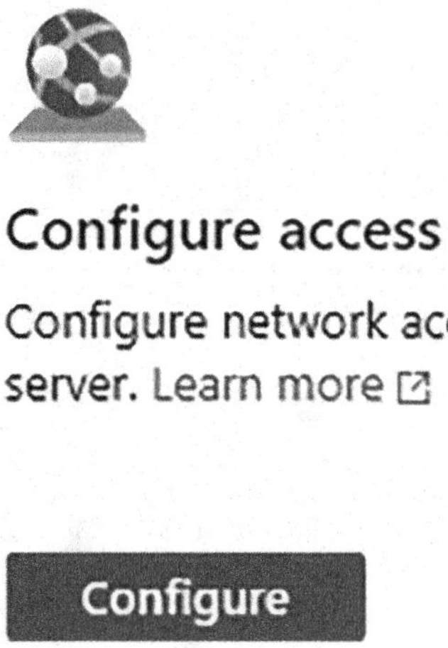

Configure access

Configure network access to your SQL
server. Learn more 🗗

Configure

Figure 14-9. *Configure access*

- Click on Configure.

- You'll be directed to the Networking tab as in Figure 14-10.

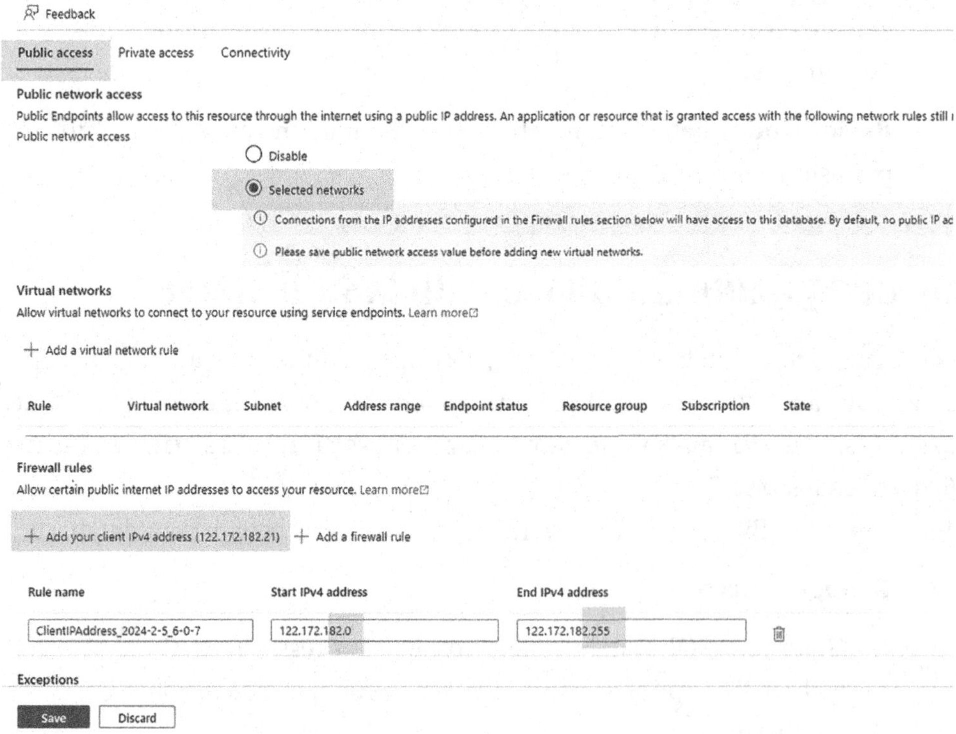

Figure 14-10. *IPv4 access*

- Here select Public Access.

- Click on Selected networks to allow your IP to access this.

- Click on Add your client IPv4 to add your IPv4.

- You can also select the range for access, like I have edited it to start from 122.172.182.0 and end at 122.172.182.255.

- **Find Connection Details**

  - Go to your database, and copy the Servername, as highlighted in Figure 14-11.

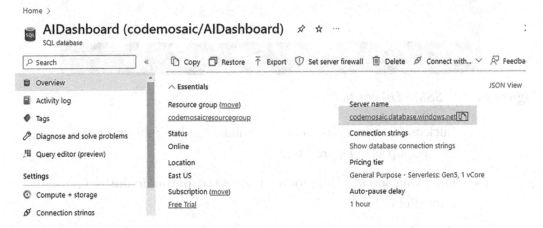

Figure 14-11. *Connection details*

- **Open Server Management Studio (SSMS)**

  Launch SSMS on your local machine.

- Connect to Your Database.

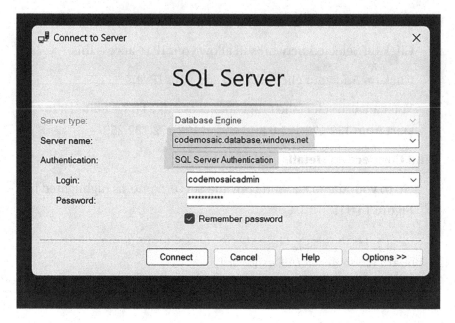

Figure 14-12. *SSMS DB connection*

- Click on "Connect" and select "Database Engine"; this will open up a popup as in Figure 14-12.

- Enter your server's URL (found in the Azure portal) in the Server Name field.

- Choose "SQL Server Authentication," and enter your login credentials.

- Click "Connect" to establish the connection.

- After successful connection, you'll be able to see the Database detail in Object Explorer as in Figure 14-13.

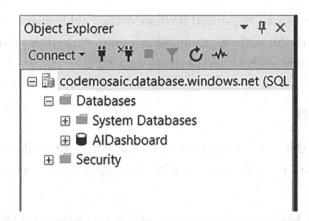

Figure 14-13. *Object Explorer*

Best Practices

- **Security:** Ensure your firewall settings in Azure allow connections from your local IP address.

- **Backups:** Regularly back up your data. Azure SQL Database provides automated backups, but it's good practice to understand and configure these settings according to your needs.

- **Monitoring:** Utilize the monitoring tools provided by Azure to keep track of performance, identify potential issues, and optimize resource usage.

In the next section, we'll explore how to structure our database effectively, aligning it with our AI Dashboard's requirements and ensuring a solid foundation for data-driven insights.

Crafting the Database Structure

In this section, we delve into the core of our AI-dashboard database by establishing the "ProjectMetrics" table. This table is pivotal, serving as the nexus where data reflecting AI's impact on software development projects is stored and analyzed. Crafting a database structure that's both robust and intuitive is crucial for the accurate representation and manipulation of data. A well-organized "ProjectMetrics" table ensures that the insights derived from the AI-dashboard are grounded in a solid, data-driven foundation, setting the stage for meaningful analysis and decision-making.

Table Creation

Creating the "ProjectMetrics" table involves precise SQL commands to structure your data effectively. Here's a step-by-step guide to creating this crucial table within your AI-dashboard database:

- **Open SQL Server Management Studio (SSMS):** Connect to your Azure SQL Database server using the credentials provided during the setup.

- **Create New Query:** Open a new query window in the SSMS connected to your AIDashboard database.

- **Define Table Structure**

  Craft a SQL statement to create the "ProjectMetrics" table. Ensure you include all necessary columns as per your schema design. Here's an example SQL command for creating the table:

  ```sql code
  CREATE TABLE ProjectMetrics (
      ProjectID INT PRIMARY KEY,
      ProjectName VARCHAR(255),
      AIIntegrationLevel VARCHAR(50),
      EfficiencyImprovement FLOAT,
      FeatureCount INT,
      AIDrivenFeatureCount INT,
      BugCountBeforeAI INT,
      BugCountAfterAI INT,
      DevelopmentTimeBeforeAI INT,
      DevelopmentTimeAfterAI INT,
      AI_Technology_Used VARCHAR(255),
      AI_Impact_Area VARCHAR(255)
  );
  ```

This SQL command sets up the "ProjectMetrics" table with columns for project details, AI integration specifics, and project metrics. It assigns appropriate data types for each column and marks ProjectID as the primary key.

- **Execute the Query**

  Run the SQL command in SSMS to create the "ProjectMetrics" table. Ensure the command executes successfully without errors.
  After executing you'll see the message similar to Figure 14-14.

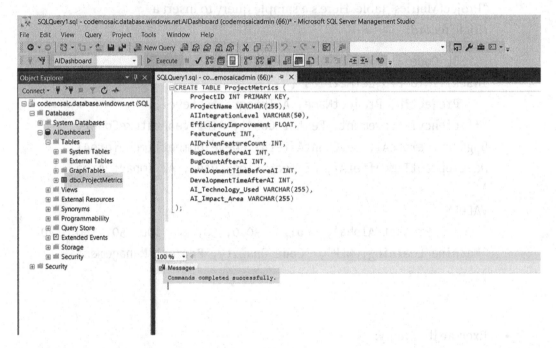

Figure 14-14. *Project metrics—table creation*

- **Validate the Table Creation**

  After executing the command, you can validate the creation of the "ProjectMetrics" table by querying the database to check if the table exists and has the correct structure.

By following these steps, you should have the "ProjectMetrics" table set up in your AI-dashboard database, ready to be populated with data for insightful analysis and visualization.

Data Insertion in ProjectMetrics

Inserting data into the "ProjectMetrics" table involves formulating and executing INSERT INTO statements. Here's how you can proceed:

- Open SSMS: Connect to your Azure SQL Database in SQL Server Management Studio.

- Craft Insert Query:

  Write SQL INSERT INTO statements to add data into your "ProjectMetrics" table. Here's a sample query to insert a single record:

```SQL Code
INSERT INTO ProjectMetrics (
    ProjectID, ProjectName, AIIntegrationLevel,
EfficiencyImprovement, FeatureCount, AIDrivenFeatureCount,
BugCountBeforeAI, BugCountAfterAI, DevelopmentTimeBeforeAI,
DevelopmentTimeAfterAI, AI_Technology_Used, AI_Impact_Area
)
VALUES (
    1, 'Project Alpha', 'Full', 30.0, 50, 20, 100, 50, 180, 120,
'Machine Learning, NLP', 'Code Quality, Project Management'
);
```

- Execute the Query:

  Run your insert query in SSMS to add the data to your table. Check for successful execution without errors.

- Validate Data Insertion:

  Query the "ProjectMetrics" table to ensure your data was inserted correctly.

For multiple insertions or dynamic data entry, you might consider a conversation with AI like GPT to generate or validate insert queries based on your specific dataset or to guide you toward resources for bulk data insertion scripts. Remember, this is a simulated interaction, and actual database changes should be handled with caution.

Creating Stored Procedure

Creating a stored procedure in SQL Server involves defining the logic for retrieving data from the "ProjectMetrics" table in a structured manner. Here's a step-by-step guide:

- **Define the Procedure**

  Start with the CREATE PROCEDURE statement. Provide a meaningful name, like usp_GetProjectMetrics.

- **Write the SQL Query**

  Inside the procedure, craft a SELECT statement to retrieve records from the "ProjectMetrics" table. Specify the columns you wish to retrieve or use * for all.

- **Add Parameters (Optional)**

  If you want to filter or customize the retrieved data, define input parameters using the @parameterName syntax.

- **Execute the Procedure**

  After creation, execute the procedure using the EXEC command followed by the procedure name and any necessary parameters.

Here's a basic template for your stored procedure:

```SQL code
CREATE PROCEDURE usp_GetProjectMetrics
AS
BEGIN
    SELECT * FROM ProjectMetrics;
END;
```

Remember, this is a basic structure. Depending on your specific needs, you might include additional SQL clauses or parameters to refine the data retrieval process. For us, we will be using this one, to get the data to our Data layer, and there we will be writing the business logic based on the API.

Conclusion

This chapter marks a significant milestone in our journey through "Mosaic Tile 3: Data Dynamics." We have intricately woven the threads of structured database practices, seamlessly integrating AI-driven strategies to enhance data management in our AI-dashboard. This cohesive blend of technology and strategy ensures that our data infrastructure is not only robust but also poised to adapt and evolve with our dynamic application needs.

Key Takeaways

- **Structured Database Foundation**

  Established a solid database structure within Azure SQL, ensuring data integrity and efficiency.

- **AI-Driven Data Management**

  Leveraged AI capabilities to streamline query writing, scripting, and stored procedure creation, showcasing the potential of AI in automating and optimizing database tasks.

- **Practical Implementation**

  Demonstrated practical steps in setting up Azure, creating databases, and managing data, providing readers with hands-on experience and actionable insights.

- **Security Best Practices**

  Emphasized the importance of maintaining secure and responsible data handling practices, particularly when working with cloud services like Azure.

- **Preparation for API Integration**

  Laid the groundwork for seamless API integration by ensuring the database structure and data are primed for the subsequent stages of our AI Dashboard development.

Onward

As we conclude this chapter, let's mark our user story and associated tasks as "Completed" on our Agile board. We're now ready to gracefully step into "Mosaic Tile 4: Backend Ballet—.NET Core Choreography." Here, we will connect our well-structured database to the Data layer and embark on creating three APIs using the crafted stored procedure, further enhancing the functionality and interactivity of our AI Dashboard. Let's continue our journey into the intricate dance of backend development and API choreography.

CHAPTER 15

Mosaic Tile 4: Backend Ballet—.NET Core Choreography

In this chapter we'll weave the intricate threads of backend development to support a dynamic AI-driven dashboard. Building on the Agile foundations set in Chapter 12 and the API designs from Chapter 13, and the robust data structures of Chapter 14, we now embark on a journey to implement RESTful APIs that breathe life into our data flow, ensuring a seamless interaction between our Azure SQL database and the frontend application.

As we delve into the creation of our three pivotal APIs—each serving a unique aspect of our dashboard's data presentation—we recall the valuable lessons from Chapter 6, ".NET Narratives." The knowledge we've gained about .NET Core setup, Visual Studio configurations, and the fundamentals of WebAPI architecture is the bedrock upon which we'll construct our backend services.

In this chapter, we not only build upon these principles but also integrate AI to optimize our development process, ensuring our APIs are not only functional but also intelligent and efficient. We invite you to engage hands-on, creating tasks for each API as we progress: one for the grid data, another for the pie chart data, and a third for the stacked bar chart data. Let's begin by rolling up our sleeves and preparing to craft APIs that are not just code, but a symphony of smart, seamless, and sophisticated services.

As we step forward, create three tasks corresponding to the User Story outlined in Sprint 1 of the AIDashboard project. This practical approach will ensure that you're not just following along but actively participating in the development of a truly intelligent dashboard.

393

© Arpit Dwivedi 2024
A. Dwivedi, *CodeMosaic*, https://doi.org/10.1007/979-8-8688-0276-8_15

Best Practices for .NET Core API Development

In the digital tapestry of software development, APIs are the threads that connect disparate services and data into a cohesive application. In .NET Core API development, mastering best practices is not just about writing code; it's about crafting secure, robust, and performant web services that stand the test of time and scale. This section unfolds the essential practices that elevate API development from good to great, ensuring your backend services are secure, reliable, and optimized for performance. Let's delve into the strategies that will fortify your API development in .NET Core.

- **Understanding Security Principles**

    - Grasp the "AAA" of security: Authentication, Authorization, and Accounting. Recognize threats like SQL injection, cross-site scripting, and data breaches.

    - Utilize threat modeling to identify and mitigate potential security risks early in the design phase.

- **Implementing Authentication**

    - Utilize built-in .NET Core Identity for user authentication, which supports a range of options from passwords to two-factor authentication.

    - For token-based authentication, leverage OAuth2 and OpenID Connect with IdentityServer4 for a more secure API.

- **Authorization Techniques**

    - Implement role-based authorization to assign permissions based on user roles. In .NET Core, this can be managed using the `[Authorize(Role="RoleName")]` attribute.

    - Policy-based authorization provides more granularity and is expressed as a set of requirements with the `[Authorize(Policy="PolicyName")]` attribute.

- **Data Protection Strategies**

  - Employ encryption for data at rest and in transit. For example, utilize the Data Protection APIs in .NET Core to encrypt sensitive information before storing it.

  - Enforce SSL/TLS for all communications. In development, use tools like Let's Encrypt for free SSL certificates.

- **Exception Handling Mechanisms**

  - Centralize error handling using middleware to catch and log exceptions, allowing for consistent responses and easier debugging.

  - Create custom exception classes for different error scenarios, which helps in providing more informative responses to the client.

- **Logging Best Practices**

  - Choose structured logging tools like Serilog, which allow for easy querying of logs and integration with monitoring systems like ELK Stack or Seq.

  - Log useful information including timestamps, user IDs, and stack traces, but avoid logging sensitive information.

- **Performance Optimization Basics**

  - Implement response caching to reduce server load and speed up responses. Use in-memory caching for frequently accessed data.

  - Use profiling tools like MiniProfiler or Application Insights to identify and address performance bottlenecks.

- **Asynchronous Programming**

  - Make use of the async and await keywords to improve scalability by freeing up threads while waiting for I/O-bound tasks.

  - Avoid common pitfalls of asynchronous programming such as deadlocks by understanding the synchronization context.

- **API Documentation and Versioning**

  - Integrate Swagger (OpenAPI) to auto-generate interactive API documentation, which provides clarity to consumers and ensures proper testing.

  - Implement versioning using query string, URL path, or media type to maintain backward compatibility and ease the transition for clients when updating your API.

These detailed points provide a roadmap for integrating best practices into .NET Core API development, ensuring that you have a clear understanding of not just what to do, but how to effectively apply these practices.

Influence of AI on .NET Core Development

The integration of Artificial Intelligence (AI) into .NET Core development heralds a new era where the conventional processes of writing, reviewing, and testing code are transformed. AI's impact is multifaceted:

- **AI-Assisted Code Review and Debugging Tools**

  - AI enhances code quality by suggesting improvements and identifying patterns that may not be immediately obvious to human reviewers.

  - Debugging is expedited as AI tools predict potential faults and offer automated fixes, leading to a more robust codebase.

- **Predictive Analytics for Backend Performance Enhancement**

  - AI algorithms analyze application data to predict future system behavior, allowing for preemptive optimization.

  - Predictive analytics can anticipate load spikes and resource bottlenecks, enabling developers to proactively refine performance.

- **Automated API Testing and Quality Assurance**

  - AI-driven testing frameworks can automatically generate test cases, simulate complex user behaviors, and validate API responses more efficiently.

  - Quality assurance processes are bolstered by AI's ability to learn from previous defects, enhancing test accuracy over time.

By harnessing AI, .NET Core developers can not only improve the efficiency and reliability of their development cycle but also pave the way for innovative solutions that were once beyond reach.

API Structurization and Layered Architecture

In the realm of software design, a layered architecture is a blueprint for separating the concerns of an application into distinct sections, each with its specific responsibility. This modular approach not only simplifies development and maintenance but also enhances the scalability and reusability of the code. At its core, a layered architecture typically involves a presentation layer handling the user interface, a business logic layer managing the core functionality, and a data layer for data storage and retrieval. By adhering to this structure, developers create a clear roadmap for their application that streamlines the development process and paves the way for future enhancements. As we embark on building our AI Dashboard, understanding and applying these principles will be crucial for crafting a well-organized, efficient, and manageable codebase.

Setting Up the .NET Application

To set up our application, we need to follow these simple steps, and among these, you'd probably have Step 1 and 2 already done:

- **Start by installing the .NET SDK** from the official Microsoft website, which includes the .NET runtime and command-line tools necessary for .NET development.

- **Install Visual Studio**, ensuring that the ASP.NET and web development workload is included in your installation options. Visual Studio will serve as the integrated development environment (IDE) for building our application.

- **Create a new project**

  - Start by selecting "ASP.NET Core Web API." This will scaffold a new project with the necessary files and folder structure.

  - Click new project, and fill in the required info (Figure 15-1).

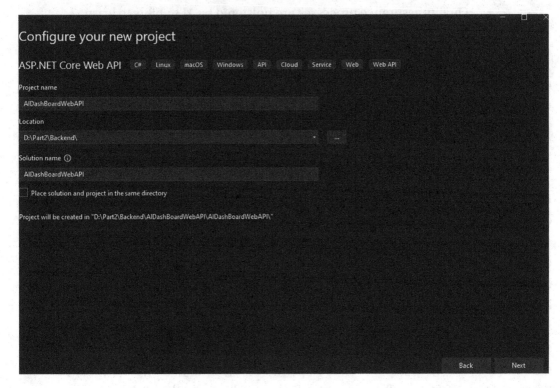

Figure 15-1. Configure project

And click next.

- In next window, you can see Additional information, verify and click Create (Figure 15-2).

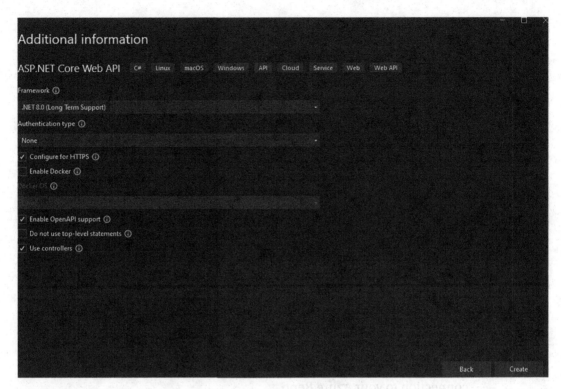

Figure 15-2. *Additional information*

- **Set up version control** by initializing a Git repository. This is an
  essential step for tracking changes and collaborating with others.To
  set up version control with Azure Repositories, you would

  - Initialize a Git repository in your project folder by using the
    command git init in the terminal.

  - Commit your initial project files to the repository with `git add`
    `.` and `git commit -m "Initial commit."` You might see an
    Identity issue while committing (Figure 15-3).

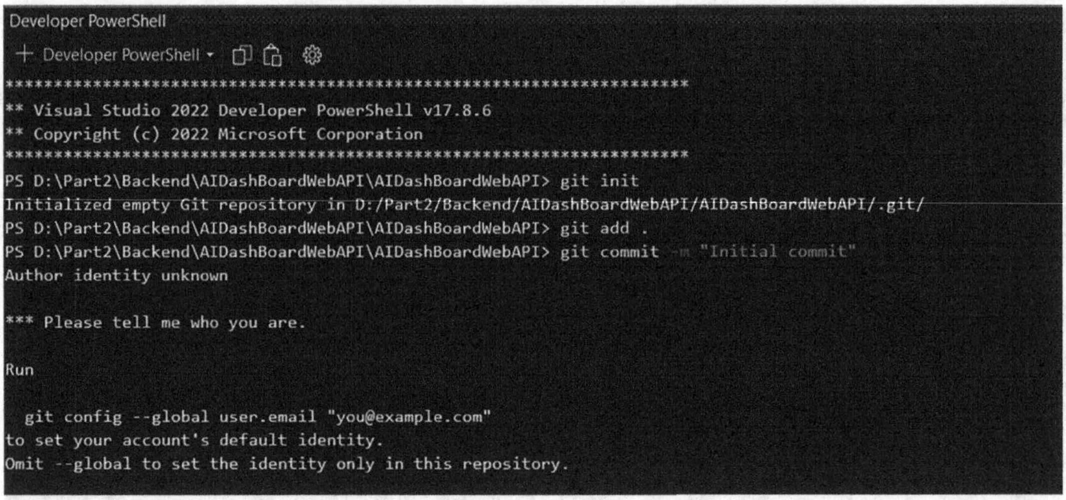

Figure 15-3. *PowerShell—Git issue*

- For this, in Visual Studio, you can then connect to Azure
  Repositories by navigating to "Team Explorer" (Figure 15-4),
  signing into your Azure DevOps account, and setting up a new
  connection to your Azure Repo.

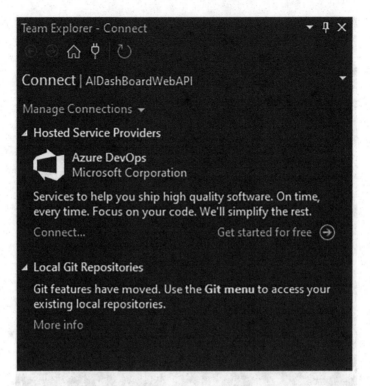

Figure 15-4. *Connect Azure Devops*

- Click connect, and you'll see a screen to connect to your Azure devops (Figure 15-5).

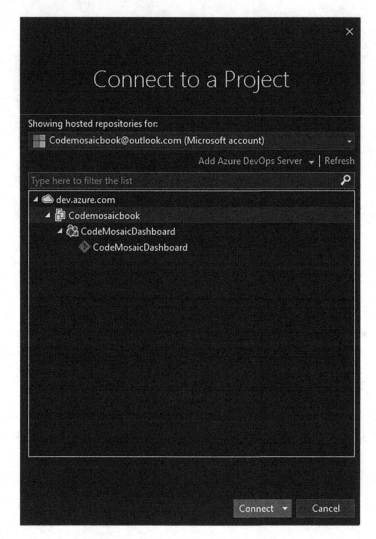

Figure 15-5. *Connect to project*

- If not then you can sign in and again open using Team Explorer.

- Once done, you can even use VI's GUI to do the rest. To do so:

    - Open Git Changes tab, and click configure (Figure 15-6).

Git Changes - AIDashBoardWebAPI
Configure your user name and email address before committing changes.
master
Push
0 View all commits
Enter a message <Required>
Commit Staged
Amend
Staged Changes (48)
D:\Part2\Backend\AIDashBoardWebAPI\AI...
bin\Debug\net8.0

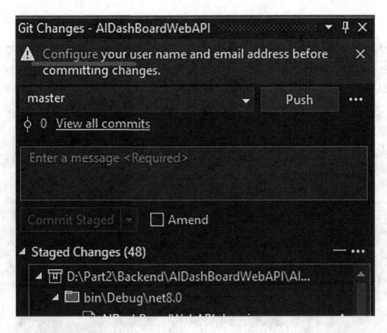

Figure 15-6. *Configure—Git*

- Fill in and Save (Figure 15-7).

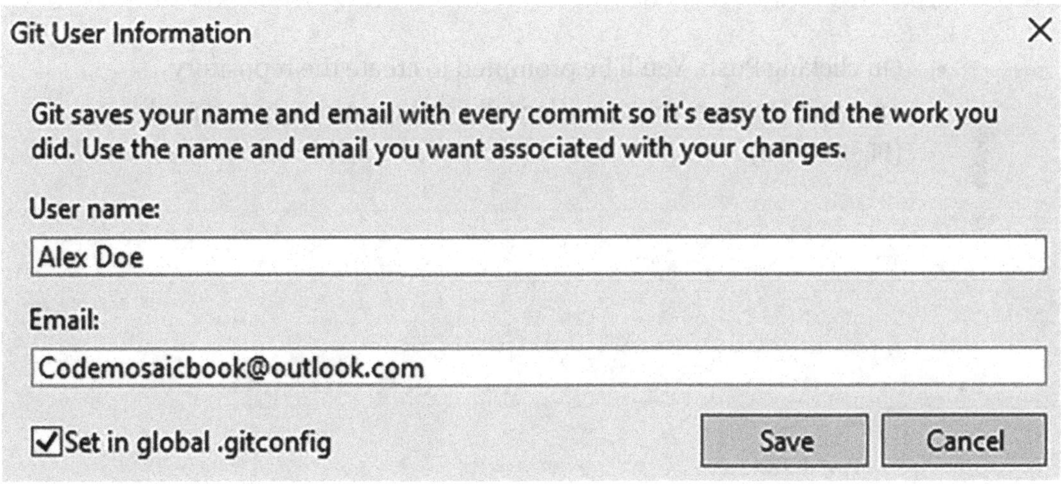
Git User Information
Git saves your name and email with every commit so it's easy to find the work you did. Use the name and email you want associated with your changes.
User name:
Alex Doe
Email:
Codemosaicbook@outlook.com
Set in global .gitconfig
Save
Cancel

Figure 15-7. *Git User information*

- Once connected, you can Commit (Figure 15-8).

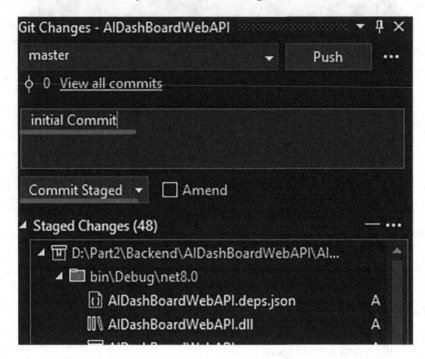

Figure 15-8. *Commit first change*

- On clicking Push, You'll be prompted to create the repository on Azure Devops. You can select all fields accordingly and push (Figure 15-9).

Figure 15-9. *Repository setup*

Now you have pushed your initial commit to the Azure Repository, making it available for collaboration and CI/CD pipelines.

- **Explore** the default project structure to familiarize yourself with the layout. Understand the purpose of the Startup.cs, Program.cs, and the Controllers and Models folders.

- Remember to select **IIS Express** for running (Figure 15-10).

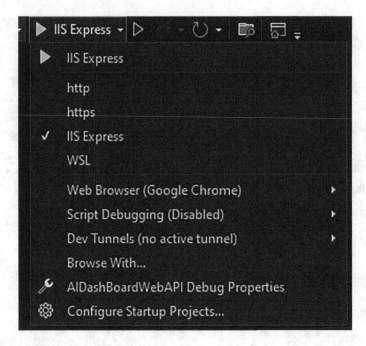

Figure 15-10. *IIS Express selection*

- Run the project to ensure everything is set up correctly. You should see a default weather forecast API running (Figure 15-11), which confirms your environment is ready for development.

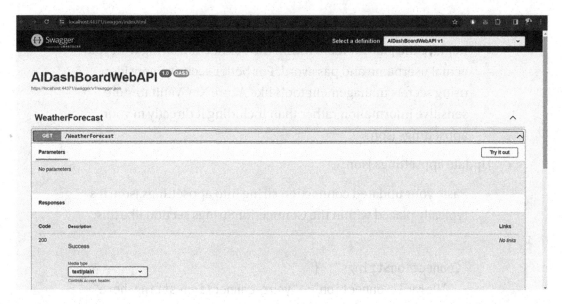

Figure 15-11. *Swagger view—API running*

Following these steps sets the stage for our next task: configuring the connection string and preparing the architecture's individual layers.

Configuring the Connection String

This is a crucial step for connecting our Azure SQL Database to our API. Follow these steps to do the same:

- Locate the **appsettings.json** File:

  - In your .NET Core project, find the **appsettings.json** file, which is where you will store the connection string for your Azure SQL database.

- Retrieve Your Azure SQL Connection String:

  - In the Azure portal, navigate to your SQL database resource. Under the "Connection strings" section, you'll find a pre-formatted connection string. Copy it.

- Secure Your Credentials:

    - Replace the placeholders within the connection string with your actual username and password. For better security, consider using secrets management tools like Azure Key Vault to store sensitive information rather than including it directly in your appsettings.json.

- Update appsettings.json:

    - Paste your updated connection string into appsettings.json. It's typically placed within the ConnectionStrings section like this:

        ```
        "ConnectionStrings": {
            "DefaultConnection": "your-connection-string-here"
        }
        ```

Creating Layer Files

Transitioning from the initial project setup, we now focus on scaffolding the core architecture of our AI Dashboard application. This involves creating specific files that will form the foundation of our Data, Business, and Controller layers. Each file will house distinct aspects of the application logic, ensuring a separation of concerns that promotes a clean and maintainable codebase.

Data Layer: AIDashboardData.cs

- Before making changes for Data Layer, Install EntityFrameworkCore using nuget if you don't have. For that:

    - Open NuGet Package Manager by following underlined steps in Figure 15-12.

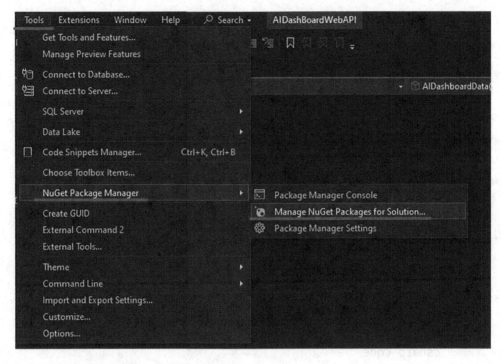

Figure 15-12. *Navigate to NuGet package manager*

- Search For EntityFrameworkCore and install it in your project (Figure 15-13a).

Figure 15-13a. *Entity framework NuGet*

- Similarly, install these other 2 as well (Figure 15-13b).

Figure 15-13b. *Remaining entity framework NuGets*

- Create a new folder in your project named **Data**.

- In the Data folder, create AIDashboardData.cs. This will contain our DbContext and entity configurations.

- Within this file, we'll set up our DbContext with DbSet properties for each entity model that corresponds to a table in Azure SQL.

```csharp code
using Microsoft.EntityFrameworkCore;

namespace AIDashBoardWebAPI.Data
{
    public class AIDashboardData : DbContext
    {
        public AIDashboardData(DbContextOptions<AIDashboardData>
        options)
            : base(options)
        {
        }

        // Define DbSets for your entities here
    }
}

```

Business Layer: AIDashboardBusiness.cs

- Create a new folder named **Services**.

- In a new Services folder, create AIDashboardBusiness.cs for our
  business logic.

- Here, we will define the business services, one for each type of data
  we're handling. Each service will include methods for processing and
  transforming data.

```csharp code
public class AIDashboardBusiness
{
    // Inject data context or other services if needed
    // Define methods for business operations
}
```

Controller Layer: AIDashboardController.cs

- Within the Controllers folder, add AIDashboardController.cs. This
  controller will handle incoming HTTP requests and delegate to the
  appropriate services.

- Define actions for each type of data retrieval or manipulation the API
  will perform.

```csharp code
[ApiController]
[Route("[controller]")]
public class AIDashboardController : ControllerBase
{
    // Inject services using constructor injection
    // Define API actions here
}
```

Each class file acts as a cornerstone for the respective layer in the application, separating the concerns of data access, business logic, and request handling. This structure paves the way for a robust and scalable application, facilitating future enhancements and maintenance.

Constructing APIs for AI Dashboard

Now that our .NET Core application is configured and the foundational layers are established, we embark on crafting the APIs for our AI Dashboard. This critical phase will transform our application into a dynamic, data-driven interface, making it capable of presenting complex data through simple, intuitive visualizations. Our focus will be to ensure these APIs not only fetch data efficiently but also encapsulate the logic needed for insightful display on the dashboard. Let's begin by bringing our Azure SQL data to life with our first API calls.

Data Layer Construction

In the Data Layer, our primary goal is to establish a connection between our .NET Core API and the Azure SQL Database to retrieve data through a stored procedure. Here's how we can achieve that:

Define the ProjectMetrics Model:

- Create a new C# class file named ProjectMetrics.cs in your Data folder.

- Define properties in the ProjectMetrics class that correspond to the columns returned by the usp_GetProjectMetrics stored procedure.

```csharp code
public class ProjectMetrics
{
    // Example properties, replace with actual columns
    public int ProjectId { get; set; }
    public string MetricName { get; set; }
    public double Value { get; set; }
```

```
    // Add additional properties to match the stored
procedure output
}
```
```

To construct the Data Layer for our AI Dashboard, we'll make updates to both
AIDashboardData.cs and Program.cs.

**AIDashboardData.cs Changes:**

```csharp code
using Microsoft.EntityFrameworkCore;
using System.Collections.Generic;
using System.Threading.Tasks;

namespace AIDashBoardWebAPI.Data
{
    /// <summary>
    /// Defines the interface for AI Dashboard data operations,
particularly for managing ProjectMetrics.
    /// </summary>
    public interface IAIDashboardData
    {
        /// <summary>
        /// Asynchronously retrieves a list of ProjectMetrics.
        /// </summary>
        /// <returns>A task that represents the asynchronous operation. The
            task result contains a list of ProjectMetrics.</returns>
        Task<List<ProjectMetrics>> GetProjectMetricsAsync();
    }

    /// <summary>
    /// Provides implementation for AI Dashboard data operations and acts
        as a data context for Entity Framework.
    /// </summary>
    public class AIDashboardData : DbContext, IAIDashboardData
    {
        /// <summary>
```
```

```csharp
    /// Initializes a new instance of the AIDashboardData class.
    /// </summary>
    /// <param name="options">The options to be used by the
        DbContext.</param>
    public AIDashboardData(DbContextOptions<AIDashboardData> options) :
    base(options) { }

    /// <summary>
    /// Gets or sets the DbSet for ProjectMetrics entities.
    /// </summary>
    public DbSet<ProjectMetrics> ProjectMetrics { get; set; }

    /// <summary>
    /// Asynchronously retrieves project metrics by executing a stored
        procedure and returning the results.
    /// </summary>
    /// <returns>A task that represents the asynchronous operation. The
        task result contains a list of ProjectMetrics.</returns>
    public async Task<List<ProjectMetrics>> GetProjectMetricsAsync()
    {
        // Call the stored procedure 'usp_GetProjectMetrics' and return
            the results as a list
        return await ProjectMetrics.FromSqlRaw("EXEC usp_
        GetProjectMetrics").ToListAsync();
    }

    /// <summary>
    /// Configures the schema needed for the model when the model is
        created.
    /// This method is called when the data context is first created to
        build the model and its mappings in memory.
    /// </summary>
    /// <param name="modelBuilder">Defines the shape of your entities,
        the relationships between them, and how they map to the
        database.</param>
    protected override void OnModelCreating(ModelBuilder modelBuilder)
    {
```

```
      base.OnModelCreating(modelBuilder);
      // Place additional model configuration here. For example,
         configuring relationships or setting default values.
   }
 }
}
```

Instead of breaking and explaining the code in steps, I've explained it in the comments in AIDashboardData.cs. For Program.cs it is quite simple:

1. Import EntityFramework:
    `using Microsoft.EntityFrameworkCore;`

2. Register the DbContext with the actual connection string name from appsettings.json:

    ```
    builder.Services.AddDbContext<AIDashboardData>(opti
    ons => options.UseSqlServer(builder.Configuration.
    GetConnectionString("AZURE_SQL_CONNECTIONSTRING")));
    ```

This setup configures the application to connect to Azure SQL using the connection string specified in appsettings.json. It also defines a method to asynchronously retrieve project metrics from the database, which will be used by the Business Layer.

Please replace "AZURE_SQL_CONNECTIONSTRING" with the exact key you've used in your appsettings.json file. This will ensure that your application can find and use the correct connection string to access your database.

Business Logic Layer

The Business Logic Layer is the cerebral cortex of our AI Dashboard, where raw data is transformed into meaningful insights. This layer's responsibility is to apply the business rules and logic that dictate how data is processed and presented. It's where the data from our SQL database begins to take shape, conforming to the specifications of our Grid, Pie Chart, and Stacked Bar Chart components. Let's start by defining the core functions that will underpin the intelligent behavior of our dashboard.

Grid Data Logic

In constructing the Grid Data Logic for our AI Dashboard, simplicity is key. For this component, we are focusing on the direct presentation of data without additional processing or business rules. This approach allows us to present the data in its most timely and unaltered state, ensuring that users have access to real-time information. Therefore, the data layer's output will feed directly into the grid component, bypassing the need for a distinct business logic layer. This direct pathway from data retrieval to presentation ensures maximum efficiency and responsiveness for the grid display on our dashboard.

Pie Chart Data Logic

Pie charts offer a visually intuitive way to represent parts of a whole, making them ideal for showcasing proportions and categories. They excel in displaying categorical data, allowing viewers to understand the relative significance of different categories at a glance.

For our AI Dashboard, the pie chart will depict the impact of AI in software development across key areas. In the GetPieChartDataAsync function, we delve into the ProjectMetrics, segregating the data by AI_Impact_Area. This segregation allows us to spotlight the direct effects of AI in distinct areas, such as Task Automation, Efficiency Improvement, and Quality Enhancement. The process involves a meticulous aggregation of relevant metrics, followed by a transformation into PieChartDataModel instances. Each instance encapsulates a category alongside its quantified impact, rendering a coherent, data-backed visualization of AI's multifaceted contributions to the software development lifecycle.

To implement the GetPieChartDataAsync function to show the efficiency improvement summed and grouped by AI_Impact_Area, you can follow these steps:

- **Retrieve and Process the Data**: Fetch the data from the data layer and process it to calculate the sum of efficiency improvements for each AI_Impact_Area.

- **Transform Data for Pie Chart**: Create instances of PieChartDataModel where each instance represents a category (AI_Impact_Area) and the corresponding sum of EfficiencyImprovement.

Here's how you might structure the GetPieChartDataAsync function:

```csharp code
public async Task<List<PieChartDataModel>> GetPieChartDataAsync()
{
    var projectMetrics = await _dataLayer.GetProjectMetricsAsync();

    // Process the data: Group by AI_Impact_Area and sum
        EfficiencyImprovement
    var groupedData = projectMetrics
        .GroupBy(metric => metric.AI_Impact_Area)
        .Select(group => new PieChartDataModel
        {
            Category = group.Key,
            Value = group.Sum(metric => metric.EfficiencyImprovement),
        })
        .ToList();

    return groupedData;
}
```

In this snippet:

- Data is grouped by AI_Impact_Area.

- EfficiencyImprovement values are summed up for each group.

- The result is transformed into a list of PieChartDataModel instances.

Stacked Bar Chart Logic

This part of the business logic aims to vividly showcase the multifaceted impact of AI integration across various projects.

The stacked bar chart will compare projects based on key performance metrics: Efficiency Improvement, AI-Driven Feature Count, Bug Reduction, and Time Saved.

Additionally, AI technology used per project will be included for detailed insights, serving as tooltips in the visualization.

Structuring the Function:

- The function will process ProjectMetrics, summing up and calculating the necessary metrics for each project.

- It will transform the processed data into a structure compatible with a stacked bar chart, emphasizing comparative insights across projects.

- The AI_Technology_Used field will be associated with each project's data for enriching the visualization with tooltips.

Since now you understand how to write the business logic, you can try writing this one yourself. If you get stuck, you can take help from the repository code provided.

Controller

In the Controller part of an ASP.NET Core Web API, you define endpoints that respond to HTTP requests. Here's how you can structure the controller and write your first endpoint, GetGridData:

- Define the Controller:

  - Controllers in ASP.NET Core inherit from ControllerBase.

  - Use the [ApiController] attribute to enable automatic HTTP 400 responses and other API-convention-based behaviors.

  - Define the route for the controller using the [Route("[controller]")] attribute.

- Writing the GetGridData Endpoint:

  - Endpoints are typically public methods of the controller, annotated with HTTP method attributes like [HttpGet].

  - The GetGridData method can call the business layer to retrieve grid data and return it.

  - Ensure proper response types are indicated using attributes like [ProducesResponseType].

Here's an example of a controller with a GetGridData endpoint:

```csharp code
[ApiController]
[Route("[controller]")]
public class AIDashboardController : ControllerBase
{
    private readonly AIDashboardBusiness _businessLayer;

    public AIDashboardController(AIDashboardBusiness businessLayer)
    {
        _businessLayer = businessLayer;
    }

    [HttpGet("GetGridData")]
    [ProducesResponseType(StatusCodes.Status200OK)]
    public async Task<ActionResult<IEnumerable<GridDataModel>>>
    GetGridData()
    {
        var gridData = await _businessLayer.GetGridDataAsync();
        return Ok(gridData);
    }

    // ... other endpoints ...
}
```

In this example:

- The AIDashboardController retrieves data by calling methods on the AIDashboardBusiness service.

- The GetGridData endpoint responds to GET requests and returns grid data.

- Modify GridDataModel and other method names to match your actual implementation.

With the first API successfully implemented and the controller operational, you now have a solid foundation to build upon. Encouragingly, you can apply the principles learned here to develop the endpoints for the remaining APIs. While this guide has equipped you with the necessary knowledge to proceed independently, remember that the code repository provided with the book stands as a valuable resource. Should challenges arise, consult it for guidance and inspiration. This approach not only reinforces your learning but also fosters confidence in your ability to navigate and resolve complexities autonomously.

Conclusion

Congratulations on reaching this pivotal milestone in your API development journey! With the successful creation of your first endpoint, you're now ready to mark the completion of this user story. This achievement paves the way for the exciting next phase: bringing the AI Dashboard to life through an engaging UI.

Key Takeaways

- Understanding of controller structure and routing in ASP.NET Core.

- Practical experience in connecting controllers with business logic and data layers.

- Insight into error handling and debugging during API development.

- Familiarity with Swagger for API documentation and testing.

- Confidence to independently tackle API endpoint creation.

Onward

As we transition from backend to frontend, the upcoming chapter promises an intriguing journey into UI implementation. We'll leverage the robust APIs developed here to construct a dynamic, user-friendly interface for our AI Dashboard. Stay tuned as we continue to weave the threads of this project into a cohesive and interactive masterpiece.

CHAPTER 16

Mosaic Tile 5: Frontend Finesse with Angular

Let's now delve into the realm of Frontend Finesse with Angular, marking the commencement of User Story 4: Front-End UI/UX Implementation. This journey is not just about building interfaces; it's about crafting experiences that resonate and engage. Angular, renowned for its prowess in developing dynamic Single Page Applications (SPAs), stands as our framework of choice. In this chapter, we'll explore how Angular's robust features, coupled with AI-driven development tools, can revolutionize frontend development, ensuring a seamless, responsive, and accessible user interface. Prepare to transform the intricate data from our APIs into a coherent, interactive dashboard, setting a new standard for UI/UX excellence. As you follow along, consider this an opportunity to create tasks, track progress, and witness your dashboard come to life, one component at a time.

Reflecting on the comprehensive insights from Chapter 5, "Angular Adventures: Crafting the User's Realm," we've already journeyed through the vibrant landscape of Angular, understanding its core elements like components, services, and the magic of data binding. Now, poised at the threshold of practical implementation, we aim to translate these foundational concepts into tangible solutions. Let's pivot from theory to practice, embracing best practices to enrich our CodeMosaic project. As we transition, our focus sharpens, channeling the Angular knowledge into crafting a UI/UX that's not just functional but also intuitively resonates with its users.

Angular for Dynamic SPAs

Single Page Applications (SPAs) have revolutionized the web experience, offering fluid, seamless interactions akin to desktop applications. Angular, with its advanced capabilities, empowers developers to build SPAs that are not only responsive and fast but

421

A. Dwivedi, *CodeMosaic*, https://doi.org/10.1007/979-8-8688-0276-8_16

also maintainable and scalable. The benefit of SPAs includes improved user experience with minimal page reloads, efficient data communication with APIs, and a modular architecture that enhances code management and collaboration. Some of the best Practices in Angular:

- **Component-Based Architecture**

  - **Problem:** Managing a large codebase can be complex and unwieldy.

  - **Description:** Angular's component-based architecture divides the application into logical, reusable pieces.

  - **Solution:** Structure your app into components, each responsible for a specific piece of the UI, promoting reusability and testability.

  - **AI-Assisted Prompt:** Use AI code completion tools to scaffold components quickly, ensuring best practices in structure and naming conventions.

- **Reactive Forms for Robust Validation**

  - **Problem:** Handling complex form inputs and validations can be tedious and error-prone.

  - **Description:** Angular's reactive forms provide a model-driven approach to handle form inputs and validations.

  - **Solution:** Implement reactive forms to manage complex form controls, ensuring a reactive and immersive user experience.

  - **AI-Assisted Prompt:** Leverage AI to generate form validation rules based on your specific requirements, reducing manual coding and potential errors.

- **Efficient State Management**

  - **Problem:** Managing the state in large applications can lead to performance bottlenecks and maintainability issues.

  - **Description:** State management libraries like NgRx or Akita provide structured ways to manage state, improving predictability and performance.

- **Solution:** Integrate a state management library to centralize state handling, ensuring a consistent and performance-optimized user experience.

- **AI-Assisted Prompt:** Utilize AI tools to model your application state, suggesting optimal structuring and data flow strategies.

- **Optimizing Performance with Lazy Loading**

  - **Problem:** Large applications can suffer from slow initial load times, affecting user engagement.

  - **Description:** Angular's lazy loading feature allows for splitting the application into chunks, loading them on demand.

  - **Solution:** Implement lazy loading for feature modules, reducing the initial load time and improving the user experience.

  - **AI-Assisted Prompt:** Use AI insights to identify bottlenecks in your application's load time, recommending modules and components ideal for lazy loading.

- **Implementing Automated Testing**

  - **Problem:** Ensuring application reliability and stability manually is time-consuming and prone to human error.

  - **Description:** Automated testing frameworks like Jasmine and Karma provide a robust platform for writing and executing tests.

  - **Solution:** Integrate automated testing into your development process, ensuring each component and service is tested and reliable.

  - **AI-Assisted Prompt:** Generate test cases and scenarios based on your application's functionality, ensuring comprehensive coverage and reliability.

As in this section, we've explored the transformative potential of Angular in crafting dynamic SPAs. From best practices that address real-world development challenges to AI-assisted solutions that streamline processes, Angular positions itself as an invaluable asset in the modern developer's toolkit. As we transition from these foundational concepts to practical implementation, the stage is set for bringing these principles to life in your AI Dashboard project.

Angular Application Creation

Creating an Angular Application within a .NET Solution:

- Prepare the Development Environment:

  - Ensure Node.js and npm (Node Package Manager) are installed.

  - Update npm to the latest version using `npm install npm@ latest -g`.

- Install Angular CLI:

  - Install Angular CLI globally using `npm install -g @angular/cli`.

  - Verify installation with `ng version`.

- Initialize Angular Project:

  - Navigate to the root directory of your .NET solution.

  - Create a new directory for the Angular project, for example, AIDashboardUI.

  - Within this directory, initialize the Angular app using `ng new client-app` (replace client-app with your desired app name).

- Using Standalone Components:

  - With Angular 17, you can leverage standalone components for a more modular and lightweight application structure.

  - When generating new components, use the `--standalone` flag or configure your default component schematics accordingly.

- Integration and Initial Run:

  - Run npm install inside your Angular project directory to install all required dependencies.

  - Ensure your .NET backend is running.

  - Start your Angular application with ng serve.

  - Verify that the Angular app can communicate with the .NET backend by testing API endpoints.

These steps lead you through setting up an Angular application within your existing .NET solution, ensuring that both frontend and backend are seamlessly integrated for a smooth development process.

Writing Services for API Interactions

For the AI Dashboard project, the Angular framework provides a robust structure to handle API interactions efficiently. Services in Angular act as a bridge between our frontend components and backend API endpoints. This segment delves into creating and utilizing Angular services to fetch and display data from our AI Dashboard backend.

Introduction to Angular Services in Context

In the AI Dashboard project, services are instrumental in performing API calls to fetch data related to AI project metrics, pie chart data for AI impact areas, and stacked bar chart data for project efficiencies. We utilize Angular's `HttpClient` to make these API requests and handle the responses.

Generating the AiDashBoardService

Utilizing the Angular CLI, we created a service specifically for our AI Dashboard:

`ng generate service services/ai-dash-board-api`

This command creates a service file named ai-dash-board-api.service.ts within the services directory, setting the stage for our API interaction code.

Structuring the AiDashBoardApiService with HttpClient

The HttpClient module is Angular's mechanism to communicate with backend services. Here's how we structure our AiDashBoardApiService:

```typescript code
import { Injectable } from '@angular/core';
import { HttpClient } from '@angular/common/http';
import { Observable } from 'rxjs';
```

```
@Injectable({
  providedIn: 'root'
})
export class AiDashBoardApiService {
  private BASE_URL = 'https://localhost:44371/AIDashboard';

  constructor(private http: HttpClient) {}

  // API method implementations will go here
}
```

With **HttpClient** injected, we can now define methods in our service to call specific API endpoints.

Defining API Interaction Methods

We've defined several methods within AiDashBoardApiService to interact with our backend:

```typescript code
getGridData(): Observable<any> {
  return this.http.get(`${this.BASE_URL}/GetGridData`);
}

getPieChartData(): Observable<any> {
  return this.http.get(`${this.BASE_URL}/GetPieChartData`);
}

getStackedBarChartData(): Observable<any> {
  return this.http.get(`${this.BASE_URL}/GetStackedBarChartData`);
}
```

These methods correspond to the three key data visualizations in our dashboard: grid data, pie chart data, and stacked bar chart data.

Utilizing the Service in AppComponent

In our master component, app.component.ts, we inject AiDashBoardApiService and call these methods to retrieve data:

```typescript code
import { Component, OnDestroy } from '@angular/core';
import { CommonModule } from '@angular/common';
import { RouterOutlet } from '@angular/router';
import { AiDashBoardApiService } from '../app/services/ai-dash-board-api.
service';
import { HttpClientModule } from '@angular/common/http'; // <-- Import
HttpClientModule
import { Subscription } from 'rxjs';

@Component({
  selector: 'app-root',
  standalone: true,
  imports: [CommonModule, RouterOutlet,
    HttpClientModule],
    providers: [AiDashBoardApiService],
  templateUrl: './app.component.html',
  styleUrls: ['./app.component.scss']
})
export class AppComponent implements OnDestroy {
  title = 'AIDashboard-UI';
  private subscriptions: Subscription[] = [];
  gridData: any[] = []; // Variable to store grid
  pieChartData: any[] = [];
  stackedBarChartData: any[] = [];

  constructor(private aiDashboardApiService: AiDashBoardApiService) {
    this.fetchData();
  }

  private fetchData(): void {
    this.subscriptions.push(
      this.aiDashboardApiService.getGridData().subscribe({
```

```
      next: data => this.gridData = data,
      error: error => console.error('Error fetching grid data:', error)
    }),

    this.aiDashboardApiService.getPieChartData().subscribe({
      next: data => this.pieChartData = data,
      error: error => console.error('Error fetching pie chart
      data:', error)
    }),

    this.aiDashboardApiService.getStackedBarChartData().subscribe({
      next: data => this.stackedBarChartData = data,
      error: error => console.error('Error fetching stacked bar chart
      data:', error)
    })
  );
}

ngOnDestroy(): void {
  // Unsubscribe from all subscriptions
  this.subscriptions.forEach(sub => sub.unsubscribe());
}
}
```

Each subscription is managed within the fetchData method, which is called when the component initializes.

Through the AI Dashboard project, we've demonstrated how to construct an Angular service to handle API interactions, inject the service into our main component, and utilize it to fetch and display data. This structure is not just theoretical but has been practically applied in our ongoing project, reinforcing Angular's capacity to streamline complex data interactions in a web application.

Navigating Common Challenges in the AI Dashboard Project Setup

Developing a cutting-edge application like the AI Dashboard involves overcoming a variety of challenges, especially when working with the latest technologies. Our journey was no exception, and here we'll share the common hurdles you may have encountered and how you can tackle them head-on.

Embracing the New Structure of .NET 6+ and Angular 17

Our project uses the latest versions of .NET and Angular, which introduced significant changes to project structures. Gone are the days of **Startup.cs** in .NET Core and **app. module.ts** in Angular. Instead, .NET 6+ uses a streamlined **Program.cs** file, and Angular 17 introduces standalone components, eliminating the need for **NgModule** boilerplate code. This can be a source of confusion for developers accustomed to earlier versions.

Handling CORS in .NET 6+ with Program.cs

Cross-Origin Resource Sharing (CORS) is a security feature that can often trip up developers. In .NET 6+, the CORS setup is done directly in Program.cs. We encountered CORS errors initially when our Angular app tried to access the .NET backend. Here's how we configured CORS to allow our Angular app to communicate with the backend:

```csharp code
var builder = WebApplication.CreateBuilder(args);

// ... Add services

builder.Services.AddCors(options =>
{
    options.AddPolicy("AllowWebApp",
        policy => policy.WithOrigins("http://localhost:4200") // Angular
        app's URL
                    .AllowAnyMethod()
                    .AllowAnyHeader());
});
```

```
var app = builder.Build();

// ... Configure the HTTP request pipeline

app.UseCors("AllowWebApp");

// ... Other app configurations

app.Run();
```

Addressing Angular 17's Standalone Components

In Angular 17, we leverage standalone components, which allow us to import modules directly into the components that require them. This new feature simplifies the app structure but also requires a new understanding of dependency management. For instance, **HttpClientModule** must now be imported directly in any standalone component that makes HTTP requests:

```typescript code
import { HttpClientModule } from '@angular/common/http';

@Component({
  // ...
  imports: [HttpClientModule],
  // ...
})
export class AppComponent {
  // ...
}
```

Resolving Errors and Debugging Tips

During development, we encountered several errors that required careful debugging. Here are some common issues and how we resolved them:

- **NullInjectorError for HttpClient**

  This error occurred because **HttpClientModule** was not imported where needed. Once we added the import directly to our standalone component, this issue was resolved.

- **CORS Error**

  Initially, our Angular app was blocked from accessing the .NET backend due to CORS policy restrictions. By configuring the CORS policy in our Program.cs, we allowed our Angular app to make cross-origin requests to the backend.

- **HTTP Error Responses**

  We observed HttpErrorResponse in our console when API calls failed. To handle these, we enhanced our service methods with error handling logic, ensuring graceful degradation of the user experience.

Working with the latest versions of frameworks can lead to a steep learning curve, but it also brings numerous advantages in terms of performance and simplicity. By sharing the challenges we faced and the solutions we implemented in the AI Dashboard project, we aim to prepare you for a smoother development experience. Stay curious, and don't shy away from exploring the new features that modern frameworks have to offer.

Basic Data Representation with HTML Tables in the AI Dashboard Project

As part of our UI/UX development in the AI Dashboard project, we'll start with a simple yet effective way to present data fetched from our backend services. The most straightforward method is using HTML tables. This method allows for quick implementation and provides a clear view of the data, making it a go-to choice for initial data visualization.

Implementing Basic HTML Tables

Our approach was to utilize Angular's data binding capabilities alongside standard HTML table tags to render the data returned from three distinct API endpoints: Grid Data, Pie Chart Data, and Stacked Bar Chart Data. Here's an overview of the process:

- **Fetching Data**

  - Using AiDashBoardApiService, we subscribed to our API endpoints within the **app.component.ts** to fetch the data, which is already discussed in the previous section.

- **Structuring Tables**

  In the **app.component.html**, we crafted three separate tables using Angular's *ngFor directive to iterate over the data arrays and display each item within table rows.

  Here is an example of the first simple HTML table we created:

  ```HTML code

<h1>AI in Software Development</h1>
<table>
  <thead>
    <tr>
      <th>Project ID</th>
      <th>Project Name</th>
      <th>AI Integration Level</th>
      <th>Efficiency Improvement (%)</th>
      <th>Feature Count</th>
      <th>AI-Driven Feature Count</th>
      <th>Bug Count Before AI</th>
      <th>Bug Count After AI</th>
      <th>Development Time Before AI (days)</th>
      <th>Development Time After AI (days)</th>
      <th>AI Technology Used</th>
      <th>AI Impact Area</th>
    </tr>
  </thead>
```

```
<tbody>
    <tr *ngFor="let item of gridData">
      <td>{{ item.projectID }}</td>
      <td>{{ item.projectName }}</td>
      <td>{{ item.aiIntegrationLevel }}</td>
      <td>{{ item.efficiencyImprovement }}</td>
      <td>{{ item.featureCount }}</td>
      <td>{{ item.aiDrivenFeatureCount }}</td>
      <td>{{ item.bugCountBeforeAI }}</td>
      <td>{{ item.bugCountAfterAI }}</td>
      <td>{{ item.developmentTimeBeforeAI }}</td>
      <td>{{ item.developmentTimeAfterAI }}</td>
      <td>{{ item.aI_Technology_Used }}</td>
      <td>{{ item.aI_Impact_Area }}</td>
    </tr>
  </tbody>
</table>
```

- **Basic Styling**

  We applied minimal CSS to ensure readability, focusing on the
  essentials such as borders, padding, and headers to distinguish
  data points.

```
/* app.component.scss */
table {
    width: 100%;
    border-collapse: collapse;
}
table, th, td {
    border: 1px solid black;
}
th, td {
    padding: 8px;
    text-align: left;
}
```

```
thead {
    background-color: #f2f2f2;
}
```

- This approach demonstrates how quickly data can be presented in an Angular application. However, the simplicity of basic HTML tables also comes with limitations in terms of visual appeal and user engagement.

Visual Impact and the Need for Enhanced Solutions

While HTML tables serve their purpose for straightforward data display, they lack the visual impact necessary for a compelling user experience. Figure 16-1 shows the tables we implemented.

AI in Software Development

Project ID	Project Name	AI Integration Level	Efficiency Improvement (%)	Feature Count	AI-Driven Feature Count	Bug Count Before AI	Bug Count After AI	Development Time Before AI (days)	Development Time After AI (days)	AI Technology Used	AI Impact Area
1	AlphaNet	Full	40	50	20	100	60	180	108	Copilot, ML Algorithms	Code Quality
2	BetaStream	Partial	25	30	5	80	70	150	112	NLP, Data Analytics	Project Management
3	GammaCloud	None	0	40	0	90	90	200	200	None	None
4	DeltaSys	Full	50	60	30	120	48	240	120	RL, GNNs	Code Quality

Pie Chart Data

Category	Value
Code Quality	90
Project Management	25
None	0

Stacked Bar Chart Data

Project Name	Efficiency Improvement (%)	AI-Driven Feature Count	Bug Count Reduction	Time Saved (days)	AI Technology Used
AlphaNet	40	20	40	72	Copilot, ML Algorithms
BetaStream	25	5	10	38	NLP, Data Analytics
GammaCloud	0	0	0	0	None
DeltaSys	50	30	72	120	RL, GNNs

Figure 16-1. *Table view*

This effectively presents the data but does not capture the user's attention or aid in data interpretation beyond basic organization.

Conclusion

In this journey through Chapter 16, "Frontend Finesse with Angular," we have navigated the comprehensive landscape of Angular to build a dynamic, intuitive, and engaging user interface for our AI Dashboard project. From the initial setup of our Angular environment within the cutting-edge frameworks of .NET 6+ and Angular 17 to the implementation of basic data representation using HTML tables, we have laid a solid foundation for our frontend architecture.

We embraced the modern structures introduced in the latest versions of .NET and Angular, transitioning from Startup.cs and app.module.ts to Program.cs and standalone components. We tackled common challenges such as CORS configuration and dependency management in Angular 17, ensuring seamless communication between our frontend and backend.

Our journey through data representation began with the simplest approach: using HTML tables. We leveraged Angular's data binding capabilities to render API data into structured tables, providing clear and organized views. However, we also recognized the limitations of basic HTML tables in terms of visual appeal and user interaction.

As we wrap up the enriching journey through "Mosaic Tile 5: Frontend Finesse with Angular," it's time to take a step back and appreciate the strides we've made. For those meticulously tracking progress using agile methodologies, you can confidently mark your fourth user story, dedicated to UI/UX implementation with Angular, as "Completed." This milestone not only signifies the culmination of a chapter but also exemplifies your commitment to embracing agile practices, ensuring a seamless and structured development journey.

Key Takeaways

- **Modern Framework Adoption:** Embracing the new structures of .NET 6+ and Angular 17, enhancing the development workflow, and ensuring the application is future-proof.

- **Angular Services**: Effectively utilizing HttpClient within Angular services (AiDashBoardApiService) to interact with APIs and manage data efficiently.

- **Overcoming Challenges**: Successfully navigating common issues like CORS and dependency management, crucial for ensuring smooth communication between different parts of the application.

- **Basic Data Representation:** Implementing basic HTML tables for quick and clear data presentation, demonstrating Angular's simplicity and power in data binding.

- **Limitations of Simplicity:** Acknowledging the need for more advanced visualization techniques to create more engaging and insightful user interfaces.

As we conclude this chapter, we understand that while we have established a functional and structured UI, the journey toward creating a truly immersive and visually appealing user interface is just beginning. The tables have set the stage, but the need for more sophisticated visualization is clear.

Onward

We stand at the cusp of elevating our user interface from functional to fascinating. As we transition to Chapter 17, "Mosaic Tile 6: Visionary Vistas—Data Visualization Delight," we will explore how libraries like DevExtreme and Angular Material can be pivotal in transforming our data representation. These powerful libraries offer a plethora of components and tools, enabling us to create visually stunning, interactive, and intuitive visualizations with ease. This next user story will unveil the art of implementing data visualization components, further enhancing our AI Dashboard's interactivity and visual appeal. Get ready to transform abstract data into visual masterpieces, as we continue our agile journey, one user story at a time.

Join us in the next chapter as we delve into the realm of advanced data visualization, enhancing the UI/UX of our AI Dashboard to not just display data but to tell a story that resonates and engages. The journey from data to delight awaits!

CHAPTER 17

Mosaic Tile 6: Visionary Vistas: Data Visualization Delight

Welcome to "Visionary Vistas: Data Visualization Delight," where we transcend traditional data presentation to explore the artistry and impact of advanced visualization techniques. As we embark on this journey, our mission is to transform the intricate datasets of our AI Dashboard into visually engaging, insightful narratives that not only inform but also captivate and inspire action.

In the realm of modern web development, data visualization stands as a pivotal element, bridging the gap between raw data and actionable insights. It's not merely about presenting numbers and figures; it's about storytelling, uncovering the hidden patterns, trends, and correlations that lie within the data. As we delve into this chapter, we remember the foundations laid in Chapter 7, "Data Vistas: Painting with Numbers," where we initially explored the potential of charting libraries. Now, we take a step further, harnessing the full power of Angular Material and DevExtreme to craft a user interface that's not just functional but a visual masterpiece.

The AI Dashboard project serves as our canvas, and the data it generates, our palette. As developers and storytellers, we are tasked with choosing the right colors, shapes, and forms—choosing the right visualization techniques—to narrate the data's story most effectively. Whether it's displaying project metrics, depicting AI impact areas through pie charts, or showcasing project efficiencies via stacked bar charts, each choice we make in visualization plays a crucial role in how the data is perceived and interpreted.

In this chapter, we're not just coding; we're designing experiences. We're not just solving technical challenges; we're unlocking new perspectives. With each graph, chart, or map we implement, we turn numbers into insights, insights into decisions, and decisions into action.

439

© Arpit Dwivedi 2024
A. Dwivedi, *CodeMosaic*, https://doi.org/10.1007/979-8-8688-0276-8_17

Let's push the boundaries of what's possible with data visualization in Angular, turning our AI Dashboard into a testament to the power of visual storytelling. Prepare to be amazed, for you're about to witness how data, when visualized effectively, can become the most compelling story ever told.

Best Practices for Effective Data Visualization

Data visualization is a powerful storytelling tool in the digital age. It transforms complex data sets into clear, understandable visual representations, making it an essential skill for developers and analysts alike. In this section, we delve into best practices that serve as guiding principles for creating effective and impactful visualizations. Each practice is not just a technique but a solution to common challenges, ensuring that your visualizations deliver clarity, insight, and value.

1. Choosing the Right Chart Type

Selecting an appropriate chart type is crucial for accurately representing the underlying data and effectively communicating the intended message.

Problem Solved: Prevents confusion and misinterpretation of data by aligning the visualization with the data's nature and the message it aims to convey.

Solution: Assess the data's characteristics and the story you want to tell. Use bar charts for comparisons, line charts for trends, and pie charts for proportions.

GPT-3 Prompt: "Generate a guideline for selecting the most appropriate chart type based on data characteristics and desired storytelling outcome."

2. Simplifying and Decluttering

Stripping the visualization of unnecessary elements or complex jargon to make it more understandable and visually appealing.

Problem Solved: Eliminates distractions, allowing the viewer to focus on the most critical parts of the data.

Solution: Remove extraneous graphics, limit color usage, and avoid overly complicated chart types that might obscure the data's message.

GPT-3 Prompt: "Provide tips for simplifying a data visualization while maintaining its integrity and purpose."

3. Consistent and Clear Labeling

Using labels and legends accurately and consistently to describe the data and variables clearly.

Problem Solved: Enhances understanding by clearly denoting what each part of the visualization represents, preventing misinterpretation.

Solution: Ensure that all labels are easy to read, axes are clearly marked, and a legend is provided if multiple variables are present.

GPT-3 Prompt: "Create a checklist for labeling elements in a data visualization to maximize clarity and user comprehension."

4. Balanced Color Palette

Choosing a color scheme that is visually appealing and serves to differentiate data points without overwhelming the viewer.

Problem Solved: Facilitates better data interpretation and ensures that the visualization is accessible to all viewers, including those with color vision deficiencies.

Solution: Use a colorblind-friendly palette, limit the number of colors used, and apply color consistently to represent the same type of data.

GPT-3 Prompt: "Suggest a color palette for a data visualization aimed at ensuring accessibility and enhancing data distinction."

5. Highlighting Key Data

Emphasizing important data points or trends to guide the viewer's attention to the most critical information.

Problem Solved: Ensures that the main insights from the data are not lost or overlooked by the audience.

Solution: Use visual elements like contrast, size, or annotations to draw attention to significant data points or trends.

GPT-3 Prompt: "Propose methods for highlighting key data points in a visualization to ensure they capture the viewer's attention effectively."

6. Interactive Elements

Incorporating interactive features such as hover effects, clickable elements, or dynamic filters to engage the viewer and provide a deeper exploration of the data.

Problem Solved: Enhances the user experience by allowing viewers to engage with the visualization and discover personalized insights.

Solution: Implement interactive components that enable users to drill down into the data or view additional details on demand.

GPT-3 Prompt: "Outline a strategy for integrating interactive elements into a data visualization to enhance user engagement and data exploration."

7. Responsiveness and Accessibility

Ensuring that visualizations are accessible across different devices and to users with varying abilities.

Problem Solved: Guarantees that the visualization is usable and informative for all users, regardless of the device used or individual accessibility needs.

Solution: Design visualizations that are responsive to screen size changes and accessible to users with disabilities, considering factors like keyboard navigability and screen reader compatibility.

GPT-3 Prompt: "Generate guidelines for creating data visualizations that are both responsive and accessible, ensuring a wide user reach and inclusivity."

These best practices serve as a roadmap for creating data visualizations that are not only visually appealing but also meaningful and insightful. As you implement these techniques, remember that the goal is to make the data tell its story in the most compelling and understandable way possible. In the next section, we will dive into the practical implementation of these principles using Angular Material and DevExtreme in our AI Dashboard project.

Enhancing Visualization with DevExtreme

DevExtreme is a premium suite of JavaScript components that offers a rich set of capabilities for building modern web applications. Its extensive collection of UI components, including the Data Grid, Pie Chart, and Bar Chart, are designed to integrate seamlessly with Angular, providing developers with a robust toolkit for creating highly interactive and visually appealing user interfaces. DevExtreme stands out for its ease of use, extensive documentation, and adaptive rendering capabilities, making it a go-to choice for developers aiming to deliver top-notch user experiences with minimal coding effort.

Setting Up DevExtreme

Installation

- Install DevExtreme into your Angular project using npm:

  `npm install devextreme devextreme-angular --save`

- This command adds both DevExtreme and its Angular integration module.

Configuration

- Import the required DevExtreme modules into your component. For instance, for the Data Grid, Pie Chart, and Bar Chart, import the respective modules.

- Example:

```typescript code
import { DxDataGridModule, DxPieChartModule, DxChartModule } from
'devextreme-angular';
@NgModule({
  // ...
  imports: [
    // ...
    DxDataGridModule,
    DxPieChartModule,
    DxChartModule
  ],
  // ...
})
export class AppModule { }
```

Code Explanation for DevExtreme Pie Chart

HTML Structure and Styling

```html code
<div class="dashboard-container">
  <h1 class="dashboard-header">AI Dashboard</h1>

  <!-- DevExtreme Pie Chart Component -->
  <dx-pie-chart
    title="AI Advancement in Projects"
    class="pie-chart"
    [dataSource]="pieChartData"
    palette="Bright">
    <!-- ... chart configuration ... -->
  </dx-pie-chart>
</div>
```

Dashboard Container and Header

- **dashboard-container:** A wrapper div for styling and positioning your dashboard elements.

- **dashboard-header:** A header tag (<h1>) for your dashboard title, giving users an immediate understanding of what the chart represents.

DevExtreme Pie Chart Component

- **<dx-pie-chart>**

  - The main component for the pie chart provided by DevExtreme.

  - **title="AI Advancement in Projects":** Sets the title of the pie chart.

  - **class="pie-chart":** Assigns a CSS class to the pie chart for additional styling.

- **[dataSource]="pieChartData":** Binds the pieChartData from your TypeScript component to be used as the data source for the pie chart.

- **palette="Bright":** Chooses a predefined color palette to make the chart visually appealing.

Chart Series Configuration

- **<dxi-series>**

  - Defines the series for the pie chart.

  - **argumentField="category":** Specifies which field from the data source should be used for the pie chart segments.

  - **valueField="value":** Specifies which field from the data source should be used for the segment values.

- **<dxo-label>**

  - Configures the labels for each pie segment.

  - **[visible]="true":** Ensures that the labels are visible.

  - **format="fixedPoint":** Sets the numeric format for the labels (in this case, a fixed-point format).

  - **[customizeText]="customizeText":** A method to customize the text of the labels (defined in your TypeScript component).

Tooltip Configuration

- **<dxo-tooltip>**

  - Enables and configures tooltips for the pie chart.

  - **[enabled]="true":** Turns on the tooltip feature.

  - **format="fixedPoint":** Sets the numeric format for the tooltip (fixed-point in this case).

  - **[customizeTooltip]="customizeTooltip":** A method to customize the tooltip content (defined in your TypeScript component).

Export and Legend Configuration

- **<dxo-export>**

  - **[enabled]="true":** Enables the export functionality, allowing users to download the chart.

- **<dxo-legend>**

  - **horizontalAlignment="center":** Centers the legend horizontally within the chart area.

  - **verticalAlignment="bottom":** Positions the legend at the bottom of the chart area.

TypeScript Component for Customization Functions

In your TypeScript component file, you should define the customizeText and customizeTooltip methods to format the text displayed in the labels and tooltips. Here's an example:

```typescript
export class YourComponent {
  // ... your existing component code ...

  customizeText(arg: any) {
    return `${arg.argumentText}: ${arg.valueText}`;
  }

  customizeTooltip(arg: any) {
    return {
      text: `${arg.argumentText}: ${arg.valueText}`
    };
  }
}
```

Visualization

So as we can see Devextreme gives us a lot of customization options, that too in minimal coding, for example, for this much of HTML code:

```
<dx-pie-chart
    title="AI Advancement in Projects"
    class="pie-chart"
    [dataSource]="pieChartData"
    palette="Bright">
    <dxi-series argumentField="category" valueField="value">
        <dxo-label [visible]="true" format="fixedPoint" [customizeText]=
        "customizeText"></dxo-label>
    </dxi-series>
    <dxo-tooltip [enabled]="true" format="fixedPoint" [customizeTooltip]=
    "customizeTooltip"></dxo-tooltip>
    <dxo-export [enabled]="true"></dxo-export>

    <dxo-legend horizontalAlignment="center" verticalAlignment="bottom">
    </dxo-legend>
</dx-pie-chart>
```

We'll have a visualization with chart as in Figure 17-1.

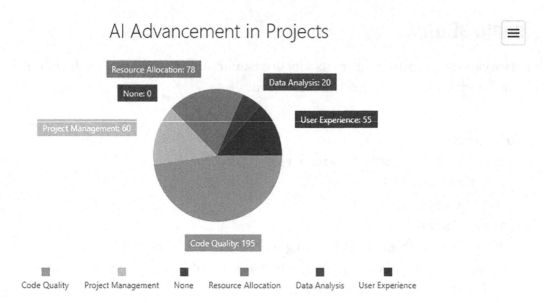

Figure 17-1. *Pie chart 1*

So using our API we can create lots of charts, on different aspects, to make our AI dashboard extremely interesting as charts in Figure 17-2.

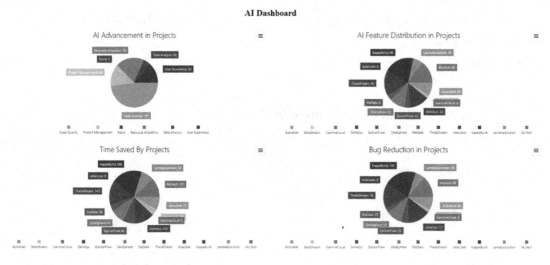

Figure 17-2. *Multiple pie charts*

And similar bar and line chart as well (Figure 17-3), that too in minimal effort.

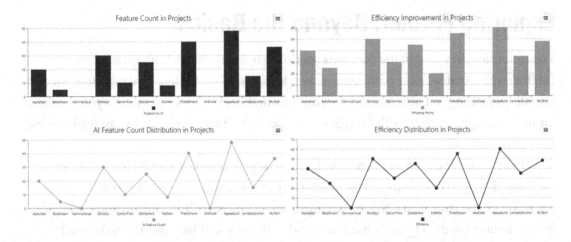

Figure 17-3. *Multiple other charts*

And some comparison charts (Figure 17-4) too.

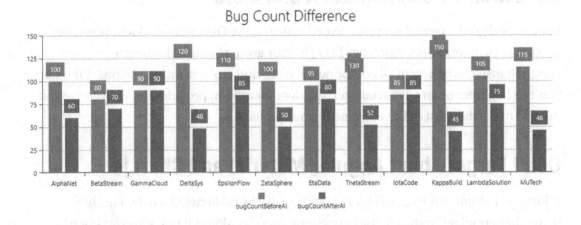

Figure 17-4. *Chart for comparison*

By customizing these aspects of your pie chart, you ensure that the visual representation of your data is not only informative but also engaging and user-friendly. The DevExtreme pie chart component's configuration options and the ability to customize text and tooltips make it a powerful tool for any data-driven Angular application.

Exploring Further: Beyond the Basics

The examples provided in the previous sections showcase just a fraction of what DevExtreme can do. These components are designed to make data visualization not only visually appealing but also interactive and informative. While we've guided you through implementing a pie chart with DevExtreme, there's a whole world of possibilities waiting for you to explore.

The code for these charts, along with many other examples, can be found in our code repository. We encourage you to dive into these resources, tweak the examples, and even create your own unique visualizations. If you're feeling adventurous, why not try implementing the DevExtreme Data Grid or the Stacked Bar Chart? The extensive documentation and community support make DevExtreme a valuable tool in any developer's arsenal.

DevExtreme Documentation and More

For detailed guidance and more advanced features, the DevExtreme Documentation (`https://js.devexpress.com/Angular/`) is your go-to resource. It offers a comprehensive overview of all components, APIs, and customization options. Whether you're a beginner or an advanced user, the documentation provides the knowledge you need to make the most of DevExtreme in your projects.

Don't Forget About Angular Material and Chart.js

While DevExtreme offers a rich set of features, it's always beneficial to be familiar with other popular libraries in the ecosystem. Angular Material is a powerful library that aligns with Material Design principles and integrates seamlessly with Angular applications. Explore the Angular Material Documentation (`https://material.angular.io/`) to learn about its components and how they can enhance your application's design and functionality.

If you're interested in crafting engaging charts and visualizations, Chart.js (`www.chartjs.org/docs/latest/`) is another excellent library to consider. It's simple, flexible, and provides beautiful charts with minimal code. Dive into the Chart.js documentation to discover how you can bring your data to life in new and exciting ways.

Conclusion

As we conclude Chapter 17, we've embarked on a transformative journey, unraveling the art and science of data visualization with a particular focus on DevExtreme. We ventured beyond mere data representation, bringing to life the complex datasets of our AI Dashboard through vibrant, interactive visual narratives. This chapter was not just about understanding the technicalities of DevExtreme but also about appreciating the immense power of visual storytelling in the digital age.

For those meticulously tracking their progress using agile methodologies, it's time to mark a significant milestone. You may now confidently close the tasks associated with this chapter and mark the corresponding user story as "Completed." This accomplishment is a testament to your dedication and skill in harnessing cutting-edge tools to transform raw data into compelling insights.

Key Takeaways

- **Visual Storytelling with DevExtreme:** Embraced the power of DevExtreme to transform complex datasets into engaging, interactive, and insightful visual narratives.

- **Best Practices for Data Visualization:** Learned the art of choosing the right visualization techniques, simplifying and decluttering visuals, and ensuring clarity and consistency in presentation.

- **Ease of Implementation:** Discovered the simplicity and effectiveness of DevExtreme in creating sophisticated visual components with minimal coding effort.

- **Resourcefulness:** Explored comprehensive documentation and resources, empowering you to further customize and refine your data visualizations.

- **Agile Progression:** Successfully integrated the principles of agile development, tracking progress, and achieving milestones in a structured and efficient manner.

- **Exploration and Innovation:** Encouraged to explore beyond the basics, leveraging the vast capabilities of DevExtreme, Angular Material, and Chart.js to innovate and create unique visualization experiences.

Onward

As we close this chapter on data visualization, we stand at the threshold of yet another exciting phase in our development journey. Get ready to embark on "Mosaic Tile 7: Integration Ingenuity with Small Tools," where we will delve into the realm of seamless integration strategies.

In the upcoming chapter, our focus will shift to integrating the frontend, backend, and databases cohesively, harnessing AI for enhanced integration efficiency. We will explore the nuances of utilizing AI tools for integration, testing, troubleshooting, as well as performance and optimization, setting the stage for a holistic and streamlined development experience.

Prepare for your next Mosaic Tile and the forthcoming user story, where the intricacies of integration await your mastery. The journey continues, and with each step, we're not just building applications; we're crafting a symphony of technology and innovation.

CHAPTER 18

Mosaic Tile 7: Integration Ingenuity with Smart Tools

As we pivot to the pivotal sixth user story of our digital odyssey, "Code Mosaic," we find ourselves at a juncture where the pieces of our software tapestry begin to weave together, forming a coherent and functional whole. This chapter, "Mosaic Tile 7: Integration Ingenuity with Smart Tools," is dedicated to the art and science of integration, a phase in the software development lifecycle where the magic of collaboration between various components unfolds.

Integration is not just about making different pieces of code work together; it's about doing so efficiently, securely, and in a way that enhances the overall quality and performance of the application. In this user story, we delve into the realm of established tools and technologies that have proven their worth in the trenches of software development. These tools are not just aids; they are the silent heroes that ensure the symphony of software components performs in perfect harmony.

As we venture through this chapter, remember that each tool and technology we explore is a tile in our mosaic, adding strength and beauty to the final picture. From code quality guardians like SonarCloud to the seamless orchestration of CI/CD pipelines with Azure DevOps, we will uncover the ingenuity behind successful integration practices. These are the tools that, when wielded with skill and understanding, can transform a fragmented set of code into a streamlined and robust application.

So, let's gear up to explore, understand, and master these integral instruments of software craftsmanship. By the end of this journey, you'll not only be acquainted with the tools that make integration a seamless process but also be ready to employ them in crafting your own masterpiece, the AI dashboard, ensuring it stands as a testament to the prowess of smart development in the modern digital era.

© Arpit Dwivedi 2024
A. Dwivedi, *CodeMosaic*, https://doi.org/10.1007/979-8-8688-0276-8_18

Established Tools for Code Quality and Review

In the labyrinth of software development, the quest for excellence is continuous. The quality of the code not only defines the integrity of the final product but also reflects the craftsmanship of its creators. As our sixth user story unfolds, we find ourselves in the realm of precision and perfection, where every line of code is scrutinized, and every potential flaw is addressed. Here, we introduce the stalwarts of code quality and review—tools that have become indispensable in the pursuit of impeccable software.

Code quality is the cornerstone of software development that determines its maintainability, scalability, and efficiency. It's not just about writing code that works but about crafting code that endures and evolves. Code review, on the other hand, is the art of collaboratively examining the code to not only catch bugs early but also to share knowledge and ensure adherence to coding standards. This is where our trusted tools come into play, automating and enhancing the process of ensuring code quality.

SonarQube/SonarCloud

Enter SonarQube and SonarCloud, the sentinels of code quality. These tools offer continuous inspection, providing developers with the means to analyze and measure the health of their codebase. They stand out by offering

- **Static Code Analysis:** SonarQube/SonarCloud scrutinizes your code for bugs, code smells, and security vulnerabilities, ensuring that quality is embedded from the very first line of code.

- **Integration with CI/CD Pipelines:** Seamlessly integrating with your CI/CD pipelines, these tools provide continuous feedback, allowing teams to address issues promptly and efficiently.

- **Customizable Rules and Quality Gates:** Tailor the rules and set quality gates according to your project's needs, ensuring that only code that meets the highest standards makes it to production.

In a real-world scenario, consider a project where introducing SonarQube drastically reduced the bug rate, significantly improving the maintainability of the codebase and reducing technical debt.

Linting Tools: ESLint, JSLint, StyleCop

Linting tools are the vigilant guardians of coding standards, ensuring consistency and preventing potential errors before they turn into bugs.

- **ESLint (for JavaScript/TypeScript):** ESLint goes beyond mere syntax checking; it's about enforcing coding styles, finding problematic patterns, and even fixing code as you type. It's like having a vigilant pair of eyes reviewing your code, ensuring it's not just correct but clean and consistent.

- **JSLint (for JavaScript):** A more stringent tool, JSLint, takes a no-compromise approach to code quality. While it might be stricter, it instills discipline, ensuring that your JavaScript code is not just functional but also well-structured and maintainable.

- **StyleCop (for C#):** For the C# aficionados, StyleCop is like the grammar police of coding. It enforces a set of style and consistency rules, ensuring that your C# code is not just powerful but also beautifully crafted and easy to read.

Integrating Quality Tools into the Development Workflow

Integrating these tools into your development workflow isn't just about automating reviews; it's about fostering a culture of quality. Automation ensures consistent checks, while continuous feedback ensures that quality is a constant, not an afterthought. Configuring these tools to align with your team's standards transforms code review from a task into a seamless part of your development process.

Benefits of Embracing Code Quality and Review Tools

Adopting these tools is an investment in your product's future. They ensure that your codebase remains clean, efficient, and secure. They facilitate knowledge sharing and collaboration, making your team not just developers but craftsmen. The result? A product that's not just built but engineered to stand the test of time.

In the narrative of "Code Mosaic," quality is not a checkpoint but a journey. As we navigate through our user stories, tools like SonarQube, ESLint, JSLint, and StyleCop are our companions, guiding us toward excellence. They are not just tools; they are the embodiment of our commitment to crafting software that's not just functional but exemplary. As we gear up for the next chapter in our saga, we carry with us the lessons of diligence, precision, and the unyielding pursuit of quality.

Effective Integration and Continuous Deployment Tools

In the tapestry of "Code Mosaic," the threads of code intertwine not just at the level of syntax but through a symphony of processes and practices that ensure every piece fits perfectly. This chapter of our narrative takes us into the world of Continuous Integration (CI) and Continuous Deployment (CD), where the rhythm of development is maintained by a suite of tools designed for harmony and efficiency. Let's explore the stalwarts of CI/CD, tools that have redefined the paradigms of software development.

In the realm of software development, CI/CD stands as the backbone of a streamlined, efficient, and error-resistant production pipeline. Continuous Integration ensures that code changes are automatically tested and merged into a shared repository, fostering a culture of collaboration and early bug detection. Continuous Deployment takes it a step further, automating the software release process, ensuring that any validated changes to the codebase are quickly reflected in the production environment. Together, they create a dynamic, agile, and responsive development ecosystem.

Jenkins: The Automation Server

Jenkins, the revered automation server, stands at the forefront of CI/CD innovation. Its prowess lies in its

- **Versatile Plugin Ecosystem:** Jenkins' extensive plugin ecosystem allows it to adapt and extend its capabilities, catering to virtually every need of the development and deployment process.

- **Support for Diverse Projects**: Whether it's a simple website or a complex multi-component app, Jenkins brings its automation magic to projects of all sizes and complexities.

- **Flexible Configuration and Management**: Jenkins provides developers with the freedom to craft their unique automation scenarios, ensuring that the tool bends to the project's needs, not the other way around.

In practice, Jenkins has transformed the development landscape. Consider a scenario where introducing Jenkins reduced deployment errors by a significant margin and cut down release times, proving its mettle as a game-changer in CI/CD.

Travis CI: The Trusted Solution for Open Source Projects

Travis CI emerges as a beacon of reliability and simplicity, particularly cherished in the open source community. Its prominence is marked by

- **Seamless GitHub Integration:** Travis CI integrates effortlessly with GitHub, ensuring that every Pull Request is a trigger for automated builds and tests.

- **Automated Testing**: Each commit is an opportunity for improvement, and Travis CI ensures that by automatically running your test suite and providing immediate feedback.

- **Multi-language Support:** Travis CI speaks the language of developers, supporting multiple programming languages and platforms, making it a versatile choice for diverse projects.

A real-world example of Travis CI could involve an open source project where the introduction of Travis CI led to a more streamlined, error-free development process, enhancing the project's reliability and quality.

Azure DevOps: The Complete DevOps Solution

Azure DevOps stands as a testament to Microsoft's commitment to comprehensive development solutions. It offers

- **End-to-End DevOps Capability:** From agile planning to source control, from CI/CD to monitoring, Azure DevOps is the one-stop solution for all DevOps needs.

- **Reliable CI/CD Pipelines:** Azure DevOps ensures that your builds are consistent and your deployments are smooth, driving reliability and predictability in the release process.

- **Integrated Monitoring and Feedback:** Continuous improvement is at the heart of Azure DevOps, with integrated monitoring and feedback mechanisms ensuring that your software is not just developed but continually enhanced.

Consider a complex enterprise scenario where Azure DevOps orchestrated the development, ensuring consistent builds, reliable deployments, and a level of agility that matched the enterprise's dynamic needs.

Benefits of CI/CD Tools

Embracing CI/CD tools is akin to setting the rhythm for a well-orchestrated performance. They bring

- **Reduced Integration Issues:** CI/CD tools ensure that integration issues are caught early and are less likely to escalate into larger problems.

- **Faster Delivery Times:** By automating testing and deployment, these tools significantly cut down on the time it takes to deliver new features and fixes.

- **Improved Quality and Predictability:** With consistent builds and automated tests, the quality of the product improves, and the release process becomes more predictable.

- **Enhanced Collaboration and Transparency:** CI/CD tools foster a culture where collaboration and transparency are not just encouraged but ingrained in the development process.

Integrating CI/CD Tools with Established Quality Tools

The real power of CI/CD tools is unlocked when they are integrated with code quality tools like SonarQube and linting tools. This integration ensures that not only is the code continuously integrated and deployed but also that its quality is continuously scrutinized and enhanced.

In our journey through "Code Mosaic," CI/CD tools are not just tools; they are the catalysts of change, driving efficiency, quality, and collaboration. They are the silent forces that ensure our digital creations are not just built but are woven with the threads of precision, reliability, and excellence. As we gear up for the next chapter, we carry with us the assurance that our development process is bolstered by the robustness and agility that these CI/CD tools provide.

Version Control Systems

As we weave through the intricate patterns of "Code Mosaic," the thread that consistently binds the fabric of our digital creation is the Version Control System (VCS). A robust VCS is the bedrock upon which the pillars of integration, collaboration, and quality assurance stand. In this chapter, we delve deeper into the world of VCS, shining a spotlight on platforms like Git, GitHub, GitLab, and Bitbucket, and their indispensable role in the integration phase of software development.

The tapestry of software development is intricate and complex, with numerous developers contributing code to the same project. Version control systems are the guardians of this tapestry, ensuring that every change is tracked, every contribution is acknowledged, and every version is preserved. In the realm of integration, these systems are not just tools; they are the facilitators of collaboration, the arbitrators of code quality, and the architects of seamless code merging.

Git: The Foundation of Modern Version Control

Git, the cornerstone of modern version control, is more than a tool; it's a paradigm that has reshaped the landscape of software development. Its distributed nature, robust branching and merging capabilities, and its support for nonlinear development make it an invaluable asset in the developer's toolkit. Git's prowess in handling everything from small to colossal projects with speed and efficiency makes it the go-to choice for teams worldwide.

GitHub: Collaboration and Integration Hub

GitHub takes the capabilities of Git and elevates them to a new level of collaboration and integration. It serves as a hub where code meets conversation, where pull requests pave the way for code review and team discussions. With features like GitHub Actions, teams can automate workflows, ensuring that integration is not just a phase but a continuous, seamless process. The integration of CI/CD tools and project management features makes GitHub a comprehensive platform for software development and delivery.

GitLab: The Single Application for the Entire DevOps Lifecycle

GitLab stands out as an all-encompassing platform that covers the entire DevOps lifecycle. It's not just a version control system; it's a complete ecosystem that integrates project planning, source code management, CI/CD, and monitoring in a single application. Its commitment to transparency and efficiency is evident in its built-in CI/CD capabilities, comprehensive issue tracking, and agile project management features. GitLab's holistic approach ensures that from the first line of code to the final deployment, every step is aligned, integrated, and optimized.

Bitbucket: The Version Control Solution for Professional Teams

Bitbucket is the version control solution that caters to the professional needs of teams, integrating seamlessly with other Atlassian products like Jira and Trello. It extends the power of Git with pull requests, inline commenting for code review, and Bitbucket Pipelines for built-in CI/CD. The integration with Jira enhances project tracking and management, ensuring that every commit, every branch, and every release is in sync with the project's goals and timelines.

The true power of version control systems is unleashed when they are combined with CI/CD tools. This synergy creates a dynamic environment where code integration, testing, and deployment occur seamlessly and efficiently. The result is a development process that is not just faster and more reliable but also one that fosters a culture of continuous improvement and collaboration.

Automated Testing Tools

In the intricate dance of software development, automated testing tools are the choreographers ensuring every step is precise, every move is synchronized, and the entire performance flows seamlessly. As we navigate through the chapters of "Code Mosaic," we recognize the critical role of these tools in the integration phase, where they not just contribute but elevate the quality, reliability, and efficiency of the final product. Let's delve into the world of some of the most prominent automated testing tools—Selenium, JUnit, TestNG, and Mocha—and understand how they orchestrate the symphony of software testing.

Automated testing stands as a beacon of efficiency in the tumultuous seas of software development. It transcends the manual limitations, allowing tests to be run repeatedly, at any time, with speed and precision. In the context of integration, automated testing is not just a phase; it's a continuous assurance of quality, ensuring that every integration is a step toward a more stable, reliable, and high-performing application.

Selenium: Navigating the UI Testing Landscape

Selenium emerges as a versatile maestro in the realm of automated browser testing. Its ability to mimic user interactions with web applications places it at the forefront of UI testing. Here's why Selenium is a tool of choice for testers worldwide:

- **Multi-language Support:** Selenium speaks the language of the developers, supporting test scripts in Java, C#, Python, and more, ensuring that the tool adapts to the developer, not the other way around.

- **Cross-Browser Compatibility:** With its ability to run tests across different browsers and platforms, Selenium ensures that your application delivers a consistent user experience, irrespective of where it's accessed from.

- **Integration Friendly:** Seamlessly integrating with testing frameworks and CI/CD pipelines, Selenium ensures that testing is an integral part of the development, not an afterthought.

In a real-world scenario, Selenium has proven its mettle by significantly reducing the time and resources required for exhaustive UI testing, ensuring that applications are not just functional but flawlessly user-friendly.

JUnit: The Cornerstone of Java Unit Testing

JUnit stands as a sentinel of quality in the Java ecosystem, embodying the principles of precision, structure, and simplicity in unit testing. Here's how JUnit makes a difference:

- **Annotations-Based Approach:** JUnit's annotation-based approach simplifies the process of writing and organizing tests, making it more structured and intuitive.

- **Seamless Integration:** The ease with which JUnit integrates with IDEs and build tools ensures that unit testing is a cohesive part of the development process.

- **Extensibility:** The ability to write custom test runners and extensions makes JUnit not just a testing framework but a testing platform that caters to varied and complex testing needs.

Consider a Java project where the introduction of JUnit transformed the testing process, leading to more robust, maintainable, and error-free code.

TestNG: Elevating Test Automation with Flexibility

TestNG, inspired by JUnit but introduced to overcome its limitations, brings flexibility and power to test automation. It's not just a framework; it's a testing powerhouse with features that address the intricate needs of complex testing scenarios:

- **Advanced Annotations:** TestNG's sophisticated annotations provide greater control over test execution, enabling more structured and organized tests.

- **Parameterized and Data-Driven Testing:** The ability to perform parameterized and data-driven testing makes TestNG a formidable tool for ensuring application behavior across various datasets and conditions.

- **Rich Reporting:** With its detailed and insightful reporting, TestNG doesn't just point out the flaws; it provides a comprehensive overview, aiding in better analysis and decision-making.

In practical terms, TestNG has been instrumental in enhancing the testing strategies of organizations, ensuring that applications are not just tested but thoroughly validated.

Mocha: The Flavorful JavaScript Test Framework

In the world of JavaScript testing, Mocha stands out with its rich features and flexibility. It's not just a framework; it's a testament to the power and dynamism of JavaScript testing:

- **Asynchronous Testing Made Easy:** Mocha's support for asynchronous testing ensures that your tests are as dynamic and robust as your applications.

- **Flexibility at its Best:** With its compatibility with assertion libraries and tools for mocking and spying, Mocha adapts to your testing needs, ensuring that your tests are as comprehensive as they need to be.

- **Informative Reporting:** Mocha's reporting is not just about the results; it's about providing insights, making it a tool for learning and improvement.

Mocha has revolutionized the way JavaScript applications are tested, ensuring that every function, every API, and every asynchronous call is scrutinized to perfection.

The Impact of Automated Testing Tools on Software Integration

Automated testing tools are the unsung heroes of software integration. They work silently in the background, catching bugs, ensuring compatibility, and validating functionality. When integrated into the CI/CD pipeline, they transform the integration process, making it more reliable, efficient, and devoid of human error. The result is software that's not just built but fortified with the principles of quality and performance.

As we script the chapters of "Code Mosaic," automated testing tools are the critical instruments ensuring that our code not only functions but excels. Tools like Selenium, JUnit, TestNG, and Mocha are not mere utilities; they are the cornerstones of quality assurance, the guardians of code integrity, and the catalysts for excellence in the integration phase of software development. As we progress in our journey, we carry the assurance that our digital creation is not just coded but crafted with the highest standards of quality and reliability.

Performance Monitoring and Optimization Tools

In the intricate symphony of software development, performance monitoring and optimization tools are the conductors, ensuring each component plays in harmony, maintaining the rhythm, and elevating the overall performance. As we progress through the chapters of "Code Mosaic," we turn our focus to the guardians of system health and performance—tools like New Relic, Dynatrace, and AppDynamics. These tools don't just monitor; they analyze, optimize, and transform data into actionable insights, ensuring that the software not only functions but thrives.

In the digital age, an application's performance is a testament to its quality. Performance monitoring and optimization tools are the telescopes peering into the universe of software, tracking every star, every planet, and every comet, ensuring that the cosmic dance of bytes and bits remains flawless. These tools are pivotal in diagnosing issues, optimizing resources, and ensuring that the application's performance resonates with the expectations of users and the objectives of businesses.

New Relic: The Real-Time Performance Monitor

New Relic stands as a beacon in the realm of performance monitoring, offering real-time insights and comprehensive visibility into the application's performance. With New Relic, teams can

- **Dive Deep into Application Performance:** New Relic provides a granular view of application performance, tracing transactions from the browser to the backend, ensuring that no issue, no matter how small, goes unnoticed.

- **Stay Proactive with Custom Alerts:** Customizable alerting mechanisms ensure that teams are not just reacting to issues but are proactively managing system health.

- **Gain Insights into Infrastructure:** Beyond application performance, New Relic offers insights into the infrastructure, ensuring that the hardware and software work in tandem to deliver optimal performance.

In practice, New Relic has been instrumental in turning performance data into performance insights, aiding teams in not just maintaining but continuously improving system performance.

Dynatrace: The AI-Powered Performance Engine

Dynatrace revolutionizes performance monitoring with its AI-powered engine, offering a futuristic approach to system health and optimization. Dynatrace excels by

- **Offering Full-Stack Monitoring**: From applications to servers to infrastructure, Dynatrace provides a holistic view of the entire stack, ensuring comprehensive monitoring.

- **Automating Problem Detection:** With its advanced AI, Dynatrace not only detects issues but also pinpoints their root causes, simplifying the complex web of diagnosis.

- **Enhancing User Experience:** By monitoring user interactions and measuring user satisfaction, Dynatrace ensures that the application's performance aligns with user expectations.

In real-world scenarios, Dynatrace has proven to be a game-changer, transforming the way teams approach performance issues, from guesswork to precise, data-driven strategies.

AppDynamics: The Application Performance Management Expert

AppDynamics stands at the forefront of application performance management, offering not just monitoring solutions but business insights. AppDynamics distinguishes itself by

- **Correlating Performance with Business Outcomes:** AppDynamics goes beyond technical metrics, linking application performance to business results, ensuring that performance optimization aligns with business objectives.

- **Providing End-to-End Transaction Tracing:** With its ability to trace transactions from start to finish, AppDynamics ensures that every interaction, every API call, and every user click is accounted for and optimized.

- **Delivering Advanced Analytics:** Through its sophisticated analytics, AppDynamics turns data into wisdom, guiding teams on not just how to maintain but how to excel.

AppDynamics has redefined performance monitoring, turning it into a strategic asset that not only ensures system health but drives business growth.

The Benefits of Performance Monitoring and Optimization Tools

Performance monitoring and optimization tools are not just instruments; they are the compasses guiding software applications toward excellence. They offer

- **Real-Time Insights:** These tools ensure that performance data is not just historical but real-time, enabling teams to act swiftly and decisively.

- **Optimized User Satisfaction:** By continuously monitoring and optimizing performance, these tools ensure that user experiences are not just satisfactory but delightful.

- **Data-Driven Decisions:** With the wealth of data these tools provide, decisions are no longer based on intuition but on solid, actionable insights.

Integrating Performance Tools with Development and Operations

Integrating performance monitoring tools into the development and operations life cycle ensures that performance is not an afterthought but a continuous priority. This integration fosters a culture of proactive performance management, where every code commit, every deployment, and every release is an opportunity for optimization and excellence.

As we etch the chapters of "Code Mosaic," performance monitoring and optimization tools are the lighthouses guiding our journey. Tools like New Relic, Dynatrace, and AppDynamics are not just monitoring solutions; they are the partners in our quest for excellence, ensuring that our software not only meets but exceeds the loftiest performance expectations. They ensure that our digital creation is not just operational but exceptional, setting a new benchmark in the realm of software performance.

Database Integration Tools

In the mosaic of software development, databases are the bedrock upon which the integrity and consistency of applications are built. The "Database Integration Tools" chapter is dedicated to the art of managing and integrating these critical components of software systems. This section delves into the world of database versioning tools like Liquibase and Flyway, and integration frameworks, highlighting their indispensable role in maintaining database stability, performance, and evolution.

Databases are the repositories of knowledge, the custodians of data that drive applications. Integrating these databases seamlessly into the development lifecycle is paramount. Proper database versioning and integration ensure not just the stability and performance of applications but also their capability to evolve and adapt in the face of changing requirements. In this landscape, database integration tools are the architects, ensuring that the foundation of our applications remains solid and secure.

Database Versioning Tools

In the dynamic world of software development, databases too must evolve. Database versioning tools are the guardians of this evolution, ensuring that every change is tracked, every version is accounted for, and every transition is smooth.

- **Liquibase**

  Liquibase stands as a sentinel of database schema changes, offering a comprehensive suite of tools to track, manage, and apply changes across various database types. Its support for multiple formats, including XML, YAML, and SQL, coupled with its integration capabilities with build and deployment tools, makes Liquibase a versatile and indispensable asset in database versioning.

- **Flyway**

  Flyway brings simplicity and elegance to database versioning. Known for its intuitive approach, Flyway ensures that versioning and migration are seamless and straightforward. Its extensive database support, coupled with its focus on simplicity and reliability, makes Flyway a preferred choice for teams that value ease of use alongside robust functionality.

Database Integration and Migration Frameworks

Beyond versioning, integrating and migrating databases with application code is pivotal. Integration and migration frameworks ensure that databases are not just static entities but dynamic components that evolve with the application.

- Entity Framework (for .NET):

  Entity Framework is the bridge between databases and .NET applications. It simplifies database operations by enabling code-first and database-first development, ensuring that database schema changes are synchronized with application code. Its capabilities in terms of database schema migration, code-first development, and comprehensive data query facilities make it an integral tool in the .NET ecosystem.

- Hibernate (for Java):

  Hibernate stands as a robust solution for database integration in Java applications. Renowned for its object-relational mapping capabilities, Hibernate simplifies data query and retrieval, ensuring that database interactions are not just efficient but intuitive. Its performance and scalability make it a cornerstone in the world of Java database integration.

Performance Implications of Database Integration

Efficient database integration is not just about maintaining stability; it's about optimizing performance. Proper versioning and migration strategies are critical in minimizing downtime, optimizing database queries, and ensuring data consistency. These strategies ensure that the database remains a catalyst for performance, not a bottleneck.

Best Practices for Database Integration

Navigating the realm of database integration demands adherence to best practices:

- **Maintain Backward Compatibility**: Ensuring that new changes do not disrupt existing functionalities is paramount.

- **Document Database Changes**: A well-documented change log is a roadmap that guides teams through the evolution of the database.

- **Test Database Migrations Thoroughly**: Rigorous testing ensures that migrations are not just successful but seamless.

- **Integrate Database Changes into CI/CD Pipeline**: Incorporating database changes into the CI/CD pipeline ensures that deployments are holistic, encompassing both application code and database schema.

In the journey of "Code Mosaic," database integration tools are not just tools; they are the pillars supporting the edifice of our applications. Tools like Liquibase, Flyway, Entity Framework, and Hibernate ensure that our databases are not just integrated but are integral to the performance, stability, and evolution of our software systems. As we script the next lines of our saga, we carry with us the assurance that our data, the lifeblood of our applications, is managed, integrated, and evolved with the utmost precision and care.

Security Integration Tools

In the intricate tapestry of software development, security is not just a thread but the very fabric that holds the entire tapestry together. The "Security Integration Tools" chapter is an essential narrative in the "Code Mosaic," emphasizing the significance of embedding security into every phase of the development lifecycle. This section explores the realm of security tools, focusing on Static Application Security Testing (SAST), Dynamic Application Security Testing (DAST), and the integration of these tools into the development pipeline, ensuring the creation of a secure, robust final product.

In the digital world, security is paramount. As threats evolve and vulnerabilities become more sophisticated, integrating security measures early in the software development process is not just a practice but a necessity. Security integration tools are the sentinels, standing guard from the inception of the code to its deployment, ensuring that every line of code, every integration, and every deployment is not just functional but fortified.

Static Application Security Testing (SAST) Tools

SAST tools are the meticulous inspectors of the code, scrutinizing every line for potential vulnerabilities even before the application is run. They are the first line of defense, identifying issues at the earliest stages of development.

- **Checkmarx**

  Checkmarx stands as a vanguard in the realm of SAST tools. Its comprehensive analysis ensures high accuracy in identifying vulnerabilities, offering insights and actionable recommendations. Integration with CI/CD pipelines ensures that security is woven into the very fabric of the development process, and its support for a wide range of programming languages and frameworks makes it a versatile ally in the quest for security.

- **Other SAST Tools**

  The arsenal of SAST tools is diverse, with formidable tools like Fortify and Veracode offering their unique capabilities. Fortify, with its automated security testing of software code, and Veracode, with its scalable solutions, ensure that security is not just an aspect but the core of software development.

Dynamic Application Security Testing (DAST) Tools

DAST tools are the dynamic warriors, testing the running applications, probing into every corner, every interaction to unearth vulnerabilities that lurk within.

- **OWASP ZAP (Zed Attack Proxy)**

  OWASP ZAP is the champion of open source DAST tools. It offers automated scanners and spidering capabilities that crawl through web applications, unearthing vulnerabilities that could have been missed. Its prowess in identifying security flaws in web applications makes it an indispensable tool in the developer's toolkit.

Interactive Application Security Testing (IAST) Tools

IAST tools combine the best of SAST and DAST, offering a comprehensive, real-time analysis of applications, making security a continuous, integrated aspect of development.

Example Tools

Tools like Contrast Security and Seeker offer unparalleled capabilities in IAST. They analyze code in real-time, providing immediate feedback, ensuring that the code is not just functional but secure. Their accuracy and efficiency in detecting security issues redefine the standards of application security testing.

Integrating Security Tools with DevOps (DevSecOps)

The integration of security tools into the DevOps process marks the evolution of DevOps into DevSecOps. This integration ensures that security is not a checkpoint but a continuous, integral part of the development and deployment process.

The Importance of Early Security Integration

Early security integration is the cornerstone of a secure application. It ensures that vulnerabilities are identified and addressed at the outset, saving costs, reducing risks, and building a product that not only meets but exceeds the security expectations of users and stakeholders.

In the odyssey of "Code Mosaic," security integration tools are not just tools; they are the guardians, the architects, and the custodians of security. Tools like Checkmarx, OWASP ZAP, and IAST solutions ensure that every phase of the software development process is secure, every product is robust, and every user's trust is upheld. As we etch the next lines of our narrative, we carry with us the assurance that our digital creations are not just built but fortified, not just functional but secure.

Conclusion

As we conclude this chapter, we reflect on the intricate tapestry we've woven together. Through our journey in "Integration Ingenuity with Smart Tools," we've explored a myriad of tools and practices that are fundamental in sculpting a robust, reliable, and efficient software infrastructure. This exploration has not just been about understanding these tools but about integrating them into our mosaic—our user story that is as diverse as it is dynamic. As we close this chapter, we also close this user story, knowing that the insights gained here are pivotal in shaping the next steps in our development odyssey.

Key Takeaways

- **Versatility of Integration Tools:** From database versioning with Liquibase and Flyway to security fortification with Checkmarx and OWASP ZAP, the versatility of these tools empowers developers to build more secure, robust, and high-performing applications.

- **Proactive Security Measures:** Integrating SAST, DAST, and IAST tools early in the development lifecycle is crucial for identifying and mitigating vulnerabilities, emphasizing the shift toward a DevSecOps culture.

- **Importance of Database Integration:** Efficient database integration, facilitated by tools like Entity Framework and Hibernate, plays a pivotal role in the application's performance and scalability.

- **Performance Monitoring:** Tools like New Relic, Dynatrace, and AppDynamics are essential for real-time performance monitoring, offering insights that guide optimization and ensuring the application meets user expectations.

- **Early Integration Benefits:** Embedding integration tools early in the development process paves the way for smoother workflows, fewer disruptions, and a more refined final product.

Onward

As we close the pages of this user story, our narrative takes a pivotal turn. The local development journey, rich with learning and integration, now seeks a broader horizon—the realm of deployment. In the upcoming chapter, "Cornerstone: Azure Awe—Smart Deployment Delight," we embark on the cornerstone phase of our project. Here, we'll navigate through the nuances of deployment strategies, leveraging the power of Azure for seamless deployment experiences. We'll delve into the practicalities of bringing our locally nurtured application into the global stage, discussing how to utilize Azure DevOps for building robust CI/CD pipelines. This chapter isn't just about deploying an application; it's about deploying a vision, a testament to our journey from a concept to a concrete solution, ready to make its mark in the real world.

CHAPTER 19

Cornerstone: Azure Awe—Smart Deployment Delight

We are now at the cornerstone that signifies the culmination of our CodeMosaic journey. This chapter marks not just the completion of a project but the realization of a vision, where every piece of code, every design decision, and every strategic plan converges into a cohesive, functional, and impactful solution. As we stand on the brink of completing our CodeMosaic, this chapter is dedicated to the critical phase of deploying our AI Dashboard, transitioning it from a local development marvel to a live, robust solution in the cloud.

Deployment is the bridge between development and real-world application, a crucial phase where your meticulously crafted solutions meet their users. It's where your code transcends the confines of the development environment and transforms into an accessible, operational service. This chapter is about ensuring that your AI Dashboard is not just a marvel in the development environment but a fully-functional, user-facing application hosted on Microsoft Azure, a platform known for its robustness, scalability, and security.

In this chapter, we will navigate through the intricacies of deploying both the .NET backend (AI Dashboard Web API) and the Angular frontend (AI Dashboard UI) to Azure. This journey will take us through the creation and configuration of Azure resources, the nuances of adjusting local development setups for the cloud environment, and the pivotal steps of building and publishing our applications to Azure. We will also delve into the automation of these processes through Azure DevOps, setting up CI/CD pipelines that streamline our deployment workflow and ensure that our application remains up-to-date and secure.

As we embark on this cornerstone, remember that it's not just about deploying an application; it's about instilling life into our CodeMosaic, making it a living, breathing entity ready to serve, solve, and innovate. Let's together bring the AI Dashboard to the forefront, ready to make an impact and serve its purpose in the real world.

Project Structure and Pre-deployment Setup

As we prepare for the deployment of our AI Dashboard to Azure, understanding the project structure and the setup of our resources is crucial. This foundational knowledge ensures a smooth transition from local development to the cloud environment.

Understanding the Project Structure

The AI Dashboard project consists of two main components: the AI Dashboard Web API (the .NET backend) and the AI Dashboard UI (the Angular frontend).

- **AI Dashboard Web API:** This .NET solution, named **AI Dashboard Web API**, is organized into a structured directory. Inside the root folder, it houses the controllers, data, and services essential for backend operations, along with the **appsettings.json** and other configuration files.

- **AI Dashboard UI:** Nested within the **AI Dashboard Web Application** directory, the Angular application, **AI Dashboard-UI**, includes standard Angular directories like **.angular, node_modules,** and **src**. It also contains the **proxy.conf.json** file, a crucial element for handling CORS during local development.

This structured approach not only makes our application modular and maintainable but also paves the way for a seamless integration and deployment process.

Azure Resources and DevOps Setup

Our Azure setup is a testament to our commitment to a structured and scalable application architecture.

- **Azure Resources**

  - **CodeMosaic Resource Group:** The umbrella under which all our Azure resources are organized, ensuring a consolidated and manageable cloud infrastructure.

  - **CodeMosaic SQL Server:** Hosts the **AI Dashboard SQL** Database, providing a robust and scalable database solution for our application.

  - **AI Dashboard SQL Database:** The heart of our data storage, meticulously designed and managed within the **CodeMosaic SQL Server.**

- **Azure DevOps Setup**

  - **CodeMosaicBook Organization:** The organizational layer in Azure DevOps, facilitating project management, collaboration, and CI/CD pipeline configuration.

  - **CodeMosaicDashboard Project:** Our specific project within the **CodeMosaicBook** organization, focusing on the development, testing, and deployment of the AI Dashboard.

  - **AI Dashboard Web API Repository:** The repository holding our .NET backend code, an integral part of our CI/CD pipeline setup in Azure DevOps.

Environment-Specific Configurations

Before we proceed with the deployment, ensuring our environment-specific configurations are accurately set is paramount.

- **Connection String for Azure SQL Database:** The lifeline that connects our .NET application to the Azure SQL Database. It's essential to ensure this connection string is correctly configured in the **appsettings.json** or through Azure App Service application settings post-deployment.

- **CORS Settings in program.cs:** To facilitate the communication between our Angular frontend and .NET backend during local development, we've adjusted CORS settings in the **program.cs** file. These settings may need further adjustments or removal post-deployment, depending on the hosting setup in Azure.

- **proxy.conf.json in Angular Application**: A pivotal configuration for local development, ensuring the Angular application can communicate with the .NET backend without CORS issues. This setup will be replaced by proper CORS configurations in Azure post-deployment.

Understanding and setting up these components correctly are the first steps toward a successful deployment. In the following sections, we will dive into the process of deploying our AI Dashboard to Azure, turning our local development success into a globally accessible, robust web application.

Deploying AI Dashboard on Azure: A Structured Approach

Deploying an application to Azure is more than just moving code from a local environment to the cloud. It's a strategic process that involves careful planning, configuration, and understanding of the cloud architecture. For our AI Dashboard, which comprises a .NET Web API and an Angular UI, adopting a structured deployment approach is crucial for ensuring scalability, manageability, and reliability.

The deployment process on Azure offers robust options for hosting, managing, and scaling applications. By leveraging Azure Web Apps (Web Slots), we can deploy our application components in isolated environments, allowing for independent management and fine-tuned control over each part of the application.

Why Separate Slots?

Separate web slots for the .NET Web API and Angular UI come with numerous advantages that align with modern cloud deployment best practices:

- **Independent Scaling:** Each component of the application can be scaled independently based on its specific resource consumption and load patterns. This ensures optimal resource utilization and cost-effectiveness.

- **Isolated Management:** Deploying to separate slots allows for individual management of the frontend and backend components. This isolation simplifies maintenance, monitoring, and updates, as changes to one component don't necessarily affect the other.

- **Flexibility in Updates and Rollbacks:** With separate deployment slots, updates or rollbacks can be performed on the frontend or backend independently. This reduces the risk associated with deployments and enables a more agile and controlled update process.

Considerations for Separate Deployments

While separate deployment slots offer numerous benefits, they also require careful consideration and planning:

- **CORS Configuration:** Cross-Origin Resource Sharing (CORS) settings become crucial when the frontend and backend are hosted separately. Proper configuration ensures that the Angular UI can securely communicate with the .NET Web API without facing cross-origin issues.

- **Interdependency of UI and API:** Even though the UI and API are deployed separately, they are closely interconnected. The Angular UI needs to know the endpoint URL of the .NET Web API. Ensuring this connection is correctly configured is pivotal for the seamless operation of the AI Dashboard.

- **Best Practices for Seamless Deployment:** Adopting best practices such as thorough testing in staging environments, monitoring after deployment, and setting up alerting and logging mechanisms are key to a successful and seamless deployment process.

- **Environment Configuration:** Environment-specific configurations, such as database connection strings and application settings, need to be carefully managed and set up in the Azure portal to ensure the application functions correctly in the cloud environment.

Understanding these aspects and planning accordingly sets a solid foundation for a successful deployment to Azure. It ensures that the AI Dashboard is not only deployed efficiently but also operates smoothly, providing a robust and scalable solution in the cloud.

Deploying the .NET Web API

Deploying the .NET Web API is the first critical step in making our AI Dashboard operational in Azure. This section outlines the rationale behind deploying the backend first, preparing it for deployment, creating necessary Azure resources, and ensuring a successful launch.

The .NET Web API acts as the backbone of our AI Dashboard, handling data processing, business logic, and database interactions. Deploying the backend service first is strategic, as it establishes the core functionalities upon which the Angular UI will depend. By ensuring that the Web API is operational and accessible in Azure, we create a solid foundation for the subsequent deployment of the frontend.

Preparing the .NET Web API for Deployment

Connection String Settings

- Review and update the connection string in the **appsettings.json** file or in the Azure App Service application settings to ensure seamless integration with the Azure SQL Database.

- Ensure that the connection string is secure and that credentials are not exposed in the code or configuration files.

CORS Settings

- Implement initial CORS settings in the program.cs file to allow requests from the local development version of the Angular UI.

- Plan to update these settings once the Angular UI is deployed to its
  Azure Web Slot, specifying the exact URL to ensure secure cross-
  origin requests.

Creating Azure Web Services for .NET Web API

Setting Up Azure Web Apps (Web Slots)

- Navigate to the Azure Portal and create a new Web App within the
  CodeMosaic Resource Group (Figure 19-1).

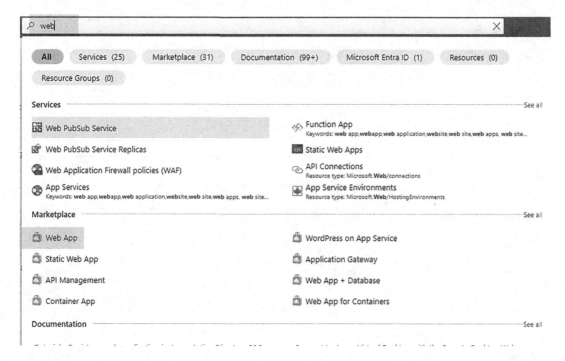

Figure 19-1. *Search web app*

- Choose the appropriate runtime stack (e.g., .NET Core) and region
  that aligns with your project requirements.

- Assign a descriptive and unique name to the Web App for clear
  identification.

- You'll be doing something like Figure 19-2.

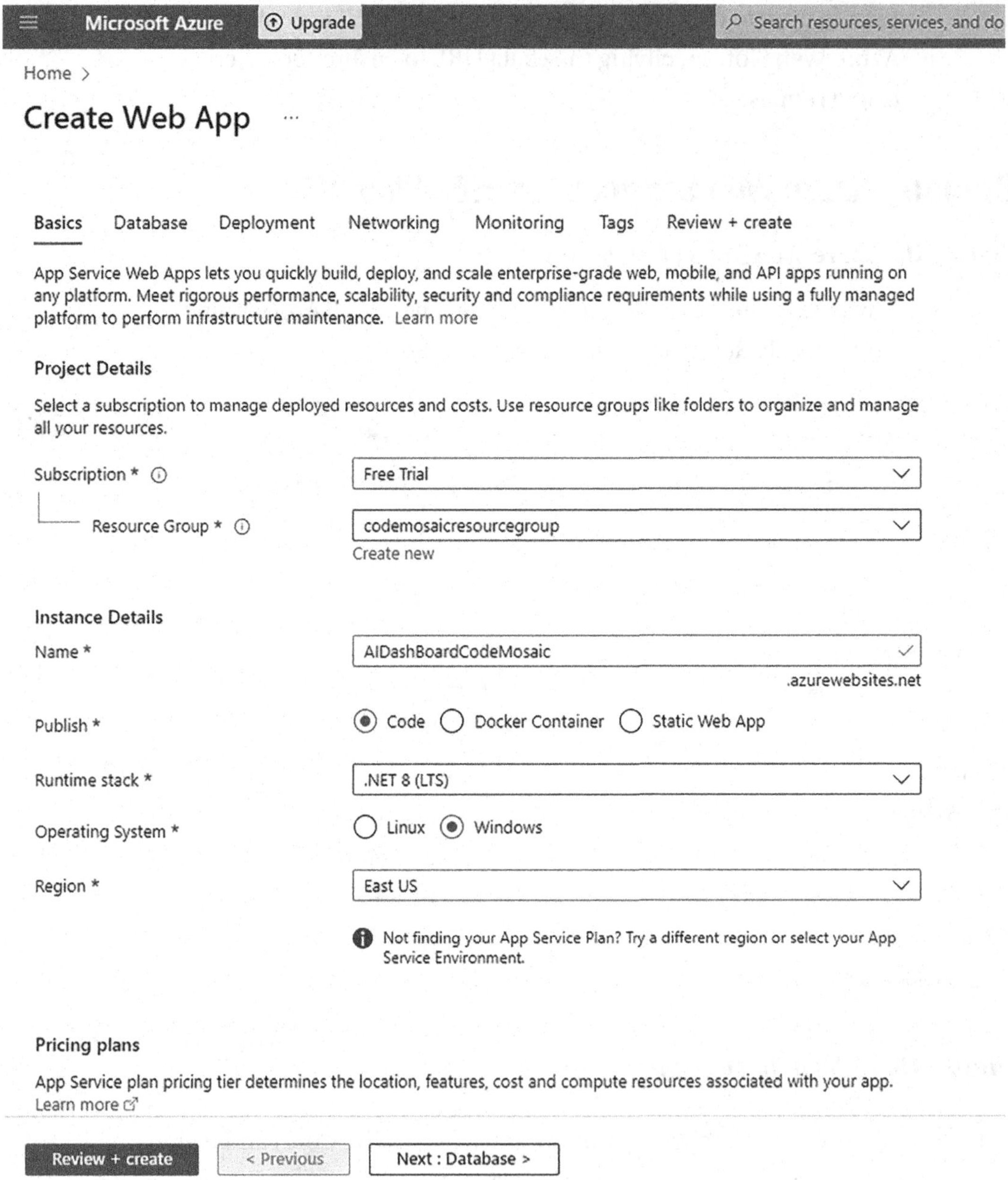

Figure 19-2. *Create web app*

Click on review and create.

Configuring App Settings and Connection Strings

- In the Azure portal, navigate to the newly created Web App's settings.

- Add or update the connection strings and app settings to match the production environment, ensuring the Web API connects to the Azure SQL Database correctly.

Local Build and Publish Process for .NET Web API

Building the .NET Project Locally:

- Open the AI Dashboard Web API project in Visual Studio.

- Build the project to verify that there are no compilation errors and that all dependencies are resolved correctly.

Publishing to Azure:

- In Visual Studio, right-click the AI Dashboard Web API project and select "Publish" (Figure 19-3).

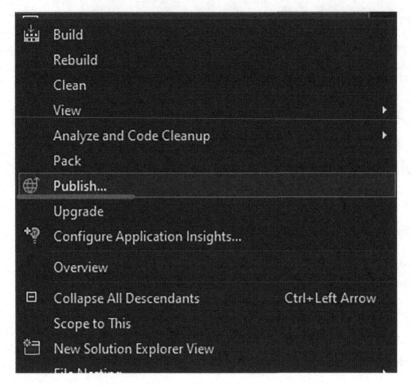

Figure 19-3. *Navigate to Publish*

- Follow the publishing wizard to select the target Azure Web App created earlier.

  - Select Azure.

  - Select Azure App Service (Windows), in Specific Target (Figure 19-4).

Figure 19-4. *Set specific target*

- In App Service, You can use the API service we just created or create a new instance:

  In case of using the slot we created, select the Service and Next (Figure 19-5).

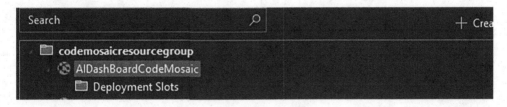

Figure 19-5. *Use the existing web app*

  If you did not create any service via azure, VS gives you option to do that too (Figure 19-6).

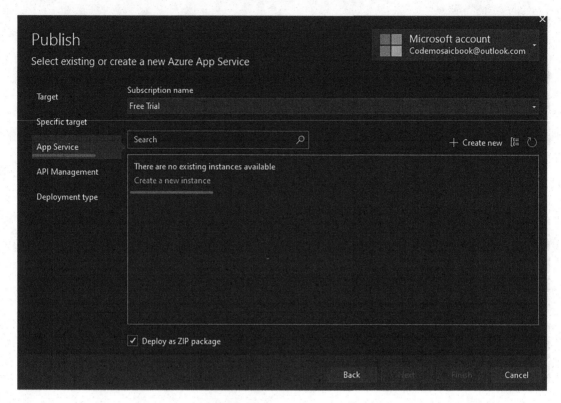

Figure 19-6. *Create new web app via VS*

- Fill and select the required fields for the new instance as in
  Figure 19-7.

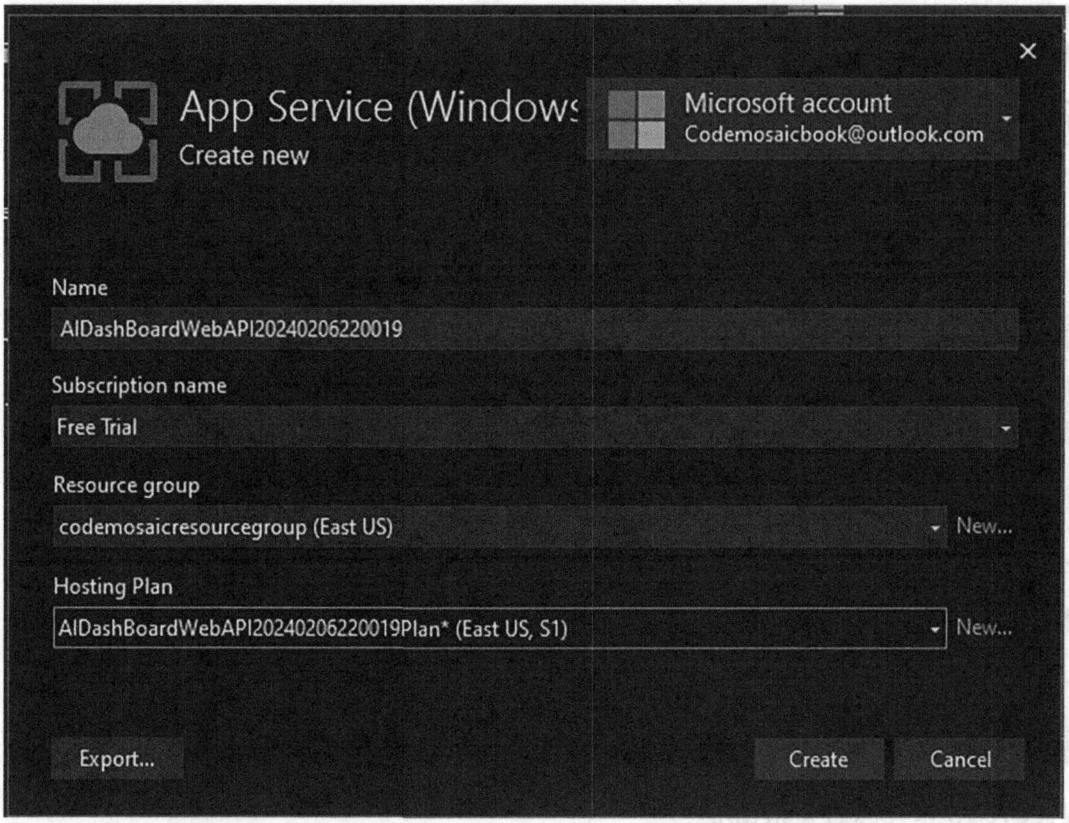

Figure 19-7. *Setup web app*

- Select the newly created web app, and check on Deploy as Zip
  Package (Figure 19-8).

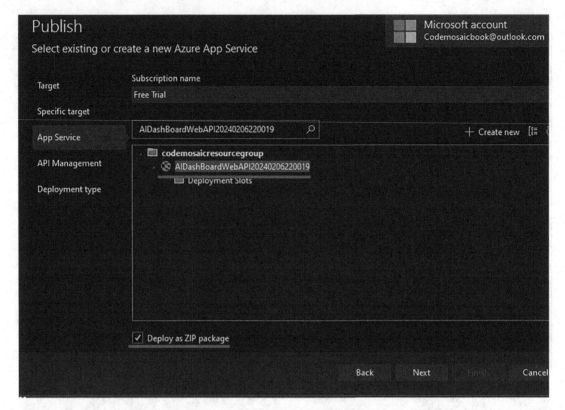

Figure 19-8. *Select web app*

- You'll be asked to select API management; you can skip it for now.

- Next click Publish in deployment type (Figure 19-9).

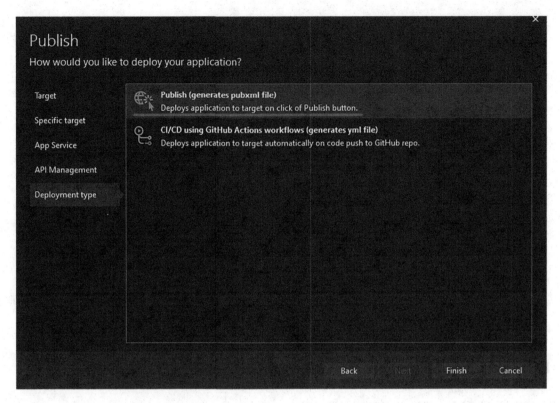

Figure 19-9. *Select deployment type*

And Finish.

- Once this is done, you'll be able to see a publish profile on screen (Figure 19-10).

+ Add your client IPv4 address (122.172.182.21)   + Add a firewall rule

Rule name	Start IPv4 address	End IPv4 address	
ClientIPAddress_2024-2-5_6-0-7	122.172.182.0	122.172.182.255	🗑

Exceptions

☑ Allow Azure services and resources to access this server ⓘ

Save   Discard

Figure 19-10. *Publish view*

- Here in Figure 19-10, click Publish.

- Now once this is published, remember while setting up the Azure SQL DB, we had to allow our IPv4 to access the DB; on the same page at the bottom, you'll see this option to allow our service to use the DB.

+ Add your client IPv4 address (122.172.182.21)   + Add a firewall rule

Rule name	Start IPv4 address	End IPv4 address	
ClientIPAddress_2024-2-5_6-0-7	122.172.182.0	122.172.182.255	🗑

Exceptions

☑ Allow Azure services and resources to access this server ⓘ

Save   Discard

Figure 19-11. *Allow services to access database*

Check the box and save (Figure 19-11).

Verification and Testing

After deployment, You'll see this message, which will confirm the successful deployment (Figure 19-12):

Figure 19-12. *Publish success*

And similarly for our firstly created services (Figure 19-13).

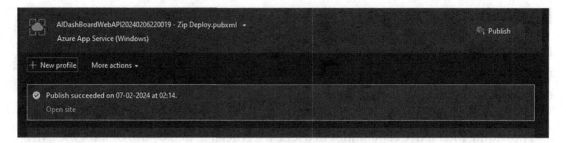

Figure 19-13.   Publish success for 1st service

Now, access the Web API through its Azure URL to ensure it's operational. For this you can use Postman:

Install Postman: `https://dl.pstmn.io/download/latest/win64`

Let's test API's from our `https://aidashboardcodemosaic.azurewebsites.net` (it will be different based on your app service) for testing, and in future setups as well.

Paste the URL along with Endpoint route to test the API (Figure 19-14).

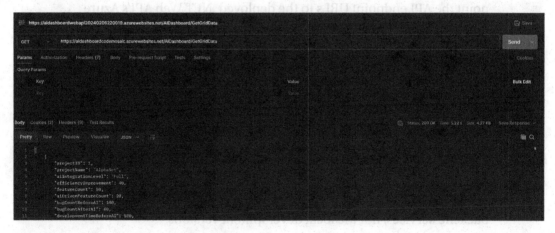

Figure 19-14.   Testing API on postman

You can see that we are getting the valid response, and 200 status code.

Verify that all endpoints are responding as expected and that the integration with the Azure SQL Database is functioning correctly.

By meticulously following these steps, the .NET Web API will be successfully deployed and operational in Azure, laying a robust foundation for the subsequent deployment of the Angular UI.

Deploying the Angular UI

Deploying the Angular UI is the final step that brings the AI Dashboard to life, providing a rich and interactive user interface to end users. This section explains the process of deploying the Angular UI to Azure, ensuring it works seamlessly with the .NET Web API.

The Angular UI is the front-facing component of the AI Dashboard, presenting data and providing interactive capabilities to users. It's crucial to deploy the UI after the .NET Web API because the UI depends on the backend services for data and functionalities. Ensuring the backend is operational before deploying the frontend minimizes issues and simplifies the deployment and troubleshooting process.

Preparing the Angular UI for Deployment

Update Environment Configuration:

- Modify the Angular application's environment configuration file to point the API endpoint URLs to the deployed .NET Web API's Azure URL (Figure 19-15).

```
export class AiDashBoardApiService {

    // Replace with your actual API URL
    private BASE_URL = 'https://aidashboardcodemosaic.azurewebsites.net';
```

Figure 19-15. *Change base URL to deployed one*

- This update ensures that the Angular UI interacts with the live backend services, not the local development versions.

Finalize CORS Settings:

- Based on the URL where the Angular UI will be hosted, update the CORS settings in the .NET Web API's program.cs file.

- Ensure that the .NET Web API is configured to accept requests from the Angular UI's Azure Web Slot, securing the cross-origin communication between the frontend and backend.

Creating Azure Web Services for Angular UI

Setting Up Azure Web Apps:

- Navigate to the Azure Portal and create a new Web App within the CodeMosaic Resource Group specifically for the Angular UI. It will be similar to what we did in the API part, except the stack will be **Node**.

- After all info is given, click on review and create, and after verifying, click Create.

Local Build and Deployment Process for Angular UI

For the purpose of this, we will use the Azure Static Web Apps extension in the Visual Studio code (Figure 19-16).

Figure 19-16. *Azure app service extension in VS code*

- Go to extensions.

- Search for Azure Static Web Apps.

- Select Azure Static Web Apps.

- Click install.

- Once done, you'll see it in the side menu, click it, and you'll find the option to sign in (Figure 19-17).

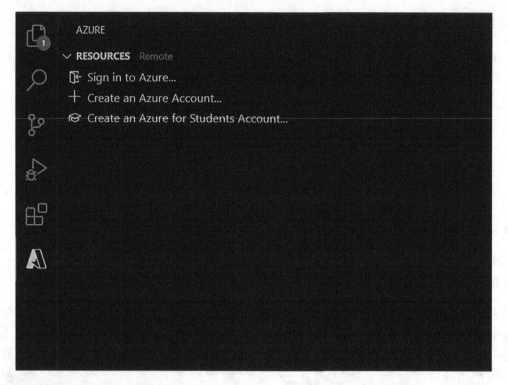

Figure 19-17. *Azure SignUp*

- Click sign in to Azure.

- Navigate to the Angular project directory and run **ng build** to compile the application for production.

- Verify that the dist/directory contains the build artifacts, including the index.html file and associated assets.

- Next got to the extension, and select your App service, and right click to deploy (Figure 19-18).

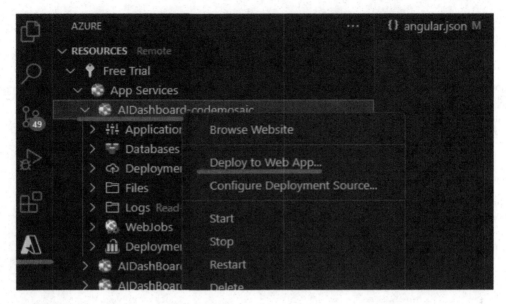

Figure 19-18. *Deploy via extension*

- It will then ask to select the folder; select the **dist** folder and deploy.

- Now one of the important parts is to edit our Program.cs file and put this UI URL in there which is currently using localhost, and redeploy the API publishing the AIDashBoardWebAPI usingVisual Studio.

- You'll be able to see our AI dashboard, on the Web App.

- There could be a case where you get the error (Figure 19-19).

You do not have permission to view this directory or page.

Figure 19-19. *UI permission error*

- In this case you can look into your dist folder, and follow that it is similar to the physical path here, and ensure that the index.html file and other assets are correctly placed and accessible (Figure 19-20).

Figure 19-20. *Synchronize physical path with dist structure*

By carefully following these steps, the Angular UI will be successfully deployed to Azure, providing a visually appealing and interactive frontend for the AI Dashboard. The deployment of both the .NET Web API and Angular UI completes the cloud setup of the AI Dashboard, making it fully operational and accessible to users.

Automating Deployment with Azure Pipelines

After successfully deploying the .NET Web API and Angular UI manually, it's essential to automate the deployment process to ensure consistency, efficiency, and reliability. Azure Pipelines in Azure DevOps provides a powerful tool for setting up Continuous Integration (CI) and Continuous Deployment (CD) workflows. This section guides you through creating and configuring pipelines for both the .NET Web API and the Angular UI.

Creating a Pipeline for the .NET Web API

- **Navigate to Azure DevOps**

  - Open your Azure DevOps project (**CodeMosaicDashboard** under the **CodeMosaicBook** organization).

  - Select the **Pipelines** section from the left navigation pane.

- **Create a New Pipeline**

  - Click on **Create Pipeline**.

  - Choose the repository where your .NET Web API code is located.

- **Configure the Pipeline**

  - Azure DevOps will try to identify the type of application and suggest a template. For a .NET application, choose the **.NET Core** template.

  - Customize the YAML file to define your build and deployment tasks. Ensure that it builds the project, runs tests, and publishes the build artifacts.

- **Define the Deployment Task**

  - Add a deployment task to the YAML file.

  - Choose the Azure Web App Deployment task and configure it to deploy to the Azure Web App (Web Slot) created for your .NET Web API.

- **Save and Run the Pipeline**

  - Review your pipeline configuration.

  - Save the YAML file and commit it to your repository.

  - Run the pipeline to validate that the build and deployment process works as expected.

Creating a Pipeline for the Angular UI

- **Set Up the Pipeline**

  - Similarly, in the Azure DevOps project, create a new pipeline for the Angular UI.

  - Choose the repository where your Angular code is located.

- **Configure Build Tasks**

  - Select an appropriate template or start with an empty job.

  - Define tasks to install dependencies (**npm install**), build the Angular project (**ng build --prod**), and publish the build artifacts.

- **Define the Deployment Task**

  - Add a deployment task tailored for a static website or a Node. js application, depending on how your Azure Web App is configured for the Angular UI.

  - Ensure it deploys the contents of the **dist/** directory to the designated Azure Web App (Web Slot) for your Angular UI.

- **Triggering and Monitoring**

  - Configure triggers to automatically run the pipeline on code changes or pull requests.

  - Monitor the pipeline runs and review logs to ensure that the deployment process is smooth and error-free.

By setting up Azure Pipelines for both the .NET Web API and the Angular UI, you automate your deployment process, making it more robust and less prone to human error. Automation also ensures that your application is always in a deployable state, reflecting the latest changes in your codebase.

Certainly! Below are example YAML files for setting up Azure Pipelines for both the .NET Web API and the Angular UI. These YAML files are templates with comments explaining each section. You may need to adjust paths, tasks, or settings based on your specific project configuration.

.NET Web API Azure Pipeline YAML Example

```yaml
```yaml code
trigger:
- main

pool:
  vmImage: 'windows-latest'

variables:
  buildConfiguration: 'Release'

steps:
- task: DotNetCoreCLI@2
  displayName: 'Restore .NET dependencies'
  inputs:
    command: 'restore'
    projects: '**/*.csproj'

- task: DotNetCoreCLI@2
  displayName: 'Build .NET project'
  inputs:
    command: 'build'
    projects: '**/*.csproj'
    arguments: '--configuration $(buildConfiguration)'

- task: DotNetCoreCLI@2
  displayName: 'Run .NET tests'
  inputs:
    command: 'test'
    projects: '**/*Tests.csproj'
    arguments: '--configuration $(buildConfiguration)'

- task: DotNetCoreCLI@2
  displayName: 'Publish .NET project'
  inputs:
    command: 'publish'
    publishWebProjects: true
```
```

```yaml
    arguments: '--configuration $(buildConfiguration) --output $(Build.
    ArtifactStagingDirectory)'
    zipAfterPublish: true

- task: PublishBuildArtifacts@1
  displayName: 'Publish .NET artifacts'
  inputs:
    PathtoPublish: '$(Build.ArtifactStagingDirectory)'
    ArtifactName: 'webapi'
    publishLocation: 'Container'

- task: AzureWebApp@1
  displayName: 'Deploy .NET Web API to Azure'
  inputs:
    azureSubscription: '<Your Azure Subscription>'
    appType: 'webApp'
    appName: '<Your .NET Web App Name>'
    package: '$(Build.ArtifactStagingDirectory)/**/*.zip'
```

Angular UI Azure Pipeline YAML Example:

```yaml
yaml code
trigger:
- main

pool:
  vmImage: 'ubuntu-latest'

variables:
  buildConfiguration: 'Release'

steps:
- task: NodeTool@0
  displayName: 'Install Node.js'
  inputs:
    versionSpec: '14.x'
```

```
- script: |
    npm install -g @angular/cli
    npm install
  displayName: 'Install npm packages and Angular CLI'

- script: |
    ng build --prod
  displayName: 'Build Angular project'

- task: PublishBuildArtifacts@1
  displayName: 'Publish Angular artifacts'
  inputs:
    PathtoPublish: 'dist'
    ArtifactName: 'angularapp'
    publishLocation: 'Container'

- task: AzureWebApp@1
  displayName: 'Deploy Angular UI to Azure'
  inputs:
    azureSubscription: '<Your Azure Subscription>'
    appType: 'webApp'
    appName: '<Your Angular Web App Name>'
    package: 'dist'
```

In these YAML files:

- The **.NET Web API** pipeline includes steps for restoring dependencies, building the project, running tests, publishing the project, and deploying it to Azure.

- The **Angular UI** pipeline installs Node.js, installs npm packages, builds the Angular project, publishes the build artifacts, and deploys the application to Azure.

Be sure to replace placeholders like **<Your Azure Subscription>**, **<Your .NET Web App Name>**, and **<Your Angular Web App Name>** with your actual Azure subscription and web app names. Also, adjust the paths and task parameters based on your project's specific structure and requirements.

Conclusion

As we bring Chapter 19, "Cornerstone: Smart Deployment Delight," to a close, we don't just conclude a chapter; we celebrate the culmination of a transformative journey—from the inception of technology in the initial chapters to the practical application in the last eight mosaic tiles. This journey through the Code Mosaic has been a testament to the evolution and application of software development, encapsulating everything from D2D—design to deployment.

Completing the Code Mosaic is not merely an academic accomplishment; it's an embodiment of the comprehensive learning and real-world application. Across 19 chapters, we've traversed through the theoretical foundations, brainstormed ideas, and executed them into tangible solutions. Each mosaic tile contributed to building a complete picture, reflecting both the complexity and beauty of software development.

In the spirit of our agile journey, it's time to mark a significant milestone:

- **Mark Deployment Tasks as Completed:** Navigate to your project's agile tracking system and mark all tasks associated with the deployment of the .NET Web API and Angular UI as Closed.

- **Close the User Story:** If the deployment of the AI Dashboard was encapsulated in a user story, now is the time to close it. This closure signifies the completion of a significant milestone in your project lifecycle.

- **Reflect and Acknowledge**: Reflect on the learnings, challenges, and successes. Acknowledge the collective effort, resilience, and ingenuity that brought the AI Dashboard to life.

Key Takeaways

- **Strategic Deployment:** Mastery over deploying complex applications to Azure, understanding the nuances of cloud architecture.

- **Structured Deployment:** The importance of a structured approach to deployment, emphasizing planning, environment configuration, and a clear understanding of cloud architecture.

- **Separate Slots Advantage:** The benefits of deploying the .NET Web API and Angular UI to separate web slots, including independent scaling, isolated management, and flexibility in updates.

- **CORS and Configuration Management:** The critical role of proper CORS configuration and environment-specific settings in ensuring seamless interaction between the frontend and backend.

- **Architecture Best Practices:** Insights into the benefits of separating frontend and backend deployments for scalability and manageability.

- **Comprehensive Learning Journey:** The journey from theoretical concepts to practical applications, encapsulating a holistic view of software development.

Transition to Next Chapter

As we transition from completing our Code Mosaic, our journey in the realm of software development continues to evolve. Chapter 20, "More on AI Tools: Developers' Magic Wand," opens up a new horizon, delving deeper into the expanding universe of AI tools in software development.

In this upcoming chapter, we will

- **Explore Various AI Tools:** Provide a detailed overview of diverse AI tools that are reshaping the landscape of software development.

- **Real-World Applications:** Unearth practical applications of these tools, demonstrating how they can be effectively integrated into everyday development tasks.

- **Future Trends and Innovations:** Peer into the future of AI in software development, discussing upcoming trends and how they will influence the industry.

Onward

Chapter 20 is not just a continuation; it's a gateway to the future, empowering you with knowledge and insights about the next frontier in software development. Join us as we venture into this exciting new chapter, expanding our toolkit with AI-driven solutions and preparing for the future innovations in our field.

More on AI Tools: Developer's Magic Wand

As we embark on the final leg of our journey through "Mosaic," we pause to reflect on the ground we've covered. From the vast expanse of software development history to the intricate workings of Angular, .NET, and Agile methodologies, we've navigated the rich landscape of IT. Our expedition through GitHub, GitHub Copilot, and OpenAI has revealed the transformative power of technology, guiding us through practical applications and theoretical insights alike. The "Mosaic tiles," our practical chapters, have allowed us to craft our masterpiece, piecing together Azure boards, UI/UX design, databases, and deployment into a cohesive whole.

Yet, as we stand on this precipice of knowledge, we recognize that our toolkit is far from complete. The realm of Artificial Intelligence (AI) beckons with a promise of endless possibilities, a vast ocean of tools and technologies beyond the familiar shores of GPT and GitHub Copilot. In this chapter, "More on AI Tools: Developer's Magic Wand," we delve deeper into this world, exploring the myriad ways in which AI is reshaping the fabric of software development.

Our aim is not just to acquaint you with the tools that dot this landscape but to inspire you to wield them with the confidence of a seasoned artisan. We venture beyond the boundaries of Microsoft technologies, into a universe where SonarCloud enhances code quality, and the Atlassian suite streamlines project management. This exploration is about broadening horizons and embracing the diversity of tools that make modern software development such an exhilarating field.

This chapter is a compass for navigating the future, a guide to the AI tools and platforms that are revolutionizing how we develop, test, and deploy software. But it's also a reflection on how these tools are reshaping the industry, creating new opportunities and challenging us to reimagine our roles as developers.

© Arpit Dwivedi 2024
A. Dwivedi, *CodeMosaic*, https://doi.org/10.1007/979-8-8688-0276-8_20

As we embark on this final chapter together, let's open our minds to the possibilities that AI presents. Let's explore how these tools can become the developer's magical wand, empowering us to create, innovate, and transform the digital landscape. Welcome to the future of software development—a future where human creativity and AI's computational prowess unite to usher in an era of unprecedented innovation.

The Evolution of Software Development Tools

The journey of software development is one marked by constant evolution and innovation. As we embark on this section, we trace the lineage of tools and methodologies that have shaped the landscape of technology. This voyage from the rudiments of programming to the sophisticated environments of today lays the foundation for our exploration into the future.

The Dawn of Development Tools

The genesis of software development was characterized by manual processes and basic tools. Early programming languages and text editors were the first stepping stones, enabling developers to communicate with machines in a more natural language. As technology progressed, integrated development environments (IDEs) and version control systems like Git emerged, revolutionizing the way developers wrote, shared, and maintained code.

Transition to Modern Development Practices

The advent of Agile methodologies marked a significant shift in the development process, emphasizing flexibility, collaboration, and customer feedback. Tools such as Jira and Confluence became staples for project management and documentation, fostering a culture of continuous improvement and adaptability. Similarly, CI/CD pipelines, enabled by platforms like Jenkins and Azure DevOps, automated the build and deployment processes, significantly reducing the time to market and increasing the reliability of software releases.

Enhancement Through Quality and Collaboration Tools

Quality assurance and collaboration have always been at the heart of successful software development. SonarCloud, with its automated code analysis, has become an indispensable tool for maintaining code quality, ensuring that projects adhere to the highest standards of reliability, security, and maintainability. On the collaboration front, Bitbucket's integration with the Atlassian suite has streamlined code sharing and review processes, enhancing team synergy and productivity.

Broadening the Toolkit: From Docker to Kubernetes

The containerization movement, led by Docker, introduced a paradigm shift in how applications are developed, shipped, and run. Containers offered a lightweight, portable solution for application deployment, making it easier to manage dependencies and environments. Kubernetes further built on this foundation, providing a platform for automating deployment, scaling, and operations of application containers across clusters of hosts, facilitating even greater efficiency and scalability.

This narrative of progress sets the stage for our next exploration: the integration of AI tools into the fabric of software development. As we delve into the realm of AI, it's essential to recognize that these advancements are not just new tools in our arsenal but represent a fundamental transformation in how we approach development challenges. The next section will guide us through this exciting landscape, showcasing the AI tools and platforms that are defining the future of our industry.

Navigating the AI Landscape: Tools and Platforms for Modern Developers

In the swiftly evolving realm of software development, the advent of Artificial Intelligence (AI) stands as a beacon of transformation, heralding a new dawn of creativity, efficiency, and innovation. This shift is not merely about automation; it's a fundamental enhancement of the developer's toolkit, enabling a leap from conventional practices to groundbreaking methodologies. Let's explore the essence of this revolution:

- **Revolutionizing Development:** AI tools are transforming the landscape from code completion to complex problem-solving.

- **Empowering Creativity:** Beyond automation, these tools unlock unprecedented levels of creativity and innovation.

- **Enhancing Efficiency:** AI-driven solutions streamline development processes, from debugging to deployment.

The Tools Shaping Tomorrow:

- **AI-Enhanced IDEs:** Tools like Codota and Kite are redefining code writing, offering real-time, context-aware suggestions.

- **Automated Code Reviews:** Platforms such as GitHub Copilot and DeepCode scrutinize code for improvements, much like a seasoned reviewer.

- **Quality at Speed:** Testing tools like Testim.io and Applitools leverage AI to automate and enhance testing processes, ensuring robustness while saving precious time.

Behind every AI tool lies a vision of making software development more intuitive, efficient, and accessible. Organizations, from tech giants to dynamic startups, are investing heavily in these technologies, signaling a unanimous belief in AI's role as a cornerstone of future development.

Why This Matters:

- **For the Novice:** These tools offer a ladder to quickly climb the steep learning curve of software development.

- **For the Veteran:** They provide a palette for painting solutions to complex problems with strokes of efficiency and creativity.

As we delve deeper into the AI tools and platforms modernizing software development, our journey is not just about understanding what these tools do. It's about appreciating the broader narrative of progress they represent, highlighting a future where development is not just faster and easier but also more aligned with the human desire to create and innovate.

AI-Enhanced Development Environments

In the rapidly evolving world of software development, the introduction of Artificial Intelligence (AI) into Integrated Development Environments (IDEs) marks a pivotal shift toward a smarter, more efficient coding process. This transformation is not just a leap in technology but a redefinition of how we approach coding challenges. Let's explore the essence of AI-enhanced IDEs and understand their significance in the modern development landscape.

Why AI-Enhanced IDEs?

The advent of AI-enhanced IDEs is a response to the growing complexity of software projects and the continuous search for improved efficiency and accuracy in coding. These IDEs incorporate AI-driven features that automate repetitive tasks, suggest code optimizations, and even identify potential errors before they become problematic. This level of assistance transforms the coding process, making it not only faster but also more intuitive for developers at all levels.

AI-Enhanced vs. Traditional IDEs

The difference between AI-enhanced and traditional IDEs lies in their capability to learn and adapt. While traditional IDEs offer a static set of features designed to facilitate coding, AI-enhanced IDEs leverage machine learning algorithms to offer dynamic support tailored to the developer's coding style and the project's specific needs. This means suggestions for code improvement, predictive coding assistance, and even automated refactoring based on the context of the development project.

- **Predictive Coding Assistance:** AI-enhanced IDEs predict what a developer is likely to write next, offering code completion suggestions that are contextually relevant.

- **Automated Error Detection:** These IDEs can foresee and highlight potential errors in real-time, often before the developer has even finished typing the line of code.

- **Code Optimization Suggestions:** Beyond identifying errors, AI-driven IDEs suggest optimizations, making code cleaner and more efficient.

The Role of Tools

The surge in AI tool adoption underscores a broader trend: the pursuit of innovation and excellence in software development. Developers are increasingly relying on these tools not just for their efficiency gains but for their ability to enhance creativity. AI-enhanced IDEs serve as the cornerstone of this new toolset, enabling developers to focus on solving complex problems and innovating, rather than getting bogged down in routine coding tasks.

- **Boosting Developer Productivity:** By reducing the time spent on repetitive tasks, developers can allocate more time to design and problem-solving.

- **Enhancing Code Quality:** AI-driven insights ensure that the code is not only functional but also optimized and maintainable.

- **Learning and Improvement:** AI-enhanced IDEs can be a source of learning, exposing developers to best practices and new ways of thinking about code.

The emergence of AI-enhanced IDEs is a testament to the software development industry's relentless drive for improvement and efficiency. By melding the analytical power of AI with the creative prowess of developers, these tools are not just changing how we code; they're redefining what's possible in software development. As we delve deeper into specific tools like Codota, Kite, IntelliJ IDEA, and Visual Studio Code, we'll explore how each embodies this blend of innovation and utility, propelling the software development process into a new era of efficiency and creativity.

Exploring Key AI-Enhanced Tools

As we venture into the realm of AI-enhanced development environments, a few standout tools are reshaping how developers interact with their IDEs, making coding more intuitive, efficient, and error-free. Each tool, backed by robust technology and innovative minds, brings its unique strengths to the table. Here, we'll dive into the details of Codota, Kite, IntelliJ IDEA with Codota integration, and Visual Studio Code with IntelliCode, exploring their origins, functionalities, and the benefits they offer.

- **Codota**

  - **Introduction:** Codota is an AI-powered code completion tool that supports a wide range of programming languages and IDEs. It offers real-time, context-aware suggestions that improve coding speed and accuracy.

  - **Who's Behind Codota:** Founded by Dror Weiss and Eran Yahav, Codota is backed by significant investments from leading venture capital firms, underscoring its innovation and market potential.

  - **How to Use Codota:** Install Codota as a plugin in your preferred IDE, and it immediately starts providing suggestions as you type, learning from your codebase to offer tailored advice.

  - **Benefits of Codota:** Codota drastically reduces coding time, helps avoid bugs by catching them early in the development process, and assists in adhering to coding best practices.

- **Kite**

  - **Introduction:** Kite enhances coding with AI-powered code completions based on the context of your work. It supports various languages and integrates seamlessly with multiple IDEs.

  - **Who's Behind Kite:** Kite Technologies, Inc., led by Adam Smith, has garnered attention and funding for its innovative approach to leveraging AI in coding, with significant contributions from venture capital.

  - **How to Use Kite:** After installing Kite for your IDE, it runs in the background, analyzing your typed code to provide relevant suggestions and documentation.

  - **Benefits of Kite:** Developers find that Kite accelerates coding, improves code quality, and enhances learning by exposing them to efficient coding patterns and practices.

511

- **IntelliJ IDEA (with Codota Integration)**

  - **Introduction:** IntelliJ IDEA, renowned for its robust set of developer tools, further enhances its capabilities with Codota integration, offering AI-powered code completions and insights.

  - **Who's Behind the Integration:** JetBrains, the creator of IntelliJ IDEA, collaborates with Codota to integrate this AI technology, providing an even more powerful development environment.

  - **How to Use IntelliJ IDEA with Codota:** Enable Codota through IntelliJ IDEA's plugin marketplace to start receiving AI-driven code suggestions within the IDE.

  - **Benefits of This Integration:** This combination offers a sophisticated coding experience with advanced error detection, code completion, and optimization suggestions, making it a favorite among Java developers and beyond.

- **Visual Studio Code (with IntelliCode)**

  - **Introduction:** Visual Studio Code, Microsoft's lightweight but powerful source code editor, is supercharged with IntelliCode, Microsoft's AI-assisted coding feature.

  - **Who's Behind IntelliCode:** Developed by Microsoft, IntelliCode exemplifies the company's commitment to integrating AI into developer tools to boost productivity and code quality.

  - **How to Use Visual Studio Code with IntelliCode:** IntelliCode is available as an extension for Visual Studio Code, easy to install and activate from the Visual Studio Marketplace.

  - **Benefits of IntelliCode:** IntelliCode saves developers time by predicting the most likely correct API and coding patterns based on the context, significantly speeding up the development process and reducing errors.

Each of these tools exemplifies the incredible potential of AI to enhance the software development lifecycle. By integrating these AI-enhanced tools into their workflow, developers can not only streamline their development process but also elevate the quality of their code, ultimately leading to more robust and reliable software solutions.

The backing of these tools by established organizations and their widespread adoption across the industry further attest to their effectiveness and the value they bring to the development community.

Automating Code Reviews and Maintenance

The integration of AI into the process of code reviews and maintenance has revolutionized the way developers approach coding, ensuring that the highest standards of quality and efficiency are met. Let's delve into how AI is reshaping this crucial aspect of software development.

- **Enhancing Accuracy:** AI tools can detect issues that human reviewers might overlook, including complex bugs and potential vulnerabilities.

- **Speeding Up Reviews:** Automating reviews with AI significantly reduces the time it takes to vet code, accelerating development cycles.

- **Consistency in Standards:** AI ensures that every piece of code is reviewed with the same high standards, promoting uniformity across the project.

- **Learning and Improvement:** AI-driven insights help developers learn from errors, improving their skills over time.

Exploring Tools for Code Reviews and Maintenance

As we explore the tools that are leading the charge in automating code reviews and maintenance, each offers unique advantages to the development process.

- **DeepCode**

  - **Introduction:** DeepCode brings AI-powered code review to the forefront, scanning code for bugs and security vulnerabilities across multiple programming languages.

  - **Who's Behind DeepCode:** Acquired by Snyk, a leader in digital security, DeepCode benefits from Snyk's extensive expertise and resources in making software more secure.

- **How to Use DeepCode:** Integration with popular IDEs and version control systems allows DeepCode to seamlessly scan your code repositories for issues.

- **Benefits of DeepCode:** By catching potentially catastrophic errors before deployment, DeepCode maintains code integrity and prevents future headaches.

- **Sourcery**

  - **Introduction:** Sourcery refines code by providing real-time refactoring suggestions, making code cleaner and more efficient.

  - **Who's Behind Sourcery:** Developed by a dedicated team of software engineers passionate about improving code quality, Sourcery is on a mission to make coding more efficient for everyone.

  - **How to Use Sourcery:** Easily integrated into your IDE, Sourcery works alongside you, suggesting improvements as you code.

  - **Benefits of Sourcery:** Sourcery helps developers write high-quality Python code faster, automating the improvement process and teaching best practices.

- **Amazon CodeGuru**

  - **Introduction:** Amazon CodeGuru is a machine learning service for automated code reviews and application performance recommendations, supporting Java and Python.

  - **Who's Behind Amazon CodeGuru:** Backed by Amazon's vast resources, CodeGuru leverages the tech giant's deep learning expertise to improve code quality.

  - **How to Use Amazon CodeGuru:** Integrating with GitHub, Bitbucket, and AWS CodeCommit, CodeGuru reviews pull requests, identifying costly lines of code and critical issues.

  - **Benefits of Amazon CodeGuru:** CodeGuru helps optimize application performance by identifying line-level issues and suggesting fixes, potentially saving costs and improving efficiency.

- **CodeDefect AI**

  - **Introduction:** CodeDefect AI, by Microsoft, uses machine learning to predict and identify defects in coding projects, enhancing the quality of software development.

  - **Who's Behind CodeDefect AI:** Leveraging Microsoft's extensive experience in AI, CodeDefect AI is part of Microsoft's broader initiative to incorporate AI into developer tools.

  - **How to Use CodeDefect AI:** Available for integration with Azure DevOps, CodeDefect AI provides insights and predictions directly within the development workflow.

  - **Benefits of CodeDefect AI:** It streamlines the development process by predicting defects, allowing teams to address issues proactively, saving time, and reducing the cost of late-stage fixes.

The advent of AI in automating code reviews and maintenance is not just a trend but a significant leap forward in software development practices. By embracing these AI-powered tools, developers can ensure their code meets the highest standards of quality and efficiency, all while accelerating development timelines and fostering a culture of continuous improvement. As AI technology evolves, its integration into code reviews will undoubtedly become more sophisticated, further enhancing the capabilities of developers worldwide.

AI for Testing and Quality Assurance

The integration of Artificial Intelligence (AI) into testing and quality assurance (QA) marks a significant evolution in ensuring software reliability and performance. By harnessing AI, teams can automate complex testing processes, predict potential issues before they arise, and enhance the overall quality of software products. Let's explore the transformative role of AI in testing and QA, followed by a deep dive into the tools revolutionizing this domain.

AI-driven testing and QA tools are reshaping the approach to software validation, offering unprecedented capabilities that streamline testing processes and elevate product quality:

- **Automated Test Creation:** AI algorithms can generate comprehensive test cases and scripts, covering a wide array of scenarios with minimal human input.

- **Predictive Bug Detection:** Leveraging historical data, AI can predict where bugs are most likely to occur, allowing teams to preemptively address potential issues.

- **Dynamic Test Adjustment:** AI tools adapt testing strategies based on real-time code changes and feedback, ensuring relevant and effective test coverage.

- **Enhanced Efficiency:** By automating routine testing tasks, AI frees up human testers to focus on more complex and high-value testing activities.

Exploring Tools for Testing and Quality Assurance

Each of these AI-powered testing tools offers unique advantages, streamlining the QA process and ensuring software meets the highest standards of quality.

- **Testim.io**

  - **Introduction:** Testim.io utilizes AI to automate the creation and execution of end-to-end tests, making them more reliable and easier to maintain.

  - **Who's Behind Testim.io:** Founded by Oren Rubin and backed by a team of testing and AI experts, Testim.io is at the forefront of AI-driven testing solutions.

  - **How to Use Testim.io**

    - Sign up for Testim.io and integrate it with your development environment.

    - Use the platform to record a series of actions in your web application.

    - Testim.io's AI will analyze these actions to create automated test cases.

- Run these tests across different environments and browsers, with AI optimizing and maintaining them over time.

  - **Benefits of Testim.io:** Testim.io significantly reduces the time required to create and maintain tests, while improving test coverage and reliability.

- **Applitools**

  - **Introduction:** Applitools provides an AI-powered Visual Testing and Monitoring platform that ensures your application's UI looks and functions correctly across devices.

  - **Who's Behind Applitools:** Developed by a team dedicated to modernizing how visual testing is performed, Applitools is leading the charge in AI-assisted QA tools.

  - **How to Use Applitools**

    - Integrate Applitools with your testing framework.

    - Write test scripts that navigate your app and capture screenshots.

    - Applitools compares these screenshots against baseline images using AI to detect differences.

    - Review and manage detected visual discrepancies through the Applitools dashboard.

  - **Benefits of Applitools:** Ensures pixel-perfect accuracy of your app's UI, significantly reduces manual testing efforts, and improves the quality of the final product.

- **mabl**

  - **Introduction:** mabl is an end-to-end test automation service that uses machine learning to identify application issues quickly.

  - **Who's Behind mabl:** Founded by experienced software and QA professionals, mabl is designed to simplify and improve the testing process.

- **How to Use mabl**

  - Connect mabl to your CI/CD pipeline.

  - Train mabl by navigating through your application; mabl learns and creates tests based on these interactions.

  - Automatically run these tests for every deployment or on a scheduled basis.

  - Utilize mabl's insights to improve test efficiency and application quality.

- **Benefits of mabl:** Offers seamless integration with development workflows, provides detailed insights for improving test strategies, and enhances the speed and accuracy of testing.

- **TestCraft**

  - **Introduction:** TestCraft is a codeless Selenium test automation platform, driven by AI, for creating and managing automated test scenarios without programming.

  - **Who's Behind TestCraft:** With a focus on bridging the gap between manual and automated testing, TestCraft is supported by a team committed to quality assurance.

  - **How to Use TestCraft**

    - Design your test scenarios in TestCraft's drag-and-drop interface.

    - TestCraft's AI algorithms translate these scenarios into Selenium code.

    - Execute tests across various browsers and environments directly from TestCraft.

    - Analyze the results and leverage AI recommendations to refine tests.

  - **Benefits of TestCraft:** Accelerates the transition from manual to automated testing, minimizes maintenance efforts for test scripts, and enhances test coverage and effectiveness.

AI in testing and QA is not just a trend; it's a pivotal shift toward more intelligent, efficient, and reliable software development. By incorporating these AI-powered tools into their workflows, teams can achieve higher quality standards, reduce time-to-market, and allocate human resources to more strategic tasks. As AI technologies continue to advance, their integration into testing and QA processes promises even greater improvements in software quality and development efficiency.

AI-Powered Continuous Integration and Deployment

In the dynamic world of software development, Continuous Integration (CI) and Continuous Deployment (CD) practices are crucial for maintaining efficiency and ensuring high-quality outputs. Integrating Artificial Intelligence (AI) into these processes elevates their effectiveness to new heights, enabling smarter decision-making, predictive analytics, and enhanced automation. Let's delve into the transformative impact of AI on CI/CD practices and explore the leading tools in this space.

- **Predictive Analytics:** AI can predict the outcomes of code integrations and deployments, identifying potential issues before they occur.

- **Enhanced Automation:** Beyond automating tasks, AI can optimize workflows, deciding the best times for integrations and deployments based on complex data analysis.

- **Quality Assurance:** AI improves the detection of errors and vulnerabilities, ensuring that only the highest quality code is deployed.

- **Efficiency and Speed:** By streamlining CI/CD processes, AI significantly reduces manual overhead, leading to faster development cycles and quicker time-to-market.

Exploring Tools for AI-Powered CI/CD

The integration of AI into CI/CD tools represents a leap forward in software development efficiency and reliability. Here are some of the pioneering tools setting the standard for AI-powered CI/CD:

- **Launchable**

  - **Introduction:** Launchable leverages AI to predict the likelihood of test failures, enabling teams to prioritize tests that are most likely to catch critical issues.

  - **Who's Behind Launchable:** Founded by veterans from the software development and open source communities, Launchable is backed by expertise and innovation.

  - **How to Use Launchable:** Integrate Launchable with your existing CI pipeline to analyze your codebase and test suite, providing insights on test prioritization.

  - **Benefits of Launchable:** By focusing testing efforts where they are needed most, Launchable reduces test cycle times and accelerates the feedback loop for developers.

- **Harness**

  - **Introduction:** Harness utilizes AI to simplify and automate the entire CI/CD process, offering smart automation, intelligent rollbacks, and performance monitoring.

  - **Who's Behind Harness:** With strong backing from venture capital and industry support, Harness is poised at the cutting edge of CI/CD technology.

  - **How to Use Harness:** Implement Harness into your software delivery pipeline to take advantage of its machine learning capabilities for deployment and monitoring.

  - **Benefits of Harness:** Harness ensures safer deployments, faster iterations, and reduced downtime, all while maintaining a focus on quality and efficiency.

- **CircleCI**

  - **Introduction:** CircleCI, a stalwart in the CI/CD space, has embraced AI and machine learning to optimize build processes and predictively flag potential issues.

- **Who's Behind CircleCI:** Supported by a robust community and significant industry investment, CircleCI is a trusted platform for software delivery.

- **How to Use CircleCI:** Incorporate CircleCI into your development process to automate builds, tests, and deployments with AI-enhanced insights.

- **Benefits of CircleCI:** CircleCI streamlines the development lifecycle, enabling rapid delivery of high-quality software with fewer errors and optimized build times.

- **Jenkins X**

  - **Introduction:** Jenkins X extends the Jenkins ecosystem with cloud-native technology, incorporating AI to automate CI/CD for Kubernetes applications.

  - **Who's Behind Jenkins X:** As an open source project, Jenkins X benefits from contributions from CloudBees and the wider Jenkins community.

  - **How to Use Jenkins X:** Leverage Jenkins X for your Kubernetes-based projects to automate your pipelines and apply AI-driven optimizations.

  - **Benefits of Jenkins X:** Jenkins X facilitates cloud-native development, offering scalability, resilience, and enhanced pipeline automation with predictive insights.

AI-powered CI/CD tools are transforming the landscape of software development, offering unprecedented levels of efficiency, accuracy, and speed. By adopting these intelligent solutions, development teams can not only streamline their processes but also achieve higher-quality standards and faster delivery times. As AI continues to evolve, its integration into CI/CD practices promises even greater advancements, making it an exciting time for developers and organizations alike to explore these cutting-edge tools.

Platforms for AI and Machine Learning Development

The emergence of AI and Machine Learning (ML) development platforms has been a game-changer for businesses and developers alike, enabling the creation of intelligent applications with unprecedented efficiency and scale. These platforms provide comprehensive environments that simplify the complexities of AI and ML development, from data preprocessing and model training to deployment and monitoring. Let's explore the significance of these platforms and delve into some of the leading solutions in the market.

The integration of AI and ML into applications and services is no longer just a competitive edge but a necessity for staying relevant in today's technology-driven market. Development platforms specialized in AI and ML democratize access to these advanced technologies, offering

- **Streamlined Development Processes:** Simplify the lifecycle of AI development from idea to deployment.

- **Scalable Infrastructure:** Provide the computational power necessary to train complex models efficiently.

- **Collaborative Environments:** Facilitate collaboration across data scientists, developers, and subject matter experts.

- **Comprehensive Toolsets:** Offer a wide range of tools and libraries to support various stages of AI and ML development.

Some Selected Platforms

- **Google AI Platform**

  - **Introduction:** A comprehensive suite that allows developers to build, train, and deploy machine learning models at scale. It's designed to accommodate both novice and experienced ML practitioners.

  - **Who's Behind It:** Developed by Google, it leverages the same technologies that power Google's own AI-driven products and services.

- **How to Use It**

  - Access the platform through Google Cloud Console.

  - Use Google Cloud's storage services to manage your datasets.

  - Select or create a model using Google's pre-built ML models or custom TensorFlow code.

  - Train your model on Google's scalable infrastructure.

  - Deploy the trained model to Google Cloud for predictions.

- **Benefits:** Offers a seamless and integrated environment for ML development with access to Google's advanced ML capabilities, vast computational resources, and robust security features.

- **Microsoft Azure Machine Learning**

  - **Introduction:** A cloud-based platform for building and deploying ML models, designed to streamline the ML lifecycle with a focus on machine learning operations (MLOps) best practices.

  - **Who's Behind It:** Microsoft, leveraging its cloud infrastructure and software expertise to make ML more accessible and manageable.

  - **How to Use It**

    - Create an Azure Machine Learning workspace through the Azure portal.

    - Prepare and import data using Azure data services.

    - Build and train models using Azure's automated ML capabilities or custom code.

    - Deploy models as web services on Azure Containers or AKS (Azure Kubernetes Service).

  - **Benefits:** Integrates deeply with other Azure services, offering a robust, scalable environment for ML projects with enterprise-grade security and governance.

- **Amazon SageMaker**

  - **Introduction:** A fully managed service that provides every developer and data scientist with the ability to build, train, and deploy machine learning models quickly.

  - **Who's Behind It:** Amazon Web Services (AWS), drawing from its extensive cloud computing experience to simplify ML model development.

  - **How to Use It**

    - Start by creating a notebook instance in SageMaker.

    - Use the notebook to preprocess data and experiment with different models.

    - Train your model with SageMaker's optimized algorithms or bring your own.

    - Deploy your model to production with automatic scaling.

  - **Benefits:** SageMaker simplifies the ML model development process by automating complex tasks like model tuning, making it easier to get models from concept to production.

- **IBM Watson Studio**

  - **Introduction:** A collaborative environment that empowers data scientists, developers, and domain experts to dynamically collaborate on AI projects.

  - **Who's Behind It:** IBM, leveraging its extensive research and development in AI and cognitive computing.

  - **How to Use It**

    - Sign up for IBM Cloud and access Watson Studio.

    - Utilize Watson Studio's tools to clean and prepare your data.

    - Choose from various ML and deep learning models to train your data.

    - Deploy models within Watson Studio or integrate them into existing applications.

- **Benefits:** Watson Studio offers a wide range of data science and ML tools within a unified environment, supported by IBM's powerful AI and hybrid cloud technologies.

AI and ML development platforms are essential tools in the modern developer's arsenal, offering the power and flexibility needed to harness the full potential of AI and ML technologies. By choosing the right platform, developers can accelerate the development cycle, enhance model performance, and drive innovation in AI applications. Whether you're a seasoned data scientist or a developer looking to explore AI, these platforms provide the resources and support necessary to turn your ideas into reality.

Enhancing Development with AI-Powered Tools

The landscape of software development is continually evolving, with AI-powered tools playing a pivotal role in transforming how developers work. From automating documentation to providing intelligent code completion and ensuring code quality, AI is making development faster, more efficient, and error-free. Let's explore some innovative tools that leverage AI to enhance various aspects of development.

AI is not just revolutionizing the core aspects of coding but is also enhancing peripheral development activities, making the entire software development lifecycle more efficient:

- **Automating Tedious Tasks:** AI tools are automating time-consuming tasks, allowing developers to focus on more complex problems.

- **Improving Code Quality:** Through intelligent analysis and suggestions, AI helps maintain high standards of code quality.

- **Enhancing Developer Productivity:** By reducing manual effort and introducing smarter workflows, AI tools significantly boost productivity.

Selected Tools

- **Mintlify**

  - **Introduction:** Mintlify uses AI to automate the creation and maintenance of documentation, making it easier for developers to keep documentation up-to-date with the codebase.

  - **Who's Behind Mintlify:** A team of developers passionate about solving the perennial challenge of outdated documentation through innovative AI solutions.

  - **How to Use Mintlify**

    - Integrate Mintlify with your code repository.

    - Use Mintlify's AI to scan your codebase and generate initial documentation drafts.

    - Review and refine the documentation with Mintlify's suggestions.

    - Keep Mintlify synced with your repository for continuous documentation updates.

  - **Benefits:** Ensures that documentation stays aligned with code changes, significantly reducing the manual effort required in documentation maintenance.

- **Gitpod**

  - **Introduction:** Gitpod streamlines the development workflow by providing automated, ready-to-code development environments in the cloud, accessible from anywhere.

  - **Who's Behind Gitpod:** Developed by a team committed to removing friction from the development process, Gitpod makes setting up and sharing development environments effortless.

  - **How to Use Gitpod**

    - Connect Gitpod to your GitHub, GitLab, or Bitbucket repository.

- Configure your project's Gitpod file to specify the development environment setup.

- Open a new Gitpod workspace for your project directly from your browser.

- Code, build, test, and run your projects in a fully configured, containerized dev environment.

- **Benefits:** Eliminates the "works on my machine" problem, enhances collaboration, and significantly reduces the setup time for new development environments.

- **Tabnine**

  - **Introduction:** Tabnine is an AI-powered code completion tool that supports over a dozen languages and integrates with any editor. It offers highly accurate code suggestions, improving coding speed and accuracy.

  - **Who's Behind Tabnine:** Created by a team dedicated to enhancing developer productivity, Tabnine utilizes deep learning models trained on millions of lines of code.

  - **How to Use Tabnine**

    - Install the Tabnine plugin in your preferred code editor.

    - Start coding, and Tabnine will automatically offer completion suggestions.

    - Customize Tabnine's settings to tailor its suggestions to your coding style.

  - **Benefits:** Increases coding speed, reduces bugs, and helps developers learn new coding patterns and best practices.

- **SonarLint**

  - **Introduction:** SonarLint is an IDE extension that uses AI to perform real-time code quality analysis, helping developers identify and fix quality issues and security vulnerabilities as they code.

- **Who's Behind SonarLint:** Part of the SonarSource suite of tools, SonarLint benefits from the company's extensive experience in code quality and security.

- **How to Use SonarLint**

  - Install SonarLint as a plugin in your IDE.

  - Write code as usual, and SonarLint will highlight issues in real-time.

  - Follow SonarLint's suggestions to improve code quality and security.

- **Benefits:** Enhances code quality, ensures adherence to coding standards, and helps prevent security vulnerabilities from making it into the final product.

AI-powered tools are indispensable allies in the quest for more efficient, error-free software development. By adopting tools like Mintlify, Gitpod, Tabnine, and SonarLint, developers can automate mundane tasks, ensure higher code quality, and focus their efforts on innovation and problem-solving. As AI continues to evolve, we can expect even more sophisticated tools to emerge, further enhancing the capabilities of developers and the quality of software products.

The Criteria for Selecting AI Tools

When integrating AI tools into the software development lifecycle, selecting the right tools is crucial to enhance efficiency, quality, and innovation. The landscape of AI tools is vast, with solutions addressing different aspects of development, from coding to testing, deployment, and beyond. To navigate this landscape effectively, developers and organizations should consider several key criteria that ensure the chosen tools not only meet immediate needs but also align with long-term objectives.

Longevity and Support

- **Well-Established or Rapidly Growing Organizations:** Choosing tools developed by reputable companies or those demonstrating rapid growth and innovation is vital. These organizations are more likely to provide continuous updates, support, and a roadmap for future enhancements.

- **Community and Ecosystem:** Tools backed by a robust community or ecosystem offer additional resources, such as plugins, integrations, and a wealth of shared knowledge, which can be invaluable for solving complex challenges.

Integration with Existing Workflows

- **Seamless Integration:** The tool should seamlessly fit into your current development practices without requiring significant changes to your workflow. This ease of integration ensures that the tool enhances productivity rather than becoming a bottleneck.

- **Compatibility with Existing Tools:** It's essential to consider how well the new AI tool integrates with the rest of your development stack, including IDEs, version control systems, CI/CD pipelines, and project management tools.

- **Customization and Flexibility:** The ability to customize the tool according to specific project requirements or development practices is crucial. A flexible tool can adapt to various scenarios, making it a valuable asset across different projects.

Scalability

- **Support for Project Growth:** As projects evolve, their complexity and scale can increase significantly. The chosen AI tool should be capable of handling this growth, providing consistent performance and functionality as demands rise.

- **Resource Management:** Consider how the tool manages computational resources, especially for AI and ML development platforms. Efficient resource management ensures that the tool remains cost-effective and performs well under different loads.

- **Future-Proofing:** Look for tools that are not just relevant to current trends but are also positioned to adapt to future developments in AI and software engineering. A tool that evolves with emerging technologies offers a longer-term investment.

Selecting the right AI tools for software development requires careful consideration of their longevity, integration capabilities, and scalability. By focusing on these criteria, developers and organizations can choose tools that not only address immediate needs but also support continuous improvement and innovation in their projects. The goal is to leverage AI tools that enhance the development process, improve product quality, and adapt to the changing landscape of technology, ensuring long-term success and competitiveness.

The Impact of AI on Software Development

The integration of Artificial Intelligence (AI) into software development heralds a transformative era in the tech industry. This paradigm shift is not merely about streamlining processes but redefining the very nature of how we build, deploy, and maintain software. In this section, we delve into the multifaceted impact of AI on the software development landscape, examining both the opportunities it presents and the challenges it poses.

Revolutionizing Development Workflows

AI tools are revolutionizing development workflows by automating repetitive tasks, offering predictive insights, and facilitating rapid prototyping. These advancements free developers from the tedium of manual coding and debugging, allowing them to focus on more strategic and creative aspects of software development. For instance, AI-powered code completion tools not only speed up coding but also help in learning new programming languages and frameworks by suggesting syntax and code snippets.

Enhancing Efficiency and Accuracy

The accuracy and efficiency of software development have significantly improved thanks to AI. Tools that automatically review code and suggest optimizations help maintain high-quality standards, reducing the likelihood of bugs and vulnerabilities. Moreover, AI-driven testing tools can quickly identify issues that might take human testers much longer to find, ensuring that software products are both robust and reliable.

Facilitating Personalized User Experiences

AI extends its influence beyond the development process to impact the end product directly. By leveraging machine learning models, developers can create applications that offer personalized user experiences, adapt to user behaviors, and make intelligent recommendations. This capability is particularly beneficial in sectors like e-commerce, entertainment, and healthcare, where customization enhances user engagement and satisfaction.

Navigating the Job Market Landscape

The advent of AI in software development has sparked a debate around job displacement. While AI automates certain tasks, it also creates opportunities for developers to upskill and engage in more complex and rewarding work. The demand for professionals skilled in AI and machine learning is growing, highlighting the importance of continuous learning and adaptability in the tech industry.

Shaping the Future of Software Development

The future of software development, augmented by AI, is poised for unprecedented innovation. As AI tools become more sophisticated, the potential for creating complex, intelligent, and adaptive systems grows. This evolution will not only change how developers work but also expand the possibilities of what can be created.

Preparing for an AI-Driven Era

To thrive in this AI-driven era, developers must embrace a mindset of lifelong learning and curiosity. Engaging with AI technologies, understanding their capabilities and limitations, and exploring how they can be applied to solve real-world problems are essential steps in this journey. Additionally, developers should cultivate skills in AI and machine learning, data analysis, and ethics in AI to ensure responsible and effective use of these technologies.

The impact of AI on software development is profound and far-reaching. By enhancing efficiency, accuracy, and creativity, AI tools empower developers to push the boundaries of what's possible. As we continue to explore these technologies, we not only witness the evolution of software development but also participate in shaping its future.

Preparing for the Future: Skills and Mindsets for the AI-Enhanced Developer

As we stand at the intersection of software development and artificial intelligence, it's clear that the landscape of our industry is undergoing a monumental shift. The future belongs to those who are prepared to navigate this new terrain, armed with both the technical skills and the mindsets necessary for success in an AI-enhanced world. This section outlines the key competencies and attitudes that developers will need to cultivate to thrive in the era of AI-driven development.

Embracing Continuous Learning

The rapid pace of AI technology development means that what is cutting-edge today may become obsolete tomorrow. Developers must adopt a mindset of continuous learning, staying abreast of the latest tools, languages, and methodologies. This doesn't just apply to AI technologies but also to the evolving landscape of software development practices influenced by AI.

Cultivating AI Literacy

Understanding the fundamentals of AI and machine learning is becoming increasingly important, even for developers not specializing in these fields. A basic grasp of AI concepts, algorithms, and data processing techniques will be essential to leverage AI tools effectively and responsibly. Developers should seek to understand the capabilities and limitations of AI, recognizing when and how to integrate AI solutions into their projects.

Developing a Problem-Solving Mindset

AI-enhanced development is as much about solving problems in innovative ways as it is about coding. Developers should cultivate a problem-solving mindset, thinking critically about how AI can address complex challenges. This involves not just technical proficiency but also creativity, ethical consideration, and an understanding of the human impact of AI solutions.

Building Ethical and Responsible AI Systems

As AI becomes more integrated into software development, ethical considerations and the potential societal impact of AI systems take on heightened importance. Developers must be equipped to make decisions that prioritize fairness, privacy, and transparency, ensuring that AI technologies are used responsibly and for the benefit of all.

Collaborating Across Disciplines

The future of software development will increasingly require collaboration across disciplines, including data science, design, and ethics. Developers should be prepared to work in multidisciplinary teams, communicating effectively with professionals from diverse backgrounds to create holistic AI-enhanced solutions.

Conclusion

As we bring the curtains down on this exploration of "Mosaic," we reflect on a journey that has taken us through the vast and intricate landscape of AI in software development. From the foundational tools that enhance coding efficiency to the advanced platforms enabling machine learning and AI innovation, we've traversed a terrain rich with technology that is reshaping the future of development.

Throughout this book, key insights have emerged, illustrating the transformative power of AI across various aspects of software creation. We've seen how AI-enhanced IDEs make coding more intuitive and error-free, automating code reviews and maintenance to uphold high-quality standards. The advent of AI in continuous integration and deployment has streamlined processes, ensuring faster delivery times without compromising on quality. Moreover, AI's role in testing and quality assurance has underscored its importance in building resilient, user-centric software.

But the completion of this mosaic does not signify the end. Instead, it marks the beginning of a continuous journey in the ever-evolving domain of software development. The landscape of AI is dynamic, with new tools and technologies emerging at a rapid pace. The possibilities that lie ahead are limitless, inviting us to keep exploring, learning, and innovating.

Epilogue: Looking Ahead—the Developer's Next Steps

The path forward is one of perpetual growth and exploration. As developers, the quest for knowledge never ceases, and the drive to harness the latest technologies for better software solutions is ever-present. Here are some steps and resources to guide you on your ongoing journey:

- **Continuous Learning**

    - **Online Courses and Tutorials:** Many platforms offer courses on AI, machine learning, and advanced software development techniques.

    - **Workshops and Webinars:** Attend industry workshops and webinars to stay updated on the latest trends and practices in AI and software development.

- **Community Engagement**

  - **GitHub and Open Source Projects:** Contributing to open source projects can provide practical experience and insight into real-world problem-solving with AI.

  - **Forums and Social Media Groups:** Engage with communities on Reddit, Stack Overflow, and LinkedIn groups dedicated to AI in software development.

- **Stay Informed**

  - **Read Widely:** Keep abreast of the latest research and developments in AI and software development through blogs, journals, and news articles.

  - **Tech Conferences and Meetups:** Participate in conferences and local meetups to network with fellow developers and learn from their experiences.

- **Experiment and Innovate**

  - **Personal Projects:** Apply what you learn by working on personal projects. Experimenting with new tools and technologies is one of the best ways to understand their capabilities and limitations.

  - **Collaboration:** Collaborate with peers on innovative projects. Teamwork can lead to breakthrough ideas and solutions.

The journey of a developer is marked by continuous learning and adaptation. As we venture into the future, let us embrace the challenges and opportunities that come with the territory, leveraging AI to not just streamline our work but to also create more intelligent, efficient, and impactful software solutions. The mosaic of software development is ever-expanding, and each of us has a unique piece to add to this vast and beautiful picture. Let the journey continue.

Index

A

© Arpit Dwivedi 2024
A. Dwivedi, *CodeMosaic*, https://doi.org/10.1007/979-8-8688-0276-8

B

Printed in the United States
by Baker & Taylor Publisher Services